READINGS IN ANTHROPOLOGY

Revised Printing

Eugene Cooper and Andrei Simić

University of Southern California

KENDALL/HUNT PUBLISHING COMPANY
4050 Westmark Drive   Dubuque, Iowa 52002

CONTENTS

iii

SOCIAL ORGANIZATION

ECONOMICS

MYTH AND IDEOLOGY

1 TAKE ME TO YOUR LEADER

—NIGEL BARLEY

Days begin early in Africa. In my London life I had been used to rising about half past either of a morning; here everyone was afoot at five-thirty, as soon as it was light. I was wakened punctually by sounds of beating metal and screaming and guessed that my local missionary was about his business. At the time I had no idea what luxury I was enjoying; this was the last time I was to see running water, not to mention electricity. I was intrigued to find a paraffin refrigerator next door, the first time I had seen one of these monsters. Capriciously unpredictable, these erstwhile staples of bush life have become rare and expensive as electricity has been introduced into the towns. Out of sheer perversity, they will spontaneously defrost and destroy a month's meat supply or give out so much heat as to incinerate anyone in the room. They must be protected from draughts, damp, unevenness of the floor and with luck they may consent to exert a mild cooling effect. In Cameroon, with numerous languages and pijins, there are other dangers. English paraffin and petrol get mixed up with French *pétrole* and *essence,* American kerosene and gas. It is not unknown for helpful servants to top paraffin refrigerators up with petrol, with devastating results. I peered inside; carefully stacked were bags of large yellow termites. Even in death they seemed to seethe. I was never able to bring myself to eat more than one or two of these African delicacies, of which Dowayos are inordinately fond. The insects swarm at the beginning of the rains and are attracted by any light. The standard means of collecting them is to place a light in the midst of a bucket of water. When they reach the light, the insects drop their wings and fall into the water whence they can be collected and their fatty bodies either roasted or eaten raw.

After a day's respite it was time to deal with the administration again. At the N'gaoundere mission I had been urged not to forget to register with the local police and to introduce myself to the local *sous-préfet,* the government representative. Accordingly, I armed myself with all my documents and set off on foot into town. Although it was something less then a mile, it was clearly a major eccentricity for a white man to walk. One man asked me whether my car had broken down. Villagers rushed out and shook hands with me jabbering in garbled Fulani. I had learned the rudiments of this tongue in London so I was able at least to say, 'I am sorry, I do not speak Fulani.' Since I had practiced this sentence many times, it came out rather fluently and added to the incomprehension.

The police post was manned by about fifteen gendarmes, all armed to the teeth. One was polishing a sub-machine gun. The commandant turned out to be a huge Southerner of about six foot five. He summoned me into his office and inspected my documents minutely. What was my reason for being here? I displayed my research permit, a most impressive document, covered with photographs and stamps. He was clearly very unhappy as I tried to expound the essential nature of the anthropological endeavour. 'But what's it for?' he asked. Choosing between giving an impromptu version of the 'Introduction to Anthropology' lecture course and something less full, I replied somewhat lamely, 'It's my job.' Subsequently, I came to realize what a highly satisfactory explanation this was to an official who spent most of his life in pointlessly enforcing rules that seemed an end in themselves. He considered me lengthily under hooded eyes. I noticed for the first time that he was chewing on a needle. He would balance it, blunt ends outwards, on his tongue. With a deft flick, he drew it wholly inside his mouth and performed an adroit adjustment so that it reappeared at the other side of the mouth with the point outwards. Back in, and there was a blunt end again. It was horribly like a snake's tongue. I felt there would be problems here, and I was to be proved right. For the time being, however, he let me go with the air of one allowing a rogue enough rope to hang himself. My name and personal details were recorded in a large volume that recalled the tomes of prohibited persons from the Embassy.

The *sous-préfet* lived in a dark and peeling house dating from the French colonial period. Moss and mould clung to every crack and crevice in its facade. On a hill above the town he has constructed a gleaming new palace but it stood empty, its air-conditioning unused, its tiled floors untrodden. Several explanations were given for this. Some said that the government had confiscated it as proof of corruption. The Dowayos, when I got to know them, told a different tale. The house had been built on an old Dowayo burial ground, despite their protests. They had not threatened, they claimed, they did not need to; they knew the spirits of their ancestors. They had simply informed the *sous-préfet* that the day he moved in was the day he would die. Either way, he never did move in but was doomed to look at his new house from the window of the old.

Having listened to my tale, a dour servant showed me in. I was struck by the fact that he knelt down before daring to address his superior.

I had been tipped off in advance that a present of some cigars would be 'acceptable', so these were duly produced and graciously accepted, disappearing swiftly inside the flowing robes. I was still standing up, the servant was still on his knees, the *sous-préfet* sat. My documents were once more examined with minute attention. I began to fear that they might wear out before I left the country. 'Out of the question,' he declared impassively. 'I cannot have you in Poli.' This was something of a setback; I had regarded this as a courtesy visit. 'But my research permit, from Yaounde,' I emphasized carefully, 'gives me permission to be here.' He lit one of my cigars. 'Yaounde is not here. You have not my permission.' Clearly this was not a situation where the passage of currency between us would be politic since the venerable retainer was still on his knees, taking in every word. 'How might I obtain your permission?' I persisted. 'A letter from the prefect, absolving me of responsibility, would be sufficient. He is to be found in Garoua.' He turned away and busied himself with papers. Our interview was at an end.

Back at the mission, Pastor Brown seemed to regard this as a vindication of his pessimism. He was touchingly cheered by my misfortune. He doubted whether I would ever get to see the prefect even it he happened to be where they claimed he was and not away in the capital; it was virtually certain he would not return for months. His own life had been fraught with many such frustrations. There was no hope; this was Africa. He walked off chuckling.

Calculating that I had just enough petrol to reach Garoua, about a hundred miles away, I resolved to set off at dawn the following day.

When I left the house next day, I was rather taken aback to find a sea of expectant faces confidently intending to accompany me. It has always been something of a mystery how such information circulates. Westerners often fail to realize with what minute attention they are observed. Being seen checking the fuel level is enough to trigger a barrage of requests for transport. To refuse is held to be inadmissible. Those who reproach Europeans with paternalism fail totally to perceive the relations that traditionally exist between rich and poor in much of Africa. A man who works for you is not just an employee: you are his patron. It is an open-ended relationship. If his wife is ill, that is as much your problem as his and you will be expected to do all in your power to heal her. If you decide to throw anything away, he must be given first refusal on it. To give it to someone else would be most improper. It is almost impossible to draw a line between what is your concern and what is his private life. The unwary European will get caught up in the vast range of loose kinship obligations, unless he is very lucky indeed. When an employee calls you 'father', this is a danger sign. There is surely a story about an unpaid dowry or dead cattle to follow and it will be perceived as a genuine betrayal not to assume part of the burden. The line between 'mine' and 'thine' is subject to continual renegotiation and Dowayos are as expert as anyone else in trying to get as much as they can out of a link with a rich man. The failure to realize that the relationship is being seen in very different terms from either side has led to much friction. Westerners are always complaining of their workers' (they are not called 'boys' or 'servants' nowadays) 'cheek' or 'nerve' in their bland expectation that employers will look after them and always bail them out when in trouble. Initially, I was much put out on occasions such as that which now presented itself. It seemed as if I could never do anything spontaneously or go anywhere without dragging a hugh burden of obligation behind me. When in the city, it was even more galling to find that people one had given lifts to would be most annoyed if loans to finance their stay were not also readily forthcoming. I had brought them to this strange place; to forsake them here would be unthinkable.

However, on the first occasion I understood none of this and embarked as many as seemed possible. Here again, European and African notions are strongly divergent. By local standards, a car with only six people in it is empty. Any claim that there is no more room in it is greeted as a patent falsehood. It is a further annoyance, having finally limited numbers by striking those rather firm attitudes that Africans expect from Westerners who really mean what they are saying, only to find that all manner of baggage is suddenly dragged forth from concealment to be tied to the roof with the inevitable strips of rubber cut from inner tubes.

By now much delayed, I finally set off, the car heaving and groaning, for Garoua. Various other features dependent on numerous passengers soon became apparent. Dowayos are not enthusiastic travellers and react badly to motion. Within ten minutes, three or four of them were vomiting with great gusto all over the car, none of them bothering to use the window for this purpose. It was a decidedly seedy driver who finally reached the city limits for more inspection of documents. Whereas a lone white man attracts very little police attention, he is a matter of some concern when hauling around Africans. The police were very interested indeed in my movements and motives.

The appearance of the word 'doctor' on my passport seemed to do more than anything else to dispel doubts, but my passengers were not so lucky. While I was seeking to explain the absence of a registration card for the car by leading the sergeant through the dossier I had prudently brought from N'gaoundere, my passengers were dolefully lined up and required to produce receipts for tax for the last three years, identity cards and membership cards of the sole political party. Inevitably, they fell somewhat short of perfection and this caused further delays. It became clear that little would be achieved before the midday siesta.

Garoua is a strange town situated on the river Benoue, a watercourse of sporadic appearance that varies from raging Mississippi in the rainy season to damp sand in the dry. Its dedication to its wayward river explains the smell of ripe fish that hangs over it like a pall of smoke. Dried fish is one of its main industries, the others being beer and administration. The beer is a particular source of fascination of Dowayos. They are keen customers of the breweries that produce the '33' beer, a mark of a previous French administration. Its peculiar quality is that it enables one to pass directly from sobriety to hangover without an intervening stage of drunkenness. The factory has a glass wall through which it was possible to see bottles of beer gliding, without the intervention of human agency, from one stage of the process to another. This deeply impressed the Dowayos and they spent hours watching the miracle. To describe it, they used the word *gerse* which means 'miracle', 'wonder', 'magic'. It was in this context that I first heard the term that was later so to occupy me as an anthropologist. It was also a fertile source of metaphor for their most metaphysical concepts. The Dowayos believed in reincarnation. It was like the beer at Garoua, they explained; people were like bottles that had to be filled with spirit. When they died and were buried, it was like sending the empty bottle back to the factory.

Fearing the worst, I now expected my encounter with the prefect, if it occurred at all, to take some days. A sort of calm fatalism had settled upon me. Things would take as long as they took; there was no point in worrying about it. It is one of the marks of the fieldworker that he has a supplementary gear into which he can shift such moments and let the slings and arrows do their worst.

Not yet having made those contacts that stand the city-visiting anthropologist in such good stead, I checked into a hotel. Garoua boasted two of these, a modern Novotel at a mere £30 a night for the tourist trade and a seedy French colonial establishment for a fraction of that amount. The latter was clearly more my style. It had apparently been built for the rest and recreation of suncrazed French officers from the forlorn stations of empire, and consisted of separate huts with grass roofs and furnished in military fashion; but it had water and electricity. It also possessed a large terrace on which the élite would sit and drink as the sun went down behind the trees. It was especially romantic since it was impossible to forget the presence of the rest of Africa: the roars of the lion in the zoo next door recalled it.

It was in this establishment that I first made the acquaintance of the woman who came to be known as the 'Coo-ee lady'. Whatever the season, Garoua is at least ten degrees hotter than Poli and, thanks to the river, has a profusion of mosquitoes. After being cloistered with vomiting Dowayos, I was therefore keen to have a shower. I was hardly under the tap when there came a persistent dry scratching noise at the door that ignored all attempts at interrogation. Swathing a towel round myself, I opened the door. Outside was an extremely large Fulani woman in her mid-fifties. She began simpering coyly, making little circular motions in the dust with her expansive feet. 'Yes?' I queried. She made drinking motions: 'Water, water.' My suspicions were aroused; dim memories of the rules of hospitality of the desert stirred. While I was considering the problem, she sailed blandly past me and seized a glass, filling it from the tap. To my horror she began to unwrap her vast form. The porter chose this moment to bring me some soap and, misinterpreting the situation, began to back out muttering apologies. I was trapped in a farce.

Fortunately, my few lessons in Fulani at the School of Oriental and African Studies stood me in good stead, and crying 'I do not wish it', I disclaimed any desire of physical contact with this woman, who reminded me strangely of Oliver Hardy. As if by some prearranged sign, the giggling porter seized one arm, and I the other and we got her outside. Thereafter she came back every hour, unable to accept that her charms were unappreciated and roamed outside calling 'Coo-ee', like a cat miaowing to come in. In the end, I tired of this. It was clear that she was operating in connivance with the management, so I declared that I was a missionary, come from the bush to see my bishop, and strongly disapproved of such goings-on. They were shocked and embarrassed; thereafter she ignored me.

The story became a favorite of the Dowayos as we sat around the fires in the evening when one of the chief occupations is spinning yarns. I had my assistant rehearse me in telling the 'fat Fulani woman story', as it came to be known, and when I got to the part where she called 'Coo-ee' they would scream with laughter, hug their knees and roll about on the ground. It did much to establish good relations between us.

My visit to the prefect's office the next day turned out to be an anticlimax. I was shown right in. The prefect was a tall, very dark Fulani who listened to my problem, dictated a letter over the telephone and chatted to me most amiably about government policy with regard to establishing schools in pagan areas. The letter was brought to him, he signed it, stamped it and wished me good luck and 'bon courage'. Thus armed, I returned to Poli.

The first priority was to find an assistant and settle down to learning the language. The anthropologist's assistant is a figure who seems suspiciously absent from ethnographic accounts. The conventional myth seeks to depict the battle-scarred anthropologist as a lone figure wandering into a village, settling in and 'picking up the language' in a couple of months; at the most, we may find references to translators being dispensed with after a few weeks. Never mind that this is contrary to all known linguistic experience. In Europe, a man may have studied French at school for six years and with the help of language-learning devices, visits to France and exposure to the literature and yet find himself hardly able to stammer out a few words of French in an emergency. Once in the field, he transforms himself into a linguistic wonder-worker. He becomes fluent in a language much more difficult for a Westerner than French, without qualified teachers, without bilingual texts, and often without grammars and dictionaries. At least, this is the impression he manages to convey. Of course much may be done in pijin or even in English, but as often as not this isn't mentioned either.

It was clear to me that I needed a native Dowayo who also spoke some French. This meant that he would have been to school which also, given the nature of things in Dowayoland, would imply that he was a Christian. For me that would be a considerable disadvantage since the traditional religion was one of the areas that interested me most. But there was nothing for it; I decided to go along to the local secondary school and see if they had someone suitably qualified. In fact, I never got there.

I was pre-empted by one of the preachers being trained at the Poli mission who knew what I was looking for; it so happened that he had twelve brothers. With rare entrepreneurial flair he swiftly mobilized them, marched them in from the village twenty miles out in the bush and presented them to me. This one, he explained was a good cook and very cheerful. Alas, he did not speak French. This one could read and write, was a terrible cook, but very strong. This one was a good Christian and told stories well. Each, it seemed, had great virtues and was an outstanding bargain. In the end, I agreed to hire one on trial, nobly settling for one who could not cook but spoke the best French, and could read and write. I realized at the time that the preacher himself was the man I should have taken on but his present employment prevented that. He was subsequently thrown out of the mission because of his promiscuous tendencies.

The time had come, if indeed it was not overdue, to move into a village. Dowayos divide into two sorts, mountain and plains. Everyone I had spoken to had urged me to live among plains Dowayos. They were less barbarous, supplies would be easier, more of them spoke French; I would be able to go to church more easily. Mountain Dowayos were savage and difficult, they would tell me nothing, they worshipped the Devil. Given such information, an anthropologist can only make one choice; I opted for mountain Dowayos. Some nine miles outside Poli was the village of Kongle. Although on the plains between two sets of hills, it was a mountain Dowayo village. Here, I was told, lived a very old man who was a stern traditionalist and had much arcane knowledge from the ancestors. The road was just passable. I decided to install myself here.

I consulted Matthieu, my new assistant. He was horrified to hear that I intended to live in the bush. Did this mean I should not have a fine house and other servants? Alas, it did. But surely I did not intend to live in Kongle—the people were savages. I should leave it to him; he would speak to his father, a plains Dowayo, who would arrange for us to live near the Catholic mission. I explained again the nature of my work. The only similar endeavour in Dowayoland had been the establishment of the linguists who had begun the analysis of the Dowayo language. They had spent some two years building a fine cement house and had been supplied by aeroplane. Matthieu was distressed to learn that my operation was much more a shoestring affair. It became clear that his status was dependent on my own, and he managed to make any lapse from dignity on my part seem like a bitter betrayal.

The moment for initial contact had come. Taking Matthieu's advice I brought some beer and tobacco and we set off for Kongle. The road was not too bad, though there were two rivers I did not much like the look of; indeed they proved rather a nuisance. My car would make a habit of developing faults half-way across. This was more serious than it might otherwise have been since they were liable to flash-flood. The mountains were pure granite, and should it rain there the water came straight off and caused almost a tidal wave in the river valleys. To either side of the road were fields with people working in them. They stopped and stared as we crawled past. Some fled. Later I found that they had assumed we were from the *sous-préfet;* outsiders usually meant trouble to Dowayos. At the foot of the mountains the road simply came to an end, and behind a palisade of millet stalks and cacti lay the village.

Dowayo huts are circular mud constructions with conical roofs. Being built of the mud and grass of the countryside, they assume a picturesque quality that is a relief after the ugliness of the cities. On the roofs grow long, trailing melons like the rambling roses of an English cottage. Following Matthieu's lead, I entered the circle that stands before every Dowayo village. This is the place where all public meetings and courts of law are conducted, where rituals are held and the various shrines important in religious life are to be found. Behind it lies a second circle where the communally owned cattle are kept. We passed through these and into the courtyard of the chief. It is not strictly accurate to use this term: the Dowayos have no real chiefs in the sense of leaders with power and authority. The French tried to create such men so that they would have figureheads to rule through and someone to collect taxes. The Dowayo term for such men, *waari*, is based upon an older classification. Chiefs are simple rich men, that is, men with cattle. Such men can organize the various religious festivals that are an essential part of ritual life. Poor men can associate themselves with rich celebrants and so complete rituals that they would not otherwise be able to afford. Chiefs are therefore very important people. Some have modelled themselves on the dominant local tribe, the Fulani, and sought to improve their status by refusing to speak Dowayo to their own people. They pretend that they can only understand it with difficulty, although it is their first language. Hence their astonishment when I refused to talk Fulani, like all the other white men, and insisted on learning Dowayo. Several of the chiefs have adopted all the panoply of pomp with which Fulani nobles surround themselves. They wear swords and have someone carrying a red sunshade over their heads. Some even have praise singers who precede them beating drums and wailing out a stereotyped list of their singular accomplishments and virtues, always in Fulani.

The Chief of Kongle was a rather different kettle of fish. He despised such acculturated Dowayos and made a point of only speaking Dowayo to them.

We came to a halt before a bare-breasted woman who knelt down before me and crossed her hands in front of her genitals concealed by a minute bunch of leaves. 'She is greeting you,' whispered Matthieu, 'shake hands with her.' I did so and she began to rock backwards and forwards on her heels crooning 'Thank you' repeatedly in Fulani and clapping her hands together. Faces appeared furtively over walls and round the side of huts. To my huge embarrassment a child appeared with a single folding chair and stood in the middle of the courtyard. I was required to sit. There was nothing else for it; I sat in splendid isolation, feeling rather like one of those stiff and very British figures in the photographs from colonial days. Status differences are clearly marked in much of Africa; Africans go in for heavy overstatement. People grovel and scrape, kneel and bow in a way that Westerners find hard to swallow; yet to refuse to accept such gestures is extremely impolite. Initially, whenever I would sit on a rock at the same level as everyone else it would cause acute embarrassment. People would desperately attempt to arrange matters so that they were lower than me or insist that I sit on a mat. Sitting on a mat, though lower than on a rock, carries higher status. Thus a compromise was reached.

By now the silence was becoming very strained and I felt it incumbent upon me to say something. I have already said that one of the joys of fieldwork is that it allows one to make use of all sorts of expressions that otherwise are never used. 'Take me to your leader,' I cried. This was duly translated and it was explained that the Chief was coming from his field.

Zuuldibo later became a good friend. He was in his early forties, invariably grinning all over his face, and somewhat running to fat. He was resplendent in Fulani robes, a sword and sunglasses. I now realize that whatever he had been up to when I arrived had not been in his field. No one cultivated the land in such attire; moreover, Zuuldibo had never touched a hoe in his life. He found the whole business of agriculture so unspeakably boring that he looked pained if anyone even mentioned work in the fields to him.

I launched into my prepared speech, saying how I had come many miles from the land of the white men because I had heard of the good ways of the Dowayos and especially of the good nature and kindness of the people of Kongle. This seemed to go down rather well. I wanted to live among them for a while and learn their ways and language. I made great play of the fact that I was not a missionary, which no one believed initially because I was living at the mission and driving a car that they recognized as belonging to the mission. I was not connected with the government, which no one believed because I had been seen hanging around the *sous-préfecture*. I was not a Frenchman, which no one even understood; to Dowayos all white men are the same. However, they listened politely, nodding their heads and muttering 'It is good', or 'true, true'. It was swiftly agreed that I would return in one week and the Chief would have a hut for myself and accommodation for my assistant. We drank a beer together and I gave them some tobacco. Everyone looked ecstatic. As I left, an old woman fell on the ground and embraced my knees. 'What did she say?' I asked. Matthieu giggled, 'She said God had sent you to hear our voice.' It was a better start than I had dared to hope for.

In the following week I made another trip to the city to lay in supplies and buy tobacco. The black Nigerian tobacco that Dowayos so like sells in Dowayoland for four times the price in Garoua. I bought a large bag of it to pay informants with. My financial situation remained acute. I had arranged for my salary to be sent from England to my Cameroonian account. Since it came from England, it was sent to the old capital of British Cameroons, Victoria, thence to Yaounde, thence to N'gaoundere, thence to Garoua. In fact it never made it; the bank at Victoria simply deducted ten per cent 'expenses' and returned it to England, leaving me biting my nails and building up an ever larger debt at the Protestant mission. It was impossible to contact the bank at Victoria; they simply ignored letters, and the phones did not work.

It was during this final trip that I caught malaria for the first time. It manifested itself initially as a mild, light-headed sensation as I left the city. By the time I reached Poli, I had double vision and could barely see the road. A high fever was accompanied by shivering bouts and red-hot knives in the belly.

One of the sadder aspects of the disease is that it causes loss of control of the sphincters; when you stand up, you urinate on your feet. Even worse, there is an almost infinite list of remedies, some of which merely offer protection against the disease, others cure it once contracted. Unluckily, the pills I swallowed so hopefully were not curatives and so my condition worsened and the fevers rapidly reduced me to a whimpering wreck. Pastor Brown passed by to draw encouragement from my physical dissolution and lent me some curatives, warning me that 'Out here you can never be sure anything's gonna work.' Work, however, they did and I was rather shakily back on my feet in time to move into the village as planned—not, however, until I had spent several fever-racked nights tormented by the bats that came down into the house through holes in the ceiling. Much has been written on the excellence of bats' navigation equipment. It is all false. Tropical bats spend their entire time flying into obstacles with a horrible thudding noise. They specialize in slamming into walls and falling, fluttering onto your face. As my own 'piece of equipment essential for the field', I would strongly recommend a tennis racket; it is devastatingly effective in clearing a room of bats. Pastor Brown had taken the time to tell me that bats carried rabies. They occupied a large place in my fevered fantasies.

It was not until I packed to leave that I found the house had been broken into and half my food stolen.

2 CHINESE TABLE MANNERS: YOU ARE HOW YOU EAT

—EUGENE COOPER

"Etiquette of this kind (not putting half eaten meat back in the bowl, [not] wiping one's nose on one's sleeve) is not superficial, a matter for the surface rather than the depths; refined ways of acting are so internalized as to make alternative behavior truly 'disgusting,' 'revolting,' 'nauseous,' turning them into some of the most highly charged and deeply felt of intra-social differences, so that 'rustic' behavior is not merely quaint but barbarous" (Goody 1982: 140).

"Probably no common practise is more diversified than the familiar one of eating in company, for what Europeans consider as correct and decent may by other races be looked upon as wrong or indelicate. Similarly, few social observances provide more opportunities for offending the stranger than the etiquette of the table" (Hammerton 1936:23).

The anthropological literature on food habits reveals three modes of understanding. The first mode assumes that food habits, usually taboos, fulfill a practical positive function in the adaptation of a population to its habitat (Harris 1974; Farb and Armelagos 1980). The second assumes that food habits represent a symbolic order, generally reverberating sympathetically with other such orders in a given culture (Douglas 1966; Goody 1982). The third assumes that food habits serve as social markers (de Garine 1976) with the expectation that rules of commensality will parallel rules applying to sex (Douglas 1975:249; Rubel and Rosman 1978). As Goody has pointed out, "To eat alone is tantamount to marrying in" (1982:206).

The functionalist perspective is represented in Farb and Armelagos's work (1980) in which the origin of food taboos is explained by the "evolutionary mechanism of bait shyness" (1980:126). Once burned, twice shy, leads to the imposition of taboos on certain foods. It is almost as though Sahlins had never written *Culture and Practical Reason*. In Farb and Armelagos's work, we have an entire book (deceptively well-named *Consuming Passions*) in which the most arbitrary and capricious of human inclinations and habits do their part for human evolutionary adaptation.

As regards the subject at hand, it is hard to see how table manners, as varied and diverse as they are in world ethnography, could be incorporated into a framework of positive adaptive significance. Rules of etiquette are subscribed to or not as a result of one's membership in a group and inculcation by group members, and as an affirmation or rejection of one's membership. Food habits communicate symbolic messages, and as Douglas

(1975:249) has stated, encode social events. The message of that code is about different degrees of hierarchy, inclusion and exclusion, boundaries and transactions across boundaries. The significance of food habits in any given social group, and table manners more particularly, is the subject of continuous negotiation, as each generation devises its own praxis in opposition to, or in accord with, the precedents of the past (see Myerhoff 1979 on the importance of the negotiation of the significance of ritual). Thus the latter two modes of understanding seem most suited to this study, and allow for a role for the culture bearer other than simply slavish prisoner of tradition or environment.

Surprisingly, for a civilization which has generated so many handbooks of its various cuisines, China has not produced any popular guidebooks for table manners of the Emily Post variety. The field, of course, has for the most part been preempted by the *Li Chi*—records of etiquette and ceremonial—most of which is said to date from the early Han. Indeed, many of the themes which characterize contemporary Chinese table manners are present in the minute descriptions of behaviors appropriate to people of various stations in all the gradations of Han social structure, such as the prescription to yield or defer. However, one is hard pressed to find a general rough and ready guide to contemporary Chinese table manners of anything more than the most superficial kind, usually present in popular Chinese cookbooks for Western audiences.

The absence of attention to table manners may be the result of the fact that table manners are among those habits most taken for granted—rules no grown-up needs instruction in. A Chinese culinary enthusiast of my acquaintance assures me that table manners are not important in Chinese history, being far outweighed by the scarcity of food generally as the major issue. Nevertheless, an examination of Chinese table manners provides sufficient contrast with Western table habits in terms of structure and performance, as to make significant features of Chinese etiquette emerge in comparison—features taken for granted by the native.

Those few who have written on the subject (Chang 1977; Hsü and Hsü 1977) generally qualify as bi-cultural individuals with sufficient experience of both Chinese and Western rules to tease out the areas of contrastive significance. My five years of field research (and eating) in Hong Kong, and eight years of marriage to a Chinese woman who taught me Chinese table manners as to a child, also qualify me for the assignment, although my former European colleagues at the University of Hong Kong might question my credentials as an expert on Western etiquette, to be sure.

The spirit in which this inquiry is carried out is aptly captured in the following quote from the master in the Chü Li (Li Chi 1971:17):

> When entering a country inquire of its customs. When crossing a border inquire of the prohibitions.

Among such customs and prohibitions, those associated with behavior at the table make an enormous difference in the way one is perceived by a Chinese host. The way one handles oneself at the table gives off signals of the clearest types to most Chinese as to what kind of a person one is. Thus, it behooves the would-be intercultural communicator to learn the basics of the rules of the Chinese table.

BASIC STRUCTURES AND PARAPHERNALIA

To begin with, it is useful to consider K. C. Chang's (1977) broad outline of the important distinctions in Chinese food between food (*shih*) and drink (*yin*), and then within the category food, between *fan* (grain/rice) and *ts'ai* (dishes). Chang establishes a hierarchy with grain as the base, vegetables and fruit as next least expendable, and meat as most expendable in the preparation of a meal. Fish would probably fall between vegetables and meat at least as far as contemporary Hong Kong is concerned, particularly if one includes the enormous variety of preserved fish available.

In any event, it is fair to say that a Chinese meal is not a meal without *fan*. The morning food event, at which rice is not normally taken, or if so is taken as gruel, is not thought of as a meal. When Chinese speak of a full day's eating fare, it is two square meals per day rather than three. Thus rice (or grain) defines a meal, and its treatment and consumption are circumscribed in a number of ways.

It will be helpful, however, to lay out the general paraphernalia with which the diner is equipped, and the structure in which it is deployed before returning to the rules governing rice. On this subject, Hsü and Hsü (1977:304) have written:

> The typical Chinese dining table is round or square, the *ts'ai* dishes are laid in the center, and each participant in the meal is equipped with a bowl for *fan*, a pair of chopsticks, a saucer, and a spoon. All at the table take from the *ts'ai* dishes as they proceed with the meal.

The *ts'ai* dishes are typically shared by all, and must be treated much as common property, whereas one's bowl is a private place which comes directly in touch with the mouth. The chopsticks are of both the mouth and the table, and mediate between. They are thin, and when employed appropriately only touch the one piece or small quantity a person touches first. Many Westerners find the habit of sharing from a common plate potentially unhygienic, and one might be tempted to dismiss this as a bit of ethnocentricity. However, the point has recently been made by no less an authority than Communist party secretary Hu Yaobang, who called attention to the unsanitary character of traditional Chinese eating habits and urged change.

One employs the chopsticks to take from the common plate and place food in one's bowl, then one raises the bowl to the mouth and pushes food into the mouth with the chopsticks. Hsü and Hsü state, "The diner who lets his *fan* bowl stay on the table and eats by picking up lumps of *fan* from the bowl is expressing disinterest in or dissatisfaction with the food. If he or she is a guest in someone's house, that is seen as an open insult to the host" (1977:304). Since one's bowl is a private place, "good manners do not preclude resting a piece of meat (or other items) in one's bowl between bites" (1977:304). However, one never puts a partially chewed piece of anything back into one of the common plates (I would not have thought this necessary to mention; however, an otherwise culturally sensitive person I know had the audacity to do so recently so it may bear mentioning). Also, it is extremely poor manners to suck or bite your chopsticks.

In some cases the bowl may be substituted for by a spoon, as, for example, when one goes out to lunch with one's workmates, and each diner is supplied with a flat plate piled high with rice topped with roast pork, chicken, duck and/or *lap cheong* (Chinese sausage), or with a helping of a single *ts'ai* dish (the latter known as *hui fan*).

Eating rice off a flat plate with chopsticks alone is not an easy task. Westerners exasperated with the use of chopsticks often feel their most intense frustration when trying to accomplish this task, and are often reduced to picking up small bits of rice with the ends of their chopsticks and placing them in the mouth. Seeming to pick at one's food in this way is not good manners and marks one as an incompetent foreign devil, confirming in most Chinese minds all of their previous prejudices about *guailos*.

No self-respecting Chinese would attempt to eat rice directly from a flat plate without first piling the rice onto, or scooping the rice into, a spoon. One eats the *ts'ai* or meat with one's chopsticks, but rice is most often carried to the mouth in a spoon. The spoon stands in for the bowl in the mini-context of an individual serving, and one can also think of the bowl itself as serving in the capacity of an enlarged spoon in the context of regular dining as well.

Rice is usually doled out from a common pot by the host or hostess. When someone has filled your rice bowl for you, it is accepted with two hands. To accept rice with one hand suggests disinterest, disrespect and carelessness. One places the full bowl in front of oneself and waits until everyone else has been served. It is very impolite to begin eating before everyone at the table has had his bowl filled with rice. When one has finished the rice in one's bowl, one does not continue to eat of the common *ts'ai* dishes. To eat *ts'ai* without rice in one's bowl is to appear a glutton interested only in *ts'ai*, of which one must consume a great deal to get full without rice. Depending on the degree of intimacy of a relationship, one may, when eating at the home of a friend or acquaintance, rise from the table to refill one's bowl with rice from the rice pot in the kitchen. However, at formal occasions one's host will usually be alert enough to notice when one's rice bowl is empty and move to fill it before one might be forced to request more rice. When one rises to get more rice, the host will usually insist on taking one's bowl and filling it. One may decline such assistance if the host is a close friend by simply saying "I'll serve myself."

At banquets one is expected to fill up on *ts'ai*, and consumption of too much rice may be a sign of disrespect to the quality of the *ts'ai* dishes. No rice should ever be left over in one's bowl at the end of a meal.

> As children we were always taught to leave not a single grain of *fan* in our bowl when we finished. Our elders strongly impressed on us that each single grain of rice or corn was obtained through the drops of sweat of the tillers of the soil (Hsü and Hsü 1977:308).

A corollary of this rule is never to take so much rice, or anything else for that matter, in your bowl as to be unable to finish it. It is also extremely disrespectful of the meal and of one's host to leave bits of rice on the table around one's bowl, and Chinese children are often told that each of these grains will materialize as a pockmark on the face of their future spouse.

As regards the *ts'ai* it is important to note again that it is arrayed for all to share. Generally speaking, especially on formal occasions, one does not serve oneself without first offering to others, at least those seated immediately to either side. This applies also to the taking of tea, and one generally fills a neighbor's cup before taking tea for oneself. When tea is poured for you, it is customary to tap the table with your fingers to convey your thanks.

The overriding rules of Chinese table customs is deference. Defer to others in everything. Be conscious of the need to share what is placed in common. This means don't eat only from those dishes that you like.

> One very common point of instructions from parents to children is that the best mannered person does not allow co-diners to be aware of what his or her favorite dishes are by his or her eating pattern (Hsü and Hsü 1977:304).

When taking from the common dishes one should also only take in such proportions that everyone else will be left with a roughly equivalent amount. It is polite to take the remains of a common *ts'ai* dish after a new dish has been brought out. The desirability of the remains is diminished by the introduction of a new dish, and the remains of the old become fair game. However, it is rather poor manners to incline a common plate toward oneself and scrape the remains into one's bowl. This "looking in the mirror" evokes the idea of narcissistic concern with oneself.

In general, young should defer to old in order of eating, and on formal occasions when guests are present children may even be excluded from the dining table until the adults are finished, or seated at a table separate from the adults. In the household of the boss of the factory where I did my fieldwork, apprentices commonly sat with the boss at the family table, but were relegated to the children's table at the New Year's feast.

A host will usually signal that it is appropriate to begin eating, after each person at the table has taken rice, by picking up his chopsticks and saying "*sik fan.*" When a guest has eaten his fill, he indicates that he is finished by putting down his chopsticks and encouraging others still eating to take their time. They in turn will inquire if the guest if full, and if he is he should say so. Upon finishing one may either remain at the table or leave. A guest of honor is expected to remain until all are finished.

In addition, one should be careful not to take large mouthfuls, to refrain from making noise while chewing, and to try to maintain the same pace of eating as others at the table. In contrast to Western etiquette in which "toothpicks are never used outside the privacy of one's room" (McLean 1941:63), toothpicks are provided at most Chinese tables and it is not impolite to give one's teeth a thorough picking at the table, provided one covers one's mouth with the opposite hand.

Spitting is not good manners at a Chinese table, although this is a rule often honored more in the breach. Spittoons are often provided in Chinese restaurants, both as a repository for waste water and tea used to sterilize one's utensils, and for expectorations of various sorts. Often the contents of the spittoons threaten to get up and walk away, so vile are the contents. The floor is fair game in many restaurants for just about anything remaining in one's mouth not swallowable, such as small bits of bone or gristle. Hong Kong has improved considerably in this regard in recent years, but in working-class restaurants and *daipaidongs,* spitting is still quite common.

INFLECTIONS OF GENERAL PRINCIPLES

Having laid out these basic ground rules, it remains to explore how these rules are inflected in the various contexts in which food events occur in contemporary Hong Kong. These contexts are many and varied, ranging from informal and intimate occasions when the family is together at home for a meal, to the more formal occasions involving elaborate feasts usually held in restaurants. Somewhat intermediate between these are the meals eaten out, but in somewhat less formal contexts—from breakfast taken at *dim saam* houses, lunches taken at foodstalls with workmates, to evening meals prepared in restaurants for individual diners (*hak fan*), and midnight snacks. Expectations as to appropriate comportment at the table will also vary with region of origin, age and class position.

For example, for Cantonese a full meal usually includes soup, and many Cantonese feel uncomfortable leaving the table without having partaken of soup. The minimal structure of the Cantonese meal includes not just *fan* (grain) and *ts'ai* (dishes), but also soup. This minimal structure is served up in what is known as *hak fan*, a specialty of some restaurants (usually Shanghainese) in which one may choose from a daily set menu of *hak* dishes, served with an extra large bowl of rice and the soup of the day. *Hak fan* is designed for people who must eat alone for some reason, not considered the most desirable circumstances. Two Chinese who knew each other would not sit down at the same table and order two individual orders of *hak fan.* They would surely grasp the opportunity of sharing the greater variety available to each through social eating.

Jack Goody has likened eating alone to defecating in public (1982:306) because of the absence of the social in meeting essentially biological needs. *Hak fan* assures that even taken alone, the minimum structural entity of a Cantonese meal is available to be consumed. This basic structure is also revealed in a variety of thermos containers used for carrying lunch to work which are equipped with compartments for rice, *ts'ai* and soup. Since the contexts in which food events occur in Hong Kong are so varied, soup is not always the focus of attention. Proceeding through the ordinary day's food events from morning to evening will give us occasion to note context-linked inflections of our general principles.

As mentioned previously, the morning food event does not pass muster as a meal, largely due to the absence of rice. Still, there are a variety of contexts in which this event may take place. At home, the morning food event usually involved rice from the evening before boiled down to congee with a variety of pickles and condiments tossed in or served on the side. This is usually grabbed quickly in the kitchen on the way out to work, if it is eaten at all, and seldom involves the entire family seated at a single table.

Eaten out, the morning food event may take several forms. Consistent with the quick and superficial character of the event at home is the food event taken at a food stall or *daipaidong,* of which several different types serve suitable breakfast fare—congee (most commonly with preserved egg and pork), *yautiu* (unsweetened fried dough strips), hot *daojeung* (soy bean milk), *jucheung fen* (rolled rice noodles), all served with tea, usually in a glass.

Eating at a *daipaidong*, and even in some restaurants, one assumes the probability that the chopsticks, stuffed together in a can and set at the center of the table for individual dinners to take, as well as one's cup, bowl and spoon, will not have been properly washed. A brief ritualized washing usually precedes the meal in which one pours a glass of boiling hot tea into one's glass, stirring the ends of the chopsticks in the water to sterilize them, pouring the still hot water into one's bowl where one's cup and spoon are immersed and sterilized. The wash water is then thrown out, usually on the street in the case of a *daipaidong*, or in a spittoon at a restaurant, and one is prepared to commence eating. Occasionally, one is even provided with a separate bowl for washing one's eating implements, filled by one's waiter with boiling water from a huge kettle.

At a *daipaidong* for breakfast, one usually shares a table with a stranger, or perhaps a neighbor or workmate, depending on whether one eats near home or near work. In any case, one's portion is usually one's own, and the rules of formal dining apply only in the most general terms. Food is usually taken with dispatch, as one is usually rushing to work or to school, and the idea is just to put something in one's stomach to suppress hunger till the first meal of the day— *ng fan* (lunch).

The slightly more formal morning food event is *dim saam,* referred to most often as *yam ch'a* (drink tea). "Drinking tea" again refers to something less than a "meal," although on weekends, taken with one's family at a large table, *dim saam* often involves the consumption of large quantities of buns, dumplings, rice noodles in various shapes, a variety of innards, and the like. One sits down, is approached by one's waiter, or in fancier restaurants by a host or hostess, who will inquire what kind of tea one will be drinking—*sao mei, bo lei, soy sin,* and that old perceived favorite of *guailos—heung pien* (jasmine). When the tea arrives the host will fill everyone's cup and the meal may begin.

One acquires food from carts pushed around by young children and/or aged women, and less frequently by older men. One may find oneself sharing a table with strangers, or with regular customers who eat at the same restaurant at the same time every morning. Going to *yam ch'a* on a regular schedule assures one of continuous contact with the usual crowd, and it is common to find oneself seated at the same table with many of the same people each morning. While polite conversations is the general rule, more juicy gossip is not inappropriate as the relationship between morning diners becomes more familiar.

Generally, each diner is aware of what he has consumed and the position of plates may be adjusted where they have been ambiguously placed so the waiter can figure the tab. One eats from one's own plates under such circumstances, and one pays for one's own plates; however, it is polite to fill the tea cup of one's neighbor from one's own pot if one is acquainted with him or her. There are still some restaurants in Hong Kong which serve tea in a covered bowl, quite literally stuffed with tea, and poured into a cup to be drunk, extremely dark, but the standard tea pot has replaced the bowl as a tea vessel in most restaurants.

A table shared with strangers or neighbors is usually an informal arrangement in which one eats one's own food. However, taking *dim saam* may also be a more formal occasion, especially on weekends, or when one has been *cheng*-ed (asked out). In such circumstances many of the rules of formal dining apply, i.e., the food on the table is common and should only be taken in such proportions that enough is left for others. One may order dishes one likes from the passing wagons, but one should always offer to others before taking from the dish for oneself. The dishes accumulate somewhat at random due to the vagaries of the itinerary of the carts, so there is no formal order to the dishes' arrival, although sweeter dishes are usually taken last.

Dim saam often trails off into lunch on formal or informal occasions, and by noon after the diners have warmed up with a few *dim saam* dishes, it is polite to inquire of one's fellow diners whether a plate of noodles or rice (a real meal) is in order, and if so, to order such dishes from the kitchen from one's waiter. Varieties of *dim saam* are also available from *daipaidong* as well, sometimes served up in individual portions to go.

The midday food event in Hong Kong includes rice or a reasonable substitute (rice noodles, bean noodles, wheat noodles), and is most often taken during a lunch hour break from factory or office labor. A variety of choices confront the Hong Kong worker eating out for lunch. Food stalls serve a variety of dishes, usually in individual portions on flat plates heaped high with rice, and covered with a single *ts'ai* dish. A glass of tea is usually served, and doubles again as a vessel for sterilizing one's chopsticks and spoon. Blue collar workers I knew in Hong Kong would often consume a full-to-the-brim tea tumbler of high octane spirits with such meals, and trundle back to work with the warm glow and slightly glazed look of a two-martini-lunch executive.

A plate of noodles may also be ordered from stalls specializing in such things. These may be served in individual portions, but given the easy divisibility of noodle dishes it is common for workmates to order a variety of noodle dishes and share them in common. A portion is lifted from the plates to one's bowl; with chopsticks initially, when the noodles are easily grasped in quantity; with help from the spoon as the plate gets progressively emptied. The setting of shared common dishes makes the general rules of the table outlines above once again applicable.

Co-workers will often go out to lunch at large *dim saam* restaurants, catch the tail end of the morning *dim saam* and order a variety of more substantial noodle or rice dishes. Where eating has taken the place in common, and occasionally even where individual portions have been served, it is unusual for the check to be divided. Someone usually pays the whole tab. Among workmates, or those who often eat together, there is an implicit assumption that in the long run reciprocity will be achieved. It is not impolite among status equals to grab the check and pay for one's fellow diner, but this is not polite if the status difference is too great. Fights over the check occasionally occur in a way which evokes the potlatches of Northwest Coast Indians in which a status hierarchy is confirmed. Paying the check validates one's status superiority over one's fellow diners. Of course, the wider social setting must also be taken into account. One may be desirous of seeking a favor of an important person, in which case paying the check may serve as a mild form of pressure in which the obligation of reciprocity is finessed, enjoining one's fellow diner to comply with one's request. Food events are first and foremost social events.

The evening meal taken at home usually includes some warmed over *ts'ai* from the previous day's meal plus an increment of newly prepared dishes. It is not good manners to ignore the leftovers, despite the fact that they may not be quite as attractive as when served the day before. The general rules of the table apply, although the intimate setting of the family at home makes their application somewhat less formal. Still and all, parents will most commonly instruct children as to the appropriate forms of behavior at the table in this setting, and the children must show that they understand and are learning. In many working-class homes in Hong Kong it is still common for the men to eat first, with the women joining later and/or hovering over the meal without ever formally sitting down.

At more formal dinners or at banquets or feasts associated with weddings, New Year's, funerals or festivals, the primacy of the *fan* and secondary character of the *ts'ai* is reversed, with attention devoted to the quality of the *ts'ai* dishes (Hsü and Hsü 1977:307), and rice not served till last. Thus at a banquet one may eat *ts'ai* without rice in one's bowl, and one is expected to fill up on *ts'ai* such that when the rice is finally served, one can only take a token portion, which is to say, this has been a real feast.

> During festivals and especially when acting as hosts all Chinese seem to ignore their sense of frugality and indulge in extravagance, *Ts'ai* dishes are served in abundance. The host or hostess will heap the guests' saucers with piece after piece of meat, fish, chicken and so on, in spite of repeated excuses or even protests on the guests' part. When *fan* is finally served, most around the table are full and can at best nibble a few grains (Hsü and Hsü 1977:307).

By the time the rice has been served at a banquet the diner has already had a share of cold appetizer, several stir fry dishes, or whole chickens, ducks, fish, soup and a sweet/salty dessert. The emphasis on whole items (with head and tail attached) symbolizes completeness and fullness, and evokes these meanings at the table. One tries to serve fish, *yü*, a homophone for surplus, *yü*, to sympathetically bring about that condition in one's guests.

It is not polite to turn over a fish at the table. Rather, when the side facing up has been finished, the skeleton is lifted off to leave the meat underneath exposed. Apparently, turning over the fish is taboo among boat people, since the fish symbolizes the boat which will capsize sympathetically if a fish is turned over. Waiters in Hong Kong are never sure which of their customers are boat folk and might take offense, so they generally refrain from turning over any fish and apparently the practice has now become general.

A variety of prestige foods, such as shark's fin soup and the various eight precious dishes, are served at banquets more for the social recognition they confer than for the pleasure derived from their consumption (see de Garine 1976:150).

Conceptually, whiskey belongs with grain from which it is distilled and may be taken with food as rice substitute. On formal occasions in Hong Kong scotch or VSOP Cognac is the rule, served straight in water tumblers, and often diluted with Seven-Up.

Another food event of note in Hong Kong is *siu yeh*—loosley translated as snacks. Usually taken late in the evening, they may include anything from congee, noodles and won ton, to roast pork, duck or chicken, to *hung dao sa* (sweet red bean soup—hot or iced) and *daofufa* (sweet bean curd usually flavored with almond). *Siu yeh* is usually served in individual portions. If you go out for won ton mien, everyone gets his own bowl. If you order duck's neck soup with rice, you are served an individual helping of soup, and an individual bowl of rice. Depending on the class of restaurant you take your *siu yeh* in, you may or may not find it advisable to wash your utensils with tea.

Itinerant street vendors with wheeled carts dispense a variety of prepared *siu yeh* in some residential neighborhoods, calling housewives and amahs to the street clutching their large porcelain bowls, or doling out cuttlefish parts to school-children on street corners.

In all these contexts the general pattern that emerges is one that centers on deference, in thinking first of the other, in suppressing one's inclination to satiate oneself before the other has had a chance to begin, in humility. One yields to the other before satisfying one's own urges. At the macro level of China's great tradition, one finds such behavior characteristic of the *chün-tzu,* the individual skilled in the *li* (etiquette, rites and ceremonies). He is one also skilled in the art of *jang*—of yielding, of accomplishing without activity, of boundless generosity, of cleaving to the *li.* There is even something of a Taoist resonance in all this, getting at things indirectly, without obvious instrumental effort.

Generally, it can be stated that the degree to which a Chinese practices the rules of etiquette marks his class position with respect to his fellow Chinese; although the degree to which the behavior of lower-class people at the table is informed by these rules should not be underestimated. Disregard of the rules on the part of a Chinese is regarded with as much distaste by their fellows as the faux pas normally committed by Westerners, except that the latter can be excused by their hopeless, if expected, ignorance.

It does not take much study for a Westerner to perform well enough at the table to impress most Chinese, since their expectations are exceedingly low. Keeping in mind a few simple things without slavishly parading one's knowledge, one can usually avoid provoking disgust and revulsion, and convince one's fellow diners that one is sensitive to others on their own terms, as well as to the world at large. Among the most basic of cultural patterns, learned early in life, the degree to which one observes these patterns has a lot to do with the way one is perceived as a person in Chinese terms.

Simple knowledge of the structural contexts, behavioral expectations and symbolic associations of food events can provide access across social boundaries that would otherwise be less easily breached, and make it possible to more easily achieve one's goals. Rather than constituting positively functioned adaptive responses, table manners and knowledge of them are better seen as an inventory of symbolic responses that may be manipulated, finessed and encoded to communicate messages about oneself. For Chinese, as for most everyone else, you are *how* you eat.

REFERENCES CITED

Chang, K. C. (ed.) 1977 Introduction, *In* Food in Chinese Culture. Hew Haven: Yale University Press

de Garine, I. 1976 Food, Tradition and Prestige. *In* Food, Man and Society. D. Walcher, N. Kretchmer, and H. L. Barnett, eds. New York: Plenum Press.

Douglas, M. 1966 Purity and Danger. London: Routledge. 1975 Implicit Meanings. London: Routledge.

Farb, P., and G. Armelagos 1980 Consuming Passions. New York: Houghton Mifflin.

Goody, J. 1982 Cooking Cuisine and Class. Cambridge: Cambridge University Press.

Hammerton, J. A. 1936 Manners and Customs of Mankind, Vol. I. New York: W. M. A. Wise.

Harris, M. 1974 Cows, Pigs, Wars and Witches. New York: Random House.

Hsü, F. L. K., and V. Y. N. Hsü 1977 Modern China: North. *In* Food in Chinese Culture. K. C. Chang, ed. New Haven: Yale University Press.

Li Chi 1971 Chü Li, Part I. Taipei: World Publishing.

McLean, N. B. 1941 The Table Graces: Setting, Service and Manners for the American House without Servants. Peoria, IL: Manual Arts Press.

Myerhoff, B. 1979 Number Our Days.New York: Dutton.

Rubel, P., and A. Rosman 1978 Your Own Pigs You May Not Eat. Chicago: University of Chicago Press.

3 AGING IN THE UNITED STATES ACHIEVING NEW UNDERSTANDING THROUGH FOREIGN EYES

—ANDREI SIMIĆ

Today there are probably very few Americans who conceive of old age as the "golden years." At every turn—in the media, in academic studies, in the pronouncements of government agencies, and in popular wisdom—we are confronted with a series of dreary images of later life, images punctuated by every sort of misery and deprivation. In effect, old age has become the negative focus of both public and private concern; it has been transformed into a so-called social problem. It seems paradoxical that this has occurred at a time when most people can reasonably expect to live in comfort and relatively good health to an age unimagined even in the very recent past. While this undoubtedly reflects the fact that there are now many more old people than ever before among us, and that our population is aging as a whole, it also mirrors substantive changes in the role of the elderly, and in our ideas concerning them. Moreover, not only has there been a shift in our attitudes towards aging, but also in the nature of ideas the elderly hold about themselves.

At one time, not so very long ago, older people were largely integrated into our society as members of families, neighborhoods, churches, voluntary associations, and the like. Thus, their participation in community life was achieved through a variety of age-heterogeneous institutions characterized by intimate, multistranded relationships. Berger and Neuhaus (1977) have referred to such small-scale social groupings as "mediating structures" since they stand between the individual and the large-scale impersonal abstractions that typify the modern industrial-urban state. However, with the weakening of these institutions, especially the family, in recent times a new self-perception rooted in growing feelings of marginality and alienation has emerged on the part of the elderly who have increasingly shifted their orientation from that of a generalized category to that of an age-homogeneous, common-interest group. Thus, for many old age itself has become an organizational principle by which to satisfy some of the most basic psychological, social, and economic needs. In part, this process has been stimulated by the activism and high visibility of other "oppressed" minorities. The feminist movement is particularly analogous since it, too, has involved a conceptual transition from a categorical identity to one of a quasicorporate nature. However, in the case of the aged, such models should not be regarded as causal per se, but rather as responses to similar cultural and social conditions. Thus, the militancy of many women and older people must be understood as symptoms of certain kinds of changes that have surfaced recently in American life, and that represent, to a large degree, the intensification of ideological elements already present in our culture.

One way of interpreting the role of older people in contemporary American society is in terms of *adaptive strategies* in response to the pervasive social and cultural discontinuities that have typified many of their lives. In essence, this addresses the perplexing theoretical problem regarding the causal connection between ideology and values on the one hand, and behavior on the other. This conceptual problem is further compounded when we attempt to study our own society, embedded as we are in a cultural system we tend to accept uncritically as part of the "natural order." Nevertheless, the obstacle is not insurmountable, and one way of achieving a greater degree of objectivity is through a cross-cultural perspective, by observing ourselves from the vantage point of others. As Kluckhohn has aptly noted, "anthropology holds up a great mirror to man and lets him see himself in his infinite variety" (1949, p 11). Implicit in this metaphor is the assertion that only through our acquaintance with this "infinite variety" can we eventually come to terms with the realities of our own lives. In other words, the exotic provides a perspective from which to view the familiar. In effect, this represents a reversal of the usual ethnological process which Bohannan (1963) has described as "the translation of strange ideas, customs, and things into familiar language" (p 10). Curiously, while this kind of cultural introspection is not at all easy, once it has been achieved, it is surprising how evident these new understandings should have been all along.

An anthropological perspective does not only entail *cultural relativism,* but also what is commonly termed the *holistic approach:* seeing things in context as parts of integrated systems of thought and behavior. This is particularly pertinent for the study of aging in America since so much of the gerontological literature has portrayed older people stereotypically as somehow existing in isolation outside the boundaries of their own culture and society. Thus, I will first turn to the description of these models of alienation, and then attempt to explain them contextually as the inevitable product of a more generalized form of social and cultural organization of which America is perhaps a prototype. Finally, I will focus on specific aspects of American culture as they affect aging. Central to this discussion will be such traditional ethnographic topics as the socialization of children, the developmental cycle of the family, and the values and world view structuring intergenerational and other family relationships. Drawing implicitly on both the anthropological literature dealing with so-called traditional societies and my own field work in Yugoslavia and among Latin Americans, I will attempt to view American culture very much as an ethnographer describes an exotic society with emphasis on those characteristics that seem somehow unusual by the standards of much of the rest of the world.

IMAGES OF AGING IN AMERICA

One of the earliest attempts to understand aging cross-culturally was that of Simmons who published *The Role of the Aged in Primitive Society* in 1945. Drawing on the Yale Human Relations Area Files, he examined the position of the elderly in 71 so-called primitive societies. Among other findings, he concluded that for most people success in aging is related to their ability to make a place for themselves in society so that as they grow older they can achieve fulfillment through prolonged strategic participation. He asserted that everywhere old people had five wishes: to live as long as possible; to conserve waning energy; to continue sharing in the affairs of life; to protect seniority rights; and to experience an easy and honorable release from life. If Simmons' conclusions are accurate, and there is little common-sense reason to doubt them, the fate of many of the elderly in our society appears to fall short of these expectations in at least the latter three instances.

Regardless of what model of success in aging is evoked, old age in America is generally viewed as a total disaster and, except for death, the ultimate form of alienation. This negative perspective is not only an artifact of academic opinion, but also of our folk culture. For instance, Clark (1967) has suggested that one of the main reasons for the neglect of the study of aging by anthropologists is that they hold the same aversion to the subject as the public at large. In many ways, both aging and death are perceived as abnormal states, and Clark (1973, p 81) further notes that frequently the only sanctioned roles the elderly are permitted to play are those of sick and dependent persons. Moreover, old age is the only stage in the life cycle that is conceptualized pathologically and in terms of losses rather than accrued gains (cf Rosow, 1974, p 23). This is particularly perplexing, since the logic of other cultures tells us that old age should ideally provide the stage for the dramatization of a lifetime of experience and accomplishment (cf Simic and Myerhoff, 1978, p 243).

It is probably not an exaggeration to state that many Americans perceive the aged as a class existing somehow outside the normal range of everyday experience as a kind of pariah group. This view has led a number of scholars to regard the elderly as either a "social minority" (cf Kiefer, 1971) or as the carriers of a distinctive subculture (Rose, 1962; 1965). The implications are clear: all too often older people have been forced to live lives segregated from those ideas and activities deemed most significant by the larger society. In one of the most influential studies of aging during the last few decades, Cumming and Henry (1961) have asserted that there is a direct relationship between aging and decreased interaction within a social system, a theory they have labeled *disengagement.*. While the authors have imputed universality to their concept, it is significant that the research was carried out among a largely white, middle-class sample from Kansas City—representatives of the dominant Anglo-American cultural mode. In a similar conceptual framework, Anderson (1972) has proposed the idea of *deculturation,* by which the elderly gradually assume a "cultureless" role in which they function largely outside of the dominant traditions that constitute the daily patterns of the rest of the population. In essence, disengagement and deculturation simply represent different facets of the same sense of alienation and anomie. However, to assert that this separation on the part of older people from significant relationships, activities, and values is the inevitable result of the aging process per se is to belie the pervasive influence of the underlying normative structure of mainstream Anglo-American culture, a subject that will be treated in greater detail below.

Another related perspective has focused on the elderly as they attempt to adapt to a hostile environment. For example, Foster and Anderson (1978) identify two strategies by which older people cope with their unenviable position on the fringes of society: the "confront-the-system model" and the "escape-the-system model". The former is exemplified by Clark and Anderson's (1967) 3-year longitudinal study of more than 1000 elderly San Franciscans. Here, the aged are depicted in a constant struggle for social acceptance and self-esteem as they attempt to endow their otherwise denigrated status with an aura of prestige. The authors' basic premise is that the elderly face the task of finding a place where they can achieve a sense of worth, however, such places do not actually exist as cultural norms, but must be discovered in the unclaimed and overlooked niches of our society. Moreover, as part of this process there is an inevitable shift from the active control over others and productive participation to a self-contained system of values not generally recognized by the culture as a whole. This adaptive strategy focuses on the conservation of physical and psychological resources, self-acceptance, and the accommodation to passivity, and as such it conflicts markedly with the dominant ethos of American society.

The escape-the-system model refers to the conscious creation on the part of the elderly of new, age-homogeneous communities where older people may again experience a sense of valued and vital participation. These self-conscious institutions may assume a variety of forms ranging from voluntary associations to retirement communities. A salient characteristic is that they all, to one degree or another, attempt not only to create a self-contained system of values, but to also exclude discordant or counterindicative elements that may impinge upon them from the outside world. An example of this model is provided by Byrne, (1974), who summarizes her findings in a California retirement community:

> The secret of Arden's success is that adaptation to life in this high-density, age-segregated, planned community requires a less drastic modification of behavior and values than growing old in the urban or suburban areas from which the majority of residents came. Moving to Arden is their personal solution to the difficulties of growing old in a society which has little regard for its elders (p 152).

Without denying that the foregoing models represent highly visible aspects of American life, they require qualification in several ways. First, they represent only a limited sample, albeit an important one, of the American population, and as such tend to ignore the heterogeneity of our society as well as the wide variability of individual experience. Secondly, there seems implicitly embedded in these views the widespread American belief in the perfectability of the human experience and the idea that contentment is somehow "natural." Similarly, when we speak of the "trials of aging," we frequently do so in the implicit comparative context of an idealized "Golden Era" thought to have existed at sometime in the past when venerable elders enjoyed unlimited love, security, and respect in the bosom of large, extended families. Regardless of the reality of this image, and there is good cause to question its authenticity, it is primarily a statement of a cultural ideal, to which we tenaciously cling in the face of our collective unwillingness to abandon more immediate values and to make the sacrifices required to transform this quasi-fiction into fact. Furthermore, if we are to judge from the evidence from contemporary societies characterized by extended kinship systems, family relationships in such cultures are frequently fraught with intergenerational tensions, conflict, and even fear (cf. LeVine 1965; Simic 1978b). Thus, if one is to read between the lines of the ethnographic data, the role of elders in many traditional societies might well be portrayed in terms of empty rituals and symbolic honors devoid of genuine respect and sentiments of affection from others. It is also worth noting that old age per se, like every other stage of the life cycle, is characterized by its own particular problems, frustrations, and potential tragedies regardless of the cultural setting. In this respect, it should be recognized that in no known society do all members have equal access to wealth, prestige, and valued modes of behavior, and everywhere desired things and attributes are distributed differentially. In light of these considerations, the cross-cultural comparison of levels of satisfaction and happiness appears particularly tenuous if not outright impossible (cf Simic, 1978a). However, other kinds of questions can be posed. Is the criterion of age a significant one for the awarding of honor and other benefits in a society? To what degree are older people integrated into those activities considered most important and central to the prime values of the culture? And, finally, to what extent do people growing old in a society experience a sense of continuity, tying together the various stages of their lives?

American society, or at least that segment associated with the dominant upper middle class, appears particularly deficient in respect to the forementioned questions. The explanation for this is obviously complex, rooted in the demographic and historical development of the United States. However, as an anthropologist I am not nearly so interested in the origins of our culture as I am in understanding how it fits into a spectrum of possibilities, and in explaining the way that it functions as a system of interrelated ideas and behavior.

MODERNIZATION AND AGING: THE UNITED STATES AS A SOCIETAL TYPE

Urban life seems to have always enjoyed an unsavory reputation, and even in the classical civilizations of the Mediterranean the countryside was idealized as a both moral and physically healthy environment in opposition to the dangerous forces embodied in the city (Caro Baroja, 1963). These models are surprisingly consistent, and urbanites today continue to dream of some idyllic and uncomplicated paradise thought to lie somewhere beyond the city limits. Such ideas are no less common in academic thought than in popular folklore. For instance, in 1938, Wirth published a now-classic essay in which he asserted that urbanism was characterized by disorganization, alienation, and social pathology. Similarly, the literature on aging has not escaped this trend. For example, Cowgill and Holmes (1972), on the basis of cross-cultural materials dealing with such diverse peoples as the

Bantu and Norwegians, concluded that there was a negative correlation between modernity on the one hand, and participation, status, and satisfaction among the aged on the other. Here again, we find ourselves in the analytically difficult position of attempting to assess levels of satisfaction. Moreover, the argument is further weakened by evidence suggesting that modernization is neither a uniform process everywhere nor necessarily a negative one (cf Lewis, 1952; Simic, 1975). Nevertheless, the opposition between so-called traditional and modern, complex societies is real, with profound implications for the manner in which individuals are integrated into their cultures.

Perhaps one of the most enduring themes in social thought is the attempt to define the direction of change. More often than not, this quest has centered around the search for a definition of "progress" or "modernization." Unfortunately, in spite of the intensity of such efforts, these concepts still remain rather nebulous. Nevertheless, consensus is not entirely lacking, and an intellectual pedigree of very similar ideas oppose, "traditional" and "complex" societies as dichotomous stereotypes. For example, from a plethora of such concepts, among the most famous are Durkheim's (1933) *mechanical* and *organic solidarity,* Tonnies's (1957) *Gemeinschaft* and *Gesellschaft* ("community and society"), Sapir's (1964) *genuine* and *spurious culture* and Redfield's *folk-urban continuum* (1941) and the *moral* and *technical order* (1953). If the obvious utopian overtones of these ideas are ignored, and allowances are made for abstractions that overlook the evidence of counterindicative cases, there nevertheless still remains a core of truth. Implicit in each of these dyads is the contrast between social systems whose cohesion stems principally from intimate, face-to-face relationships, and those held together by conscious, abstract, social contracts. Phrased in another way, these dichotomies reveal a shift from systems dependent on concrete personal ties based at least in part on accidents of birth and other ascribed characteristics, to those rooted in more remote and vicarious relationships where individual accomplishment and knowledge play a larger part.

The traditional-modern dichotomy was largely popularized in the American social sciences by Robert Redfield, who applied this venerable concept to the analysis of his field work in Yucatan (1941). The contrast was clear-cut; in what he called the *folk society* the members experienced a high level of commonality and empathy due to the homogeneity of their culture and the unity of their consciousness. Redfield referred to this kind of social cohesiveness as the *moral order.* In such a system, which presumably characterized preurban peoples everywhere, the pursuit and cultivation of interpersonal relationships within the folk community, and in harmony with traditional norms regarded as sacred, constituted an end unto itself. Thus, all other activities, including economic ones, played supportive roles to the central concern of maintaining all-important social ties within the context of ideas placing individuals in an undifferentiated continuum between the natural and supernatural worlds. Conversely, Redfield perceived urban society as an instrumental one where the ties between individuals were oriented toward goals outside of, and extraneous to, the relationships themselves. People in such a context tended to operate atomistically in terms of the contributions their specific skills and knowledge could make to the good of society as a whole. In this way, each person was alienated from kin and neighbors by his specialized abilities and the resultant niche he occupied in the social abstraction.

Another classic interpretation of the modernization process has emerged from Weber's study, *The Protestant Ethic and the Spirit of Capitalism* (1930). A dominant theme in this analysis of the relationship between religious ideology and economic behavior in Western European industrial society is the concept of *rationalism.*. Although Weber's argument is complex, it will be interpreted simply here, as an instrumentality for the achievement of economic and social ends in the most efficient way possible without reference to extraneous goals or personal social entanglements. In a thoroughly rational society social relationships would be formulated on the basis of, and subordinated to, economic and bureaucratic tasks deemed important to the maintenance of the social fabric as a whole and thus abstracted from the needs of any specific individuals or interest groups.

Closely tied to the concept of rationalism is that of *universalism*. This refers generally to the application of a single set of standards in such a way that privileges and responsibilities in a society are distributed on the basis of the same objective criteria by which everyone may compete openly in terms of his or her particular experience, knowledge, and skills. Thus, as society becomes larger and more complex, in order to function optimally, it *ideally* abandons particularistic values in favor of a more abstract morality encompassing not simply the family, clan, or tribe, but rather the society as a whole. However, in so doing, the individual's relationship to society necessarily becomes less concrete and more individualistic and vicarious. At the same time, society tends to be experienced through a multitude of institutions that are perceptually remote and limited in function. In this way, participation in social life no longer takes place exclusively in terms of membership in tight-knit, bounded, multipurposed groups, but is fragmented between many arenas each with its own particular and highly specialized characteristics (Simic, 1975, pp 48–85).

The preceding models are, of course, ideal types, and only represent reality in a general sense. However, they do summarize a set of widely held beliefs about the direction of change and the nature of the modernization process, and, more significantly for the present discussion, appear to conform closely to a number of central values in contemporary American culture that hold particular portent for the fate of the aged.

THE AMERICAN FAMILY IN CROSS–CULTURAL PERSPECTIVE[1]

What is perhaps most significant about American culture (and that of a few other highly industrial and urbanized Western countries) is its uniqueness. Not simply unique in the way that each culture differs from every other culture, but unique as a type in opposi-

---

1. This section closely follows the discussions in Simić (1977, 1979).

tion to the spectrum of economically less developed and more traditional societies. More-over, this singularity does not stem entirely from the scale, technological acumen, and ma-terial wellbeing of the United States, but rather, is also intrinsic in the very basis of human relationships, and particularly in those values focusing on such grass-roots institutions as the family. This aspect of American life was unwittingly underscored by an expatriot American journalist, living in Madrid, who once commented that "Spanish teenagers spend an inordinate amount of time at home with their parents!" The question can only be posed, "*inordinate* by whose standards?" Nevertheless, in spite of its lack of objectivity, his state-ment unintentionally revealed as much about American culture as Spanish, and at the same time alluded to some of our most revered values.

Ruth Benedict (1934) contended that each culture is integrated in terms of a dominant theme that permeates the entire substance of social life. Although our present knowledge suggests that her assertion was, at best, an oversimplification, and that real cultures encom-pass a complex web of often conflicting norms and assumptions, nevertheless, some domi-nant ideas appear to surface in every society. For example, there is little doubt that inde-pendence, self-determination, freedom of decision-making, and individuality are among some of the most widely enunciated and accepted transcendental values in contemporary American society. These abstractions have recently assumed an increasingly visible role. This has perhaps been nowhere more evident than in family life with its growing deempha-sis on corporacy, and the orientation of its members away from the home towards the exter-nal world, each person with his or her own particular focus, interests, and personal network of social relationships. Although this is not the only pattern of behavior in American life today, these atomistic, centrifugal forces have been noted repeatedly by a spectrum of ob-servers. For instance, Riesman (1972, p 38), in an essay dealing with American character in the twentieth century, observes that children, through the influence of their peers, the school, and the mass media, are oriented towards imperatives not in harmony with parental ones. Noting these same tendencies, Yugoslav anthropologist Vera Erlich (who lived for almost 10 years in California) has written the following (1972) (my translation):

> The desire for complete independence has become so strong during the past few decades that it has emerged as one of the principal causes for the isolation of older people, and although the entire American life style from its incipiency placed personal independence on a high rung of the value scale, the desire for independence has become so absolute in recent times that it is threatening family life (p 55).

Bronfenbrenner (1974) also voices alarm about the direction of change in American life and, in an essay dealing with the origins of alienation in our society, observes that "the degree of estrangement between young people and adults in the United States is currently higher than it has been in other times" (p 53). Despite counterindicative opinions, such as those of Bengtson (1970, pp 19–22), that do not entirely concur with the "generation gap model," the evidence appears to support overwhelmingly Bronfenbrenner, who attributes this schism to the failure of both the family and the larger society to maintain mechanisms and institutions that once integrated young people into meaningful sets of intergenerational relationships. This same theme of familial fragmentation also surfaces in purely literary descriptions such as that of Lindbergh (1963) who portrays the reactions of a young French-man to American family life: "They were all individuals . . . loosely but reluctantly tied to-gether into a family group" (p. 97). In short, such expressions of foreboding have become commonplace stereotypes, whose seeming ubiquitousness is noted by Demos (1979):

> There is a diffuse sense of 'crisis' about our domestic arrangements generally—a feeling that the fam-ily as we have traditionally known it is under siege, and may even give way entirely. The manifesta-tions of this concern are many and varied—and by now have high visibility. . . . There is a new flower-ing of commissions, task forces, and conferences on one or another aspect of family life (p 43).

If self-fulfillment and unfettered individualism are indeed prime values undermining the solidarity of family and other close personal ties, what are the correlates of this kind of worldview, and, in particular, how is it expressed in behavior? In part, the answers can be elucidated with reference to the socialization process, the family developmental cycle, the patterns of authority and affect within the family, and, above all else, in the light of basic assumptions about the nature and purpose of interpersonal relationships—all topics tradi-tionally treated by ethnography. In this respect, I will next attempt to describe what appears to be a very prevalent, perhaps the dominant, pattern of American family life. I will do so as much as possible from an alien perspective, and, in so doing, risk the affirmation of the obvious. However, this will lead to the illumination of the less evident origins of the unen-viable position occupied by large number of the elderly in our society.

The model of family life and aging in America suggested here is largely an impres-sionistic one consistent with the various theories of alienation discussed earlier. It is not the result of deliberate and focussed field work per se, but stems from a conscious reexamina-tion of my own experiences as a participant in American society against the background of almost 15 years of intermittent field work among Yugoslavs, Latin Americans, and immi-grant groups in the United States. The cultural patterns described typify what I believe to be a common, although not universal, complex of behavior and belief among the Anglo and Anglicized upper-middle class in our country—a complex that appears, however, to be rapidly diffusing among other elements in the population. Moreover, the ideas associated with this world view are supported by a significant segment of ostensibly "informed" opin-ion, that is, by many, perhaps most, of the "cultural elite."

One measure by which families can be compared cross-culturally is in terms of their patterns of periodic fission and fusion. From this perspective, the developmental cycle of the American family is extremely short, spanning the period from the establishment of an independent household by a young couple until their last-born child reaches the late teens or early 20s. Outside of certain ethnic groups, religious enclaves, and other conservative minorities, the almost universal expectation in our society is that from about the age of 18, all adults, married or single, will establish themselves in autonomous households that are separate from those of their parents. Encouraged by the ready availability of housing and relative economic prosperity, spatial autonomy and psychological independence have emerged as a major tenets of American ethos. The abandonment by young adults of their natal homes for work, education, marriage, or simply to enjoy an unencumbered lifestyle constitutes an abrupt and essentially permanent rupture in their lives and those of their parents, who nevertheless share essentially the same expectations, and either overtly or implicitly encourage this behavior.

The fragmented developmental cycle of the American family provides a key to understanding the culture of aging in that the modes of behavior that determine its brevity also shape the roles people are destined to play in later life. The experience of being old and the way the elderly perceive and present themselves are not only the result of the role models that were available to them as they grew up, but also stem from the entire socialization process beginning with a child's earliest years. American children are indoctrinated almost from the moment of birth in the ideology of independence. A central element in this process is a concept notably lacking in many other cultures, that of *privacy* with its connotation of the *right, pleasure*, and even *necessity* of being alone. This is expressed in a number of ways including the exclusive control of personal space and material possessions. In essence, privacy involves the positive evaluation of freedom from the intrusion of others, be it actual or symbolic. Ideally, each child, even a newborn baby in its crib, is given a room apart from that of his or her parents and/or siblings in order to respect the mutual requirement for privacy. Moreover, in the case of siblings, there is a belief that each child's uniqueness transcends the commonality of family membership, and therefore his or her interests are not identical with those of siblings, but will eventually be expressed in the circle of extrafamilial age-mates.

Underlying this early socialization process is the assumption of peer-group solidarity, and a stress on the importance of achieved relationships based on this or that narrow interest. Here we can see the assertion not only of universal standards, but also of technocracy's demand for specialists unencumbered by binding personal ties, and thus free to fill highly specific slots in the society wherever they occur. This early individualization and orientation toward the world outside the home is reflected in the realization of such crisis rites as birthday parties where parents and other family members remain discreetly offstage while active participation is limited to the child and his or her extrafamilial guests. This kind of behavior reaches its apex during the teens when children unrepentingly, even righteously, exile their parents from the home during social gatherings that may reach orgiastic proportions in their proclamation of filial independence. More often than not, this is accepted by the older and younger generation alike as part of the normal segregation of parents and children.

The orientation of American children is further directed away from their families at a very early age through participation in a myriad of voluntary associations, organized sporting events, and other planned activities. This is totally harmonious with the fact they are not generally expected to spend a significant amount of their leisure time interacting with other family members, and frequently when they choose to do so, they are apprehensively regarded as "odd," and efforts are usually made to assure greater participation in peer-group activities. "Social adjustment," (meaning "getting along with one's age-mates"), for example, has long been a prime concern of American public education. This same stress continues throughout the life-cycle, and adults together with their own peers frequently dedicate themselves to an exhausting and sometimes frenetic round of "self-improvement," benevolent, civic-minded, and recreational activities that bear little or no relationship to the needs and welfare of their families as a whole. The specificity of generational interests has, in fact, become so widely accepted in America that there is a belief in the existence of age-specific cultural matrices, the most familiar of which has been embellished with the formal designation of "youth culture."

The democratic ideal dominates American family ideology. There is both a stress on the equality of rights and on equal participation in decision-making within the limits of each member's abilities. At the same time, there is a deemphasis of hierarchal principles based on either age or sexual identity. Thus, lacking any clear-cut system for the application of power within the family, the decisive factor rests on the nature of individual personalities. Not only are the rights of adults vis-a-vis children vaguely defined by the culture, but most formal forms of deference towards older persons are also notably lacking. Moreover, what parental prerogatives do exist are rapidly eroded as children approach adulthood. Similarly, older siblings are not usually given authority over, or responsibility for, their younger brothers or sisters. On the contrary, efforts by older children to dominate younger ones are usually discouraged as an inevitable but unfortunate form of antisocial behavior.

In the same way that egalitarian and democratic ideals mitigate against any preestablished system of authority within the family, the striving for autonomy tends to limit the nature of affectual exchanges. Overt or effusive displays of affection are characteristically confined to husbands and wives, or to the interaction of adults with very young children. Certainly, with the onset of adolescence there is the expectation of diminishing signs of affect between parents and children, and marriage heralds an almost total transfer of both loyalty and sentiment from the natal family to the newly created household. Implicitly assumed is that the most enduring ties are those linking husband and wife who constitute the only theoretically corporate unit within the family. Today, even this bond is in question, and recent currents of thought suggest that husband and wife, too, should be freed from entangling mutual commitments, each to pursue his or her own individual interests.

Nowhere is the evidence for the lack of corporate sentiment within the American family clearer than in the realm of economics. For example, as soon as they are able, children are commonly encouraged to earn money, or to at least exercise control over it. This is usually rationalized in terms of "learning the value of money," although this cliche surely also implies "learning how money can make one free." At the same time, children are rarely expected to contribute any significant portion of their resources to a common family coffer. Thus, children's earnings constitute private property to be disposed of in accord with their own needs and caprices. This same compartmentalization of family resources continues throughout the entire life-cycle. Underwriting this is the belief that the financial success or bad fortune of one family member is not necessarily that of another. Although money is frequently exchanged between family members, this often occurs in the form of loans that are sometimes even negotiated on the basis of signed formal agreements stipulating the payment of interest. Similarly, although parents frequently aid their children financially after they have left home, it is almost always with the overt rationale of helping them establish themselves as "independent persons." Thus, such exchanges are not intended to create the basis of a binding and continuing reciprocity linking the two generations. This same ideology also prevails in later life, and what the elderly seem to fear more than anything else is "demeaning dependence" on their children or other family members. In essence, the limiting factor in intrafamilial economic exchanges is the quasimoral concern of always remaining "one's own person."

Behavior outside the home is largely shaped by a predisposition toward universal standards and a concomitant antipathy toward all forms of personalism including familism. These values assume the aspect of a moral imperative, and by their very definition blur and transcend the boundaries of the family. The result is that in the United States, unlike much of the rest of the world, the family does not constitute the focus of an acutely defined moral double standard differentiating behavior considered characteristically "good" and associated with the closed world of the household from that permitted in the "amoral" universe of the society at large (cf. Banfield 1958; Simic 1975, pp 48–50). In other words, in American culture the same general standards are *ideally* applied to kin and outsiders alike. Even such venerable ideas as parents' responsibility for the actions of their children have recently come under scrutiny. Thus, the weak corporate image of the family fails to evoke a compelling rationale for a lifelong cooperation linking the generations in the maintenance of a common reputation.

If the family does not provide the primary arena for social engagement and the attainment of individual esteem, what does? One answer can be found in a set of ideas commonly associated with Protestantism, and in particular with Calvinism (cf. Weber, 1958). Here I refer to the familiar concept of *work* as a moral commitment containing its own intrinsic rewards. Perhaps nowhere in the world has this idea enjoyed greater ascendancy than in the United States where, for many, it has assumed the aspect of an absolute imperative. And, even though recently there has been considerable movement away from this ethos in the direction of a variety of popular philosophies focussing on "self-improvement," transcendence, and hedonism, these new ideologies appear to be functionally very similar to the work ethic in their stress on the self-contained and atomistic nature of people. In whatever form it may assume, the work ethic has become almost a cliche of American national character, and as such, merits restatement in the context of ideas about the family. Most significantly, occupational status has largely replaced kinship as the primary marker of social identity. With reference to this, an Indian anthropologist (Triloki Pandey, personal communication) once commented that upon meeting a stranger in India, one does not first ask personal name and occupation as in the United States, but rather, simply the identity of his or her kinship group. This observation points to the primacy of both individualism and work in America, and suggests that the family, in many cases, constitutes little more than a logistic mechanism for the support of its individual members in their various occupational statuses. In other words, activities outside the home are not regarded as a common effort uniting family members, but constitute unrelated sets of moral obligations for the attainment of individual psychic wellbeing and emotional fulfillment. The implication is not that work is valued in American culture and not in others, but rather that the values attributed to it differ from those in many other societies, and as such hold profound consequences for both family relationships and social life in general.

As mentioned before, I have chosen to describe those characteristics of American family life that contrast most strikingly with the norms of more traditional cultures. In this regard, a brief summary of family relationships and the values associated with them in such socially conservative environments as those typifying Yugoslavia and the Latin American upper and middle classes will serve to make this comparison overt and underscore the uniqueness of many aspects of our world view.

In the traditional Balkan and Latin American family the nourishment of corporate sentiments starts early in childhood with a constantly reinforced orientation away from extrafamilial interests. In this way, boundaries against "outsiders"—all those other than family members, kin, fictive kin, and very close friends—are continually strengthened through the application of parental authority, appeals to moral absolutes, and negative stereotyping. At the same time, the family or larger kinship unit is emphasized as the sacred bastion of fulfillment and security. Within the home there is a concomitant deemphasis on the concept of privacy and private property (the word "privacy," in the American sense, cannot even be directly translated into such languages as Spanish or Serbo-Croatian, and the closest dictionary synonyms focus on concepts of loneliness and withdrawal), and the sharing of space, material property, and information is combined with a prevailing ethic of secrecy toward persons outside the tight-knit family group. The social universe is sharply demarked in terms of *we* and *they*, and in more conservative homes the slightest bit of information leaked to the outside, no matter how seemingly trivial, may represent a potential chink in the family's protective armor, and as such, a potential weapon in the hands of others.

The ideal of family corporacy inevitably leads not only to economic cooperation, but also to the development of a common reputation. In turn, common reputation acts as a powerful lever for the support of traditional values particularly as they apply to family norms. Thus, behavior is never regarded as simply an individual concern, but as that of the entire family or kinship group whose members will exert a variety of moral and social pressures, sometimes even resorting to physical force or violence, to bring deviants back into conformity and to protect the common reputation. Another, perhaps even more significant correlate of this familistic ethos is the firm expectation, albeit not always realized, that each person will use his or her particular talents, position, resources, or power to the advantage of the entire group, which, in Yugoslav society, for instance, often includes even very distant kin. This ethic is, in a sense, tied to the expectation that a leveling process will always occur, with those possessing more giving to those with less. It is seemingly paradoxical that one of the underlying dynamics of the system is the frequent dissatisfaction of those engaged in such negotiations; those who give feel they are doing more than their fair share, and those who receive believe that they have not benefitted sufficiently. Nevertheless, in spite of such conflicts, few opt out of the game. Not only are there not many other options available, but there is also a deep love of, and commitment to, this kind of negotiation and reciprocity. Moreover, when close extrafamilial friendships are established, they are structured according to this same model.

Although the traditional family may appear homogeneous from the outside, internally it consists of a number of highly differentiated roles. The principle of age is dominant whether it corresponds to the difference between generations or to the order of birth among siblings. Interacting with the criterion of seniority is that of sex. The male is associated with overt authority, particularly in relations with the outside world, and the female with positive affect and the power associated with it. In fact, the influential role played by many women toward their children and grandchildren suggests that many overtly patriarchal societies such as those in Yugoslavia and Latin America can also be characterized as *crypto-matriarchies*. Nevertheless, regardless of the sources of power and influence, the constraints and privileges associated with age and sex lead to the inevitable logic that "only likes may compete" since those who differ in these respects also contrast in terms of their particular contributions, obligations, and privileges in both the household and the society as a whole (cf Friedl, 1962 pp 87–91).

One of the points of greatest variance between the model of the Yugoslav or Latin American family and that of its American, middle-class counterpart is the concept of an ideal marriage. Among the most venerable and ubiquitous American images is that of a married couple joined together by intense bonds of communication, affection, and mutual sexual and spiritual love. In this frequently unrealized dream, husbands and wives behave towards each other as inseparable companions and confidantes. Such a concept would appear alien, even indecent, in many other parts of the world. In contrast with the American norm, marriage is not a matter of personal predilection in most traditional societies, but rather, the product of an inevitable and pragmatic decision to create a reproductive and economic unit whose cohesion is based on the authoritative and affectual links *between* generations. It is not surprising that in such an atmosphere it is considered unusual, even improper, for unmarried children of any age to live outside the parental-home unless compelled by economic or educational necessity. Similarly, postmarital neolocality is not, as in our country, the universal pattern. Thus, it is unlikely, though it does occur, that older people will find themselves alone and dependent entirely on their own resources in their declining years.

In contrast with the way that many elderly Americans somehow exist *in* our society but not as *part* of it, in the more traditional settings just described, as a person grows older there is a progression from one age- and sex-specific role to another, each integrated within a series of interlocking family relationships. I remember once asking a Yugoslav villager, "How do older people and children spend their time?" He replied with some surprise, "Doing old people's and children's things, of course!" In other words, his culture provides specific models for each defined span in the life cycle, and these roles are not isolatory but serve to strengthen the intense reciprocity that underwrites all important relationships. The significance of this reciprocal ideal for the aged is succinctly summarized by Yugoslav family sociologist, Olivera Buric, who describes intergenerational relations (1976):

> Such obligations are regarded as part of the "natural order," and people uncritically strive to fulfill them. As in the normal course of events in other societies, most parents attempt to rear their children to the best of their ability. In return, Yugoslav children also consider it their duty to care for their parents in old age and infirmity, wherever they live and whether or not social services and help are available (p 131).

CONCLUSIONS

This chapter has proposed two opposing models of family organization, intergenerational relationships, and aging. These correspond to very different visions of society and the individual's place in it. Nonetheless, the contrast between these conceptual modes should not be interpreted as absolute but as one of degree. Family solidarity is not totally lacking among the American middle-class, nor is individualism and self-assertion unknown in traditional cultures. In this respect, then, the stereotypes presented here represent abstractions that only vaguely approximate real life. Nevertheless, certain overall trends and dominant ideas can usually be discerned in every culture.

There is an axiom in anthropology that culture does not determine behavior but simply limits choices, and this is the case with the aged in our society. Thus, it seems inevitable that the elderly, caught in a value system stressing individual psychological and economic independence, and evaluating excellence in terms of virtuosity and dedication in the performance of occupational tasks, once deprived of their work statuses, and lacking an ideology focusing on intergenerational reciprocity, will experience a deep sense of alienation, isolation, and anomie. Similarly, it is not surprising that, excluded from these routes to security and prestige, the elderly either withdraw from active competition for goals they cannot hope to achieve, or turn to the deliberate creation of age-homogeneous social settings where they can dramatize their own worth to each other. It is not fortuitous that such familiar slogans as "be self-sufficient" and "stay active" provide rallying cries for the aged, since these bits of popular wisdom echo core values in our culture as a whole. At the same time, it should be noted that in spite of their sense of exclusion and loneliness, many, perhaps most, of the older people in the United States enunciate and support the world view that has contributed to their own alienation. They are, in effect, unwilling to forego the reputed pleasures of independence and individualism to commit themselves to the kinds of give and take that typify interpersonal relationships in other more traditional societies. The fact is, for better or worse, older Americans share the same vision of what constitutes "the good life" as our population as a whole.

REFERENCES

Anderson, Barbara G. (1972) The process of deculturation: Its dynamics among United States aged. Anthropol Q 45:209–216.

Banfield, E.C. (1958) The Moral Basis of a Backward Society. Chicago: Free Press.

Benedict, Ruth (1934) Patterns of Culture. Boston: Houghton Mifflin.

Bengtson, Vern L. (1970) The generation gap: A review and typology of socio-psychological perspectives. Youth Society 3:7–32.

Bengtson, Vern L. (1973) The Social Psychololgy of Aging. New York: Bobbs Merrill.

Berger, Peter L. Neuhaus, Richard John (1977) To Empower People: The Role of Mediating Structures in Public Policy. Washington, D.C.: American Enterprise Institute for Public Policy Research.

Bohannan, Paul (1963) Social Anthropology. New York: Holt, Rinehart and Winston .

Bronfenbrenner, Urie (1974) The origins of alienation. Sci Am 231:53-61.

Buric, Olivera (1976) The Zadruga and the contemporary family in Yugoslavia. *In* Byrnes, Robert F. (ed.), Communal Families in the Balkans: The Zadruga. Notre Dame: University of Notre Dame Press.

Byrne, Susan W. (1974) Arden, an adult community. *In* Foster, George M. and Kemper, R.V. (eds.), Anthropologists in Cities. Boston: Little, Brown.

Caro Baroja, Julio (1963) The city and country: Reflections on some ancient common-places. *In* Pitt-Rivers, Julian (ed), Mediterranean Countrymen Paris: Mouton .

Clark, Margaret M. (1967) The anthropology of aging: A new area for studies of culture and personality. Gerontologist 7:55–64.

Clark, Margaret M. (1973) Contributions of cultural anthropology to the study of the aged. *In* Nader, Laura and Maretzki, T.W. (eds.), Cultural Illness and health. Washington, D.C.: American Anthropological Association, Anthropological Studies 9.

Clark, Margaret M. and Anderson, Barbara G. (1967) Culture and Aging: An Anthropological Study of Older Americans. Springfield, IL.: Charles C. Thomas .

Cowgill D.O. and Holmes, L.D. (eds.) (1972) Aging and Modernization. New York: Appleton-Century-Crofts.

Cumming, Elaine and Henry, William E. (1961) Growing Old: The Process of Disengagement. New York: Basic Books.

Demos, John (1979) Images of the American family, then and now. *In* Tufte, Virginia and Myerhoff, Barbara, (eds.), Changing Images of the Family. New Haven: Yale University Press.

Durkhiem, Emile (1933) The Division of Labor in Society. New York: Macmillan Company.

Erlich, Vera St. (1972) Americki Zivotni Stil [The American Life Style]. Zagreb: Sociologija.

Foster, George M. and Anderson, Barbara G. (1978) Medical Anthropology. New York: John Wiley.

Friedl, Ernestine (1962) Vasilika: A Village in Modern Greece. New York: Holt, Rinehart and Winston.

Havighurst, Robert J., Neugarten, Bernice L., and Tobin, Sheldon S. (1968) Disengagement and patterns of aging. *In* Neugarten, Bernice L (cd.), Middle Age and Aging. Chicago: University of Chicago Press.

Kiefer, Christie (1971) Notes on anthropology and the minority elderly. Gerontologist 11:94–98.

Kluckhohn, Clyde (1949) Mirror for Man: The Relationship of Anthropology to Modern Life. New York: Whittlesey House.

LeVine, R.A. (1965) Intergenerational tensions and extended family structures in Africa.*In* Shanas, E. Streib, G.F. (eds), Social Structure and the Family Generational Relations. Englewood Cliffs, N.J.: Prentice-Hall.

Lewis, Oscar (1952) Urbanization without breakdown: A case study. Sci Monthly 75:31–41.

Lindbergh, Anne Morrow (1963) Dearly Beloved: A Theme and Variations. New York: Popular Library.

Redfield, Robert (1941) The Folk Culture of Yucatan. Chicago: University of Chicago Press.

Redfield, Robert (1953) The Primitive World and Its transformations. Ithaca, N.Y.: Cornell University Press.

Riesman, David (1972) Some questions about the study of American character in the twentieth century. *In* Feldman, Saul D. and Thielbar, Gerald W., (eds.), Life Styles: Diversity in American Society. Boston: Little, Brown.

Rose, Arnold M. (1962) The subculture of aging: A topic for sociological research. Gerontologist 2:123–127.

Rose, Arnold M. (1965) The subculture of aging: A framework in social gerontology. *In* Rose, Arnold M. and Peterson, W.A. (eds.), Older People and Their Social World. Philadelphia: F.A. Davis.

Rosow, Irving (1974) Socialization to Old Age. Berkeley: University of California Press .

Sapir, Edward (1964) Culture, Language and Personality. Berkeley: University of California Press.

Simić, Andrei (1975) The Ethnology of Traditional and Complex Societies. Washington, D.C.: American Association for the Advancement of Science.

Simić, Andrei (1977) Aging in The United States and Yugoslavia: Contrasting models of intergenerational relationships. Anthropol Q 2:53–64.

Simić, Andrei (1978a) Introduction. Myerhoff, Barbara G. and Simic, Andrei (eds), Life's Career—Aging: Cultural Variations on Growing Old. Beverly Hills: Sage Press.

Simić, Andrei (1978b) Winners and losers: Aging Yugoslavs in a changing world.*In* Myerhoff, Barbara G. and Simić, Andrei (eds), Life's Career—Aging: Cultural Variations on Growing Old. Sage Press.

Simić, Andrei (1979) White ethnic and Chicano families. Continuity and adaptation in the new world. *In* Tufte, Virginia and Myerhoff, Barbara G. (eds.), Changing Images of the Family. New Haven: Yale University Press.

Simić, Andrei and Myerhoff, Barbara G. (1978) Conclusion. In Myerhoff, Barbara G. and Simić, Andrei , (eds.), Life's Career—Aging: Cultural Variations on Growing Old. Sage Press.

Simmons, Leo W. (1945) The Role of the Aged in Primitive Society. New Haven: Yale University Press.

Tonnies, Ferdinand (1957) Community and Society. East Lansing, MI: Michigan State University Press.

Weber, Max (1930) The Protestant Ethnic and the Spirit of Capitalism. London: George Allen and Unwin.

Wirth, Louis (1938) Urbanism as a way of life. Am J Sociol 44:1–24.

4 SCIENCE AND RACE

—JONATHAN MARKS

RACE AS AN EMPIRICAL ISSUE

Teaching that racial categories lack biological validity can be as much of a challenge as teaching in the 17th century that the earth goes around the sun—when anyone can plainly see the sun rise, traverse a path along the sky, and set beyond the opposing horizon. How can something that seems so obvious be denied?

Of course, that is the way all great scientific breakthroughs appear, by denying folk wisdom and replacing it with a more sophisticated and analytic interpretation of the same data. We can break down race into four separate empirical issues, each of which has been comprehensively answered by anthropology in this century.

IS THE HUMAN SPECIES NATURALLY DIVISIBLE INTO A SMALL NUMBER OF REASONABLY DISCRETE GROUPS?

Whether we examine people's bodies or sample their genes, the pattern that we encounter is very concordant. People are similar to those from geographically nearby and different from those far away. We refer to this pattern as *clinal,* a cline being simply a geographic gradient of a particular biological feature (Huxley, 1938; Livingstone, 1962).

Dividing human populations into a small number of discrete groups results in associations of populations and divisions between populations that are arbitrary, not natural. Africa, for example, is home to tall, thin people in Kenya (Nilotic), short people in Zaire (Pygmies), and peoples in southern Africa who are sufficiently different from our physical stereotypes of Africans (i.e., *West* Africans) as to have caused an earlier generation to speculate on whether they had some southeast Asian ancestry (Hiernaux, 1974). As far as we know, all are biologically different, all are indigenously African, and to establish a single category (African/Black/Negroid) to encompass them all reflects an arbitrary decision about human diversity, one that is not at all dictated by nature.

Further, grouping the peoples of Africa together as a single entity and dividing them from the peoples of Europe and the Near East (European/White/Caucasoid) imposes an exceedingly unnatural distinction at the boundary between the two groups. In fact, the

From AMERICAN BEHAVIORAL SCIENTIST, November–December 1996, Vol. 40, No. 2. Reprinted by permission of Sage Publications, Inc.

"African" peoples of Somalia are far more similar to the peoples of, say, Saudi Arabia or Iran—which are close to Somalia—than they are to the Ghanaians on the western side of Africa. And the Iranis and Saudis are themselves more similar to the Somali than to Norwegians. Thus associating the Ghanaians and Somalis on one hand and Saudis and Norwegians on the other generates an artificial pattern that is contradicted by empirical studies of human biology.

The reason why this clinal pattern exists lies in the processes of microevolution in the human species. Natural selection adapts people to their environment, yet environments generally change gradually over geography—consequently, adaptive differences in the human species might be expected to track that pattern. In addition, people interbreed with people nearby, who in turn interbreed with people nearby, and over the long run this reinforces the gradual nature of biological distinctions among populations. Indeed, the "isolation" of traditional indigenous peoples is a feature that has been consistently overestimated in the history of anthropology—all peoples trade, and where goods flow, so do genes (Terrell & Stewart, 1996; Wolf, 1972).

We know very little about the time frame in which these clines originated, but genetic and paleontological evidence points to a recent origin for the genetic diversity within our species. For example, we find two randomly chosen chimpanzees or gorillas to be considerably more different genetically than two randomly chosen humans, even though chimps, gorillas, and humans diverged from one another about 7 million years ago and are all consequently the same age (Ferns, Brown, Davidson, & Wilson, 1981; Ruano, Rogers, Ferguson-Smith, & Kidd, 1992). Genetic diversity in the human species is surprisingly ephemeral—only on the scale of tens of thousands of years—and seems in some large measure to have been replaced by cultural diversity.

The reason why Americans tend to see three "races" of people is simply an artifact of history and statistics. Immigrants to America have come mostly from ports where seafaring vessels in earlier centuries could pick them up—hence our notion of African is actually *West* African, and our notion of Asian is actually *East* Asian (Brace, 1995). When we realize that people originating from very different parts of the world are likely to look very different and combine that with the fact that most European immigrants came from north-central Europe, it is not hard to see why we might perceive three types of people.

If there were a larger immigrant presence in America representing the rest of the world—western Asia, Oceania, East or South Africa, the Arctic—we would be more struck by our inability to classify them easily as representatives of three groups. Perhaps the most obvious example involves the people of South Asia (India and Pakistan), who are darkly complected (like Africans), racially resemble Europeans, and live on the continent of Asia!

To an earlier generation, dividing humans into three types harmonized well with a mythical history that saw humans as descended from Noah's three sons. Although the far reaches of the continents were unknown to them, the ancient Hebrews ascribed the North Africans to the lineage of Ham, central and southern Europeans to the lineage of Japheth, and West Asians (including themselves) to the lineage of Shem, "after their families, after their tongues, in their lands, in their nations" (Genesis 10:20). This origin myth spread in the Roman Empire through the popularity of the *Antiquities of the Jews* by Flavius Josephusili (Hannaford, 1996).

However, if there were three geographic types of people in nature, it is difficult to know in the light of modern knowledge what they might represent bio-historically. Did one ancestral lineage (Ham) settle near Ghana, one (Shem) settle near Korea, and one (Japheth) settle near Norway, their descendants becoming rather distinct from one another and remaining rather homogeneous as they spread outward and mixed at the fringes—as some 19th-century writers essentially believed? No; humans have always been living and evolving in the in-between places, and there is no basis on which to regard the most divergent peoples as somehow the most primordial.

Actually, our racial archetypes represent not some pure ancestors but symbolic representations of the most biologically extreme peoples on earth. We may note in this context that the father of biological classification, Linnaeus, defined Europeans as blond and blue-eyed. Linnaeus, of course, was Swedish. But people with these features are the most *extreme* Europeans, not the most European, nor the most representative.

Dividing and classifying are cultural acts and represent the imposition of arbitrary decisions on natural patterns. This is most evident in the legalities of defining races, so that intermarriage between them could be prohibited—the miscegenation laws (Wright, 1995). In general, a single black great-grandparent was sufficient to establish a person as "Black," whereas seven white great-grandparents were insufficient to establish one as "White." Here, race can be seen as inherited according to a symbolic or folk system of heredity, in contrast to biological inheritance. Thus racial heredity is qualitative, all or nothing, whereas biological heredity is quantitative and fractional.

CAN WE COMPARE PEOPLE FROM DIFFERENT PARTS OF THE WORLD?

The primary basis of all science is comparison. Peoples of the world differ from one another, and to understand the nature of those differences we are obliged to compare them. The social issues overlaying such comparisons, however, necessitate considerably more introspection than would be taken for granted by a scientist accustomed to comparing spiders or earthworms (Marks, 1995).

The skin, hair, face, and body form all vary across the world's populations. In humans, these biological differences are complemented and exaggerated by differences in language, behavior, dress, and the other components of the cumulative historical stream we call culture. The skeletal differences among the world's most different peoples are actually quite subtle, however, so that although a trained forensic anthropologist can allocate modern remains into a small number of given categories, it is virtually impossible to do so with prehistoric remains (Clark, 1963).

The fact that skeletal remains can be sorted into preexisting categories does not mean that those categories represent fundamental divisions of the human species (Brace, 1995;

Sauer, 1992). When asked to sort blocks of various sizes into large and small, a child can do so easily and replicably, but that is not a testimony to the existence of two kinds of blocks in the universe. It is a testament only to the ease with which distinctions can be imposed on gradients.

By the 18th century, European sailors had demonstrated unambiguously that all known human populations were interfertile and were thus biologically a single taxonomic unit in spite of the perceptible differences among them. Indeed, reconciling the obvious differences among humans to a single creative act in the Bible led 18th-century European scientists (such as Buffon) to the first theories of microevolution. On the other hand, theories of multiple origins of different peoples (polygenism, as opposed to monogenism) persisted in the United States through the Civil War. These biological theories helped to justify the subjugation of non-Whites by emphasizing their biological separation (Stanton, 1960). In the 1920s, geneticists still debated whether race-crossing might be genetically harmful because of the apparently profound differences among human populations (Davenport & Steggerda, 1929; Provine, 1973). Those differences are not so genetically substantial, however, for such interbreeding among human populations has not shown evidence of biologically harmful effects (Shapiro, 1961).

ARE CONSISTENTLY DETECTABLE DIFFERENCES BETWEEN HUMAN POPULATIONS GENETIC?

This is quite possibly the most widely misunderstood aspect of human biology, in spite of nearly a century of study. If I study 1,000 Ibos from Nigeria and 1,000 Danes from Denmark, I can observe any number of differences between the two groups. One group, for example, is darkly complected; the other is lightly complected. This difference would probably be the same whether I selected my sample in the year 1900, 2000, or 2100, and it is presumably genetic in etiology.

On the other hand, one group speaks Ibo and the other speaks Danish. That difference would also be there if I selected my sample in 1900, 2000, or 2100, but it is presumably *not* genetic. At least, generations of immigrants attest to the unlikelihood of a genetic component to it.

How, then, can we know from the observation of a difference whether the difference is biologically based or not?

European explorers were well aware that the people who looked the most different from them also acted the most differently. Linnaeus had invoked broad suites of personality ("impassive, lazy") and culture traits ("wears loose-fitting clothes") in his diagnosis of four geographic subspecies of humans in 1758. The next generation of researchers recognized that these traits were both overgeneralized (if not outright slanderous) and exceedingly malleable, and they sought to establish their formal divisions of the human species solely on biological criteria. (One can also observe that cultural boundaries [political, linguistic, etc.]

are generally discrete, in contrast to clinal biological variation, which makes it unlikely that the two are causally connected.)

It was widely assumed by the middle of the 19th century that regardless of the degree of malleability of mental or behavioral traits of human groups, the features of the body were fundamentally immutable. Thus traits like the shape of the head could be taken as an indicator of transcendent biological affinity-groups with similarly shaped heads were closely related, and those with differently shaped heads were more distantly related (Gould, 1981).

The first to challenge this assumption empirically was Boas (1912), who measured skulls of immigrants to Ellis Island and compared them to those of relatives already living in the United States. He found that the human body is indeed very sensitive to the conditions of growth and that there was a decided tendency of diverse immigrant groups to become more physically convergent in America—in spite of marrying within their own groups—than they were when they arrived.

In particular, the shape of the head turned out to be very malleable, and not at all a reliable indicator of genetics or race. Subsequent studies of other immigrant groups, notably Japanese immigrants to Hawaii by Shapiro and Hulse (1939), supported this discovery. Thus the observation of consistent difference between groups of people—even of the body—is not necessarily indicative of a genetic basis for that difference (Kaplan, 1954; Lasker, 1969). This work effectively shifted the burden of proof from those who *question* a genetic basis for the observation of difference to those who *assert* it.

To establish a genetic basis for an observed difference between two populations, therefore, requires more than just observing the difference to be consistent It requires presumably genetic data. The inference of a genetic difference in the absence of genetic data thus represents not a scientific theory of heredity but a folk theory of heredity. To the extent that behavioral and mental traits—such as test scores and athletic performances—are even more developmentally plastic than are strictly physical traits, the same injunction must hold even more strongly for them. Genetic inferences require genetic data.

DO DIFFERENT GROUPS HAVE DIFFERENT POTENTIALS?

One of the catch-phrases of 1995's best-selling *The Bell Curve* (Hermstein & Murray, 1994) was "cognitive ability." Eluding a scientifically rigorous definition, the phrase is left to be explained by a commonsense or folk definition—cognitive ability presumably means the mental development possible for a person under optimal circumstances. But it would take an extraordinarily naive or evil scientist to suggest seriously that such circumstances are, in fact, broadly optimized across social groups in our society. Consequently, not only can we not establish that abilities are different, we have no reliable way even to measure such an innate property in the first place. What we have is performance—on tests or just in life—which is measurable, but which is the result of many things, only one of which is immeasurable innate ability.

Once again, we encounter the problem of a burden of proof for a biological assertion. If the concept itself is metaphysical, the burden of proof must obviously be very heavy. On one hand, it is not at all unreasonable to suggest that different people have different individual "gifts"—we all possess unique genetic constellations, after all. On the other hand, those gifts are not amenable to scientific study, for they are only detectable by virtue of having been developed or cultivated. Thus no scientific statements can be responsibly made about such genetic gifts in the absence of the life history of the person to whom they belong.

In other words, ability is a concept that is generally easy to see only in the past tense. I know I had the ability to be a college professor, because I *am* one; but how can I know in any scientifically valid sense whether I *could have been* a major-league third baseman? I can't, so it is simply vain for me to speculate on it. A life is lived but once, and what it could have been—while fascinating to contemplate—is not a scientific issue.

There is also an important asymmetry about the concept of ability. A good performance indicates a good ability, but a poor performance need not indicate poor ability. As noted above, many factors go into a performance, only one of which is ability. Thus, when we encounter the question of whether poor performance—even over the long term—is an indication of the lack of cognitive ability, the only defensible position from the standpoint of biology is agnosticism. We do not know whether humans or human groups differ in their potentials in any significant way. More than that, we *cannot* know—so this question lies outside the domain of scientific discourse and within the domain of folk knowledge.

Further, this raises a darker question: What are we to make of scientists who assert the existence of constitutional differences in ability? If we cannot gauge differences in ability in any reliable manner, it is a corruption of science to assert in its name that one group indeed has less ability than another. From the mouth or pen of a politician, the assertion might reflect ignorance or demagoguery; from that of a scientist, it reflects incompetence or irresponsibility. Scientists are subject to the cultural values of their time, place, and class and historically have found it difficult to disentangle those values from their pronouncements as scientists. We now recognize the need to define the boundaries of science in order to distinguish the authoritative voice of scientists speaking as scientists from the voice of scientists speaking as citizens. This distinction is vital to keeping science from being tarnished by those few scientists who have chosen to invoke it as a validation of odious social and political doctrines.

A reliable inference of differences in ability from the observation of differences in performance requires the control of many cultural and life history variables. The first step toward controlling those variables is to develop a society in which children from diverse social groups and upbringings have equal opportunities to cultivate their diverse gifts.

HUMAN BIOLOGY THROUGH THE LENS OF HISTORY

Because ability is a metaphysical concept, there is no valid evidence from the fields of science that groups of people have similar abilities, any more than there is evidence that they have different abilities.

There is evidence bearing on this issue from the humanities, however—namely, history. Ours is not the first generation in which the claim has been put forward that human groups are of unequal worth, ostensibly based on science. Leading geneticists of the 1910s and 1920s avidly promoted the recent discoveries of chromosomes and Mendel's laws. Breakthroughs in genetics suggested that it might be fruitful to look there for a solution to America's social problems. Crosscutting political lines, Americans widely embraced a social philosophy known as eugenics, whose cardinal tenet was that antisocial traits represented the effects of a gene for "feeblemindedness," which had a very uneven distribution in the world (Davenport, 1911). It was found commonly among the rural and urban poor, and across the world in the techno-economically backward nations.

Among the most widely cited data was the pseudonymous Kallikak family, whose 18th-century genitor had sired a child by a "feeble-minded tavern girl" and another by his lawful Quaker wife. Several generations later, the descendants of the illegitimate son were primarily social outcasts, whereas those of the legitimate sons were upstanding citizens (Goddard, 1912). This was cited for decades, even in genetics textbooks, as evidence for the transmission of feeblemindedness through one side of the family—in spite of the fact that it could hardly be diagnosed as a biological trait.

Scientific solutions to America's problems readily presented themselves on this basis: (a) restriction of immigration for the "feebleminded" hoping to enter the country and (b) sterilization for the "feebleminded" already here (Grant, 1916). The latter was upheld by the Supreme Courts 1927 decision in *Buck v. Bell,* in which the right of the state to sterilize the feebleminded, who "sap the strength of our nation" was upheld, on the grounds that "three generations of imbeciles are enough." This was not about enabling the poor to control their own reproduction, by giving them both the life options and the technology to implement them, but rather about the elimination of the gene pool of the poor, on the basis that it was irredeemably corrupt. Immigration restriction was enacted by the Johnson Act of 1924 and had an ultimate effect of denying asylum to many who would later suffer at the hands of the Nazis. Both were based on the expert voices of geneticists (Alien, 1983; Kevles, 1985; Paul, 1995).

The eugenics movement was not so much racist as classist—asserting the genetic superiority of the rich over the poor—but the Depression showed widely that economic status was not a reliable basis on which to infer genetic constitution. It was, curiously enough, geneticists themselves whose blind faith in (and promotion of) their subject proved them to be the least able to distinguish their own science from the folk prejudices that merely claimed that particular science as its basis.

Nearly a century later, however, some of these ideas are undergoing a renaissance. Promoting the Human Genome Project, James Watson declared that "we used to think our fate was in the stars. Now we know, in large measure, our fate is in our genes" (Jaroff, 1989; p. 67). With such a blank check for the power of genetics, it is no wonder we now hear routinely about hypothetical genes for crime, personality, intelligence, and sexual preference—often with evidence no more substantive than was presented in the 1920s (Nelkin & Lindee, 1995).

The eugenics movement was predicated on the apocalyptic fear that high reproductive rates in the lower classes would doom the nation to ever-growing numbers of constitutionally stupid people. And yet the descendants of those poor people became educated and socially mobile, and they have shown themselves indeed capable of running the nation. Ironically, the group targeted most strongly by I.Q. zealots of that era—poor immigrant Ashkenazi Jews—are now identified in *The Bell Curve* as comprising a "cognitive elite." With such extraordinary intellectual leapfrogging documentable in the history of this subject, we are consequently obliged to regard skeptically any broad criticisms of the gene pools of large classes of people. The issue revealed itself to be a social one—how to allow the children of the poor access to the means to develop their abilities—not a biological one, their lack of abilities.

CONCLUSIONS

Racial classifications represent a form of folk heredity, wherein subjects are compelled to identify with one of a small number of designated human groups. Where parents are members of different designated groups, offspring are generally expected to choose one, in defiance of their biological relationships.

Differing patterns of migration, and the intermixture that accompanies increasing urbanization, are ultimately proving the biological uselessness of racial classifications. Identification with a group is probably a fundamental feature of human existence. Such groups, however, are genetically fluid, and to the extent that they may sometimes reflect biological populations, they are defined locally. Races do not reflect large fundamental biological divisions of the human species, for the species does not, and probably never has, come packaged that way.

Merely calling racial issues "racial" may serve to load the discussion with reified patterns of biological variation and to focus on biology rather than on the social inequities at the heart of the problem. Racism is most fundamentally the assessment of individual worth on the basis of real or imputed group characteristics. Its evil lies in the denial of people's right to be judged as individuals, rather than as group members, and in the truncation of opportunities or rights on that basis. But this is true of other "isms"—sexism, anti-Semitism, and prejudices against other groups—and points toward the most important conclusion about human biology: Racial problems are not racial. If biologically diverse peoples had no biological differences but were marked simply on the basis of language, religion, or behavior, the same problems would still exist. How do we know this? Because they *do* exist, for other groups. The problems of race are social problems, not biological ones; and the focus on race (i.e., seemingly discontinuous bio-geographic variation) is therefore a deflection away from the real issues (Montagu, 1963).

The most fundamental dichotomy we can emphasize from the standpoint of biology is that between identity and equality. Identity is a relationship defined by biology; equality is a relationship conferred by culture and society. Genetic processes operate to guarantee that we are not biologically identical to others, although we are more or less similar to others; however, our laws guarantee equality, independently of biology (Dobzhansky, 1962). A society in which individual talents can be cultivated without regard to group affiliations, social rank, or other a priori judgments will be a successful one—acknowledging biological heterogeneity while developing the diverse individual gifts of its citizenry.

APPENDIX

For Further Information

Marks, J. (1995). *Human biodiversity.* Explores the overlap between genetics and anthropology, searching for areas of mutual illumination.

Montagu, A. (1963). *Man's most dangerous myth.* A classic work by an outstanding and outspoken scholar.

Nelkin, D., & Lindee, M. S. (1995). *The DNA mystique.* A popular account of the American infatuation with heredity, and the ways in which it has been exploited by science in mis century.

REFERENCES

Alien, G. (1983). The misuse of biological hierarchies: The American eugenics movement, 1900–1940. *History and Philosophy of the Life Sciences,* 5,105–127.

Boas, F. (1912). Changes in the bodily form of descendants of immigrants. *American Anthropologist,* 14, 530–562.

Brace, C. L. (1995). Region does not mean "race"—Reality versus convention in forensic anthropology. *Journal of Forensic Sciences,* 40, 171–175.

Buck v. Bell, 274 VS. 200 (1927).

Clark, W. E. Le Gros. (1963, January 12). How many families of man? *The Nation,* pp. 35–36.

Davenport, C. B. (1911). *Heredity in relation to eugenics.* New York: Henry Holt.

Davenport, C. B., & Steggerda, M. (1929). *Race crossing in Jamaica* (Publication No. 395). Washington, DC: Carnegie Institution of Washington.

Dobzhansky, T. (1962). *Mankind evolving.* New Haven: Yale University Press.

Ferris, S. D., Brown, W. M., Davidson, W. S., & Wilson, A. C. (1981). Extensive polymorphism in the mitochondrial DNA of apes. *Proceedings of the National Academy of Sciences, USA, 78*, 6319–6323.

Goddard, H. H. (1912). *The Kallikak family: A study in the heredity of feeblemindedness.* New York: Macmillan.

Grant, M. (1916). *The passing of the great race.* New York: Scribner.

Gould, S. J. (1981). *The mismeasure of man.* New York: Norton.

Hannaford, I. (1996). *Race: The history of an idea in the West.* Baltimore: Johns Hopkins University Press.

Herrnstein, R., & Murray, C. (1994). *The Bell Curve.* New York: Free Press.

Hiernaux, J. (1974). *The people of Africa.* London: Weidenfeld & Nicolson.

Huxley, J. (1938). Clines: An auxiliary taxonomic principle. *Nature, 142,* 219–220.

Jaroff, L. (1989, March 20). The gene hunt. *Time,* 62–67.

Johnson Act (Immigration) ch 190, 43 Stat. 153 (May 26, 1924).

Kaplan, B. A. (1954). Environment and human plasticity. *American Anthropologist, 56,* 780–800.

Kevles, D. J. (1985). *In the name of eugenics.* Berkeley: University of California Press.

Lasker, G. W. (1969). Human biological adaptability. *Science, 166,* 1480–1486.

Livingstone, F. (1962). On the non-existence of human races. *Current Anthropology, 3,* 279.

Marks, J. (1995). *Human biodiversity: Genes, race, and history.* Hawthorne, NY: Aldine.

Montagu, A. (1963). *Man's most dangerous myth: The fallacy of race.* Cleveland: World Publishing.

Nelkin, D., & Lindee, M. S. (1995). *The DNA mystique: The gene as cultural icon.* New York: Freeman.

Paul, D. B. (1995). *Controlling human heredity.* Atlantic Highlands, NJ: Humanities Press.

Provine, W. (1973). Geneticists and the biology of race crossing. *Science, 1982,* 790–796.

Ruano, G., Rogers, J., Ferguson-Smith, A. C., & Kidd, K. K. (1992). DNA sequence polymorphism within hominoid species exceeds the number of phylogenetically informative characters for a HOX2 locus. *Molecular Biology and Evolution, 9,* 575–586.

Sauer, N. (1992). Forensic anthropology and the concept of race: If races don't exist, why are forensic anthropologists so good at identifying them? *Social Science and Medicine, 34,* 107–111.

Shapiro, H. (1939). *Migration and environment.* London: Oxford University Press.

Shapiro, H. (1961). Race mixture. In *The race question in modern science* (pp. 343–389). New York: Columbia University Press/UNESCO.

Stanton, W. H. (1960). *The leopard's spots: Scientific attitudes toward race in America, 1815–59*. Chicago: University of Chicago Press.

Terrell, J. E., & Stewart, P. J. (1996). The paradox of human population genetics at the end of the twentieth century. *Reviews in Anthropology, 25*, 13–33.

Wolf, E. (1972). *Europe and the people without history*. Berkeley: University of California Press.

Wright, L. (1995, July 25). One drop of blood. *The New Yorker*, pp. 46–55.

5 MATRILINEAL KINSHIP

—DAVID M. SCHNEIDER
AND KATHLEEN GOUGH

INTRODUCTION: THE DISTINCTIVE FEATURES OF MATRILINEAL DESCENT GROUPS

The aim of this introduction is to develop an initial theoretical rationale for certain features of matrilineal descent groups which distinguish them from their patrilineal counterparts. The patrilineal descent group is used as a point of contrast throughout.[1]

The problem is to put forward theoretical statements, not empirical generalizations. That is, I am concerned with some of the logical implications of a set of definitions, and the task is to show how the implications follow from the definitions so that they may have both predictive and analytic utility. For if certain conditions indeed follow logically from the way in which matrilineal descent groups are defined, then they should in real life (when they do match these definitions) be concretely constituted as predicted, and such conditions would be constant for such groups.

By concerning myself with the descent system it might seem that I somehow assume that descent is "causal" or "primary" or "important." I would explicitly disavow such assumptions. In order to say what is "important" or "causal" one must first specify "in respect to what." Descent may be "important" with respect to the patterning of certain relationships, such as marriage, or it may be but one of a series of relevant conditions. Descent may be unimportant to the techniques by which certain pottery designs are executed. I am therefore exploring the nature of matrilineal descent groups, not evaluating their importance for culture, for evolution, or for anything of that sort. I only assume that descent is a limiting condition in every kinship system; that there is a "coherence" or "logic" to a particular type of descent system such that it is not compatible with some forms of social organization but may be more or less so with others. My aim is, in a sense, to try to lay bare the

1. Most of the central ideas in this chapter were developed during the course of the SSRC Summer Seminar so that D. F. Aberle, H. Basehart, E. Colson, G. Fathauer, K. Gough, M. Sahlins, and F. Eggan were particularly important to it. Each of them then contributed specific comments on earlier drafts which materially advanced both the thinking and its presentation. In addition, Raymond T. Smith, Erving Goffman, Robert F. Murphy, Richard N. Henderson, Clifford Geertz, and Melford Spiro offered helpful comments and suggestions. The reader will immediately note how much is owed to the pioneering work of Dr. Audrey I. Richards, and particularly to her very important paper (1951), "Some Types of Family Structure Amongst the Central Bantu" (*in* Radcliffe-Brown and Forde (eds.), *African Systems of Kinship and Marriage*).

structure of one particular type of descent group and the implications of this and so illuminate its internal "logic." My aim is definitely not to argue for the priority of descent in any sense—functional, causal, or historical.

Kinship must be distinguished from descent. Kinship defines a number of statuses and their interrelationships according to a variety of rules or principles and distinguishes kinsmen from non-kin. Descent as the term will be used here, forms a unit of consanguineally related kinsmen. It is the existence of a unit which is crucial here, and the unit must be culturally distinguished as such. Such a unit cannot include all kinsmen, nor can it include kinsmen who are related in any way other than consanguineally. Descent as such thus refers to the socially stipulated rule by which the unit is constituted. Since the unit is a consanguineal one, each member is affiliated with the unit through his parents[2] and in no other way.

There may be, for instance, a patrilineal or matrilineal line which an observer can trace, or which a member of the society can trace, but unless this line is culturally distinguished in some way it does not constitute a descent unit.

A descent unit has members affiliated according to a particular rule, systematically applied. *Unilineal* rules or principles for the affiliation of descent unit members are those in which sex is systematically used as the distinguishing criterion, so that those kinsmen related through one sex are included and those related through the opposite sex are excluded. When male sex is the distinguishing criterion the descent principle or rule is called *patrilineal.* Ego is thus patrilinealy related *to* females, but *not through* females for the purpose of constituting a particular descent unit. His initial relationship is of course through his father. From the point of view of the observer, either within the society or outside it, a patrilineal descent unit consists in consanguineal kinsmen related through males. When female sex is the distinguishing criterion the principle is called *matrilineal.* In the latter case the individual's initial relationship is to his mother and through her to other kinsmen, both male and female, but continuing only through females.

In unilineal descent, by definition here, an individual's affiliation is only rarely maintained for less than his lifetime.[3] His affiliation is ascribed automatically according to the

2. See text below for definitions of the terms "parents," "mother," and "father." The usual definitions of "kinship" and aspects of kinship like "descent" tend to rest on assumptions of biological relatedness used either as an element in the definition of analytic categories or as a formal assumption implicit or explicit in some concrete system. There is no doubt whatever that many concrete systems, such as the American kinship system, use notions of "blood" and biological relationship in defining certain kinship relations. But my conviction is that biological relatedness, *used as an analytic category in terms of which kinship systems may be compared and analyzed,* has been as much of an impediment as a useful tool in understanding kinship in general. This is obviously not the place for an essay on this subject, but it is necessary to point out that I avoid biologically based definitions so far as possible.

3. The particular problem to which this provision is addressed is that of the stability of group membership and the stability of an individual's commitment to a particular descent group. Two likely sources of instability are those which arise through adoption or similar circumstances, and those which arise through voluntary or involuntary shifts of group membership.

Adoption, given the definition of "mother" used here, is simply that situation where the formal responsibility for the child's care is relinquished by one woman and taken over by another. It is necessary that the capacity for placement and affiliation are transmitted at the same time. This is not, of course, the case in some concrete systems. But the specific provision against such a contingency is introduced here since, if there were a high rate of adoption and if each adopted person could retain his ties through his first mother as well as his ties by adoption, a large number of persons might gain membership in two or more unilineal descent groups.

rule of descent and follows from his association with his mother (or, in patrilineal descent, through her to his father). Choice is open to the affiliating individual only under rare and unusual circumstances.[4]

A particular society may use one or more different principles of descent. The descent *system* of a society is defined by the inventory of the different principles of descent which are employed in that society. If a society uses only one of the two unilineal principles, regardless of what other principles occur, the system is designated by the name for the particular unilineal principle which is used. Thus a system which includes the matrilineal principle but does not include the patrilineal principle will be called a *matrilineal system*, regardless of what other principles may also be used. If both matrilineal and patrilineal principles occur, the system is called *double descent* and is thus clearly separated from a matrilineal system. My assumption is that the presence or absence of principles of descent other than the unilineal principle does not seriously affect the theory being developed here. Even under conditions of double descent what follows concerning matrilineal descent is not seriously altered.

A particular principle of descent affiliates a number of kinsmen, but these kinsmen may or may not be socially defined as a kinship *unit*. That is, unilineal lines may be traced or unilineal affiliation between two kinsmen may be traced, but all unilineally affiliated kinsmen may still not be accorded the status of a unit. When kinsmen, affiliated according to one or the other of the unilineal principles, are treated as a unit for some purpose I will speak of a *descent unit*.

The descent units of a unilineal descent system may have different forms of organization. This theory applies only to one such form of organization, that is, to *that descent unit or portion thereof which engages as a whole in activities with respect to which decisions must be made from time to time and in which all adult male members do not have equal authority.* I will call this a *descent group* to distinguish it from descent units otherwise organized, as well as from aggregates or categories or other collectivities. The term "descent group" is thus similar to what has elsewhere been called a "corporate descent group."

A descent group is a decision-making group. In order to reach decisions and to carry them out effectively the group must have the power to mobilize its resources and capacities. To do this it must somehow structure authority so that the necessary decisions can be reached and enforced and so that sanctions can be applied in cases of failure to conform. The minimal condition for such a structure is that authority be differently distributed among the members of the group.

Thus a lineage or clan which owns property, which assembles for legal, administrative, ceremonial, or other purposes, and which has a head, is an example, though not the only example, of a descent group as here defined. The Nayar *taravād* fits this definition. The *taravād* holds property jointly, acts as a unit with respect to ceremonial as well as property

---

4. Firth (1957) and Goodenough (1955) have drawn attention to certain systems in which the individual elects to join one or another descent group, that of his mother or that of his father. As they have clearly shown, the membership of such groups is quite different from what are here defined as unilineal descent groups, and so must be ruled out of consideration here. The crucial definitional element appears to me to be the element of choice between mother's or father's group.

matters, assembles on certain ceremonial occasions, and has at its head the *kāranavan*. On the other hand, a named clan whose members are dispersed over hundreds of miles, which never meets or acts as a whole, which has no leader (such as the Navaho clan), though it may be a significant kinship unit in terms of which exogamic rules are phrased and recipro-cal hospitality granted, is not a descent group by this definition. However, descent groups may be found within such dispersed unilineal units, as is the case with the Trukese lineage. Further, there may be more than one kind of unilineal descent unit present, or more than one level of unit organization in any given society.

There are, finally, three conditions which are, by definition here, constant features of unilineal descent groups regardless of the principle in terms of which the descent group is formed. They are "constants," of course, strictly in the sense that the theory requires them as characteristics of descent groups. These three constants, in combination with matrilineal descent, give matrilineal descent groups their distinctive characteristics. These are: first, women are responsible for the care of children, with every child being the primary respon-sibility of one woman; second, adult men have authority over women and children; and third, descent-group exogamy is required. I will discuss each of these briefly.

It is necessary in defining descent, descent principles, and hence the descent group, to define the terms "mother" and "father," since descent principles depend on the affiliation of each person through one or the other of these statuses.

The woman who has primary responsibility for the early care of the infant and child is its *mother*. The *father* of the child, for present purposes, is that person who is married to the child's mother at that time during the child's early life when the child is formally affiliated according to some descent principle.[5]

In the definition of "mother" the words "primary responsibility" are critical. I do not mean by this that the woman who has "primary responsibility" for the early care of the child must bear the child, or nurse it at her own breast or wash it with her own hands or, later on, actually prepare its food herself. Nannies, mammies, or servants of all sorts may very well be engaged to do the actual work, but they must be distinguished from that woman who has "primary responsibility" for the child. Indeed, the mother may have no ac-tual say in the selection of the nurse or servant, and the mother may not even see the child for long periods of time, but she is "primarily responsible" for it in that these tasks are done for her; when such tasks are undertaken by others it is not "their" child but the "mother's" child.

From these definitions the role of the mother entails three analytically separable ele-ments which may, in any concrete system, be fused into one. *Responsibility* for early care, the *actual care* itself, and *social placement* or *affiliation*. The woman who is primarily re-sponsible for the care of the child is by definition here the woman through whom the child is affiliated with other kinsmen, either through his mother (matrilineal descent) or through his mother's husband—the father (patrilineal descent).

5. I am well aware of the difficulties of defining "married to" and so leave the term undefined here except to indicate that as a minimal definition, the person through whom the child is affiliated, if it is not the child's mother, is, therefore its "father."

The role of mother has been defined as that of the woman primarily responsible for the care of a particular child. I add that this is one aspect of the role of women in general. This means that by and large all women, or almost all women, are expected to be responsible for the care of children. This does not mean that in fact each and every female member of any particular society must care for at least one child. It only means that this is part of the definition of the role of a woman, and that so far as it is possible women will play this allotted role. Whatever other roles are allotted to women (that they hoe corn, make beer or beds, or become possessed by spirits), at least child care is required by this theory.

A second aspect of sex-role differentiation has to do with authority. It has already been stated that a necessary condition of this theory is that adult members of the descent group do not all have equal authority; this is required by the definition of the descent group as a decision-making group. Quite apart from the roles of men and women in the descent group itself is the general question of the roles of men as men and women as women. The role of women as women has been defined as that of responsibility for the care of the children. I now add that the role of men as men is defined as that of having authority over women and children (except perhaps for specially qualifying conditions applicable to a very few women of the society). Positions of highest authority within the matrilineal descent group will, therefore, ordinarily be vested in statuses occupied by men.

The responsibility for the care of children is quite different from the distribution of authority. The responsibility for the care of children is one aspect of the role of adult women regardless of what other statuses they occupy. A woman may be a sister as well as a wife, a daughter as well as a mother, but none of these need alter her responsibility for the care of children. But the authority allocated to one status may very well be directly affected by the other statuses which the person occupies. Hence status stipulations may be of the utmost significance. Statuses in turn become relevant within a particular context or sphere of action. The status of wife has relevance to the domestic sphere; the status of mother's brother in matrilineal systems, to the descent-group sphere. The allocation of authority within the domestic sphere must be distinguished from the allocation of authority within the descent-group sphere and these in turn distinguished from the religious sphere, the political sphere, and so forth. Within a particular sphere of activity the authority of men and women, occupying the statuses appropriate to that sphere, may be differentially distributed. And if all spheres are compared to see how authority is distributed between men and women, there may be a systematic correlation such that male-held statuses have authority over those statuses occupied by women or children. For our purposes only two spheres are immediately important: the domestic sphere and the descent-group sphere. It is sufficient, then, to define the male sex role as having authority over the statuses occupied by women within the context of each of these spheres. This means that men of the descent group have authority over the women and children of that descent group, that adult males of the domestic group have authority over the women and children of that domestic group.

The matrilineal descent group—for this theory to hold—must be exogamous. Note however that it is the matrilineal descent group as such which must be exogamous, not the larger unit within which it may be imbedded. Thus the clan of which any particular matrilineal descent group may be a segment may be without a rule of exogamy in the sense that marriage may be permitted within it, but the matrilineal descent group itself must be exogamous.

From these definitions it might seem that matrilineal and patrilineal descent groups are precise mirror images of each other, identical in their structure except for the superficial point that in one group membership is obtained through the father, in the other through the mother. Otherwise, every element is identical. The groups are both defined as decision-making units which hold some activity in common. The roles of men and women are identically defined in both groups, men having authoritative roles and women having responsibility for child care. Both groups, by definition, are exogamous.

Despite the fact that the elements are the same, there are certain very obvious differences between matrilineal and patrilineal descents. Perhaps the first and most profound is that in patrilineal descent groups the line of authority and the line of descent both run through men. That is, both authority and group placement are male functions. In matrilineal descent groups, on the other hand, although the line of authority also runs through men, group placement runs through the line of women. The lines of authority and group placement are thus coördinate in males in patrilineal descent groups, but separated between males and females in matrilineal groups.

This is, I believe, the fundamental structural difference between matrilineal and patrilineal descent groups. From this difference all others follow.

The two differences which are consequences of this structural difference and which are in turn fundamental to all others are, first, that matrilineal descent groups depend for their continuity and operation on retaining control over both male and female members. Second, that the sex role of the "in-marrying affine" is different in matrilineal and patrilineal descent groups.

By "in-marrying affine" I mean simply the spouse of the person whose children belong to his or her own descent group. That is, the husband is an in-marrying affine with respect to his wife and her children in a matrilineal descent group; the wife is an in-marrying affine with respect to her husband and his children in a patrilineal descent group. However, once the term "in-marrying affine" is so defined, one can go on to ask about the role of the in-marrying affine with respect to his own group, the descent group into which he is married, the nuclear family into which he is married, and the kind of linkage he constitutes between his own and affinally related descent groups.

1. *Matrilineal descent groups depend for their continuity and operation on retaining control over both male and female members.* Women are required to care for the new members of the descent group and to give these new members their membership in the group (since a child belongs to the group of its mother). The control which the matrilineal descent group exercises over its female members must ensure that the children will achieve primary orientation to the matrilineal descent group and develop primary ties of loyalty to it. If males are required for authority roles then they, too, cannot be relinquished by or alienated from the group.

Male members of a matrilineal descent group might be of three kinds: those who now play authority roles and hence are required for the current operation of the group; those who are likely to succeed to those roles and who cannot be lost to the group if it is to continue when the present incumbents become incapacitated or die; and those unlikely to succeed to authoritative roles.

It is conceivable that the matrilineal descent group might exercise either no control whatever, or very little control, over this last category of males, for they are not directly required for the maintenance and perpetuation of the group. Thus it might be possible for men of this category to break all ties with their own groups. That this would then constitute a serious source of strain which would tend toward the weakening or disruption of the system of matrilineal descent groups is, however, clear on analysis.

If a portion of the men of the matrilineal descent group broke all ties with their group, but still recognized the rule of exogamy, they would marry women who were members of other matrilineal descent groups. Having neither authoritative roles in their own group, nor the prospect of gaining any, such men would be put in a position where three alternate courses of action were open to them.

First, they might attempt to become assimilated into the matrilineal descent groups of their wives, competing for authoritative roles via avenues of influence with members of those groups—an inherently unstable situation.

Second, they might attempt to gain control over their wives and children and remove them from the control of their matrilineal descent group. Such a situation would seriously weaken the matrilineal descent group, though it might not destroy it.

Third, they might remain unassimilated and yet not attempt to gain control over their wives and children, but just "live in peace" with their affines. Men in such a position, without ties to, or the backing and support of their own group, would find themselves in a difficult position against their organized affines. They would become dependents, and at the mercy of their affines. A group of "second-class citizens" might thus emerge and, if they could not be drained from the society, might constitute a serious threat to its continuation as a system of matrilineal descent groups. In short, this last alternative would result in an unstable situation which would tend to shift toward either of the first two.

I have argued here exclusively in terms of authority roles and succession to such roles and without reference to one of the important "givens" of the situation: namely, that the matrilineal descent group is being treated here, by definition, as a unit which has decision-making functions with respect to some activity. Such an activity and such corporate organization directly entail an "interest" on the part of each member which in turn implies "rights." Perhaps the matrilineal descent group holds an estate in common from which its members derive their sustenance. Even though a man has no prospect of succeeding to an authority role, he has the right in that estate as a member and has an interest in maintaining that right, and though he may never succeed to headship, he need not, for that reason alone, become alienated from the group. He remains bound to that group by the commonalty of its members' interests.

If we consider those men who have no prospect of succeeding to positions of authority, the crucial consideration—which requires that even these men cannot be completely released from their matrilineal descent groups—cannot be such rights alone. For it would seem perfectly possible for a man to exchange his rights in his matrilineal descent group for equivalent rights in the matrilineal descent group of his wife. It is precisely the fact that such an exchange constitutes a threat to the integrity of his own group as well as to his affinal group that makes this the crucial consideration. For it follows directly that if an in-marrying affine obtains the same rights as a member, he becomes in effect a member, and the organization and membership of the group cannot long remain that of a matrilineal descent group. The only condition under which men of this sort do not constitute a direct threat is when they can be kept in the position of in-marrying affines and not permitted to share rights equally with members.

But the question of rights is not an all-or-none matter, though the question of membership is, by definition. There may, thus, be degrees of *alienation* of a man from his own matrilineal descent group, and degrees of *assimilation* into his wife's group, just as there are obviously degrees to which he is *depended* on by either his own or his affinal group.

The *dependence* of a member on his matrilineal descent group and of his group on him thus varies inversely with his *alienation* from his group. His alienation from his own group would vary inversely with his *assimilation* into his affinal group. One extreme of this relationship would be the case where a member was completely independent of his own group and alienated from it, and completely assimilated into his affinal group. In such a situation it would not seem possible for matrilineal descent groups, as defined here, to continue. The opposite extreme would define the strongest kind of matrilineal descent group; namely, where members were (except for the requirement of exogamy) completely dependent on their own group, not alienated from it in any way, and in no way (beyond the minimum conditions for marriage) assimilated into their affinal groups. The weakest groups would be those in which some proportion of members were alienated from their descent groups, independent of them, and greatly assimilated into their affinal groups.[6]

---

6. The idea of variable descent-group "strength" requires more specialized treatment than can be given here. Suffice it to say that certain simple distinctions can profitably be made in dealing with this matter. First, consistency of descent principle as a factor should be kept apart from the question of descent-group "strength" until its role in whatever is defined as "strength" is determined. The not uncommon device of continuing a patrilineal line by the fiction that the daughter's husband is really the son is an example of inconsistency of descent principle. Similarly, the patrilineal principle is clearly transgressed when parts of a patrilineal unit are related through a woman. Second, the notion of "strength" has at least two distant references which might well be kept apart. On the one hand it may be used as a statement concerning the mode of internal organizations of a unit, as is done here, where the focus is on the strength of the bonds among members. On the other hand it may be used to refer to the position of the unit vis-á-vis other units in the society. Thus, for example, "strength" in the first sense refers to the degree of loyalty which can be expected from members of a descent group. In the second sense "strength" refers to the position of the descent group in the total social structure as crucial or not, as playing a "vital" role or not, as "strategic" or not. Although there is some reason to believe that any group which commands extraordinary degrees of loyalty from its members is likely to play a strategic role in the social structure, it is possible that a single, crucial function can be performed by a social unit which commands little loyalty from its members, but just enough to maintain that group.

What I have said thus far contrasts with the situation in patrilineal descent groups. Patrilineal units cannot afford to relinquish control over male members, who fill authoritative roles as in matrilineal descent groups, but they can afford to lose a considerable degree of control over their female members, provided that they gain proportionate control over the woman marrying into their group. Thus the patrilineal descent group can lose complete control over its female members in exchange for complete control over its wives. This follows from the stated conditions that female members of a patrilineal descent group cannot add new members to their group, and are *not* required for authoritative roles in their group, though females of other groups are required for the perpetuation of the group. Further, the women of patrilineal descent groups can exchange rights in their own group for rights in their affinal groups without becoming a source of strain or a threat to the system of patrilineal descent groups.

This dependence of a matrilineal descent group on both its male and female members might be phrased as an interdependence of brother and sister. A brief review of the difficulties inherent in this phrasing raises certain points worth noting.

Such a view of the problem might argue that a sister depends on her brother for protection, care,and managerial and authority functions; while the brother depends on his sister for the perpetuation of his descent line and the provision of an heir.

The interdependence is not, and indeed structurally cannot be of *one* brother on *one* sister or even of brothers on sisters. All too often there may be no brother, or the ratio between brothers and sisters may be far out of balance, so that there may be many brothers and one sister or many sisters and but one brother. What *may* happen is that all women of a descent group may depend *for a time* on a single man, the head of the group, who may be a brother or the eldest male of the group, while other males are away for longer or shorter periods.

It is true however, that the symbolic statement of the interdependence of male and female members of a matrilineal descent group is often *phrased* by the people themselves as an interdependence of brother and sister and this may be particularly so where the descent group itself is organized as if it were composed of siblings. Or, the problem of binding the allegiance of out-marrying females of a matrilineal descent group may be solved by providing them with food; in order to make a definite assessment of the responsibility for the one who provides the food which is sent, particular brothers may be paired with particular sisters when this is possible. But because a woman's husband receives his wife's food from a particular brother of his wife does not mean that her children perpetuate only that brother's descent line, nor does it mean that the woman depends on that particular brother alone for providing her children with guidance, with a village, and with plots in a village to which they may go when grown. Thus in these cases too, despite the symbolic phrasing of the relationship in terms of brother-sister interdependence, the basic interdependence is between members of a group, not between particular persons or statuses.

The interdependence of male and female members in matrilineal descent groups is thus primarily a phenomenon of descent *groups*, not of pairs of persons or pairs of statuses.

Further, the real or symbolic interdependence of brother and sister is by no means distinctive to matrilineal descent groups but occurs among patrilineal descent groups as well. Where patrilineal descent groups practice marriage by sister exchange the interdependence of brother and sister is clearly evident. Among such people a woman's marriage may be directly dependent on her brother's marriage, and where one fails for any reason the other must necessarily fail too. Similarly, among those patrilineal people where bridewealth is a significant element of marriage, the marriage of a man may depend on the bridewealth which his sister first brings in, so that in some groups brother and sister may be paired off and the brother cannot marry until his sister's marriage brings in the bridewealth necessary for his marriage. Also, the partial dependence of a woman on her brother's protection is quite clear in many patrilineal groups.

The interdependence between men and women in matrilineal descent groups does have one important implication for brother-sister relationships where the kinship system defines group membership in terms of birth and the group views birth as a consequence of sexual relations. Let us take as a given feature of the descent groups with which we are concerned the prohibition of sexual relations between brother and sister. Patrilineal descent is consistent with the demands of this incest taboo in a way that matrilineal descent is not. In the patrilineal case a woman's sexual and reproductive activities are the primary concern of her husband and her husband's group, and not of her brother. In this sense there is a consistency between the prohibition against sexual interest between brother and sister and the locus of concern with a woman's sexual and reproductive activities. On the other hand, in matrilineal descent groups a woman bears children who perpetuate her own and her brother's group, and her sexual and reproductive activities are a matter of direct concern for her brother—although she is a tabooed sexual object for him.

2. *In matrilineal descent groups there is an element of potential strain in the fact that the sister is a tabooed sexual object for her brother, while at the same timer her sexual and reproductive activities are a matter of interest to him.*

There is no reason to believe that this potential strain is always recognized and adapted to, implicitly or explicitly. Nevertheless, the fact that this strain is implicit in matrilineal descent groups but absent in patrilineal descent groups means that it may, under certain conditions, generate modes of adaptation to it which will be distinctive to matrilineal and not patrilineal descent groups.

It is possible that the occasionally reported "ignorance of paternity" may have such adaptive functions, among others. Where, along with matrilineal descent the belief exists that the sexual act bears *no* relation whatever to conception and reproduction, this belief might be interpreted as a condition which separates sexual from reproductive activity. By thus separating these two activities and denying the relationship between them, it is possible that both brother and sister gain firmer control over their incestuous impulses. The brother's unqualified interest in his sister's reproductive activity may thus be uncontaminated by any implications of interest in her as a sexual object. Similarly, his renunciation of her as an object of sexual interest need not impair his concern for her reproductivity or her offspring nor need it infuse these relationships with more or less disguised sexual overtones.

A second possible adaptation to this potential strain is that of brother-sister respect[7] or avoidance. Respect and avoidance, which almost always prohibit elements of a sexual nature, might be seen in this context as special devices over and above those usually associated with the maintenance of the incest taboo. They are especially appropriate in minimizing the strain imposed by the brother's and sister's prohibited sexual interest in each other and yet maintaining their common concern for the continuity of their matrilineal group through the reproductive activity of the sister.

Here again, however, we must be explicit in noting that this strain need not necessarily generate specific institutionalized modes of adaptation, nor need brother-sister avoidance or respect be the only possible adaptation to it. Nor does it follow that brother-sister avoidance or respect has this and *only* this function. It may very well occur in patrilineal descent groups with quite different functions than this.

I turn now to those distinctive features of matrilineal descent groups which follow from the sex role of the in-marrying affine alone, or from the combination of this factor with that of the interdependence between men and women of matrilineal descent groups. These center on the in-marrying male in matrilineal descent groups, first as husband-father, second as husband, then as father. From there I proceed to the situation of the children as a sibling group.

3. *Matrilineal descent groups do not require the statuses of father and husband.* The statuses of mother and wife, on the other hand, are indispensable to patrilineal systems.

The bond between mother and child has a certain base in the nursing and care situation which is not paralleled by the genitor-child relationship. It is the psychobiological quality of the mother-child relationship which makes the status of mother indispensable to the maintenance of patrilineal descent groups. It is precisely the psychobiological quality of the genitor-child relationship which makes no such requirement of matrilineal descent groups. All that is required is that the genitor belong to a descent group which is different from that of the mother.

In matrilineal descent groups it is the fact of responsibility for care by a particular woman that validates membership in a particular matrilineal descent group, and the psychobiological bond between a child and the mother who cares for it will be overlaid by these social elements. Every mother will be a member of a descent group and every descent group will look to the authority of its males. Though every woman must depend on one or more males for authority functions these males are by definition members of her group. Genitors, therefore, may come and go with only the weakest links to the mothers of their children and with no more formal ties than those required by the fact that sexual activity

---

7. I do not include those relations between brother and sister which are primarily limited to deference in this conception of "respect." By respect I mean those types of relationships which tend to minimize contact and narrowly channel interaction between the two.

must be ordered and regulated. Where the father-husband status is present in matrilineal societies, it must be accounted for on grounds other than that of matrilineal descent.[8]

In patrilineal descent groups the relations between mother and child are of an irreducible minimum and are necessarily present, while in matrilineal groups the relations between father and child have to be built from the ground up, from the little which is inherent in the situation. Therefore, (3a) *the status of father-husband can vary within fairly wide limits in matrilineal descent groups.* The status of mother-wife, on the other hand, can vary within much narrower limits in patrilineal systems.

In patrilineal descent groups recruitment of new members is through the males of the group. In those concrete societies where sexual reproduction and birth are conceived as crucial criteria there is an important sense in which men, in such patrilineal descent groups, have child-bearing functions which are symbolized in what Richards has called "the ideology of descent" (Richards, 1950: 213). Women may be regarded as mere receptacles, or they may be believed to contribute nothing more than a favorable medium for the development of the foetus. But there are distinct limits to how far women may be regarded as irrelevant to the recruitment process, for by definition here women do care for the children and men do not.[9]

3b. In matrilineal descent groups the position of the in-marrying male is such that even his biological contribution can be socially ignored to some advantage to the matrilin-

---

8. This is perhaps an important point at which to reiterate the fact that this attempts to be a theoretical statement and that this is a deduction from the theory. It does *not* say that since matrilineal descent groups do not require husband-fathers, it follows that a statistical survey of concrete cases will show them to be consistently absent in matrilineal descent groups and invariably present in patrilineal descent groups. No such contention is expressed or implied in this chapter. All that is argued is that matrilineal descent groups do not require the status of husband-father. That social conditions other than matrilineal descent *do* require such a status seems self-evident from its prevalence in concrete systems.

9. There is a line of thought which I cannot follow up here but which merits some attention. By the definitions used here, it is only required that some woman be primarily responsible for the care of the child from its very early years, and that this role is expected of women generally. It is not stipulated that the woman who bears the child must be the woman who cares for *that* child. Given these definitions, the question arises as to whether it is necessary to this theory that women actually bear children. All that would be required is that some woman be primarily responsible for its care after birth, and that the child become a member of the matrilineal descent group of the woman who cares for it. There is the added stipulation that the ascription of descent-group membership cannot be arbitrarily repeated with great frequency and that it cannot be multiple. That is, the definitions insist on the stability of group membership and the stability of membership of the vast majority of individuals, ruling out multiple or sequential memberships.

There must be some provision for obtaining new members for a group if old members die. Otherwise the group would become extinct. Such provision might be met by women bearing children, or it might be met equally well by test tubes bearing children. The only argument which I can imagine at this time which might challenge this view is that there is some inherent connection between birth and child care such that the woman who bears the child is, in some statistical long run, even if not in each particular case, the only woman who could properly assure that child of survival and proper socialization. Implicit here is the notion that childbirth somehow motivates women to care for children, a task that no one would want to undertake otherwise. This argument does not seem tenable.

Here again I am interested in showing the practical *analytic* irrelevance of biological links to kinship relations and descent systems. The social recognition of biological facts obviously occurs in some concrete kinship systems and obviously has certain functions, but I have difficulty in seeing that these are in any sense *required* by kinship systems or crucial to their analysis.

eal descent group, and an ideology of descent developed which ignores the male role in conception.[10]

The basic limit on the variability of father-husband roles in matrilineal descent groups is that of the degree to which he can be incorporated into the descent group of his wife, or the degree that his wife can be incorporated into his group. These limits are simply that, on the one hand, if women's children are assigned to their father's descent group the system ceases to be matrilineal. Therefore the tie between women and their own groups must be such as to permit the allocation of the child to the mother's group and to no other. On the other hand, so long as the woman's descent group locates authority functions over that group in the hands of its male members, the authority of a husband over his wife and her children is thereby limited.

4. *The institutionalization of very strong, lasting, or intense solidarities between husband and wife is not compatible with the maintenance of matrilineal descent groups.* This is not true for patrilineal descent groups (cf. Gluckman, 1950; Fallers, 1957; Schneider, 1953).

By institutionalizing I do not mean the relatively random occurrence of such solidarities in a very small portion of the population. This would constitute a source of strain, but not a systematic source of strain. What I mean essentially is that where stable marriage is a normative element such that there is strong and consistent pressure on *all* husbands and wives to be firmly bound to each other, this will constitute a source of strain on the matrilineal descent group.

There is always potential conflict between the bonds of marriage and the bonds of descent; given exogamy, they are bonds which cannot coincide but pull each party to a marriage in different directions. If the bonds of marriage are maximized as against the bonds of descent this means that in any situation of conflicting loyalties the bonds of marriage are more likely to be sustained than those of descent. Conversely, where the bonds of descent are maximized, narrow limits are set on the degree to which the bonds of marriage may develop. In such a situation there are a variety of modes of adaptation to such potential conflict. Interests may be sharply segregated, various rights clearly delineated and allocated, or situations distinguished so that when one set of loyalties applies another is held apart and so on. But every such adaptive device is in one sense merely an impairment and a limitation on the maximization of one or the other set of ties which stabilizes the conflict.

If matrilineal descent groups are to be maintained, therefore, and if women are necessary to those groups for continuity, women's ties to their husbands must not be such that

---

10. Here again is a theoretical statement. It does not follow that in the real world the biological role of the genitor is only ignored in matrilineal descent groups and is invariably present in patrilineal descent groups. There are well-known cases where the role of the genitor is ignored in both matrilineal and patrilineal descent groups. All that is argued here is that, other things being equal, matrilineal descent groups can ignore the biological role of the male in conception without in the least disturbing the system and it is implied that from the point of view of the matrilineal descent group alone there might be certain advantages to this. Where, in concrete matrilineal descent groups, the social recognition of the male's biological role in conception is evident, this cannot arise from the fact that this recognition is *required* by, or even a likely consequence of, matrilineal descent-group organization.

the priority they assign their marital ties supersedes that which they give to their matrilineal decent group. Similarly, if man is needed to fill authoritative roles in his matrilineal descent group, he cannot accord such priority to his marital relationship that he fails to play this crucial role in his own group.

Strong bonds of solidarity between husband and wife, and stable marriage, are possible with patrilineal descent groups in proportion to the degree to which the tie of the wife to her own unit is relaxed. Precisely because a woman can be practically entirely freed from obligations to her patrilineal descent group, her ties to her husband can be maximized to the point where they take first priority, and a system in which stable marriage is institutionalized can ensue. In the extreme case, therefore, there need be no conflict between the bonds of marriage and descent for a woman in a patrilineal descent group when her bonds of descent become practically nonexistent for her. Where a woman's tie to her own unit is greatly weakened or nearly severed she may become largely if not wholly dependent on her husband and his patrilineal descent group and the stability of the marriage may in such a case be a direct function of the degree of her dependency. Her severed or weakened tie to her own unit means, in such a case, that she is not free to return to her unit in divorce. Where a woman's tie to her own unit is so severed, her husband and his patrilineal descent group may gain a considerable degree of control over her, thus enforcing her bond to her husband and her dependence on him and his patrilineal descent group, regardless of her own inclinations. In short, the *independence* of men and women in patrilineal descent groups permits a degree of *alienation* of women from those groups, which in turn permits a high degree of *assimilation* of wives into their affinal groups.

Dependence and control are not, however, the only directions which the relationship between husband and wife may take in patrilineal descent groups. Strong, emotionally intense solidarity may develop between a woman and her children, and these may further reinforce her ties with her husband. I will return to this point shortly.

Thus far I have spoken of the bonds of marriage versus the bonds of descent and suggested that there is a necessarily inverse relationship between them: the greater the priority accorded to the bonds of marriage, the weaker the bonds of descent and the lower their priority. This is, of course, not only true for matrilineal and patrilineal descent groups, but for certain other descent systems as well. The only significant difference between matrilineal and patrilineal descent groups that I have pointed out thus far is that the bonds of marriage can be fully stressed in patrilineal descent groups because the bonds between a woman and her own unit can be practically severed. It should be quite clear, however, that this statement only holds true from the point of view of the woman as in-marrying affine. It cannot hold true for her husband, since his membership in and obligations to his patrilineal descent group require that from his point of view, no matter what the bonds of marriage may be, his own descent bonds must take priority; otherwise he will tend to be pulled out of and away from his descent group in situations of conflict of interest between his marriage bond and his descent-group bond.

I have been concerned only with the very general point that the development of strong bonds in any kind between husband and wife tend in the long run to be incompatible with the maintenance of matrilineal descent groups. It is appropriate now to consider a particular kind of bond likely to be significant, namely, that of authority.

The sex role of men makes them more difficult to manage as in-marrying affines than women, and hence in-marrying men are a special source of potential strain for matrilineal descent groups. In patrilineal descent groups the allocation of authority by sex is such that men as men have authority both within their descent group and over its in-marrying affines. The lines of descent and authority are thus coördinate. In matrilineal descent groups, on the other hand, such lines are not coördinate. Men have authoritative roles within their descent group, but their authority over their wives must be sharply limited. Conversely, the authority of a woman as in-marrying affine is no threat to her husband's patrilineal descent group because by definition here, her husband has authority over her.

Males as in-marrying affines in matrilineal descent groups thus pose a problem in that they are in the position where they have a firm base upon which to develop the kind of authority over their wives that can lead to the disruption of the system of matrilineal descent groups.

4a. Matrilineal descent groups require the institutionalization of special limits on the authority of husbands over wives. Although every social system will necessarily set limits on authoritative roles patrilineal descent groups do not, by their nature, require any other limits than those inherent in the problem of maintaining any system of social relations. Matrilineal descent groups, as I have suggested, do require special limits over and above those minimally necessary to systems of social relations in general.

The essence of the limitation of the husband's authority over his wife is, of course, the clear allocation of spheres of male authority so that males as descent-group members have kinds of authority which males as in-marrying affines do not have. On the other hand, men by definition here have authority over women and children. It follows, therefore, that husbands will have some authority as men over their wives and children, and the problem then becomes one of the specifications of spheres of husbands' authority as against the spheres of male descent-group members. It is thus to be expected that a domestic sphere over which the husband has some authority will be clearly distinguished in concrete cases from the descent-group sphere. Since the woman must act as a descent-group member and as a wife-mother she will tend to find herself in a position where her loyalties are in some degree split between her descent group and her husband. In part this is a problem of the integration and balancing of opposing loyalties, minimized to a great degree by the clarity with which her role toward her husband and her role toward her descent group are defined. Nevertheless, the husband's tendency to maximize his sphere of authority will be balanced by the male descent-group members' tendency to maximize and maintain their sphere of authority.

Relations between male in-marrying affines and male descent-group members will thus necessarily reflect this state of affairs. On the one hand, and perhaps as an extreme situation, it would seem very unlikely that wife's brother and sister's husband would have a warm, intimate, supportive relationship in matrilineal descent groups. A joking relationship similarly seems unlikely. However the relationship is specifically structured, one central element in it is the problem of maintaining the limitation over the husband's authority and its confinement to a domestic sphere and correspondingly maintaining and limiting the authority of the male members of the descent group to the descent-group sphere.

In this connection there is another problem entailed in matrilineal descent groups which is different in patrilineal descent groups.

5. Matrilineal descent groups have special problems in the organization of in-marrying affines with respect to each other.

In patrilineal descent groups it is possible for the woman, as in-marrying affine, to be so alienated from her own group and so assimilated to her husband's group that she can, in effect, be fully identified with her husband's position with respect to their son's wife. A woman may thus become her husband's executive and judicial arm with respect to her son's wife, and the son's wife, alienated from her own group, may be clearly subordinated to her mother-in-law. From the point of view of the son's wife, of course, her alienation from her own group is proportional to the degree to which she can be so subordinated. The stronger her tie to her own group, the weaker the control which can be exercised over her. However, because men cannot be alienated from their matrilineal descent group they present problems with respect to their organization as in-marrying affines.

Two problems are particularly evident. The first is that the daughter's husband represents a position more difficult to control than does the son's wife. Second, the father-in-law cannot be in a strong position to exert authority over daughter's husband or any other in-marrying affine.

The crucial condition for each of these problems lies in the attachment of males to their own matrilineal descent group. Where each daughter's husband retains a tie with his own unit, and where the bond of marriage is not strongly binding and he may leave it easily, the clear subordination of the daughter's husband would not seem easy, though it may be possible under certain limited conditions. Correspondingly, the father-in-law cannot be so closely assimilated to his wife's matrilineal descent group as to become his wife's executive and judicial arm with respect to their daughter's husband. The executive and judicial arm of the woman of a matrilineal descent group lies elsewhere than with her husband. Though a man may indeed have an interest in his daughter and thereby in his daughter's husband, he is not in a position to exercise a great degree of authority lest he usurp this descent-group function. The generational difference between father-in-law and son-in-law may provide a base on which their relations can be structured, but the degree of authority which one can wield over the other cannot be expected to approximate that of mother-in-law over daughter-in-law in patrilineal descent groups.

One situation in which relations among male in-marrying affines are clearly organized is that of prescribed cross-cousin marriages (matrilineal, patrilineal, or bilateral). Here relations among the in-marrying men are structured prior to marriage and continue after marriage.

6. Where bridewealth or bride service occurs with matrilineal descent this transfer of goods or services cannot establish such rights in children as allocate them to any group other than that of their mother.

This is perhaps so self-evident as to require almost no comment. Matrilineal descent groups are replenished by the children cared for by its female members. Where rights over children are formally vested in the father and his descent group, the claims of the matrilineal descent group are vacated. Such transfer of goods and/or services are more likely to establish rights in the wife, particularly to labor or sexual activity.

7. The bonds which may develop between a child and his father tend to be in direct competition with the authority of the child's matrilineal descent group. The bonds between mother and child in patrilineal descent groups do not necessarily constitute such a source of competition.

Father-child bonds are of two kinds: those of authority and those of positive affect. The father, when present, is likely to participate in some degree, however small, in the process of socialization. As a male, and as an adult male, he is thus—by definition of his age-sex role and quite apart from his kinship role—in a position of some authority over his children. For matrilineal descent groups, therefore, there is the problem of segregating and limiting the father's authority over his child so that it does not, and is not likely to, supersede the authority of the child's descent group. The situation with respect to husband and wife is, thus far, precisely paralleled by that between father and child. Nor are these two problems independent of one another, for the statuses of husband and father are occupied by the same person. This tension between a man and the matrilineal descent group over the control of the wife and children has been called "the matrilineal puzzle" by Audrey Richards, who went on to analyze the varieties of family form which reflect various balances of this tension in Central Africa (Richards, 1950: 207–251).[11]

The second type of bond between father and child which may develop in matrilineal descent groups is that of strong, positive affect. The relationship between potestality and bonds of positive affect is such that when, as in patrilineal descent groups, the father has authority over his children, there are likely to be compensatory affective ties through the mother to the child's mother's brother. Conversely, in matrilineal descent groups, where the father's authority is necessarily limited and weak and where authority is located in the office of matrilineal descent-group head, it is precisely with the father that compensatory affective bonds are most likely to occur (cf. Radcliffe-Brown,1924; Homans and Schneider, 1955).

(7a) In matrilineal descent groups the emotional interest of the father in his own chil-

---

11. Richards phrases this conflict as one between father and mother's brother. I suggest that the structural conflict is essentially between the father and the children's matrilineal descent group. It is certainly true that often the mother's brother is the head of the descent group and is its spokesman. It is equally true that the mother's brother is often perceived by the father as the locus of his difficulties. In fact, it is the descent-group head as much (who may or may not be the particular wife's brother) who must actively counter the father's efforts to control wife and children, but the locus of the strain is in the maintenance of the authority structure of the descent group against threats from outside it.

dren constitutes a source of strain, which is not precisely replicated in patrilineal descent groups by the emotional tie between the mother and her children.

As was indicated in the discussion of marriage in patrilineal descent groups, emotionally intense solidarity may develop between a woman with her children. Her alienation from her own unit may leave her free to develop such bonds with her children without affecting her own unit since she is not required to play a role in it. Thus the stability of her marriage may contribute to the unity and integrity of her husband's patrilineal descent group—partly by the loyalty she brings to it, partly by reinforcing the bonds between her children and their father and, through him, to their own descent group. Again, this need not necessarily be the case, but is a direction which it is possible for such relationships to take in patrilineal descent groups.

In patrilineal descent groups, the stronger the authority of the husband over his wife and the father over his children, the stronger the compensatory affective bond is likely to be between the mother and her children. But the strength of this bond is unlikely to become a base upon which the mother can build that kind of authority relationship which subverts the authority of the patrilineal descent-group over those children. This is unlikely because the mother does not have at the same time, an important political or authoritative role in her own patrilineal descent group, and because her authority as a woman is limited by the authority of her husband over her. That this bond may become an avenue for political alliance between two distinct patrilineal descent groups is obvious and too familiar to dwell upon here. But the analytically crucial question is whether or not this bond has significant potentialities for disrupting or subverting the authority of the patrilineal descent group over its members.

In matrilineal descent groups, on the other hand, the strong affective bond between father and child is one which can more easily become the basis for the kind of authority relationship which, as Richards' analysis shows so clearly, can easily run counter to the authority of the matrilineal descent group. That the father has some authority over both his wife and children, that he is independent of his wife's matrilineal descent group through the weakness of his marital tie, that he has a firm base in his own group, and that as a man his role tends generally to have significant political aspects, all put him in a strong position to subvert the authority of the children's group over them by inviting them to yield rights in their own group in exchange for rights in his group. This is especially so for the son, less acute for the daughter.

Economic coöperation between father and child, especially son, and the advantages of politically important rank in a father, where these occur, are two common kinds of especially serious threats to the integrity of matrilineal descent groups. Where a father and child can collaborate in economic relations and where such collaboration is in part based on a bond of strong positive affect, the alignment of the father and child against the child's descent group poses a particularly serious threat. Similarly, where the father can confer the privileges and advantages of a superior prestige position on his child, as against the position which he obtains through his own matrilineal descent-group membership, his child becomes particularly vulnerable to the temptation to exchange his rights in his natal group for such gains as can be had through his father.

There is, however, one very significant difference between the development of strong ties of positive affect between father and child and mother and child which is constant for both matrilineal and patrilineal descent groups, but which nevertheless functions differently in each. The psychobiological relationship between mother and child, by its nature, is such that strong positive affect is most likely to be developed, and since it is the first such bond in the child's life it becomes an element of more than superficial value. It is not necessary to detail the very profound psychological meaning of the mother for the child. It is only necessary to reiterate that by definition, in this theory, mothers are necessary to children as fathers are not, and to assume that the bond between the child and its mother is particularly likely to be a firm and enduring one. The bond between the child and its father, in matrilineal descent groups as in all others, tends to become established somewhat later than that of the child with its mother, and tends too to be ambivalent in affect.

It would follow, then, that children of one woman by different fathers are still more strongly tied to their mother than children by different mothers are tied to their one father.

If this is so we might expect that the children of different mothers by one father in patrilineal descent groups would on this basis alone be more likely to constitute a consistent line of cleavage than children of different fathers by one mother in matrilineal descent groups. In other words, there will be, on the basis of affective ties alone, a tendency toward fission along the lines of half-siblings in patrilineal descent groups, while that tendency should be markedly less in matrilineal descent groups.

On the basis of the different structural relevance of affective ties alone, then, (8) *the processes of fission and segmentation in matrilineal descent groups do not precisely replicate those of patrilineal descent groups.*

But affective ties are by no means the only elements involved. Men as in-marrying affines in matrilineal descent groups are bound to their own groups and tend to develop only weak marital bonds. Men constitute a source of potential strain in matrilineal descent groups because of their authority over their wives and children. Hence special limits must be imposed on the authority of men with respect to their wives and children. One important way to limit the authority of men over their wives and children, and thereby their influence on the organization and continuity of matrilineal descent groups into which they marry, is to minimize the importance of differences in paternal origin for the children by different fathers and one mother of a matrilineal descent group. Or (8a) *differences of paternal origin are less likely to be used as criteria for creating structural divisions within a matrilineal descent group than differences of maternal origin are in the process of segmentation in patrilineal descent groups.*

Perhaps the crucial element here is the strength of the wedge which can be driven between a child (particularly a son) and his matrilineal descent group by economic coöperation and the transfer of property between father and child. This does not mean that the different fathers of children by one woman in matrilineal descent groups cannot undertake such economic coöperation or such transfer of property. It only means that this constitutes a potential threat of considerable significance which, if matrilineal descent groups are to survive as such, must be carefully countered by some mechanisms which offset or diminish that threat. Thus for instance the children of one mother may constitute a sibling group which holds property in common, and the property which the father of one sibling gives him must be pooled with the property which another father gives another sibling. For when siblings hold different property through different fathers, the first and most important division among them has taken place. This first and firmest link with their fathers constitutes the first break with their matrilineal descent group. This alone may not break up matrilineal descent groups. But it does constitute a focus of great importance for the realignment of bonds which may very well bring about the termination of the matrilineal descent group.

I have spoken here of children of different fathers by one mother and children of different mothers by one father. This very general construction to cover certain situations. In either form of descent group these situations could occur as a result of polygamy of serial monogamy, that is, the children of one father by different mothers might, in patrilineal descent groups, be the children of polygynous wives, while the children of one mother by different fathers might, in matrilineal descent groups, be the children of a polyandrously married woman. Similarly, the children of one father by different wives in a patrilineal descent group might be the children of one father's successive wives, while the children of one mother by different fathers might, in a matrilineal descent group, be the children of one mother by a series of successive husbands.

There are other considerations which make the processes of fission and segmentation different in patrilineal and matrilineal descent groups.

In a patrilineal descent group any man who can acquire a wife is a potential head of a new segment. In any concrete case there may be insuperable obstacles to his founding a new segment, but in one respect he is self-sufficient: the new unit has its authoritative member (the male) and its "socially reproductive" member (the male) and a wife to care for children, the new members. In a matrilineal descent group no male can found a new segment unless he is able to pair off with one or more sisters or other matrilineal kinswomen (and their husbands), through whom social placement will occur, and no female can found a new segment without a male from her own group to fulfill the authoritative roles.

It is clearly more probable that any male can find a wife to care for his children than that he can find a sister or other female kinswoman to perpetuate a matrilineal descent group. The same situation holds in reverse: it is clearly more probable that any female can find a husband than that she can locate a brother or other matrilineal kinsman to act in the necessary authoritative roles. If we examine this proposition in the context of a single generation, then (8b) *brothers can more easily be the foci for the process of segmentation in patrilineal descent groups than can either brothers or sisters in matrilineal descent groups.*

In a patrilineal system, succession to authority may occur through unigeniture (e.g., succession by a son). The precise analogue for matrilineal systems would be from mother to selected daughter. This analogue does not apply, however, since authority is vested in male-held statuses. The nearest available analogue is that from a man to his eldest sister's eldest son, and so on. This system is possible, but unlikely in matrilineal systems. (8c) *Precise pairing of a male and a female member of a matrilineal descent group is relatively more difficult to achieve and, other things being equal, lateral succession (elder brother to younger brother, etc.) would be more likely than unigeniture in matrilineal descent groups.*

Further, (8d) *in dividing property, lateral processes would be more likely.* If property is divided among sons in a patrilineal system, it can be managed by each of those sons. If it is divided among daughters, the problem of allocating managers (brothers of those daughters) still remains. If it is divided among sons for the benefit of the daughters and their children, we still have the same problem.

Given these problems in the area of segmentation, succession, and inheritance, there would be a marked tendency to keep female siblings together in matrilineal descent groups under the leadership of one or more elder males. Succession would go from one male to another; even when it went from eldest sister's son to eldest sister's son, younger sisters and their children would be expected to remain with the group. Hence, (8e) *two or three generations of matrilineal kinsmen are more likely to stay together than to split up.* Where splitting occurred, it would likely be with reference to relatively remote matrilineal kinswomen. This bears on the possibilities of ranking lineage segments. Such ranking depends on perceptible splitting and, although it is not precluded in matrilineal descent groups, large descent groups with internally ranked segments can occur more easily in patrilineal than matrilineal descent groups.

Finally, the difficulties in separating collateral lines as social groups should be reflected in kinship terminology. (8f) *Matrilineal descent groups would be more likely to merge lineal and collateral relatives terminologically than would patrilineal descent groups.*[12]

9. *Isolated communities (or smaller groups) consisting of a matrilineal core and in-marrying spouses are extremely difficult to maintain.*

The monolineage community implies the special segregation of the descent-group members of one sex from the other. Patrilineal descent groups, which can sever or radically reduce its bonds with its female members, face no difficulty here. The women are not needed to reproduce for the group nor are they required for the exercise of authority; the group can survive quite well without them. Where a woman's bonds to her own group are so minimized, spatial separation does not matter. For matrilineal descent groups, on the other hand, the greater the spatial separation, the less the degree to which either sex can fulfill its obligations to its group. Where communities are spatially distinct yet near each

12. This proposition must be checked after eliminating non-sororal polygynous groups from account. Non-sororal polygyny, which is associated with patriliny, is also associated with collateralizing terminology; hence a spurious relationship might be found.

other, these difficulties are minimized, so that distinct matrilineal monolineage communities might only be expected under such circumstances (cf. Murdock, 1949).

In conclusion, I would raise a problem concerning one of the definitions used at the outset, namely, that authority over the joint activity of the descent group is held by male descent-group members. If authority is not specified as allocated to male members, a wider number of possible arrangements is conceivable than can be dealt with here. For this reason I have felt it necessary to retain the definition in this form. But one possibility is also thereby excluded which merits some attention and that is the possibility that male descent-group members have no authority within their own descent group, but that that authority is held by in-marrying male affines. That is, that husbands have authority over or manage the joint activity of the descent group of their wives. What, then, would happen to such a descent group?

The crucial question is that of descent-group maintenance; that is, the problem is one of balancing those conditions which would tend to disrupt the group against those conditions which would favor maintaining the group as a group. In-marrying male affines, unrelated to each other and alienated from their own group (since they exchange authority over their wives for authority over the women of their own descent group), would gain authority over their wives, but the problem would arise of their relations with each other and of their relations to the other women of the descent group into which they marry. Each man, having authority over his own wife, would be in a position to disrupt the bonds between women and require his wife to focus her primary loyalties on him. The jointly held activity of the descent group would thus become fragmented into domestic pieces, bits shared by each woman and managed by her husband independently. The descent group would thus be disrupted primarily as a consequence of the lack of some form of organization among male in-marrying affines, comparable to that which obtained among male descent-group members. In any concrete situation the particular form which descent-group joint activities took would, of course, be an important consideration in determining the specific outcome. If the descent group held land in common the matter might be rather different than if it held rights in some ceremonial activity. But the pressure of the husband to gain control over his wife and children would not be balanced by the capacity of the women to hold their group together, since husbands have authority over their own wives and children. Such a situation would therefore tend toward the disruption of the matrilineal descent group.

But what of the situation where the in-marrying male affines are already organized prior to marriage, as would be true with matrilateral cross-cousin marriage. Would the same tendency for each husband to single out his wife and gain complete control over her prevail, or could there be, in such circumstances, a coalition of in-marrying managers acting on behalf of the descent group or their wives?

The problem in this case would center on the problem of the control over children, particularly male successors. If the husbands control the descent-group activity of their wives, and if the husbands must bring in sisters's sons as successors, then the husbands must retain such bonds with the women of their matrilineal descent group as will enable them to hold their sisters's sons to their obligations as successors. This in turn means that the husbands as husbands must relinquish enough control over their own sons to permit the sons to become the successors of their mother's brothers. This would mean that the joint activity of the descent group in the management of the joint activity of another descent group. But this simply maintains matrilineal descent groups centered on joint activities requiring decision making, and entails all the distinctive features of matrilineal descent groups thus far considered; that is, it maintains the descent group's control over its recruitment, over its male and female members, and maintains this control as against the in-marrying male affines.

Where unorganized in-marrying male affines gain authority over their wives and children, then, it is unlikely that matrilineal descent groups as defined here can persist. Where matrilineally organized in-marrying male affines undertake to manage joint activities of their wives's descent group, this merely becomes the joint activity of the matrilineal descent group of the in-marrying male affines and all the conditions distinctive to matrilineal descent groups continue to prevail.

The necessity for defining authority over the joint activity of the descent group as allocated to male members therefore arises only because failure to specify who holds this authority leaves more possibilities open than can be fully considered in this treatment, not because it is conceivable that male members can exchange authority in their own descent group for authority in the descent group into which they marry.

[handwritten: week 8]

6 POTLATCH AND SAGALI: THE STRUCTURE OF EXCHANGE IN HAIDA AND TROBRIAND SOCIETIES

—PAULA G. RUBEL, PH.D.,
AND ABRAHAM ROSMAN, PH.D.

This paper is concerned with the examination of two societies, those of the Haida and the Trobriand Islands, in different parts of the world, in terms of a model that we have called the potlatch type society. This model has been derived from our extensive reexamination of the ethnographic data on six Northwest Coast societies. We began our study by examining the types of exchange structures considered by Mauss[1] in his book "The Gift," and we then sought to link specific types of exchange to forms of social structure. One such exchange structure was the potlatch type, and investigation led us inevitably to the Northwest Coast.

3 characteristics:

There are three general characteristics of potlatch-type societies. One is the presence of positions of rank embodied in names, the ownership of property and ceremonial paraphernalia, and the power to control other individuals. Such positions of rank are not linked to individuals but persist after the death of a holder through some mode of succession. The second characteristic is the presence of a ceremony at which large-scale distributions take place which serve to validate positions of rank. The distributions are bound to the element of rank. If adequate distribution is not forthcoming, then rank is diminished or the claim not accepted. If distributions are great, then rank is enhanced. This is one dimension of flexibility in the rank system of potlatch societies. The third general characteristic is that one always potlatches to one's affines. In addition to these general characteristics there are several variables in the model. These variables relate elements of the social structure to characteristics of the potlatch, such as prescribed occasions for potlatches, frequency of potlatching, and the personae involved. In potlatch-type societies, internal ranking is always present. However, it may or may not involve flexibility. If succession to position is flexible, i.e., open to competition, then funerals will be the occasion for potlatches. The competitors for rank positions try to be the first to amass enough goods with which to claim

* This paper was presented at a meeting of the Section on April 27, 1970, and is part of a study supported by funds from the Social Science Research Council and the National Science Foundation. Results of this Research will appear in a forthcoming book, "Feasting with Mine Enemy: Rank and Exchange among Northwest Coast Societies."

Reprinted from TRANSACTION OF THE NEW YORK ACADEMY OF SCIENCES, Series II, Volume 32, No. 6, pp. 732–742, June 1970. Paper presented at a meeting of the Section of Anthropology of the Academy on April 27, 1970. Copyright © 1970 by the New York Academy of Sciences. Reprinted by permission of the New York Academy of Sciences.

the now open position by carrying out the funerary rites for the previous holder. Such claims are then validated by the acceptance of goods by the guests. If succession to position is not flexible, as, for example, when there is a rule of primogeniture, then funerals will not be the occasion for a potlatch. However, succession to the position will then entail potlatching on the occasion of the passing on of the position to the heir during the lifetime of the holder. Both of these modes of succession and their related potlatch patterns occur on the Northwest Coast.

w/in group but also rep. entire group

Individuals potlatch in order to validate their own rank position in the internal structure of the group, but they also potlatch as representatives of their entire group. Thus, there is a constant interplay between the internal structure of the group and the relationship of that group to other groups. This relationship between groups may or may not be concerned with differences in rank. When rank differences between groups exist, they are always flexible in nature and subject to shift and change. Shifts in the ranking of groups are brought about by warfare or potlatching or a combination of the two, since they are related. In potlatch-type societies, the external relations between groups entail a reciprocal exchange of goods and services, as well as an exchange of that most valuable of commodities, women. The rivalry of the potlatch is thus a manifestation of the rivalry of affines to each other. The marriage rule thus defines the category of individuals with whom one exchanges women as well as with whom one potlatches. Since external ranking is flexible, when groups are ranked with respect to one another, marriages linking groups are an element of rank manipulation. In such societies, marriage will be the occasion for a potlatch.

affines

The potlatch-type society is characterized by the distinctive rank system we have described. Critical junctures occur when the rank system is rearranged. At such points, potlatches serves as *rites de passage* for society, providing a ceremonial occasion for the affirmation of the rearranged structure. Critical junctures are also occasions when the flexibility of the structure comes into play. Therefore, potlatches concurrent with critical junctures provide the opportunity for individuals to improve their positions.

rites of passage

Our first example is the Northwest Coast society, the Haida. The Haida are matrilineal in descent and avunculocal in residence. They have a marriage rule that states that the preferred marriage is with *sqan,* i.e., the father's sister's daughter.[2] This marriage pattern, given matrilineal descent, generates the structure illustrated in FIGURE 1. The presence of this structure among the Haida is supported by evidence of various kinds. The type of structure generated by marriage to the father's sister's daughter is a three-sided one, with each group intermarrying with two other groups. In the case of the Haida, the groups intermarrying in this fashion are lineages, since it is the lineage that is concerned in contracting a marriage. As a total system, a minimum of four groups is required. The Haida also have matrilineal moieties, but this moiety system is in reality a kind of pseudo-structure and does not indicate the presence of dual organization. Each lineage intermarries with two lineages in the opposite moiety. For each Haida lineage, Swanton[3] presents two in the opposite moiety with whom it is allied in marriage, forming a triad. When analyzed the triads are shown to be linked into longer chains composing a series of up to seven lineages, but

Transactions New York Academy of Sciences

A.

D.

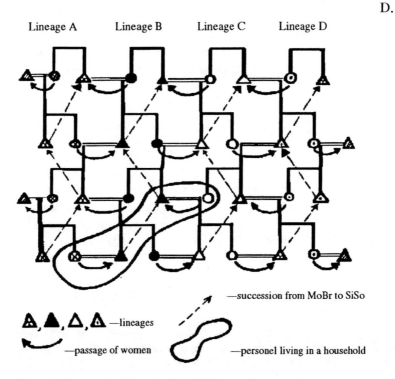

Figure 1 The structure generated by FaSiDa marriage.

not forming a circle.[3] As shown in FIGURE 1, one of the implications of this marriage rule is that the lineage of a man's father, wife, and children will be the same. This would not be the case given a pattern of random marriage in a matrilineal society. Murdock,[4] for example, speaking of some Haida songs, comments: "These songs are privileges, not of his own clan, but of a clan of the opposite moiety—his father's clan, according to my informant, but possibly the clan of his wife and children, since the two are frequently the same and were confused by my informants in other instances." Identification of father's lineage and son's lineage is further reinforced by the belief that a child is the reincarnation of his father's father and hence receives his father's father's name.[3,5] Since names are the possessions of lineages, it follows that a child and his father's father are members of the same lineage. All of these data support the structure generated by the father's-sister's-daughter marriage rule.

Rank among the Haida operates in conformity with the general structure of a potlatch-type society described above. The pattern of father's-sister's-daughter marriage, in which the direction of movement of females in marriage shifts in every generation, precludes the possibility of consistent rank differences between wife-givers and wife-takers. Therefore, as one would expect, lineages are not ranked with respect to one another. However, lineages are internally ranked. The position of chief is clearly delineated, but succession follows no hard-and-fast rule. Swanton notes,[6] "In choosing a successor to any position, the first requisite appears to have been success in amassing property. So it happened that elder sons were sometimes passed over by younger ones, or nearer relatives for those more remote." From Swanton's statement it is clear that succession to ranked positions was flexible and depended on the potential successor's ability to amass political support. This support took the form of material goods with which the claimant could then perform the mortuary potlatch, which constituted the validation of succession.

Potlatches are of two major types, mortuary potlatch and the housebuilding potlatch. In keeping with the third general characteristic of our model, the Haida potlatch only to their affines. We have noted previously that each Haida lineage is linked through exchange of wives with two other lineages in the opposite moiety. Each type of potlatch involves the host lineage with one of its two affine lineages. In the first major type of potlatch, the *sik!* or mortuary potlatch, the host, successor to the deceased chief, potlatches to men of the lineage who stood as affines to the late chief. The affines of the deceased chief have performed a number of services, including conducting the funeral of the deceased chief. At the mortuary potlatch, they bring the grave-post, paint and carve it, and finally erect it. They also perform the initiation into secret societies of young men of the deceased chief's lineage. As guests at the potlatch, they are feasted and then given large amounts of property in the potlatch distribution.

The second major form of the potlatch is the *walgal,* or housebuilding potlatch, in which the host or chief potlatches to his wife's lineage. The lineage of the chief's wife, which is so important at the *walgal* potlatch, is not present at the *sik!* potlatch. Conversely, the lineage of the previous chief's wife, which plays a major role at the *sik!* potlatch is not present at the *walgal.* Thus, it can be seen that these two types of potlatch separately relate the central lineage to the lineages with which it intermarries.

At a *walgal* potlatch, the major occurrence is the building of a new house for the potlatch donor. In contrast to some of the other societies on the Northwest Coast but similar to others, the house is built by the potlatch donor's own lineage. Initiation and tattooing of the youth of the wife's lineage, which results in raising the rank of those children, also occurs. Goods contributed by the wife's lineage are distributed to chiefs of the husband's lineage for the performance of those services. In the interactions between donor's lineage and wife's lineage, wife's lineage benefits in that the donor's children, who are members of his wife's lineage are raised in rank. On his part, the donor is now entitled to be called a housechief and to be treated as such at other individuals' potlatches. The members of the housechief's lineage receive payment for their various services.

The father's-sister's-daughter structure had been conceived of as the giving of a woman in one generation and the return of a woman in the next generation to complete the exchange. By shifting perspective to total exchange rather than simply the exchange of women, it can be seen that for the Haida, the links between groups are reiterated on a number of occasions in every generation. In referring to the accompanying diagram, when a chief in lineage B dies, his successor makes a *sik!* potlatch to which lineage C is invited and recompensed for its funerary services. Somewhat later the successor, now the chief, who has married a woman in lineage A, makes a *walgal* potlatch for lineage A. His sister's son and future successor marries a girl from lineage C. On the death of the chief and the succession of his sister's son the latter will make a *sik!* potlatch for lineage A. Thus marriages, *sik!*, and *walgal* potlatches succeed one another in an endless series of exchanges that bind the groups together in conformity with the structure of father's-sister's-daughter marriage.

The general characteristics of our potlatch model relating to rank and potlatch activity with affines are demonstrated in the Haida potlatch. In terms of the variables, internal rank is present and succession to position is flexible, so that funerals are the occasion for potlatches. External rank is absent, hence marriage is not the occasion for a potlatch. The pattern of potlatch activity mirrors the pattern of the social structure that derives from the rule of father's-sister's-daughter marriage. It is striking how little rivalry and competition occur within the context of the potlatches of the Haida.

That the Haida are a potlatch-type society will surprise no one. However, the close fit between our potlatch model and our second example—the Trobriand Islands society—which we shall now demonstrate, might well startle Professor Malinowski. Like the Haida, the Trobrianders have matrilineal descent and are avunculocal in residence. At a number of points, Malinowski firmly proclaims the Trobriand ideal of father's-sister's-daughter marriage and rules out mother's-brother's-daughter marriage. For example, he notes, "The two people who, according to native ideas are most suited for marriage with each other—a man's son and the daughter of his sister—are betrothed in infancy."[7] The manner in which such marriages are brought about and their relationship to *urigubu* payments is described as follows (REF. 7, p. 104):

> The initiative is always taken by the brother, who on behalf of his son, asks his sister for the hand of her daughter in marriage. A man has a definite right to make such a request; as the natives say: "Is he not the *kadala* (maternal uncle) of the girl? Are his sister and her child not his real *veyola* (maternal kindred)? Has he not always raised the *urigubu* (annual harvest contribution) for the household?" . . . His sister is not allowed to refuse his application.

Although others have contended that this marriage pattern is unimportant, we shall demonstrate the applicability to the Trobriand Islanders of the model generated by the rule of father's-sister's-daughter marriage, and, in our analysis of the exchanges in terms of the potlatch model, we shall verify this structure.

In one respect, the Trobrianders differ from the Haida. This is in the important role that polygyny plays for chiefs in the political system. Malinowski notes that in the old days chiefs could have up to fourscore or more wives. In addition to the giving of the wife, her close maternal relatives, in particular her brother, yearly had to contribute more than half of their harvest as *urigubu* to her husband, the chief. This payment is made each year by all brothers, commoners and chiefs alike, to their sister's husbands. The *urigubu* payments to chiefs take on the aspect of tribute. As Malinowski notes,[8] "As overlord of his district, the paramount chief has the right to marry a woman from every community, while some minor chiefs have the right to marry two or three women from adjoining villages." The chief thus fathers children for the headmen of his tributary villages, and with the yams contributed through their *urigubu* payments that he accumulates by virtue of his affinal connection he is able to demonstrate his largesse and distribute large amounts of goods. The chief performs a service by fathering children for the headmen of his tributary villages; however, at the same time, the chief is insuring the continuation of the relationship by having his sons in these important positions. But the women who are given to the chief are not part of a reciprocal relationship, since women of the chief's lineage are not given in return as wives to these headmen of tributary villages.

Malinowski gives very little information about the lineage to whom the women of chiefly lineages, especially the chief's sister, are given in marriage. Every chief of high rank was a head wife. We will use as our example the chief of the village cluster of Omarakana, who was of the highest-ranking subclan—the Tabalu, of the Malasi clan. The particular Tabalu chief whose activities concerned Malinowski was To'uluwa. In 1918, he had 12 wives, of whom the chief wife was Kadamwasila, who was of the Kwoynama subclan of the Lukwasisiga clan of Osapola village. Twelve was a much reduced number; the government no longer allowed the replacement of wives who had died. In the only genealogy given for the Tabalu, Malinowski indicates that Tabalu women intermarry with Kwoynama men. This same genealogy contains three examples of father's-sister's-daughter marriage, two classificatory and one real.[7] The Tabalu also intermarried with another subclan, the Toliwaga, also of the Lukwasisiga clan. This was the ruling subclan of Kabwaka village of the neighboring Tilataula District, who were the traditional rivals of the Tabalu.[9,10]

As noted above, father's-sister's-daughter marriage implies the equality of rank between intermarrying groups. For Trobriand Island chiefs the pattern of father's-sister's-daughter marriage characterizes the relationship between high-ranking chiefs of different villages. The chief's head wife comes to him by virtue of such a relationship with near-equals. In Malinowski's example, To'uluwa, the chief, had his favorite of his many sons—the son of Kadamwasila, his chief wife. The other group with which the Tabalu intermarry according to the father's-sister's-daughter marriage pattern are, as we have noted above, the Toliwaga of Kabwaka. The sisters of the Tabalu chiefs would be going to these two subclans in alternate generations, so that the line of Tabalu children is fathered by these two high-ranking groups. All other wives and children are of less significance and fall into the category of tributary marriages signifying subordination. This produces two distinct patterns of marriage for chiefs—the father's-sister's-daughter pattern with near-equals and the continual and unreciprocated supplying of wives for the chief by subclans and villages in subordination to him.

Despite Malinowski's explicit statements concerning father's-sister's-daughter marriage, Edmund Leach has argued that this pattern did not produce a structure since it was applicable only to chiefs. [11, 12] It can be clearly seen, however, that even if chiefs alone marry their father's-sister's-daughters, this can generate a structure that defines external relations between groups. This is because chiefs act as representatives of their groups and distribute at public ceremonies on behalf of their groups. The marriage pattern that relates to the internal structure of village clusters is the one we have categorized as tributary marriage. In his denial of the importance of father's-sister's-daughter marriage among the Trobrianders, Leach argued:[11]

> On the face of it, a marriage convention of this kind appears to be in direct conflict with the principals of *urigubu* giving. If normal residence behavior is adhered to, a patrilateral cross-cousin marriage will serve to cancel out the economic bond between Ego and his father's community. While Ego will be contributing *urigubu* to his father (*tama*), his father's sister's son (*tama*) will be contributing *urigubu* to Ego. Such direct reciprocity would make nonsense of the theme that *urigubu* payments represent among other things, tribute from a political inferior to a political superior.

In point of fact, Malinowski specifically notes this reversal of *urigubu* payments when father's-sister's-daughter marriage occurs as a result of infant betrothal: (REF. 7, p. 105):

> The natives regard *vaypokala* (infant betrothal) as equivalent to actual marriage. At the next harvest, the girl's father brings a *vilakuria* (substantial contribution of yam food) to the boy's parents. This latter fact is interesting, since it is a reversal of what happens in the previous generation. The boy's father, who is the brother of the girl's mother, has to give a harvest gift year by year to the girl's parents; and this at the time of his sister's marriage he had inaugurated by a gift of *vilakuria*. Now he receives on behalf of his infant son a *vilakuria* gift from his sister's husband, who acts as the representative of his own son or sons, that is the brother or future brothers of the bride, who later on will annually bring substantial harvest offerings to the household when it becomes such.

Thus it can be seen that the reversal of *urigubu* associated with the chiefly practice of father's-sister's-daughter marriage must be dissociated from the *urigubu* of tributary marriages. The reciprocity referred to by Leach is completely consistent with the equivalence of rank between rivalrous head chiefs and their practice of father's-sister's-daughter marriage. The tributary marriage pattern describes the relationship between the headmen of subordinate subclans and the head of the chiefly lineage within a village cluster. The former are characterized by Malinowski as *tokay* (commoners) and the latter as *guya'u* (chiefs).

Although Malinowski refers to junior and senior lines within the Tabalu subclan, there is no indication that a fixed series of ranked positions characterizes the internal structure of the subclan. However, the office of chief of the subclan is clearly delineated. There is no rule of primogeniture, and succession to the position of chief is flexible and subject to competition. As Powell notes (REF. 9, p. 128):

> The subclan leader is in effect selected on the basis of his achievements in comparison with those of others eligible by subclan membership, age and so on, and the more ambitious and dominating personalities tend in effect to compete with each other for selection. But the intensity of competition tends to vary with the rank of the subclan and its importance in local affairs . . . Where the subclan is of high rank and leads a cluster however, the personal advantages and power accruing to its leader are considerable and in olden times would-be leaders are believed regularly to have sought to eliminate rivals by fighting and by sorcery or poisoning.

As is apparent from this quotation, succession to leadership position is flexible. We would expect, in a potlatch-type society, some public ceremony with a large-scale distribu-

[handwritten: sagali = mortuary potlatch]

tion and public validation of the succession by the acceptance of gifts. Since succession is flexible, the funeral of the predecessor in office should be the occasion for a large-scale distribution of goods—the potlatch. According to Powell,[9] "The first public assertion and recognition of the new leader's position seems usually to consist in his organizing and conducting the mortuary rites for his predecessor . . ." Powell also notes,[9] "Before he (the chief) can do so he must make a display of the power which he has already achieved, in wealth and in the number of his supporters. He may do this on the occasion of the mortuary rituals for his predecessor, at which as successor he must make as lavish as possible a provision of wealth for ceremonial distribution (*sagali*) to the formal mourners, including of course the brothers of the widows of the dead leader and others." The mortuary *sagali* is a potlatch in terms of its elements. Malinowski's description of the mortuary *sagali* enables us to examine these elements in detailed interaction (REF. 7, p. 159–160).

> Immediately after the bones have been cut out and the remains buried, the dead man's sub-clan organize the first big distribution of food and valuables, in which the widow, children, and other relatives-in-law, as well as the unrelated mourners, are richly paid for the various services rendered in tending the corpse and digging the grave. Other distributions follow at stated intervals. There is one expressly for women mourners; one for the tenders of the grave; one for the rank and file of mourners; one, by far the largest, in which presents of valuables and enormous quantities of food are given to the widow and children, in so far as they, in grief and piety, have used the bones of the dead man for the lime-chewing or as ornaments. This intricate series of distributions stretches out into years, and it entails a veritable tangle of obligations and duties; for the members of the deceased's subclan must provide food and give it to the chief organizer, the headman of the subclan, who collects it and then distributes it to the proper beneficiaries. These, in their turn, partially at least redistribute it. And each gift in this enormous complex trails its own wake of countergifts and obligations to be fulfilled at a future death.

Upon the death of a man, his body becomes a dangerous substance for his consanguineal relatives, the members of his own subclan. They cannot touch the corpse. The services and rituals directly connected with the body of the deceased are therefore performed by the widow, sons, and other affines of the deceased. The formal expression of mourning is carried out by these relatives and consists of the ritual preparation of the body, the digging of the grave and the actual burial, the exhumation of the body and its examination for sorcery, and the removal of some of the bones to be used as relics by the sons. The consanguines of the deceased have nothing to do with these activities. It is clear that two sets of personae are concerned in the mortuary rites and there is a sharp separation of their roles. During the course of the life of the man now deceased, his affines, specifically his wife's brothers, yearly after the harvest period ceremonially presented him with a large proportion of the best yams they have grown as *urigubu*. After his death, his affines who have been givers all these years become receivers of mortuary *sagali*, which consists of raw yams—the same material as the *urigubu* payment.

[handwritten margin: urigubu / sagali]

This mortuary *sagali* and its accompanying distribution is hosted by the new chief, but the distribution is to the affines of the deceased chief. As can be seen in referring again to the diagram of father's-sister's-daughter marriage (FIGURE 1), the affines of the new chief are in a different lineage from the affines of the deceased chief. In terms of the diagram one would expect to find that the affines of a man would consist of his father, wife, and children. This identification is supported by Seligman in his direction of Trobriand mortuary rites:[13] "The widow, children and father of the dead man blacken themselves before this and all take part in this feast which is called *sagali* . . . ." The affine relatives of the new chief who host the *sagali* play no part in the activities.

We have assumed, that as is usually the case, the new chief, who is an adult maneuvering for power has already married his father's sister's daughter and is receiving annual *urigubu* from her brother. There is no formal ceremony of marriage. Public recognition of an acceptable marriage is through the first payment of *urigubu* by the bride's brother to her husband. This marks the beginning of the annual *urigubu* payments from wife's brother to husband, which will terminate at the husband's death. Marriage is not marked by a public [*preg-nancy sagali*] ceremonial distribution of goods and therefore is not the occasion for a potlatch.

Pregnancy, however, is the occasion for a *sagali* distribution. The pregnancy that is of structural interest to the chief is that of his sister. It is she who will produce the children who will perpetuate the lineage. She looks to the women of her own father's lineage (the father's lineage of the chief) for the performance of various services during the period of her pregnancy. They include weaving the special cloak she must wear, assisting her during her ritual bath in the sea, and performing various forms of magic to protect her during this crucial period. They take her to their own house to feed her, since she must not touch food with her hands. At the last stage of pregnancy she goes to her father's house or that of her mother's brother to deliver the baby, because of the fear of sorcery in her husband's house. The first pregnancy ritual, which includes the clothing and ceremonial bathing of the pregnant girl and her magical adornment is climaxed by the pregnancy *sagali*. Malinowski states that (REF. 7, p. 223) : " . . . the work, the magic, the ritual are performed by the female relatives of the father. In the distribution of food (*sagali*) which immediately follows the ceremony, it is the mother's brother, the brother, and the other maternal kinsmen of the young woman who do the distributing . . . . Food is divided into heaps and every heap is allotted to a single person, his or her name being called out in a loud voice."

The elements of the *sagali*, including the manner of yam distribution, are identical to the elements of a potlatch. The removal of the pregnant girl and the subsequent events, which concern her own matrilineage and that of her father, serve to separate these three lineages conceptually. Her husband's lineage is deemed to be dangerous, while the lineage of her father, in whose house she was born serves to protect her at this crucial time. The separation of these three lineages is consonant with father's-sister's-daughter marriage. The father's lineage for the chief and his sister is the one that has furnished the chief with his principal wife. Therefore that father's lineage is currently paying *urigubu* to the chief. The *sagali* payment on the occasion of the pregnancy ritual for the chief's sister thus represents a reversal in direction of the *urigubu* payment, just as the mortuary *sagali* was a reversal in direction of an earlier *urigubu* payment. [*reciprocal*]

The last *sagali* distribution we shall consider is that which accompanies the building or repair of the yam house, or *bwayma*. This is the place where the annual *urigubu* payment is displayed and stored. According to Malinowski, the chief's yam house is larger and more elaborately decorated than his dwelling house. Malinowski notes (REF. 8, p. 246): "... the owner or chief would summon his relatives in law, those who fill the storehouse with *urigubu*, to work for him. They would prepare in their villages the materials for the storehouse .... After the yam house had been constructed, the big *sagali* or distribution of food would take place at which, besides pigs and *kaulo* (vegetable food), some valuables also would probably be distributed to the most important contributors to the work." Once again, *sagali* reverses *urigubu*.

The structure generated by father's-sister's-daughter marriage has been inadequately portrayed as one in which a woman given in one generation is returned by the giving of a woman in the following generation, thus, completing a transaction and creating short cycles of exchange. As can be seen in the case of the Trobrianders, when one uses the perspective of total exchange, looking at goods and services of all sorts in addition to women, the structure is reiterated in every generation in a variety of ways. When a chief in Lineage B dies, his successor makes a mortuary *sagali* or potlatch for the dead chief's affines in lineage C who have performed the various funerary services. The new chief has been receiving *urigubu* from lineage A, from which his head wife has come. When the chief's sister becomes pregnant, the pregnancy ritual is performed at which lineage A, the father's lineage for the chief and his sister, performs various services and in return receive *sagali*. This is the same lineage from which the chief's wife comes and from which he is receiving *urigubu*. Lineage A also repairs the chief's yam house and receives *sagali* in return. On this chief's death, his sister's son will succeed him and make the mortuary *sagali*, distributing to lineage A. The new chief once again receives a wife and *urigubu* from lineage C. The sequence of exchanges thus serves to reiterate the links between the groups in the structure.

There are two other kinds of potlatch among the Trobrianders. The first, known as the *kayasa*, implies competition of a variety of types. One of them is the harvest *kayasa*, in which two subordinate villages vie in presenting *urigubu* to the chief. This type of potlatch relates to the determination of the relative rank of these subordinate villages *vis-a-vis* one another. The second form of potlatch is called the *buritila'ulo*. It implies competition between two villages in which the challenging village gives its entire harvest to the one being challenged, the latter then endeavoring to return in excess of the first amount. Like the *kayasa,* the *buritila'ulo* relates to the relative rank of subordinate villages.

In terms of the general characteristics of our model, the Trobrianders conform in that they have rank, they carry out large-scale distributions identical to potlatches, and these large-scale distributions are made to one's affines. In these general characteristics, the Trobrianders are identical with the Haida. The particular cluster of potlatch variables we have demonstrated for the Haida recurs among the Trobrianders. In both, internal rank is present and succession to position is flexible, so that funerals in Haida and Trobriand societies are the occasions for potlatches. Given the nature of father's-sister's-daughter marriage in both, marriages that take place between equals do not serve as the occasion for a potlatch.

2 other types:
Kayasa & buritila'ulo

Among the Haida, external ranking of groups is absent. The Trobrianders are more complex than the Haida. They have a two-part structure in which chiefs follow the pattern of father's-sister's-daughter marriage in marriages with women from other equally high-ranking subclans. Chiefs also take women in tributary marriage from the headmen of subordinate subclans.

We have argued that potlatching always takes place between affines. In both of these societies, potlatch exchanges serve to separate the two sets of affines. Thus, the exchanges serve as verification of the presence of the structure generated by father's-sister's-daughter marriage.

The Haida and Trobriands material are part of our ethnographic heritage, having been examined by generations of students and professionals. Their structural identity has not previously been noted. We feel that in our comparison we have followed Leach and have not been butterfly collectors but have aimed at true generalization. The most important point deriving from this analysis of two situations that are very different both culturally and ecologically is the isolation of a series of codeterminant structural variables. This series constitutes our potlatch model, to which both Haida and Trobrianders conform. The covariance of the pattern of elements in the Haida and Trobriand cases cannot be explained on cultural or ecological grounds. Only a structural explanation can account for it. From now on we hope that the term potlatch will be used in its newer, more analytical sense. From our generalizations, we conclude that in certain circumstances yams equal blankets though their caloric content differs.

ACKNOWLEDGMENT

We would like to thank our colleague, Dr. Bernard Barber, for his comments on our work.

REFERENCES

1. Mauss, M. 1925. The Gift. I. Cunnison, Trans. Cohen and West. London, England.

2. Murdock, G. P. 1934. Kinship and social behavior among the Haida. Amer. Anthropol. 36: 364.

3. Swanton, J.R. 1905. Contributions to ethnology of the Haida. Mem. Amer. Mus. Natural Hist. 8: 67, 117, & 118.

4. Murdock, G.P. 1936. Rank and potlatch among the Haida. Yale Univ. Publ. Anthropol. 13: 8.

5. Murdock, G.P. 1934. The Haida of British Columbia. *In* our Primitive Contemporaries. : 249. The Macmillan Co. New York, N.Y.

6. Swanton, J.R. 1905. Social organization of the Haida. Proc. Int. Congr. Americanists : 333.

7. Malinowski, B. 1929. The Sexual Life of Savage in Northwestern Melanesia: : 95 & 100. George Routledge & Sons. London, England.

8. Malinowski, B. 1935. Coral Gardens and Their Magic. 1: 334. G. Allen and Unwin. London, England.

9. Powell, H.A. 1960. Competitive leadership in Trobriand political organization. J. Roy. Anthropol. Inst. 90: 131 & 135.

10. Malinowski, B. 1948. Myth in primitive psychology. *In* Magic, Science and Religion. : 122–123. The Free Press. New York, N.Y.

11. Leach, E.R. 1958. Concerning Trobriand clans and the kinship category "tabu." *In* The Development Cycle in Domestic Groups. J. Goody, Ed. Cambridge Papers Soc. Anthropol. 1: 138. Cambridge University Press. Cambridge England.

12. Needham, R. 1962. Structure and Sentiment : 120–121. The University of Chicago Press. Chicago, Ill.

13. Seligman, C.S., 1910. The Melanesians of British New Guinea. : 716. Cambridge University Press. Cambridge, England.

7 THE CULTURAL ECOLOGY OF ALBANIAN EXTENDED FAMILY HOUSEHOLDS IN YUGOSLAV MACEDONIA

—C.J. GROSSMITH

The Albanians who are the subject of this paper live on the lower slopes of the mountains between Skoplje and Tetovo, ten miles west of the city of Skoplje. They are patriarchal, patrilineal, generally patrilocal, and Moslem. The twenty-five villages in the area form a more or less endogamous group.

The history of Macedonia has been a harsh one, and this area is no exception. Following five hundred years of feudalism under Ottoman rule, the area in 1913 became a part of Serbia. Bulgaria occupied it from 1916 until 1919, when the Serbs returned. From 1941 until 1944, when Tito's Yugoslavia was established, the villagers were very badly exploited and lived in conditions of extreme poverty.

Since World War II, Macedonia has made enormous strides, but the Albanian villages are only just beginning to reap some of the benefits of modern industrial society. Solid modern brick and cement block houses are now being built near the main Skoplje road. They provide a vivid contrast with the old Turkish-style houses of wood and mud bricks, clustered round the mosque in the upper part of the village. This change has occurred very recently and reflects new opportunities for employment outside the village.

In the past, village houses were grouped together in *mohullas* or neighborhoods. Each *mohulla* represented a *fis* or patrilineal descent group, some of whom can trace their origin back to Albania. Today the *fis* are scattered, and their function has diminished, since they are no longer corporate land-holding groups. *Fis* still serve as exogamous units and provide economic and moral support for marriage, circumcision, and other major financial and economic needs among their member households. Male and female members of households belonging to the same *fis* mix and talk freely, in sharp contrast to household members of different *fis* who are neither related by marriage nor proximity. Women in such households are mutually secluded, and men will visit such a household only on invitation or important business. Not a single woman in the village has employment outside her household.

Many households have left the village for Turkey or migrated to Skoplje. A number of households have moved in from surrounding villages, because the village I have studied is an administrative center for the area. It contains a school for pupils up to the eighth class, an outpatient clinic, and the headquarters of the agricultural cooperative. The villages share the overall demographic characteristics of the Albanian minority in Macedonia, who, according to the 1971 census, have a birth rate of 39.5 per 1,000 population, compared with 18.1 per 1,000 population among Slavic Macedonians.

THE EXTENDED FAMILY HOUSEHOLD

In their recent monograph,[1] the Halperns have provided an example of a large extended family zadruga in Serbia in 1905. The household of Svetozar Stojanov is reproduced here with ages. Such zadrugas can no longer be found in Serbia or elsewhere in Yugoslavia, except among Albanians, who live mainly in Kosovo, Macedonia, and Montenegro.

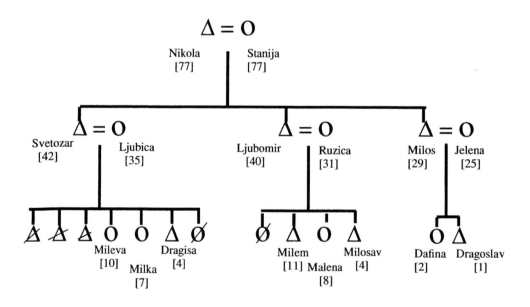

The following diagram outlines an Albanian household in 1973 in an Albania village ten miles from Skoplje and 150 miles south of the Halperns' village.

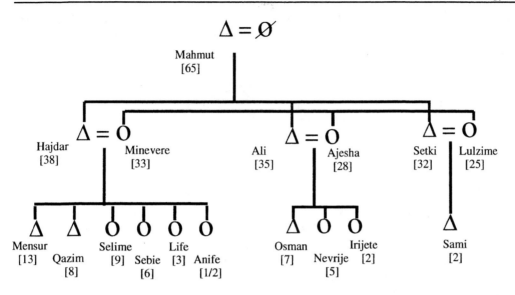

In 1973, the seventeen members of this household lived in a four-room house with a kitchen and a store room. Mahmut had a room to himself, and each of the sons had one room, in which he slept with his wife and children. The family planned in 1974 to build three smaller houses in a common compound on one of their pieces of land, so that each son would have a house of his own. The whole household eats communally. The three houses will be used only for sleeping, and the family will continue to eat together. The household provides an example of three brothers who are married to three sisters from a nearby village. One-fifth of all village households contain two or more brothers married to women who are sisters.

The Mahmut household has eighty-five *shenik* of land, registered in Mahmut's name. A *shenik* equals five hundred square meters. Mahmut inherited forty-eight *shenik* from his father, and the household bought thirty-seven *shenik* between 1943 and 1972. After the First World War, one *shenik* of land cost ten kilos of wheat. The price of one *shenik* today is about nine hundred dollars.

The work patterns of Mahmut's sons and grandsons are as follows. Mahmut's three sons, Hajdar, Ali, and Setki, began grazing the household sheep when they were six or seven years old. At the age of eleven, Hajder and Setki began to work the land with their father, continuing until age nineteen, when they went into the army for two years. From the age of ten to twelve, Ali attended a school six miles from the village. He then returned to work the land until he was nineteen, when he too went into the army. On returning from army service, all three brothers continued to work the land. Three years ago, Hajdar became a private house builder. Ali obtained a job as clerk in the village school three years after returning from the army, and still holds this position. Setki continues to work the land with his father and the occasional assistance of Hajdar. Last year, Setki took an adult evening course at the village school to complete the eighth grade. This will give him a better chance to obtain state employment in Skoplje, where he is currently registered at the employment bureau. Hajdar's sons, Mensur and Qazim, began going to school at age seven. The household no longer possesses any sheep, but Mensur grazes the draft oxen during vacations. Ali's son Osman will enter school this year.

When on private contract, Hajdar earns 6,000 new dinars ($400) a month; village construction work pays well. Ali, as a state employee, receives 1,300 new dinars ($80) a month. The household land produces 4,000 kilograms of wheat flour a year. This feeds the seventeen members of the household. In addition, the household produces all its own fruit and vegetables and collects ten liters of milk a day from its two cows. Last year, it received 14,000 new dinars from the sale of the grape harvest. A conservative estimate of the household's monthly income over and above the food consumed would be $550. Last year, they bought a second-hand Fiat for $600.

In order to put the Mahmut household in perspective, the table illustrates the frequency of different household types in the village by numbers of members. I have selected seven household types. The table shows that one-third of the village population lives in households containing two or more married brothers and their families, with or without their parents. About forty percent of the village population lives in households containing ten or more members.

HOUSEHOLD TYPES

Type 1	Nuclear Household
Type 2	Husband and/or wife, and married son with or without children.
Type 3	Husband and/or wife, and two married sons with or without children.
Type 4	Husband and/or wife, and three married sons with or without children.
Type 5	Two-generation household, with two married brothers and children.
Type 6	Two-generation households, with three married brothers and children.
Type 7	Three-generation household, with two married brothers in oldest generation.

Table of Household Type by Number of Household Members

Type	Total	1	2	3	4	5	6	7	8	9	10	11	12	13	14	15	16	17	18	19	20	20+
1	61	2	6	8	4	9	10	10	7	1	3	1										
2	25			3	2	2	2	5	2	2	4	1	1	1								
3	12								2	3	1	3	1	1						1		
4	3														1	1			1			
5	5					1	1						1			1		1				
6	1																					1
7	3							1		1											1	
Total	110	2	6	11	6	12	13	16	11	7	8	5	3	2	1	2		1	1	1	1	1

ACCUMULATION OF WEALTH

Within the Albanian extended family household, two kinds of wealth can be accumulated, material and non-material. Material wealth consists of land and income, and the latter may be described as the potential and actual contributions of household members to the prosperity of the house and the honor which they are able to accumulate.

Land is accumulated by inheritance and purchase. Inheritance involves equal division of a father's land holdings among his sons. Division may occur before or after the father's death. Daughters, although entitled by Yugoslav law to share in their father's property, in fact receive nothing. If division occurs while the father is still alive, it is ordinarily not formally registered with the taxation authorities. In this way, sons employed by the state do not declare their possession of land and therefore are entitled to child benefits. If a couple has no son, occasionally a son-in-law will come to live with them and work their land, later passing it on to his children. Such a situation occurs only if the son-in-law's father has another son to inherit his land. Alternatively, a couple without a son may sell their land and live with one of their daughters. The cash from the sale of their land may be given to the son-in-law for buying more land. A few cases of both these situations have occurred in the village I have studied.

Opportunities for buying land occur when someone leaves the village. During the last fifty years, several emigrations have occurred. After the First World War, village land became very cheap when large numbers of Turks returning to Turkey sold their land in Tetovo and Gostivar to Albanians from mountain villages nearby. A number of families from the village studied moved into the Tetovo District, buying better land and selling their village land. During the 1950's, another emigration to Turkey occurred because of the pressures on Moslems to conform to certain state regulations, such as sending daughters to school. A father who violated this law was sent to prison. More recently, about twenty households migrated to Skoplje because of favorable opportunities for employment. Occasionally, families left the village because of a *bela* or quarrel.

When a man decides to leave the village, he first offers to sell his land to members of his own *fis*, then to his *miks* (affines), then to those who have land bordering on the land he wants to sell. Then, if he has been unable to sell it, anyone can purchase it.

Since the last war, agricultural stock has been considerably reduced in size in Yugoslavia. After the First World War, many families had large flocks of sheep and goats. Goats have now been banned by law, because of the destruction they cause to the crops and vegetables on the mountainside. Flocks of sheep have also been considerably reduced. Most households are content to have a donkey, a cow, a pair of draft oxen, and perhaps a few sheep.

Today four different kinds of economic opportunity are open to male household members: work on the land, state employment, private enterprise, and migrant labor abroad. If a household has land, a member in state employment, and a member either in private enterprise or in migrant labor in Germany, it will prosper. Work on the land meets all the household's food requirements, and may in addition bring in large amounts of seasonal capital through the sale of grapes and other produce. State employment provides a low but regular income, and migrant labor abroad provides relatively large amounts of capital, which are used for buying land, building houses, arranging marriages, and buying modern luxury items, such as cars, television sets, and refrigerators.

HOUSEHOLD WORK PATTERNS

When an extended family household divides into separate nuclear families, the major economic change which occurs is that each nuclear family produces and consumes products separately from separate areas of land. This represents the basic criterion in defining a household. The saying "Who will give you bread this evening if you don't work today?" serves to emphasize the dependence of household members on their own domestic and agricultural labor.

The majority of village households still maintain many characteristics of a traditional peasant economy. The only regularly purchased domestic supplies are rice, cooking oil, matches, sugar, salt, tea, coffee, detergent, and soap. Some families grow their own sunflowers, which they have made into cooking oil in a Skoplje factory. Many families still cook on wood fires from wood gathered on privately-owned village woodland. Bread, leavened and unleavened, is baked every day from home-grown wheat and forms the staple diet. It is eaten with home-grown fruit and vegetables, eggs, domestic milk products, and vegetable conserves. Water is drawn by hand from the household or neighborhood well. Many families grow their own tobacco, and the brooms used to sweep the house and court yard are also grown on household land. Old men can still be seen wearing clothes made at home from material woven on domestic looms, and everyone possesses thick white woolen home-knitted socks from domestic sheep.

All household members from six years of age are expected to help with household work. A member who does not do his share is known as *çelepurxh*i, someone who waits for everything to be handed to him. Villagers say, "Some people live by buying everything, but we work in the fields to have something in addition."

Male members who work the land have their hardest period between May and September. During that time, the corn fields are plowed and planted. The grape vines are tied and sprayed, the meadows scythed, and the grass made into haystacks to dry. The vegetable gardens and melon patches are dug and planted, manured, and then hoed. From time to time, men go up the mountain to cut wood and graze cattle, or else to transport bags of wheat on the backs of their donkeys to the water mill in the next village. In July and August, the wheat and rye are harvested. Until two years ago, harvesting was done entirely with sickles, and threshing was done separately in the yard by a horse trampling the ears of wheat as it walked slowly round a central pole. This method is still used among village households. Now, in addition, the village has the use of a combine which threshes as it harvests. In upland fields, harvesting is done by hand, though often threshed by machine later.

During July, which is the hottest month, the kitchen gardens and cornfields have to be irrigated with water from the mountain streams which flow through the villages. By September, after the corn and beans are harvested, the agricultural work slacks off and people await Ramazan, which for the past ten years has fallen in autumn and winter.

Men who are in state employment, unless they have a job in the village, take the five o'clock bus to Skoplje every morning for work at six. They remain until three in the afternoon, when they catch the bus back to the village, arriving at three-thirty or four o'clock. If there is work to be done in the fields, they then join their brothers and fathers on the land until five or six in the evening.

Men who have retired from state jobs and are too old for heavy work on the land still contribute in numerous ways to the household. They take the oxen out to graze, or watch and feed the poultry. Some work at hand crafts, such as basket-making, or take dried corn off the cob for seed. From time to time, they may visit *fis* or *affines* to arrange some household business. In short, there are always jobs for everyone, according to his abilities.

In the extended family which contains two married brothers, the *kunata* or sisters-in-law are responsible for most of the housework. The mother-in-law directs their work and watches the children. Usually, one sister-in-law will sweep the house and yard, draw water, prepare food, and bake bread, while the other washes the children and the clothing for the whole household, milks the cows, makes the milk into yogurt, and churns it into curds and whey. Each week, the sisters-in-law change jobs. In addition, during the months from May to September, the sisters-in-law may go into the fields to work with the men, dig the vegetable garden, hoe the corn, collect fruit, harvest the wheat with a hand sickle, and pick beans. In winter, when work is lighter, they embroider handkerchiefs or head scarfs for themselves or a future bride, knit woolen sweaters for their husbands, or weave aprons on the loom. This work pattern is followed whether the sister-in-law is healthy, sick, or pregnant. During pregnancy, she works in the fields with the men until the ninth month. She usually labors in the fields when her children are old enough to be left but too small to work, and when there is an insufficiency of adult males.

When children have reached the age of five or six, they are expected to fetch and carry round the house, take trays of food to the kitchen, pour water for other household members to wash their hands, sweep the floor after meals, draw water from the well, fetch ash trays for guests, and take messages to other houses. After heavy rain, they collect sand from the bed of the village stream for use as building material. They watch the poultry, and carry the midday meal to the fields for their father or uncles working there. They also go to the cooperative store to buy cigarettes, bottles of fruit juice, and other items required suddenly when relatives arrive.

THE ROLE OF HONOR

The Albanian household is entwined in a network of relations essential to its preservation. It forms part of a patrilineal descent group and is also linked with a series of other households through marriage. In addition, it is linked with neighboring households, which, although related neither lineally nor affinally, occupy a somewhat similar status. Women of neighboring households talk to their male neighbors. Such households visit each other often and cooperate in the day-to-day round of agricultural and domestic work. In addition, the household is linked with the rest of the village households by language, religion, ethnic and village identity, common way of life, contact on ceremonial occasions, and, often, male members at work in Skoplje.

Within such a complex network of relationships, self-respect or honor is an essential ingredient of the Albanian household. A household can accumulate honor in a number of ways. Working for the household is one way, and keeping the rules is another. In a patriarchal society, one set of rules involves showing respect to one's elders and therefore, by extension, to the household. Honor also involves keeping the rules of Islam. Daughters and wives are secluded from all males who do not belong to the household *fis*, and the fast of Ramazan must be kept. A son must be circumcised and sons and daughters married in the proper manner. In the case of a son's marriage, bride wealth consisting of as much as two thousand dollars worth of Turkish gold lira and clothing must be sent to the bride's family as the daughter's personal property and insurance.

If a household has an honorable reputation as well as wealth, its sons and daughters can obtain wives and husbands easily. The families with whom their marriages are arranged become *mik* (affines) to the household, and such households then enter into a relationship of cooperation and support. Thus, a *mik* who is a builder will construct a house for half the price a non-related builder will ask. Relationships of reciprocal assistance develop with *mik* households which assist in the exchange of domestic produce and help with the agricultural work.

When either honor or wealth are in short supply, brides are obtained by the use of additional strategies. In 12.3 percent of village households, the husband had obtained a wife by exchanging a sister. In twenty percent of the households, a wife was forced to fetch her younger sister for her husband's younger brother. On occasion, sums of money have been paid directly to the bride's father, and a few families have obtained Slavic Moslem women from Bosnia.

When a man obtains a bride, he has an opportunity to have sons who will enrich the house, support him, and provide him with leisure in old age. Meanwhile, his bride will carry out the arduous domestic work essential to maintenance of the household.

The activities of the Albanian household are clearly directed towards the prosperity of a group of resident male agnates. Women serve as an important means towards this prosperity, but their benefit from it is incidental.

WOMEN AS A DIVISIVE ELEMENT

Women are often the divisive element in extended households. They lose much of their identity with their own *fis* when they move into their husband's house, and they are also strangers there. A young bride before going to her husband's house swallows a bead which she later collects from her stool and takes to the *hoxha* , or Moslem priest, who recites over it. This bead is always kept on the bride's person as protection from *seire* (witchcraft) of members of her husband's *fis*. Fear of witchcraft is only one sign of the tension which exists between women and their in-laws.

An extended family depends for its existence on subjugation of individual interests and loyalties to the common cause of the house. However, women often feel no particular loyalty to their husband's *fis* or extended family. Their loyalty crystallizes and develops with the development of their immediate nuclear families. Albanian women want children as quickly as comfortably possible. Many mention three years as the maximum period they prefer between deliveries. This enables them to recover from the previous birth, wean the child, teach it to feed itself, take it out of swaddling, and dispense with the laundry involved. After this they are ready to deliver the next child. The sooner they can produce a son, the sooner they can ensure their relationship with their husband and therefore their status in his house. Until a son is born, they are on trial. If they are unable to produce a son within a few years, they may be divorced. In any case, they must expect constant tension in the household from their husband and in-laws. The sooner they have a son, the sooner he will grow up, marry, and enable them to hand over a large part of the domestic work to his bride.

The birth of a daughter has initial advantages, because she will soon be able to provide help around the house. However, from puberty until she is married, she is a constant worry to her mother, who must protect her from contact with non-related males and ensure she marries in the proper manner, not by running away with someone. After a daughter has been married, she is of no further direct economic benefit to her household.

For a woman, one son is not enough because an extended household needs to exploit three of the four economic possibilities for male employment if it is to prosper. Two or three sons will not only enrich the house, but will act as a safeguard if one of the sons should die or enter into the non-Moslem, alien world of the city. Finally, several sons will provide the economic base which will enable a woman to bring about a division in the extended family, if intra-household relations are strained.

In extended households which have two or more married brothers, relationships between the sister-in-law and the mother-in-law are most conducive to conflict. Sisters-in-law tend to favor their own husbands and children in their daily work. As a result, constant accusations arise that the other sister-in-law is not doing her share, and mutual distrust develops. One sister-in-law will use the ethic of household equality to spite the other: "After my son was born, she got jealous, and didn't allow me to give the boy milk. We often quarrelled when I fed him biscuits, milk, or eggs. She did not have a son and therefore did not want me to feed him with those things." Mothers-in-laws often resent the threat posed to their nuclear family relationships by the arrival of a daughter-in-law. One daughter-in-law said of her mother-in-law, "She thinks she has been left without a son, and says, 'I had one and I got left without him. My daughter-in-law took him for herself.' "

Such patterns of conflict, not unique among Albanians, acquire a special significance in the Albanian extended family, where household organization is geared to the preservation of a group of resident male agnates, and female members are constantly at odds with the system.

Extended family households of fifteen or more members still exist among Moslem Albanians in Yugoslavia. These households are independent economic units and rely upon the subjugation of individual interests for the prosperity of the house. Household economies are ecologically generalized in that household members exploit several kinds of economic resource. If one resource fails, several alternatives are available. Better state employment opportunities and migrant labor abroad have increased these alternatives recently. In order to function as an economic unit, the household must maintain a network of reciprocal relations with other families. Keeping such relations in good repair provides the household honor, and thereby enables it to obtain women to produce sons and replenish the household manpower. Honor and adherence to religious beliefs have very similar functions.

Women act as divisive elements in the extended family because their loyalties center around their immediate nuclear families. Both male and female household members want several sons, but not for the same reasons. For male members, sons help replenish the work force and provide security in old age. For females, sons provide security of status in the husband's household and help create circumstances with enable a woman's nuclear family to separate from the extended family.

As long as an Albanian is group-oriented, rather than individually oriented, that is to say, as long as his household's prosperity comes before his own, Albanians will maintain a high birthrate in order to provide household manpower in both rural and urban areas.

In their relations with non-Moslem nationalities in Macedonia, Albanians still seek the maintenance of cultural separateness and distance. Integration will be a slow and painful process. In the long run, household authority among Albanians may diminish as education and employment levels among males increase. The creation of culturally acceptable possibilities for the extra-household employment of Albanian females in the near future would probably produce an immediate decline in the birthrate, particularly if emphasis were placed upon skills currently possessed by Albanian females, such as handicrafts. These do not require high educational qualifications, but would permit Albanian women to participate in extra-household activities. This would make them wage earners, and increase the number of people with whom they are in regular contact. Studies of many different parts of the world have shown that employment among women helps produce a sharp decline in the birthrate. However, opposition to such a change lies deep in the roots of the Albanian interpretation of Islam.

NOTES

1. Joel M. Halpern and Barbara K. Kalpern, *A Serbian Village in Historical Perspective* (New York, 1972), p. 36.

8 MACHISMO AND CRYPTOMATRIARCHY:
POWER, AFFECT, AND AUTHORITY IN THE CONTEMPORARY YUGOSLAV FAMILY

—ANDREI SIMIĆ

Even God has a mother.
A man is a child as long as he lives; keep him at your breast and he will always be satisfied.
    (Serbian folk aphorisms)

As elsewhere in Yugoslavia, on the northern Adriatic island of Krk elderly women constitute an influential social category. Grandmothers, swathed from head to foot in the black of mourning, are seemingly everywhere. The islanders sometimes refer to them humorously as "black crows," since like these omnipresent fixtures of Krk's rocky landscape "they see and know everything." What remains unsaid but implied is their salient role in the control and manipulation of interpersonal relationships and in the safeguarding of community mores. For example, it was rumored that a recent marriage resulted from the conspiratorial intercession of two grandmothers who engineered periods of prolonged privacy for the young couple so that the faltering romance could be rekindled and expedited by the prospective bride's anticipated pregnancy. The power of older women is equally evident in the western Serbian village of Borina, where adult male informants, some of advanced age, casually related that, while they frequently made important decisions without consulting their wives, they almost always sought the opinion of their mothers. Similar behavior is depicted in the Yugoslav feature film *Skuplijaci Perja (The Feather Gatherers)* set in the region of Vojvodina on the rich Pannonian Plain. The Gypsy protagonist, who publicly beats his wife and spends his money with wild abandon in drinking bouts that include the self-infliction of wounds with broken glasses he has smashed on a cafe table in a demonstration of machistic prowess, is also pictured as meekly acquiescing to his mother's demands, and seeking her advice in both business and love. In the light of such behavior, it is not surprising that mothers provide one of the most pervasive themes in South Slav popular culture. For instance, in the analysis of the lyrics of 71 contemporary composed folk songs dealing with courtship (Simic 1979a:30–31), mothers assume a central role in 21. In these lively commentaries on contemporary Yugoslav life (not unlike the American country-and-western tradition) mothers encourage their sons to marry (sometimes even selecting their brides), caution them about the dangers of nightlong carousing and the wiles of "inappropriate" women, protect their daughters' virginity and reputations, and act in general as confidantes to their children in unhappy love relationships. In other songs, parents, particularly mothers, emerge as the focus of intense emotional attachments. The cultural significance and emotional power of these sentiments is indicated by the fact that such lyrics are capable of moving even burly truck drivers and grizzled peasants to bouts of tearful sentimentality.

Given the overtly machistic and male-oriented nature of Yugoslav culture, the preceding examples pose a number of apparent paradoxes, and evoke questions regarding the relationship between formal ideology and social structure on the one hand and social process and the quality of interpersonal ties on the other. Specifically, the authoritative and influential positions occupied by older women appear anomalous in light of a social charter stressing patrilineality, patrilocality, and male dominance. However, this apparent contradiction can be resolved if viewed in terms of a system typified by the complementary distribution of sexually and generationally specific roles. In other words, traditional Yugoslav society is one in which the modes of behavior associated with men and women as well as with the old and young, are not generally interchangeable, and the kinds of power and authority associated with these are appropriate exclusively within the contexts of certain restricted social arenas and sets of relationships.

In order to further explain these seemingly contradictory elements in Yugoslav culture, this essay will focus on three basic characteristics of native family life.

1. In contrast to the Western European and North American variants, the South Slav family is not as isolated in regard to kinship ties or patterns of residence, and thus family process must be viewed within a framework transcending the nuclear household.

2. The apparent patriarchal nature of the family and the society as a whole is more a public than a private fact, and because of this the important affectual power of women is obscured.

3. Women achieve this power not by virtue of being wives, but as the result of becoming mothers, and, eventually, grandmothers. In this way, it will be demonstrated, women legitimatize their status within their husbands' kinship groups by giving birth to sons and through the influence they exert over their children in general.

   In this respect, the concept of affectual power stemming from the mother-child bond in patrilineal societies is not a new idea in anthropology, and as early as 1924 Radcliffe-Brown drew attention to this phenomenon in his classic study of the role of mother's brother among the South African Ba'Thonga. In a more general sense both of these ethnographic examples provide further indication of the ubiquitous disparity between formal and informal levels of social organization.

STRUCTURE AND PROCESS IN THE CONTEMPORARY YUGOSLAV FAMILY

One of the hallmarks of the anthropological approach has been the study of social phenomena in the simplest and most basic contexts possible. In this respect, the family provides an optimum medium for the analysis of sex-role behavior. However, in the Yugoslav case, the observer should take care not to be unduly influenced by apparent structural similarities between the contemporary South Slav household, particularly its urban variant, and its middle-class American counterpart. For example, in the analysis of authority within the American family there is generally little need to leave the confines of the nuclear family or even the husband wife dyad. In contrast, though many modern Yugoslav households also consist of nuclear families, the nature of interaction with other kin suggests that a larger unit of study is more appropriate. Here, the division of labor, the exercise of power, and the flow of affect, can be best understood when placed in the perspective of broader sets of relationships, in particular those linking the generations, that is, grandparents, parents and children.

In this discussion of the South Slav family the model employed has been derived from the study of over 200 households, both rural and urban, spanning the gamut from peasants and unskilled workers at one end of the spectrum, to professionals and highly placed bureaucrats at the other. Materials were collected during five field trips spanning the period from 1966 through 1978.[1] Research was carried out in such varied localities as the northern Adriatic coast (Hrvatsko Primorje), Bosnia, and Serbia. The sample included Catholics, Orthodox, and Moslems, and was supplemented by data gathered from among Yugoslav-Americans in California. However, in spite of this diversity, in no case did the rural urban dichotomy, nor regional, ethnic, or religious differences reveal any significant or widespread variations in cultural patterns in respect to family life, though a range of behavior, much of it situationally determined, could be discerned everywhere. Similarly, superficial differences in cultural styles tended to mask a deeper level of ideological and structural homogeneity underlying the ethnic and historical heterogeneity of the Yugoslav population (cf. Lockwood 1975:20–34, 47–55). At the same time, this analysis does not attempt to demonstrate the statistical distribution or modality of certain traits, but rather to simply elucidate and explain behavior that not only appears to occur with great frequency, but is also widely accepted as "normal" and even desirable by present-day Yugoslav standards.

A number of factors can account for contemporary attitudes about kinship and family life in Yugoslavia. Though urbanization and social mobility have diminished the importance of the large, corporate, patrilocally extended households (*zadruge*) that formerly typified much of rural life in this part of the Balkans, and the emergence over the last century of a strong central government has virtually eliminated the political functions of the tribal society that once dominated the Dinaric Highlands, the mentality associated with these ear-

1. Research during 1973–74 was sponsored by Grant #GI-ERP 72–03496 under the Exploratory Research and Problem Assessment Component of the Research Applied to National Needs program of the National Science Foundation.

lier forms of social organization has survived essentially intact (Halpern and Anderson 1970; Hammel 1969a, 1977; Hammel and Yarbrough 1973; Simic 1973a, b). Moreover, the generally particularistic and personalistic nature of Balkan culture has not significantly diminished under the impact of Marxism, economic development, and modernization. Thus, the system of intense, reciprocal ties linking family members and kin (and, by extension of the same principle, fictive kin and close friends) continues to provide the individual in today's Yugoslavia with what is probably his or her most vital resource in the struggle for success or simple survival (Simic 1982). In this respect, many educated Yugoslavs interested in the rapid modernization of their country view this fixation on kinship and personal relationships as a kind of "national vice" inhibiting the development of more rational (in the Weberian sense), large-scale social and economic institutions (cf. Buric 1976:117–118).

As the product of a long history of corporate and anti-individualistic ideology, the contemporary Yugoslav family thus stands in sharp opposition to the ideal of the independent nuclear household so familiar to most Americans. This contrast is not necessarily one of form and composition (though it may be), but rather one of conceptualization. Stated succinctly, the Yugoslav tends to view the family not as an entity isolated at one moment in time, but rather diachronically as one stretching endlessly backward and forward, the generations flowing almost imperceptibly one into the next without sharp ruptures or discontinuities. Therefore, regardless of the actual composition of a given household at any moment in time, ideologically and conceptually its developmental cycle is a very long one, one that is in fact theoretically infinite. In this way, for example, households may *symbolically* contain members who are physically absent, even dead.

The ramifications of this cognitive view of the family are numerous. For instance, the postmarital neolocality that typifies much of the Western world is not in key with the imperatives of a multigenerational, corporate family ethic. In much of the Yugoslav countryside patrilocality is still the rule, and in the city both patri- and matrilocality are encouraged not only by traditional norms but also by an acute housing shortage as well. As Baric (1967a,b) has observed, modernization has simply resulted in the extension of the rules governing kinship to matrilateral as well as patrilateral links. Moreover, where married couples (with living parents) form new households, the nature of ritual, material, and affectual reciprocity between the generations indicates that social and psychological separation has been complete. Needless to say, the premarital neolocality so common in the United States is utterly alien to the South Slav mentality. Even when children do leave their natal homes to attend school or to accept employment elsewhere, such individuals usually continue to consider their parental households as their "real" loci of residence. For example, the response of a 22-year-old university student was typical of attitudes observed among 56 young adults interviewed in Belgrade. When asked if she would like to have her own apartment, after some perturbation she replied simply, "What a strange idea! It would be lonely without my parents." In a similar vein, a number of married adult male informants related that they did not hold a celebration in honor their patriline saint (the *slava*) in their Belgrade apartments because their fathers performed this ritual for them "at home" in the village.

Another reflection of the multigenerational nature of the Yugoslav family is dual or even multiple residence on the part of older persons. For instance, the Belgrade sample revealed a large number of cases where elderly persons spent the cold winter months in their children's urban apartments, the men typically idling away the daytime hours or leisurely shopping for the family at the open market, and the women aiding in household chores and caring for their grandchildren. With the coming of spring these same elderly people returned to their villages, frequently with urban grandchildren in tow. In every case recorded, the presence of grandparents in either rural or urban homes was regarded as a *positive* asset. Thus, even though parents and children may live spatially apart (sometimes even in different countries), conceptually their residences can be regarded as separate loci of a single household. Even the dead continue to cast their aura on family life, and generational continuity is symbolically assured through elaborate funerary practices, regular graveside memorial feasts (*dace*), and other observances in honor of the dead. Lifelong mourning is not unusual, particularly on the part of older women who are the arbiters of ritual propriety. Mourning may be symbolized in a number of ways, including the relinquishment of most forms of recreation and pleasure. Such behavior may be manifested at any age, and, for example, a Dalmatian Catholic informant donned black and gave up his favorite pastimes upon the death of his mother when he was in his early 40s, and a dozen years later was still commemorating his loss in this manner.

In spite of the emotional trauma associated with a parent's death, especially that of a mother, the event represents a major marker in the developmental sequence of an individual. It conforms closely to Van Gennep's (1960) classic interpretation of rites of passage. Children, frequently in advanced middle age, are separated from their old status of social, economic, and psychological dependence and from those who define it (their parents); they pass through a stage of transition embodied in elaborate funerary rituals and a prolonged period of mourning, and then emerge as full adults. In this respect, feasts in honor of the dead and other commemorative practices can be interpreted as overt signs of newly achieved adulthood regardless of what other social and psychological functions they may also fulfill. To adequately interpret this *extended childhood*, it is necessary not only to examine the relationships of power and affect that bind children and parents together in a system of intense emotional and substantive reciprocity, but also to make explicit the underlying ideological basis that structures all social relationships among the South Slavs. In essence, the ethic of individualism and the belief in self-determination that constitute core values in much of contemporary American thought are notably lacking. Rather, family corporacy and interpersonal dependence provide central themes. This orientation is expressed by the strong attachment of children to their siblings, parents, and other kin in preference to extrafamilial peers. Moreover, family roles are conceived as interdependent, reciprocal, and complementary rather than replicative. At the same time, the family constitutes an almost closed universe, and is the focus of a double moral standard in a society that functions, even in the public sector, largely in terms of particularism and personalism. In other words, strict moral standards are applied in dealings among family members, extended kin, fictive kin, and a few close friends, but to very few outside this circle. One significance of this is that marriage, particularly in rural settings, is essentially an alliance between competitive and potentially antagonistic kinship groups (cf. Diaz 1967). Thus, a wife initially enters her husband's home as an outsider, and during the first years of marriage she is, in effect, *unprotected* by children of her own, who, upon their birth, will be full members of their father's lineage.

In most cultures marriage is a logical point of departure for describing family process. Where neolocality is the rule this event signifies the beginning of a new and independent social entity. In other societies, such as Yugoslavia, marriage contributes a new member to an existing social unit, a member who initially occupies an inferior position and must accommodate to the ongoing order. During the traditional period in the Balkans, which lasted well into modern times, in most areas marriages were arranged, and the bride and groom may have scarcely spoken to each other before the ceremony. Even after marriage there was little expectation of communication, positive affect, or companionship. Essentially, the conjugal pair constituted an exclusive relationship only in the realm of sexuality and procreation, a relationship that was otherwise subsumed in the context of a larger kinship group. Moreover, the open expression of affection or other overt signs of solidarity between a husband and wife was perceived as a threat to the unity of the household. For instance, Erlich (1971), in her study of 300 Yugoslav villages based on questionnaires distributed by schoolteachers throughout the country between 1937 and 1941, cites (among many similar examples) the following (pp. 39–40):

> There are cases today where a man between 50 and 60 years of age will not speak with his wife, or call her by her name in front of his own father. [Christian Macedonia]

> In front of his parents a husband doesn't dare look at his wife. . . . Even today this has really changed very little. . . . [Serbia]

In more recent times, Halpern (1958:202) calls attention to similar behavior in the Serbian village of Orasac, which he studied in 1953 and 1954:

> Although a great deal of affection is shown to children, and from children to parents and grandparents, parents are never openly demonstrative toward one another. In fact, it is still common for couples to refer to each other as He and She or My Husband and My Wife. Even in addressing one another directly, they rarely use proper names. If a man calls to his wife, for example, he shouts, "Zeno! Odi 'vamo!" (Wife, Come here!)

Even in contemporary Yugoslavia, with the increased freedom to choose one's own mate, the anonymity of urban life, the advent of datinglike behavior, and a growing ideology of sexual freedom, there appears to have been little concomitant increase in the communicative aspects of marriage. In fact, the stylized ritual and romantic idealizations that typify South Slav courtship quickly give way to emotional indifference in marriage. While the nature of private behavior between husbands and wives is difficult to verify and can only be indirectly inferred, the statements of informants and the observation of public behavior suggest that deep affection and communicative empathy are relatively rare phenomena between husbands and wives, especially during the earlier years of marriage. In contrast, the open expression of affection between parents and children (and even between more distant kin) continues to be the rule as in the past, and the following example is not atypical:

> A twenty-eight-year-old urban Moslem woman was greeted by her father, mother, aunt, and husband as she left the hospital after a prolonged stay. She rushed to her parents and aunt, kissing and warmly embracing each in turn, and then turned to her husband, and formally shook hands. [Tuzla, Bosnia]

The relationship between husbands and wives conforms to the generally sex-segregated nature of Yugoslav society, especially in those regions that were longest under Turkish domination. For instance, most married informants reported that they spent little or no leisure time alone with their spouses, but rather each chose to socialize with other family members, kin, or friends of the same sex.[2] In this respect, a visiting Yugoslav professor at a California university, impressed by laundromats, commented unintentionally on the role of South Slav wives: "In America you don't need a wife, just a pocketful of quarters!" His statement is reminiscent of the frequently cited Serbian proverb: "Muz zenu nosi na *kosulji*, a *zena muza na licu*" ("A man displays his wife on his shirt, and a wife her husband on her face"). In another case a 42-year-old married informant underscored the relative lack of emotional attachment in marriage when he observed upon the death of a friend's wife that "a man can always find household help, but he has only one mother." Similarly, a 29-year-old Belgrade woman with three children replied with great surprise when questioned if she missed her husband who had been working in Libya for almost two years: "Why should I? I have my children and my mother and father." Moreover, her statement should not be considered in any way as a sign of an unsuccessful marriage, rather the husband and wife were each fulfilling his or her proper role; he by providing an economic base and "giving her children," and she (safely chaperoned by her parents) by maintaining the home and rearing them. Another example is provided by a middle-aged informant employed by a Belgrade construction firm who returned only once a year to visit his wife and three children who lived with his parents in a village in southern Serbia. Neither he nor any other informants found this the slightest bit unusual or distressing. Nor was this type of behavior a class-specific phenomenon. For example, intellectuals, who might be expected to hold a more Western view of marriage, were fully as tolerant of long separations from their spouses as were working-class informants. The major difference distinguishing the two poles of the social spectrum was that professional women enjoyed greater freedom and autonomy than their less-educated counterparts, but apparently with only slightly higher levels of mutual affect and communication in their marriages. However, what emerges as a crucial variable for the understanding of male-female relationships within the family is the interplay of sex and age. As men grow older, they lose much of the aggressiveness and vitality that is so valued in a machistic society, and women experience a parallel decline in sexual attractiveness. It is at this point in life that many husbands and wives grow emotionally closer, with

---

2. Bott (1957) has made similar observations about the behavior of working class London families.

the wife not infrequently stepping into the power vacuum left by her husband in his declining years. Thus, as men and women age, their relationships toward each other are transformed little by little, and the overt power the man enjoys in the larger society as often as not becomes, at least in part, a facade masking the locus of other kinds of authority and control. Moreover, this metamorphosis is tacitly recognized in public life as well where older women enjoy a latitude of behavior unconstrained by what was considered in their youth as a dangerous and potentially predatory sexuality. As Halpern (1958:203) notes:

> As they advance in years women approach a status more respected than at an earlier period and which more nearly resembles the status enjoyed by males. They are permitted a greater degree of freedom of conduct, hedged in by none of the restrictions imposed on them in their younger days. For example, old women may usually go where they please, whenever they wish. They can go alone to market, social gatherings, and weddings. In the company of their cronies they can dance, drink, tell jokes, and "whoop it up" at a gathering of relatives and neighbors without being condemned for their behavior.

What is clearly reflected here is that males and females experience different life trajectories with the power of men peaking in middle age, and women gradually accruing greater and greater authority, influence, and prestige as they grow older (cf. Simic and Myerhoff 1978:236–240). Nevertheless, this is not the product of sex and seniority alone but also stems from events tied to the developmental cycle of the family itself. Of particular cogency in this respect is the nature of the relationship between mothers and sons.

MOTHERS AND SONS

Dynamics within the Yugoslav family can be modeled quite succinctly in terms of three dyadic relationships: husband/wife, mother/son, and daughter-in-law/mother-in-law. In the absence of an affectual tie to her husband, and as a reaction to the dominance of her mother-in-law, the young wife cultivates unusually strong reciprocal links with her children, validating these attachments through the inculcation of supportive moral imperatives and appeals to her children's sense of guilt phrased in the idiom of her own ostensible dedication to parental duty, self-sacrifice, and martyrdom. As Erlich (1971:75) has stated quite simply, on the basis of her observations in rural Serbia, "because love between married couples is poorly developed, the mother attaches herself to her children." However, since daughters, especially in the countryside, almost always marry into other households and even other communities, sons usually become a mother's primary focus.. Regarding this, Erlich (1971:75) notes that "a mother ties herself to her son in the battle against the dominance of his father." Nevertheless, as true as this may be, the real threat to a woman's position in her family stems not so much from her husband as from her mother-in-law, against whom a daughter-in-law's principal weapon is the status and pride that results from grandparenthood. An almost identical situation has been described by Cornelisen (1977:219) in her eloquent and moving account of the lives of women in southern Italy:

Once a woman has power, however slight her influence appears to be outside the family, she consolidates it into a hold over her sons stronger than that famous boast of the Jesuits. Only death will loosen it, but already her daughter-in-law has learned the art of day-by-day living and day-by-day power and has tied her sons to her as firmly as though they were still swaddled.

Thus, in the traditional South Slav family the son as a member of his father's lineage and the inheritor of a share of his father's property provides the validation of his mother's position in what is initially for her after marriage a "household of strangers." Moreover, as a son becomes an adult, he gradually assumes, within the limitations of his family's reputation and his own attributes, the prestigious and authoritative position the society formally bestows on a man, and it is through him that his aging mother can exert influence and power both within the family in the external world, drawing on the affectual and moral levers that are not only condoned, but overtly encouraged by the culture. At the same time, the young daughter-in-law must be patient until she too has succeeded in creating a similar position through the medium of her own sons. In today's Yugoslavia the tenacity of such behavior is attested by the fact that even the tremendous social and spatial mobility that has occurred since World War II has not significantly eroded the established pattern. For instance, a mother's manipulation of her married sons does not seem dependent upon her residence with them, and even in urban settings characterized by nuclear families, the age-old process continues. Regarding this, Yugoslav sociologist Olivera Buric (personal communication) once commented with some disgust that she was familiar with a case where "a mother had gone from household to household and ruined the marriages of her sons each in turn." Though such a situation is undoubtedly quite rare, it nevertheless reflects the fact that the success of marriage depends to a great degree on the ability of a daughter-in-law to get along with her husband's mother, who is, in the final analysis , the arbiter of her excellence as a wife. This powerful influence of mothers in the marital affairs of their sons is widely reflected in popular folklore, and for example, a composed folk song of some years ago (Svadbena Pesma—The Wedding Song) proclaimed, "I am getting married, and there is joyous music and drinking, but happiest of all is my old mother because she is getting a bride."

Another variant of the parent-child relationship is what may be termed the *sacrificial child syndrome* (cf. Simic 1979b:263–264). Here, reference is made to an unmarried adult son or daughter who remains with his or her parents until their death. Probably the most common expression of this behavior is the situation in which a son renounces marriage in order to attend to his mother's material and psychological needs. Although this clearly occurs in other cultures, including American, among the South Slavs, it is considered well within the realm of expected behavior and an essentially normal expediency. In some cases, an older sibling may assume responsibility for an aging parent so as to "liberate" younger brothers and sisters. However, family histories collected in both Yugoslavia and among Yugoslav-Americans indicate that in many cases mothers deliberately select a particular child to be socialized for this role. As a California Serbian Orthodox priest commented, "What wife could ever make such a man feel like a king from the moment he enters the door when in reality he is only a common laborer or peasant?" The incidence of the sacrificial-child syndrome may well be more frequent among Yugoslav-Americans than in Yugoslavia. In part this can be explained by a reduced need for this kind of behavior in Yugoslavia because of the presence of greater numbers of extended households that include married children, and because of the fact that the American-born children of immigrants are frequently called upon to act as culture brokers negotiating relationships between the home and the outside world, and in this way playing the role of interpreters of American life styles. The frequency of this phenomenon among American Yugoslavs in suggested by my 1976 census of a California Serbian Orthodox parish. Of 119 households surveyed there was a total of 57 married couples or individuals with living adult children. In 24 of these cases an unmarried son or daughter (a number of them middle aged) lived with his or her parent/parents; in one case a married daughter and her husband lived with her parents; in one case a son and his wife lived with his mother; and in one case an adult grandchild lived with his paternal grandmother and great aunt. Thus, in almost half of the situations in the parish where it was possible, the sacrificial-child syndrome occurred. Moreover, this fails to take into account those who lived in close proximity to their parents, and probably carried out many of the functions of the sacrificial–child except coresidence.

As was previously indicated, the power of mothers is accrued slowly over the years through the medium of their sons who occupy positions of prestige and authority in an overtly patriarchal society. This power is not only derived from the structural legitimacy bestowed by the birth of a son in a system of patrilineal descent, but also from the more subtle affectual and moral dominance exercised by mothers, a dominance that is both the product of widely accepted cultural values and a long and careful process of socialization and indoctrination. Among the most important messages conveyed to sons are those concerning sex and procreation. These imperatives are rooted in a sexual and moral double standard. On the one hand, the mother surrounds herself with an aura of martyrdom and virginal purity giving visible expression of the "pain" associated with sexuality and childbirth. At the same time, a mother sometimes tacitly encourages her sons to associate with "profane" women outside of the home. The implicit message is that women other than family members and kin are potentially "whores" to be freely exploited. Moreover, while sexual exploits involving such women are entirely excluded from acceptable household conversation, they are, at the same time, clearly taken for granted. Such attitudes are evident even in contemporary urban Yugoslavia where young men and women generally conceal contacts with the other sex from their parents, and introduce only prospective mates into their households.

Probably closely associated with the dominance of mothers and the sexual and moral double standard are the extravagant demonstrations and dramatizations of masculinity that can be observed with such frequency in many parts of Yugoslavia (cf. Simic 1969). This machistic behavior almost always takes place in public settings such as bars or cafes. A number of core elements are usually present in a generalized atmosphere of carousing, and include, among others: openhanded hospitality and the seemingly heedless expenditure of money, what might be called the "set 'em up for the house" syndrome; heavy drinking usually in the company of a small group of male friends but sometimes including prostitutes, bar girls, or female singers; the destruction of property, most often glasses, tableware, and bottles, but occasionally tables, chairs, and other barroom fixtures as well; trancelike, ecstatic behavior induced by a combination of alcohol and the performance of erotic love songs; and not infrequently, brawling and more serious forms of physical violence. Significantly, however, these dramatic exhibitions of male prowess almost never occur within the household or in any other arena typified by the interaction of family members or kin. In this way, the illusion of total male dominance is maintained through the segregation of activities that might otherwise demand the resolution of the paradox posed by the ascendancy of the mother.[3] Similar observations have been made by Halley (1980:133) in a recent essay dealing with the Yugoslav family in America:

> A mother's continuing control, coupled with interior distress at one's own dependency and bondage (which undercuts one's honor), and deep resentment at the perpetual and unpayable debt (including the deeply felt obligation to support one's mother in all her conflicts, even in conflicts between her and one's wife) could at times provoke outbursts of rage.

In effect, the culture chooses to *consciously* ignore the disparity posed by the authoritative position of older women and the principle of patriarchy, and indeed the actors appear to perceive no anomaly in the exalted and authoritative positions accorded mothers. This juxtaposition of conceptually irresolvable imperatives within South Slav culture seems to confirm Weber's view of society as "an equilibrium between opposing forces" (cf. Bendix 1962:260–267).

As is the case in most of the Mediterranean, the semi-sacred aura surrounding mothers in the Balkans is probably very ancient. For instance, the theme of the martyred and self-sacrificing mother, appears repeatedly in South Slav epic poetry. A dramatic example of this is found in the epic, "The Building of Skadar" (*Zidanje Shadra*). King Vukasin with his two brothers orders the building of the city of Skadar but they are thwarted by the constant destruction of their work by nature spirits (*vile*). To appease these spirits, the wife of one of the brothers is entombed in the city walls, leaving behind a small child in the cradle. However, on her pleas, openings are made in the masonry so that her breasts are left free to nourish her small son, and even after she dies the milk continues the flow until the child has grown up. Later, a spring of "miraculous and healing water" appears at the site.

A similar stereotyping of mothers in terms of sacredness, devotion, sublime altruism, and martyrdom was frequently expressed by informants within the context of dichotomous set opposing mothers and fathers:

> Mothers earn love and devotion, fathers our respect!
> Our mothers are angels, out fathers devils.
> Mother's advise and console, fathers command.
> Mothers suffer for their children, fathers fight for them.

---

3. Hammel has also noted the disparity between public demonstration of male pride and private behavior within the Serbian home (1967), as well as the frequent incompatibility of patriarchal ideology with the nature of affectual ties among kin (1969b). Similarly, Denich (1974:260) in a study of the role of women in traditional Balkan society notes what she terms the "patrilineal paradox" in which the formal structure "denies the . . . existence of women, while at the same time group survival depends upon them."

Thus, the South Slav mother provides a perfect conceptual counterpart to the image of the aggressive and heroic male. The power of this maternal image is rooted in a moral superiority derived from self-abnegation and suffering phrased in a mother's devotion to the well-being of her children at the expense of other forms of self-realization. In this way, "maternal sacrifice" provides the keystone for the support of a structure of guilt on the part of children, especially sons, assuring the perpetuation of a mother's influence and power throughout her lifetime. As Halley (1980:131) insightfully comments, the mother has created a debt that can never be fully paid, and "the mother's capacity for mobilizing the support of all her children against anyone who opposes her is a sort of 'calling in the chips.' "

The roles that mothers frequently play toward their sons in Yugoslav society would certainly be considered as emotionally debilitating by most middle-class American standards, as well as in terms of contemporary psychological theory. However, the question may well be raised as to whether it is, at least in part, a conceptual error to ethnocentrically impute such negative psychological ramifications to behavior considered entirely normal in another culture. For example, the Serbian mother who proclaimed at a large social gathering that her married, 46-year-old son was "his mama's spoiled darling (*mamina maza*) did so not only with pride, but also with the total assurance of the appropriateness of her words and the approbation of her audience. Moreover, it is not at all surprising in a society where sexuality and positive affect are virtually disassociated from each other that a strongly dependent and emotion-laden relationship flourishes in the overtly asexual content of the mother-son tie. Thus, in contrast to the common American model of the family with its focus on the husband-wife dyad, the flow of affect and authority within the Yugoslav family underwrites and perpetuates its multigenerational structure.

The seemingly paradoxical relationship between the subordination of men to their mothers and the machistic role assigned to them by Yugoslav culture can also be explained with reference to ideas regarding the contrasting nature of men and women, and the behavior appropriate to each. In this regard, South Slav culture clearly demonstrates its affinity to that of other Mediterranean and Middle Eastern societies (cf. Campbell 1964:150–172; Peristiany 1965; and Pitt-Rivers 1954:84–121, among many others) in that males and females are viewed as "separate orders of creation" each with particular abilities, predilections, predispositions, and innate knowledge; attributes that are different but nevertheless mutually dependent and reciprocal. Similarly, the generations are typified by the same kind of complementarity, and underlying the reciprocity between those of different age and sex is the general rule that *only likes may compete or occupy identical niches in a given social arena* (cf. Friedl 1962:87–91). Therefore, in traditional South Slav culture children do not vie with adults, nor do women (with the exception of bar girls, prostitutes, and other "unprotected women") openly usurp the roles of men in the usual course of events. Even in contemporary urban settings where the majority of women are employed outside the home, wives and mothers continue to manage the family arena, setting and maintaining the moral tone of the home while at the same time skillfully influencing the course of events in the outside world through the control and manipulation of their sons. Thus it is that the strict segregation of incompatible roles and behavior makes it mandatory for a man, who may spend large sums of money brawling in the local honky-tonk, to act only with the greatest decorum in the quasi-sacred context of his mother's home; a mother with whom he may never openly compete; and toward whom he is prohibited from expressing all forms of open hostility.

The Yugoslav family also exhibits what may be termed *long term dynamics* related to different male and female life trajectories (cf. Simic and Myerhoff 1978:236–240). Mothers eventually grow old and die, and wives become mothers, and finally mothers-in-law and grandmothers. In old age men also experience profound changes, with a decline in the physical strength and aggressiveness so valued in males by the culture. Moreover, the death of a mother leaves the son with an affectual and authoritative void that must somehow be filled. Thus, a middle-aged wife is frequently able to assume the role previously occupied by her mother-in-law, and in this way the symmetrical power relationship that typifies a young husband and wife is subsequently reversed in later life. In this way, in a society that accords a woman little public power, a female can accrue great prestige and authority through the manipulation of the moral and affectual claim she exercises over her sons on the one hand, and the exploitation of her husband's changing physical and psychological needs on the other. Moreover, this transference of dependency on the part of the husband from his mother to his aging wife is made possible by her symbolic loss of what the culture considers a dangerous and potentially defiling sexuality incompatible with a status of autonomy.

CONCLUSIONS

The model of family process and sex roles elucidated in this essay, like all models, is an abstraction conforming only approximately to reality, and glossing over very real differences in individual experience. Nevertheless, among the many informants interviewed and families studied, not a single case was totally counterindicative of the behavior and values noted here. In essence, what has been described in this disussion is a set of pervasive ideas current in Yugoslav society, ideas that appear to have considerable consequence for the structuring of family life and the molding of sex-role behavior. The Yugoslav case also has implications that transcend this particular context, and suggests that models of sex-role behavior that speak simplistically of male dominance and female submissiveness obscure the intricacies and subtleties of the sociocultural process everywhere.

The characterization of Yugoslav society as a *cryptomatriarchy* is intended to call attention to the pitfalls inherent in the cross-cultural study of power and authority. One problem in this respect is conceptual and related to the opposition commonly drawn between *patriarchy* and *matriarchy* as mutually exclusive categories with the latter all too often defined simply as a mirror image of the former. For example, Margaret Mead (1949:223) in her classic study of sex roles, *Male and Female*, has defined matriarchy precisely in accord with this formula:

> A matriarchal society is one in which some if not all of the legal powers relating to the ordering and governing of the family—power over property, over inheritance, over marriage, over the house—are lodged in women rather than in men.

There has clearly been a tendency in anthropology (and elsewhere as well) to look at differential power between the sexes in terms of formal institutional organization, that is, in the context of ideological and social structures which may or may not be the actual loci of the moral and affectual order. For example, Fisher (1979:7–8), in a recent feminist critique of traditional anthropology, points out with some justification that the typical "male cosmology" evident in the work of many famous ethnographers is based largely on the analysis of formal structural characteristics, and thus there is a failure to consider the more subtle conceptual and qualitative aspects of male-female relationships. Her contention is, to a large degree, validated by the evidence from Yugoslavia. As this essay has indicated, power may assume many forms, some formal and overt, others informal and covert. Thus, it may operate publicly and officially, or in the less visible realm of affect and moral obligation. It is reflected in concrete instrumental action on the one hand, and shrouded in symbol, innuendo, and quasi-mysticism on the other. It may be intentional or situationally determined, permanent or transitory, contractual or manipulative, ascribed or achieved. In Yugoslav culture it stems from a variety of sources including the very structure of the family. At the same time, power and affect in South Slav society are not only closely interrelated but are also inherent in, and restricted by, the nature of the various arenas in which individuals act out their lives.

REFERENCES

BARIC, LORRAINE. 1967a. Levels of Change in Yugoslav Kinship. *Social Organization* (M. Freedman, ed.), pp. 1–24. London: Cass and Company.
_____. 1967b. Traditional Groups and New Economic Opportunities in Rural Yugoslavia. *Themes in Economic Anthropology* (R.Firth, ed.), pp. 253–278. London: Association of Social Anthropologists of the Commonwealth.

BENDIX, REINHARD. 1962. *Max Weber: An Intellectual Portrait.* Garden City: Doubleday.

BOTT, ELIZABETH. 1957. *Family and Social Network.* London: Tavistock.

BURIC, OLIVERA. 1976. The Zadruga and the Contemporary Family in Yugoslavia. *Communal Families in the Balkans* (R.F. Byrnes, ed.), pp. 117–138. Notre Dame: University of Notre Dame Press.

CORNELISEN, ANN. 1977. *Women of the Shadows: A Study of the Wives and Mothers of Southern Italy.* New YHork: Vintage Books.

CAMPBELL, J. K. 1964. *Honour, Family and Patronage.* Oxford: Clarendon Press.

DENICH, BETTE S. 1974. Sex and Power in the Balkans. *Woman, Culture, and Society* (M. Z. Rosaldo and L. Lamphere, eds.) pp. 243–262. Stanford, Calif.: Stanford University Press.

DIAZ, MAY N. 1967. Opposition and Alliance in a Mexican Town. *Peasant Society* (J. M. Potter, M. N. Diaz, and G. M. Foster, eds). pp. 168–174). Boston: Little, Brown.

ERLICH, VERA ST. 1971. *Jugoslavenska Porodica u Transformaciji* (The Yugoslav Family in Transformation). Zegreb: Liber.

FISHER, ELIZABETH. 1979. *Woman's Creation: Sexual Evolution and the Shaping of Society.* New York: McGraw-Hill.

FRIEDL, ERNESTINE. 1962. *Vasilika: A Village in Modern Greece.* New York: Holt, Rinehart & Winston.

HALLEY, LORELEI, 1980. Old Country Survivals in the New: An Essay on Some Aspects of Jugoslav-American Family Structure and Dynamics. *The Journal of Psychological Anthropology* 3:119–141.

HALPERN, JOEL M. 1959. *A Serbian Village.* New York: Columbia University press.

HAMMEL, E. A. 1967. The Jewish Mother in Serbia or Les Structures Alimentaires de la Parente. *Essays in Balkan Ethnology* (W. G. Lockwood, ed.) pp. 55–62. Berkeley: Kroeber Anthropological Society Special Publications, No. 1.
_____. 1969a. Economic Change, Social Mobility, and Kinship in Serbia. *Southwestern Journal of Anthropology* 25:188–197.
_____. 1969b. Structure and Sentiment in Serbian Cousinship. *American Anthropologist* 71:285–293.
_____. 1977. The Influence of Social and Geographical Mobility on the Stability of Kinship Systems: The Serbian Case. *International Migration: A Comparative Perspective* (A. Brown and F. Neuberger, eds.), pp. 401–415. New York: Academic Presss.

HAMMEL, E. A., and CHARLES YARBROUGH. 1973. Social Mobility and the Durability of Family Ties. *Journal of Anthropoligical Research* 29:145–163.

LOCKWOOD, WILLIAM G. 1975. *European Moslems: Economy and Ethnicity in Western Bosnia.* New York: Academic Press.

MEAD, MARGARET. 1949. *Male and Female: A Study of the Sexes in a Changing World.* New York: New American Library.

PERISTIANY, J. G. 1965. *Honor and Shame: The Values of Mediterranean Society.* London: Weidenfeld and Nicolson.

PITT-RIVERS, J. A. 1954. *People of the Sierra.* New York: Criterion Books.

RADCLIFFE-BROWN, A. R. 1924. The Mother's Brother in South Africa. *South African Journal of Science* 21:542–555.

SIMIC, ANDREI, 1969. Management of the Male Image in Yugoslavia. *Anthropoligical Quarterly* 42:89–101.
_____. 1973a. *The Peasant Urbanites: A Study of Rural-Urban Mobility in Serbia.* New York: Seminar Press.
_____. 1973b. Kinship Reciprocity and Rural-Urban Integration in Serbia. *Urban Anthropology* 2:206–213.

_____. 1978a. Introduction. *Life's Career—Aging: Cultural Variations on Growing Old* (B. Myerhoff and A. Simic, eds.), pp. 9–22. Beverly Hills: Sage Press.

_____.. 1978b. Winners and Losers: Aging Yugoslavs in a Changing World. *Life's Career—Aging: Cultural Variations on Growing Old* (B. Myerhoff and A. Simic, eds.), pp. 77–165. Beverly Hills: Sage Press.

_____. 1979a. Commercial Folk Music in Yugoslavia: Idealization and Reality. *Journal of the Association of Dance Ethnologists* 2:25–37.

_____. 1979 b. White Ethnic and Chicano Families: Continuity and Adaptation in the New World. *Changing Images of the Family* (V. Tufte and B. Myerhoff, eds.), pp. 251–269. New Haven: Yale University Press.

_____. 1982. Urbanization and Modernization in Yugoslavia: Adaptive and Maladaptive Aspects of Traditional Culture. *Urban Life in Mediterranean Europe* (M. Kenny and D. Kertzer, eds.), pp. 203–224. Urbana: University of Illinois Press.

SIMIC, ANDREI, and BARBARA MYERHOFF. 1978. Conclusion. *Life's Career—Aging: Cultural Variation on Growing Old* (B. Myerhoff and A. Simic, eds.), pp. 231–246. Beverly Hills: Sage Press.

VAN GENNEP, ARNOLD. 1960. *The Rites of Passage.* Chicago: University of Chicago Press.

9 CHILDHOOD ASSOCIATION, SEXUAL ATTRACTION, AND THE INCEST TABOO: A CHINESE CASE[1]

—ARTHUR P. WOLF

Whereas most sociological and biological explanations of the incest taboo assume that intimate childhood association enhances sexual attraction, most psychological explanations assume that such association depresses it. In northern Taiwan one of several forms of marriage involves the introduction of the bride into her future husband's home as an infant; bride and groom are then raised as members of the same family, experiencing a prolonged period of intimate association. The responses of these couples to marriage and sexual relations support the psychological view of the effects of intimate association on sexual attraction and thereby challenge the basis of most sociological and biological explanations of the incest taboo.

The village of Hsiachichou is a small Hokkien-speaking community located near the town of Hsulin on the southwestern edge of the Taipei basin in northern Taiwan.[2,3] Here, as in many other areas in China, local custom recognizes two forms of patrilocal marriage and at least three forms of uxorilocal marriage. As the various forms of uxorilocal marriage differ in the extent to which the husband is incorporated into his wife's family, they produce different social arrangements and may be considered structurally distinct. The two forms of patrilocal marriage, on the other hand, with which I am primarily concerned in this paper, are structural equivalents. They differ in prestige and in the extent to which the bride's change of residence is ritually elaborated, but from a jural point of view they bring about similar rearrangements of existing social relationships. The only structural difference between them lies in the timing of the procedures by which these changes are effected. In one case a marriage creates, at one stroke, an affinal alliance between two families and the conjugal union of a man and woman, while in the other these two aspects of marriage are distinguished as two distinct stages in the marriage process.

As the people of Hsiachichou see it, three things happen in the course of a marriage of the patrilocal type. The bride leaves her natal home and relinquishes membership in her family of orientation; she steps over the threshold of the groom's home and becomes a member of his household; and she is presented to the groom's ancestors and thereby ac-

Reproduced by permission of the author and the American Anthropological Association from AMERICAN ANTHROPOL-OGIST 68:4, August 1966. Not for further reproduction.

quires the status of wife. The first two of these three events unite the two families as affines, and the third binds the bride and groom as husband and wife. What I will here refer to as the grand patrilocal marriage accomplishes these various steps of the marriage process in one day and almost simultaneously. The go-between leads the bridge over the threshold of the groom's home, and she and the groom are then immediately presented before his ancestral shrine. The girl is no sooner a daughter-in-law and a member of the groom's household than she is a partner to conjugal relationship.

The distinguishing characteristic of what I will term the alternative patrilocal marriage is that in this case these two events are separated by 10 to 15 years. Dressed in the traditional wedding costume, the bride enters her future husband's home as a child. She is seldom more than three years of age and often less than a year. In entering the home as a bride, the girl becomes a member of the household and a daughter-in-law, but in the case she is not immediately presented to the family's ancestors. This last phase in the marriage process does not take place until she is old enough to fulfill the role of wife. In the meantime she and her parents are affinally related to the groom's parents, but she is not in fact married to the groom. She takes his family surname as the first character of her own name, relegating her natal family's surname to the second position in the same manner as a woman married in the grand way. Should she later marry anyone other than the groom, she may be stigmatized as "that woman who married twice." She has married into the groom's family, but she has not as yet entered into a conjugal relationship. If the groom dies, she is not required to remain forever chaste, for she does not become a widow. She may even be acceptably married to the dead man's brother, a union that would be considered incestuous if she had been the deceased's wife.

As Chinese families living in a village are reluctant to contract marriages within their own community, couples united by the grand form of marriage are seldom acquainted at the time of their marriage. Often they do not even meet until the day of the wedding. In the case of the alternative marriage the situation is just the reverse. The couple's jural status reflects the fact that they are born into two different families, but the actual circumstances of their childhood are the same as if they had been born into the one family. They are trained and educated by the same set of adults, and in their relations with other members of the community they are both children of the same household. From the time the girl enters the family, she and the boy are in contact almost every hour of every day. Until seven or eight years of age they sleep on the same tatami platform with his parents; they eat together and play together; they are bathed with the other children of the family in the same tub; and when they work or study, they work in the same fields and study in the same school. At the age of ten or eleven, when they become aware of the implications of their jural status, they may attempt to avoid each other, but this is not socially required of them. "It is just because they are embarrassed." So far as the society at large is concerned, they are free to behave as though they were siblings until they are designated husband and wife.

The very different degrees of premarital association in these two Chinese forms of patrilocal marriage provide a rare opportunity to test the relative validity of two approaches to a traditional anthropological problem, that of the incest taboo.

Explanations of the taboo differ strikingly in their assumptions about the effects of the close association characteristic of family life. Most sociological and biological explanations, in viewing the incest taboo as an institutionalized means of protecting man from the dangers of mating or marrying within the family, assume that close association disposes men toward the choice of a primary relative as a mate. The incest taboo is interpreted as a "centrifugal force" instituted to overcome this "centripetal tendency" (White 1949:316). The most influential psychological theories make exactly the contrary assumption. The experience of family life is viewed as giving rise to an emotional resistance of the possibility of an incestuous relationship. Explanations inspired by the writings of Freud and Westermarck differ in their views of the origin and character of this resistance, but they agree in arguing that family life creates a resistance that is prior to and responsible for the institution of the taboo.

If the sociological and biological theories are correct in their view that the nature of family life favors incestuous unions, the marital relationships of those Hsiachichou couple brought together as children should be at least as satisfactory as those created by the grand form of marriage. Any difference should be in the direction of less satisfaction with the grand form of marriage and greater degree of satisfaction with the alternative form of marriage. If, on the other hand, the psychological theories are right about family life creating an emotional resistance to incest, then the relationships created by the grand form of marriage should be more satisfactory than those brought about by the alternative form of marriage. Those couples brought together as children and raised in the same household should resist marriage, and if forced to marry they should find sexual relations unsatisfactory and avoid one another as much as possible.

The reader should be aware at the outset that my purpose here is not to explain the incest taboo, but rather to test against field data the validity of a set of assumptions underlying two different approaches to an explanation of the taboo. While I argue that this test has implications for the evaluation of these two approaches, the approach that meets this test does not thereby qualify as an explanation of the taboo. The question of the effects of intimate childhood association on sexual attraction is a question of the origins of behavior within the family, and it is obviously a long step from here to the question of the origins of jural regulations prohibiting sexuality among categories of kinsmen who are often not members of the same household. In my opinion the two questions are intimately related, and I think the answer to the first points toward a solution of the second, but for the purpose of this paper I confine myself to the question of whether intimate childhood association has the effect of stimulating or depressing sexual desire.

To turn to the data, until the late 1920's all marriage decisions in the village of Hsiachichou were made by the couple's parents or grandparents. They decided the forms their descendants' marriages were to take, and they also chose the particular person a child or grandchild was to marry. Although a few young people managed by various means to influence these decisions, open defiance of one's seniors in the matter of marriage was difficult if not impossible. In an agricultural economy a young man could not support a wife and children without land, and as head of the household his father or grandfather controlled all access to land. The only man I know of who defied his parents by deserting the wife they chose for him was forced to make his way as a petty gangster and gambler. While his success in these activities earned him the envy of his fellow villagers for a time, his eventual death at the hands of jealous rivals served to discourage any young man who may have been tempted to follow his example.

Under these conditions marriages of the alternative types were almost as common in Hsiachichou as the grand form of marriage. Genealogies collected during the two and a half years I spent in the village include a total of 48 male children born before 1910 and raised in Hsiachichou. In 22 of the 48 cases the boy's parents or grandparents decided to take a girl into the family and raise her as his wife. In 4 of the 22 cases either the boy or his betrothed died before reaching a marriageable age; in one case the parents themselves decided against the completion of the arrangements; and there was also one instance in which the parents were somehow dissuaded from insisting on the marriage. In the remaining 16 of the 22 cases, the decision taken when the boy was a child was eventually implemented by the creation of a conjugal bond.

During the next 20 years, 1910 to 1930, the senior generations of the village continued to decide in favor of the alternative form of marriage at about the same rate as they had in the years before 1910. Of 50 boys born during this period and raised in Hsiachichou, 19 were matched with "little brides," or *sim-pûà*. By the time these children reached the age of marriage, however, the senior generations' position in the family had begun to deteriorate as a result of changes in the economy. In 1923 the rerouting of the Taipei-Hsinchu railroad brought Hsiachichou an hour closer to Taipei markets and stimulated the growth of local industry, most notably a large winery and several coal mines. A young man who was dissatisfied with his parents' plans for his marriage could now threaten to leave the family for a job in the winery or in a coal mine. The parents would then be forced to reconsider their decision. Without their son they would have no one to support them in their old age. The result was a sharp decline in the frequency of concluded marriages of the alternative type. Of the 19 marriages initiated between 1910 and 1930, only 2 resulted in the creation of a conjugal union. In 2 cases one of the parties to the marriage died in childhood, and in 15 cases the young couple refused to go through with the match.

While these data indicate that young people were not always happy with the alternative form of marriage, this is not necessarily a result of their having grown up in intimate association. There may be other ways of explaining their distaste for this form of marriage. We must consider these. One possibility is that the young people's reasons for rejecting the alternative form of marriage were not specific to this form of marriage. During this same period the teachings of missionaries and the example of foreigners living in the city of Taipei were gradually making young people more aware of Western conceptions of marriage and the family. It might be argued that this standard of comparison gave them a motif and perhaps also a motive for dissatisfaction with their position. Their rejection of the alternative form of marriage may have been only one aspect of a more general rejection of what came to be regarded as an overweening parental authority.

In more recent years the sim-pua and the alternative form of marriage have indeed become symbols of parental oppression. Missionaries and government agencies have worked to make them so. Yet I do not think that the rejection of such marriages in the 1920's and '30's should be interpreted in these terms. It would be closer to the truth to say that the demands of young people for more independence were created by their seniors' insistence upon the alternative form of marriage. There is clear evidence that this form of marriage was disliked for what it was long before it came to be resented for what it represented. At least 9 of the 15 men who refused to marry a sim-pua did allow their parents to choose a bride and make all of the arrangements for a marriage of the grand type. Only 2 of these 15 insisted upon marrying a particular girl against their parents' will. The majority of these men were obviously objecting to *what* their parents had arranged, not to their making the arrangements. In talking to older villagers I also discovered that as young men they had been just as opposed to marrying a housemate as their children were 20 years later. The only difference was that they were in no position to do anything about it. Perhaps the best evidence for a long-standing dislike specific to the alternative form of marriage is the colloquial way of referring to the brief ceremony that creates the conjugal bond. So long as people of Hsiachichou can remember, this has been referred to a *sàng-cûe-tui,* "pushing (them) together," the force of which my informants illustrated with rough shoving gestures.

There are, however, still other ways of explaining the younger generation's rejection of the alternative form of marriage. One possibility is that they objected to such a marriage out of a concern for social status. While a young man who marries a sim-pua is not stigmatized (as the man is who married uxorilocally), his marriage is not as prestigeful as a marriage of the grand type. A second possibility is that young people felt that by marrying within the "family" they were missing their one chance to play a central role in an important ceremonial event. Whereas the progress of a marriage of the grand type is marked by an engagement ceremony, a dowry procession, a bridal procession, and finally a wedding attended by hundreds of friends and relatives, the formalities of the alternative form of marriage tend to be quiet, even perfunctory in nature. There are no firecrackers, no bands, and often no guests, none of the *lau-ziâi,* the "noise" or "excitement," of an important event. A third possibility is that the young people were reluctant to give up the material advantages of the grand form of marriage. A girl who joins her husband's family as an adult brings with her a bed and bedding, a camphor chest, a wardrobe, jewelry, a set of candelabra, a suit of clothes for the groom, clothes for herself, a few yards of fabric, a variety of choice foodstuffs, perhaps a sewing machine, and at least a small sum of money. A sim-pua receives no dowry at all. She and her husband begin their married life with nothing more than a room of their own and such furniture as other members of the family are willing to part with.

From the point of view of the younger generation the grand form of marriage might also be seen as having certain strategic advantages. While the social arrangements effected by the two forms of patrilocal marriage are equivalent from a jural point of view, the behavior content of the relationships produced are quite different. A sim-pua's early incorporation into her husband's family tends to make her a *de facto* daughter of the family. This has the advantage of replacing the normally hostile mother-in-law/daughter-in-law relationship with a more satisfactory mother/daughter relationship. The disadvantage is that the girl's early transfer of loyalties tends to take the substance out of the affinal relationship. While the affinal ties created by the grand form of marriage often develop into alliances of some social and economic significance, the ties resulting from the alternative form of marriage seldom involve more than the use of the appropriate kinship terminology. Often the two families do not even exchange visits on such occasions as the New Year and the birthdays of the tutelary deities of their respective localities. It could therefore be argued that while the senior generation of a family might prefer the alternative form of marriage as a means of promoting domestic harmony, the junior generation might very well reject this form of marriage because of its disadvantages with respect to the family's relationship with the larger community. An older person will be primarily concerned with securing his old age and maintaining his authority over his children, but a young person is more likely to be occupied with the problems of promoting a business or finding a better job.

Any and all of these considerations may play a part in the younger generation's dislike for the alternative form of marriage. I cannot prove otherwise. There is, however, other evidence which argues that these considerations are not alone sufficient to account for their rejection of this type of marriage. In the course of my work in Hsiachichou I collected a good deal of information about the personal histories of most of the village residents. This included something of their sexual habits, the parentage of their children, the scandals in which they had been involved—in short, the substance of village gossip. Although this information is almost certainly inaccurate in some details, every effort was made to eliminate gross errors of fact. Information given by one informant was checked and rechecked with other informants, and then the entire set of data was reviewed and revised by a sophisticated informant who had grown up in the village and whose family maintains a lively interest in its affairs. While it is possible to account for the young people's rejection of the alternative form of marriage in terms of its low prestige and its practical disadvantages, these data reveal further aspects of the reaction to this form of marriage that cannot be accounted for in these terms.

It is not at all uncommon in Hsiachichou for married men to seek the services of prostitutes in the nearby market towns or the Wanhua section of Taipei. All but the very poorest make such expeditions occasionally. What is of interest to us here is that men who have married a sim-pua are more likely to frequent prostitutes than men who have married uxorilocally or in the grand way. Of a total of 119 married men, 25 had widespread reputations as frequenters of what are euphemistically referred to as "dark rooms." These 25 men included 10 of 70 men married in the grand way and 4 of 26 men married uxorilocally. The remaining 11 are all to be found among those 23 men who made marriages of the alternative type. Thus, the men married to housemates became heavy frequenters of prostitutes at three times the rate of other men, and this is true regardless of their age or the time of their marriage. Among the 119 men, 57 were married before 1930; of these, 16 were known to their fellow villagers as habitues of "dark rooms." These 16 include 10 of 20 men who married sim-pua as against only 6 of 37 men married to women who grew up in another family.

While a man is expected to visit prostitutes and perhaps even to take a mistress if he can afford to do so, a married woman's philandering is considered a serious moral offense. Although the law does not give a husband the authority to punish his wife for sexual transgressions, the villagers themselves feel that a husband has the right to beat and even kill his wife if she should become involved with another man. It is thus not surprising that the frequency of extramarital relations among women is much lower than among men. Of a total of 121 married women, only 5 were known to have engaged in extramarital relationships. The interesting and important point is that here again sexual behavior seems to be a function of the form of the person's marriage. One of these 5 women is a former prostitute whose husband married uxorilocally, and the other 4 are all women who made patrilocal marriages of the alternative type.

The alternative form of marriage thus differs from the other two forms in what might be called its internal as well as its external aspects. Less prestigeful and without some of the practical advantages of the grand form of marriage, the alternative marriage also creates a distinctive conjugal relationship. This is, I think, crucial to our understanding of the younger generation's dislike of such marriages. While the external disadvantages of this form might make young people reluctant to enter into such a marriage, I can see no reason for believing that these disadvantages should affect the conjugal relationship after marriage. There is nothing about the loss of a dowry or less solidary affinal ties that should make a man more likely to hire the services of prostitutes or a woman more prone to adultery. We must look for some characteristic of the alternative form of marriage that will explain the behavior of the married as well as the reluctance of the unmarried. My hypothesis is that there is a negative attitude toward the idea and toward the act of sexual relations with a person with whom one has been reared. A sexual aversion arising out of their early association makes people who have grown up in the same family reluctant to marry; and when they are forced to marry, the same aversion causes them to seek sexual satisfaction outside the marriage.

This interpretation assumes that those villagers who seek frequent extramarital sexual relations do so because they are dissatisfied in their sexual relations with their wives or husbands. While this seems to me a reasonable inference, it is nonetheless an inference. Perhaps, it might be argued, men who marry a sim-pua find their connubial relations so rewarding that they seek more sexual activity, both inside and outside of marriage, than do men who marry in another way. Fortunately for the sake of my argument, there is reason to reject this possibility. In Hsiachichou men who have produced children, and thus fulfilled their prime filial duty, not uncommonly take a mistress and establish a second household in the market town or in another village. These men ordinarily continue to participate in their natal families, fulfilling their roles as fathers and sons, but they neglect their role as husbands. A man with a mistress usually returns to the village during the day to work in the fields with his father or brothers, but his nights he spends elsewhere with his mistress. Such arrangements vary in duration from a few months to many years, and they sometimes involve men who have married uxorilocally or in the grand way as well as men who have married a sim-pua. The point to be made here is that men who have married sim-pua find these arrangements more attractive than men who have married in some other way. Thirteen men who lived in this fashion for two or more years include 3 of 70 men married patrilocally in the grand manner, 2 of 26 men married uxorilocally, and 8 of the 23 men whose marriages were patrilocal but of the alternative form. Among the 5 men married uxorilocally or in the grand way these extramarital arrangements never lasted more than four years. In contrast, the 8 men married to a childhood associates include at least 4 who continued an arrangement of this kind for ten or more years.

Men who marry childhood associates are not only more likely to seek extramarital relations, but are also more likely to avoid their wives. Clearly, these men are in some way dissatisfied with their conjugal relationship. The remaining question is whether or not this dissatisfaction is specific to the sexual side of the relationship. If a man avoids his wife, for whatever reason, he may seek to find a sexual partner elsewhere, but the fact that he avoid his wife is not necessarily due to a distaste for sexual relations with her. Perhaps the nature of the childhood relationship created by the alternative form of marriage gives rise to an enduring hostility. The couple may be loath to marry and happy to avoid one another because of a strong personal animosity rather than an emotional resistance to sexual relations. To maintain the interpretation I have offered there must be evidence that the dissatisfaction with the conjugal relationship is specific to its sexual aspects.

When asked why they dislike making marriages of the alternative type, people in Hsia-chichou did not refer to the matter of the dowry or to the advantages of strong affinal ties. They said nothing about prestige or the comparatively uneventful nature of the wedding. Nor did anyone mention childhood antagonisms or any other reasons for a personal animosity. Instead, they acted embarrassed. When pressed, a few people said that they didn't like the idea of making such a marriage because it was *kian-siau,* "shameful" or "embarrassing." Others admitted that they thought that such a marriage was *bou i-su,* "uninteresting" or "meaningless," a phrase commonly used to describe a dull performance or a pointless conversation. By and large, however, questions about this subject elicited no answers at all, only long and uncomfortable silences. Most of the young women questioned giggled and blushed. What is significant about this is that the only other times I obtained such responses were when I attempted to interview people about their personal sexual habits. My field notes abound with detailed accounts of family quarrels, bitter evaluations of friends and relatives, discussions of prestige and the social advantages and disadvantages of certain institutions, even accounts of such activities as gambling and prostitution. The only thing the villagers would not discuss was sex. Thus their silence when asked why they didn't want to marry a childhood associate was paradoxically eloquent. A villager who tells you that he didn't want to marry a housemate because it was "embarrassing" or "uninteresting" may or may not be referring to the sexual side of the union; but when he says this and also acts uncomfortable and embarrassed, his manner indicates that he is indeed thinking of the sexual aspects of the marriage.

Any *one* facet of the younger generation's reaction to the alternative form of patrilocal marriage can be accounted for in any of several ways. There is, however, as best I can now see, only one simple way of explaining *all* of the various facets of this reaction: the intimate childhood association of the parties to such a marriage creates a strong emotional resistance to sexual relations. But why should this be the case? Edward Westermarck (1921) was the first to suggest a relationship between childhood association and an emotional resistance to sexual relations, but Westermarck was unable to find a satisfactory explanation of the relationship. In his earlier writing he referred to the possibility of an instinct, but he himself later realized that this added nothing to our understanding of the phenomenon. To say that there is an instinct for such a resistance is simply to say that there is a resistance. An adequate explanation must specify in terms of some more general assumptions the otherwise vague condition of "intimate and prolonged childhood association." What is there about such association that might create an emotional resistance of this kind? And in what way? And why?

One possibility is suggested by Sigmund Freud's treatment of the family (1920, 1950). Sharply critical of Westermarck for his view that childhood association somehow precludes sexual desire, Freud argued that "the first choice of object in mankind is regularly an incestuous one. . ." (Freud 1920:294). As regards the effects of family life on the dispositions of adults, however, Freud was essentially in agreement with Westermarck. The child's infantile sexual attraction to family members of the opposite sex encounters frustration and rebuffs from parents and rival siblings. Ambivalence is thus generated, and the impulse if repressed. The adult's emotional resistance to the possibility of sexual relations with a childhood associate is thus to be interpreted as a normal "reaction formation" to a repressed impulse. This resistance, and indeed the incest taboo itself, exists to protect a person from temptations that have proved painful in childhood. Although Freud felt that the sexual attractions of the infant continued to play a role in the adult personality, these attractions are not normally manifest in behavior or even consciously acknowledged. In so far as our understanding of the social behavior of normal adults is concerned, the Freudian view is that the experience of family life creates a strong emotional resistance to the possibility of sexual relations with a childhood associate.

A second possibility has been suggested by Robin Fox (1962:132–133). Fox follows Westermarck in emphasizing the simple fact of childhood association rather than the more general experience of a common family life, but he also accepts the Freudian view of the significance of infantile sexuality. In Fox's view the mutual stimulation occurring in childhood play leads to a heightened state of sexual excitement. While nearing climax, this excitement cannot be consummated by a successful act of coitus. The frustration thus engendered again and again in the course of childhood acts as a form of negative conditioning. As a result, when sexual maturity is reached, persons who have grown up together and played together avoid sexual approaches to one another. The painful experience of their childhood remains to curb any temptation that might be aroused in adult life. The theory shares many of the central assumptions of the Freudian hypothesis, but has the advantage of being phrased in terms of the more explicit language of a behavioristic psychology.

While I recognize that we do not as yet have the evidence necessary to evaluate these two hypotheses, my own preference lies with a somewhat different line of argument. In a review of instinctive behavior and reproductive activities, Frank Beach notes that "male mammals often fail to copulate in an environmental setting previously associated with punishment. Dogs that have become 'neurotic' as a result of experimental treatment are slow to respond to estrous females presented in the room where the experiments were conducted, but the same males mate readily in the kennel" (Beach 1951:408). These findings suggest the possibility that the very fact they are socialized together may account for the mutual aversion of persons who have grown up in the same family. The socialization process inevitably involves a good deal of punishment and pain, and children who are socialized together must come to associate one another with this experience. While mammals such as rats and dogs identify their environment primarily in terms of its physical characteristics, men ordinarily think of their surroundings largely in terms of the people with whom they associate. It is thus not unreasonable to suppose that experiences occurring in the context of the family will be generalized in terms of the concept of the family.

This thought can be pursued one step further. Children who grow up as members of the same family are not only socialized together, they are also socialized relative to one another. Simply because a child's social world is largely made up of his parents and siblings, it is usually in relation to these people that he learns to control his impulses. His parents may tell a child not to hit "other people," but it is for hitting a parent or a sibling that a child is most frequently punished. It can be argued that a child will learn to anticipate punishment and pain in many situations involving the use of a family member for the satisfaction of strong natural impulses. Regardless then of whether the parents punish a child for sexual approaches to other members of the family, his experience should have the effect of teaching him that it is dangerous to satisfy certain impulses with respect to a family member. We need only to assume that such natural impulses as sex and aggression have a common subjective component that can serve as a basis for generalization. Because all human societies demand that children learn to control strong aggressive impulses toward other members of their family, we might expect people everywhere to exhibit an aversion to the possibility of satisfying sexual desires within the family.

If any one of these hypotheses is correct, the younger generation's rejection of the alternative form of patrilocal marriage can be cited as evidence supporting a crucial assumption of most psychological explanations of the incest taboo. In each case the condition of intimate childhood association is viewed as the sufficient cause of an emotional resistance to sexual relations. There is, however, a fourth possibility. Although other children sometimes teasingly label a sim-pua and her counterpart as "wife" and "husband," most of the circumstances of their environment identify them as "brother" and "sister." In Hsiachichou the couple even address one another with the same terms used by true siblings. As the older of the two, the boy receives from his future wife the term *a-h'a*, "older brother"; he address the girl by her personal name, in the same way that he would address any younger sister. Under these conditions it would not be very surprising if the couple came to think of each other as brother and sister, or at least as a kind of brother and sister. If so, they may dislike the idea of marrying because brother and sister never marry. This possibility was first suggested to me by the comments of a girl who had herself refused to marry a boy whose family she had joined as a child. When asked why she had refused, she answered, "I just couldn't do it. It was too embarrassing. Imagine marrying your brother!" The negative reaction to the alternative form of marriage may be the result of an inadvertent extension of the incest taboo rather than an example of the conditions that give rise to the taboo.

Although children committed to the alternative form of marriage usually grow up in the same household, I know of two couples who were separated for a number of years after their marriages were initiated. In one case the boy's father and the latter's mistress were unhappy because she had not as yet borne him a child. They therefore adopted a daughter with the understanding that she was to marry the man's son (by his wife). The girl did not join her future husband's family until she was eight or nine years of age, when her father-in-law and his mistress parted company. In the second case the girl was a real daughter of the boy's father's mistress and one of her previous "friends." While living with this woman, the boy's father decided to arrange a marriage between her daughter and his own son. Even after the initiation of the marriage, however, the girl continued to live with her mother. When she did become a member of her future husband's family, she was already 11 years old. Since these couples spent their late childhood and adolescence as unmarried members of the same family, they had ample time to come to think of one another as siblings. But while they might have reacted to the idea of their eventual union as "incestuous," they did not experience the early association that could be expected to give rise to a real emotional resistance. Of the 19 marriages of the alternative type initiated between 1910 and 1930, these two were the only ones completed by the creation of a conjugal bond.

Further evidence that the label "incestuous" is not alone sufficient to create an aversion to sexual relations is to be found in the United States. In his study of incest in Chicago, S. Kirson Weinberg found that sibling incest tends to be "transitory." In general, the couples "did not behave like marriage partners" (1963:159). Weinberg's 37 cases of sibling incest, however, included 6 exceptions, instances in which the couple did "become mutually attached" and "contemplate marriage" (1963:159). In all six cases, and in only these six cases, brother and sister were separated from early childhood. All were clearly aware that they were siblings and that the incest taboo was applicable. In attempting to marry, they lied about their names and parentage to public authorities and also to a priest. Yet they became emotionally attached to one another as lovers, and they did attempt to legitimatize their relationship as a marriage. Weinberg himself concludes, "Apparently, when siblings lack common family training, they lack guilt about incest with each other, and can consider each other as eligible marriage partners" (1963:159).

An example of the opposite situation is provided by the case of the Israeli kibbutz. Children here are raised in bisexual peer groups inhabiting common living and sleeping quarters. The members of the same group are trained and educated together, and from birth to maturity they interact constantly in the same immediate environment. Until the third or fourth grade, boys and girls sleep in the same room, shower together, sit on the toilet together, and otherwise share all of their daily experiences. But while they grow up in intimate and prolonged association, these children are not identified as siblings among whom sexual relations are incestuous. The society does not prohibit the marriage of members of the same peer group as long as they are not siblings, and the circumstances of their association are not such that they might come to view themselves as siblings. They are socialized together, but by a nurse and a teacher rather than by a common set of parents. They are raised in the same environment, but it is the environment of nursery and school rather than of the family. Unlike the parties to marriage of the alternative type in China, each of the children of a kibbutz peer group has his own parents and his own family. Their childhood association is as intimate as that of a sim-pua and her intended husband, but the circumstances of this association do not identify them as brother and sister. They are sabras,[4] and sabras are free to marry if they so desire.

The reactions of young people who grow up as members of a kibbutz peer group are exactly what we should expect in terms of the psychological assumption about the effects of intimate childhood association. Although the members of the same group do display some sexual interest in one another as small children, the final result of their association is a strong emotional resistance to both sexual intercourse and marriage. In his study of Kiryat Yedidim, Melford Spiro found not one instance in which a person married a fellow sabra, and he is confident that "in no instance have sabras from the same kevutza (or peer group) had sexual intercourse with each other" (1958:347). These results are confirmed by Yonina Talmon's more recent study of marriage patterns among the second generation of three well-established kibbutzim. Among the 125 couples examined in this study, Talmon found "not one instance in which both mates were reared from birth in the same peer group" (1964:492). "The single case of intra-peer group marriage occurred between a native and an 'outsider' who was sent to the kibbutz as an 'external pupil' at the age of 15." Sexual relations and erotic attachments are equally rare. Talmon notes that "we did not come across even one love affair or one instance of publicly known sexual relations between members of the same peer group who were co-socialized from birth through most of their childhood" (1964:493). "The very rare cases of intra-group affairs involve an 'outsider' who came to the kibbutz as an 'external pupil' long after puberty" (1964:493).

Even the reasons given by the sabras for their lack of sexual interest in one another are strikingly similar to those of my Chinese informants, who say that the alternative form of patrilocal marriage is *bou-i-su,* or "uninteresting." Talmon's second generation respondents "stressed that they knew each other 'inside-out,' or more figuratively, 'We are like an open book to each other. We have read the story in the book over and over again and know all about it'" (1964:504). Like Westermarck, "they firmly believe that overfamiliarity breeds sexual disinterest and that is one of the main sources of 'exogamy'" (1964:504). Spiro reports that one reason given by his informants for their exogamy is that "they view each other, they say, as siblings," but he specifically notes that "by stating that they view each other as siblings the sabras do not mean to imply . . . that they therefore view any sexual relationship between themselves as incestuous. They mean rather that they, like biological siblings, have no sexual interest in each other" (1958:347-348).

The question we have been considering here is not a new question. Westermarck's suggestion of a relationship between childhood association and sexual attraction has been as widely discussed as any anthropological hypothesis. Unfortunately, much of this discussion has been wide of the mark. Murdock has argued that Westermarck's hypothesis "is inconsistent with the widespread preference for levirate and sororate unions" and "contradicted by the enduring attachments between husband and wife which occur in most societies" (1949:291). But neither point is relevant to the hypothesis. The parties to a levirate or sororate union rarely grow up as members of the same family, and this is certainly not the situation of husband and wife "in most societies." Murdock has also noted that Westermarck's suggestion "does not harmonize with the not infrequent ethnographic cases where marriage with a housemate is actually favored" (1949:291). But Murdock fails to ask a crucial question: favored by whom? Many Chinese parents do favor a form of marriage involving the union of housemates, but this preference cannot be cited as evidence against Westermarck's position. It is the children, not the parents, who actually marry, and the children are opposed to this type of marriage. The same point can also be made with regard to Murdock's one ethnographic example, the Angmagsalik Eskimo. While the ethnographer, G. Holm, does say that "it is by no means uncommon for children who have been brought up together to marry" (1914:65), this alone does not argue for the absence of an aversion on the part of the children. They may have been forced into such marriages by parental pressure. Holm reports, "cases of a mother having enjoined a son to marry, because 'she could scarcely see to sew any longer'" (1914:65), and he also notes that "a girl is compelled to marry, if her father desires it" (1914:67).

The very fact that incest does sometimes occur is also not very strong evidence against Westermarck's hypothesis. The myth tells us that Oedipus married his mother, but we also know that Oedipus was cast out of his mother's home as an infant. The occasional case of incest may be due to the fact that the conditions that create a resistance were not fulfilled in childhood. Also, there is the possibility that the persons involved had no other opportunity to satisfy their sexual needs. We must remember that Westermarck argued for a relative aversion, not an absolute aversion. Still a further danger is suggested by the fact that most cases of incest come to our attention by way of the clinic or the court. The mentally ill and the criminal should not be taken as representative of the population at large. People who are for some reason immune to normal social sanctions may also be immune to those experiences that inhibit sexual desire in the great majority of the population. Of the males involved in Weinberg's 37 cases of sibling incest, 39.5 percent had previous criminal records, primarily for property offences (1963:52). To take these cases as evidence against Westermarck's proposition we would have to assume that they represent the parent population, and this would not be a very satisfactory assumption.

An adequate test of Westermarck's hypothesis must be based on observations of a normal population. The test cases must be people who have actually experienced intimate childhood association, and our evidence must refer to our subjects' behavioral preferences and not to the preferences of their parents or society. The difficulty lies in finding such a population. In most human societies people who have grown up together are close kinsmen, among whom sexual relations and marriage are prohibited. The Chinese case described in this paper constitutes one of the few exceptions. Here we have a situation in which a large segment of a population fulfills the condition of intimate childhood association and yet marries. That these marriages are resisted and tend to create highly unsatisfactory conjugal relations is strong evidence in favor of the psychological assumption about the effects of the intimate association characteristic of family life. The identification of the couple as siblings may add to the strength of these effects, but the condition of sibling identification is not alone sufficient to produce such effects. In the peer groups of the Israeli kibbutz, intimate childhood associates are not identified as siblings, and yet they are just as opposed to sexual relations as the Chinese couple committed to a marriage of the alternative type. This may be due to the dynamics of family life, as Freud suggested; it may result from the frustration engendered by premature sexual experimentation; or it may be a consequence of the very nature of the socialization process. We cannot decide because we do not have the necessary information. All we can say at present is that there is something about intimate childhood association that is sufficient to create an emotional resistance to sexual relations and hence to marriage.

Most sociological and biological explanations of the incest taboo argue that stringent prohibitions are necessary for either the good of society or the health of the species. The taboo is seen as prohibiting what men might otherwise propose. Our conclusion here challenges these interpretations. If the experience of family life creates an aversion to sexual relations with primary relatives, the taboo is not necessary to protect men from the dangers of mating or marrying within the family. Leslie White has argued that "propinquity does not annihilate sexual desire, and if it did there would be no need for stringent prohibitions" (1949:309). I argue that under the condition of intimate and early association propinquity does annihiliate sexual desire, and that there is therefore no need to be concerned with the social or biological advantages of the incest taboo. We will have to seek an explanation of the taboo elsewhere. Where we should seek remains a question. The fact that intimate childhood association creates an aversion to sexual relations and marriage does not explain the incest taboo, nor does it explain the associated and sometimes independent rules of exogamy. The point I wish to make here is that the social and biological advantages of the application of these rules to the family cannot be cited as reasons for their establishment. The advantages of marrying and mating outside of the family were the unintentional benefits of the very creation of the conditions of family life.

NOTES

1. Earlier versions of this paper were read to seminars at Cambridge University and the University of Chicago, and I am very indebted to the participants for their comments and criticisms.

2. The majority of the population of Hsiachichou are descendents of 18th-century immigrants from the Chuanchou district of southern Fukien. The exceptions include a few persons descended from early immigrants from Changchou, and a very few persons who left the mainland of China after the end of World War II.

3. Place names are always given their standard post office spellings. All other Chinese terms belong to the dialect of Hokkien spoken in Hsiachichou. The romanizations presented here follow the orthography of Nicholas C. Bodman's *Spoken Amoy Hokkien* (1955). in its first occurrence in the text each term is italicized, with the syllables marked for tone; after this, italics and tone marks are omitted.

4. While the term "sabra" commonly refers to all people born in Israel, it is apparently used in some kibbutzim to refer to "one born and raised in a kibbutz" (Spiro 1958:viii). Thus, my sabra is one born and raised in my kibbutz. This is the sense of the term as it is used in this paper.

REFERENCES CITED

Beach, Frank A. 1951 Instinctive behavior: reproductive activities. *In* Handbook of experimental psychology, S. S. Stevens, ed. New York, John Wiley and Sons.

Bodman, Nicholas C. 1955 Spoken Amoy Hokkien. Kuala Kumpur, Federation of Malaya, Grenier and Son, Ltd.

Fox, R. 1962 Sibling incest. British Journal of Sociology 13:128-150.

Freud, Sigmund 1920 A general introduction to psychoanalysis. Joan Riviere, trans. New York, Liveright Publishing Corp.
_____, 1950 Totem and taboo. James Strachey, trans. London, Routledge and Kegan Paul.

Holm, G. 1914 Ethnological sketch of the Angmagsalik Eskimo. Meddelelser om Gronland 39:1-147.

Murdock, George Peter 1949 Social structure. New York, Macmillan Co.

Spiro, Melford E. 1958 Children of the kibbutz. Cambridge, Harvard University Press.

Talmon, Yonina 1964 Mate selection in collective settlements. American Sociological Review 29:491-508.

Weinberg, Kirson s. 1963 Incest behavior. New York, Citadel Press.

Westermarck, Edward 1921 The history of human marriage. London, Macmillan and Co.

White, Leslie A. 1949 The science of culture. New York, Farrar, Strauss and Co. Ch. 11, The definition and prohibition of incest.

10 THE ECONOMIC INTEGRATION OF SOCIETY

—PAUL BOHANNAN

Economic Anthropology is probably the most difficult branch of the subject to teach to Western students. The reason is twofold: Westerners take their economy very seriously and regard it as "right" because it has been technologically successful and because they find difficulty in creating fantasies about its absence or change. Moreover, among Westerners production is complex, utilizing many technological principles, whereas allocation is simple, using primarily a single principle. Among most of the peoples of the world, production is simple but allocation may be almost unbelievably complex, even when it is not excessive. The complexity of allocation, moreover, lies not so much in quantity as in the diversity of principles employed.

In the last chapter it was noted that early anthropologists had studied and classified economies on the basis of technical processes employed in production. Such classifications are still enlightening, although we no longer believe that they are in fact classifications of "economies." Anthropologists were not the only people to make these classifications in the eighteenth and nineteenth centuries—early economists did precisely the same thing. The best-known example is probably the famous labor theory of value, which attempted to solve the problem of how items acquired value. It was postulated that they were valuable because people had expended time and effort—that is, labor—upon them. The mistake of Smith and Ricardo was that they sought the idea of value in the production process. They raised one of the factors of production, labor, to the position of cause.

There is a sense in which the labor theory of value was right and another in which it is extremely useful. One must either agree with it or do one of two things. The simplest of these two things is to say that the stronghold had been erected on the wrong factor. Some economists, notably Henry George, created a land theory of value, others a resource theory of value. Each is as sensible—and as limited—as the labor theory of value.

The other and more difficult road—it must have been difficult because it was almost a century before it was discovered—is to question the whole premise on which Smith and Ricardo were working. One can deny that value arises out of either any individual factor of production or out of the juxtaposition of factors. It was not until the end of the nineteenth century that economists solved this problem. It was not until well into the twentieth that they were able fully to understand just how the solution worked. What had happened is that the point of focus had changed from production to allocation.

One of the major insights that provided a basis for sophisticated development of economic theory came in the work of Karl Menger and Alfred Marshall when they, separately, elaborated supply-and-demand theory and the crucial role of price in the market-organized economy. Like all great ideas, this one is extremely simple. By the time a generation had grown up with it, it had become "obvious." As with all "obvious" discoveries, it is somewhat difficult to give the originators of the idea the credit that they in fact deserve. Menger and Marshall discovered that the important factor is not "value" but rather "price." The market value of an item is the price it will bring. They also discovered that price varied not with the labor expended on an item or the land involved in its creation, but rather with its total cost of production and the demand for it. Given the free market and the principle of contract, an item will change hands only in those instances in which its value to a consumer is greater than the price he must pay for it, and its value to the producer less than the price he can get for it. Here was the basis of so-called "classical" economics. Once given such a premise, economic science has never looked back from its successful course.

It is well for the anthropologist, however, to point out that what happened is that the focus had changed from concern merely with factors of production to concern with allocation of goods, services, and end products in society. That is to say, the central or focal point in the economy lay in the way that goods and products and factors moved and changed hands.

The shift in attention could have occurred unnoticed only in a market-dominated society. Only when production is primarily for the market, and the market the chief instrument for acquiring goods and services, is a common element present: the market. The market provided, in short, a bridge between the problems of the nineteenth-century economists and those of twentieth-century economists. The path the interest of the economists followed from production to allocation is a straight and narrow one, leading through the market place. In an industrial, market-dominated economy, set within a society whose integration is based primarily on the principles of contract, all the factors of production as well as the products themselves change hands according to the principle of contract at a price determined by the law of supply and demand.

In assimilating this tremendous stride forward—the shift from value to price as the dominant theme of economists—it is easy to make a mistake similar to one that led to acceptance of Adam Smith's premises for so many decades before they were finally questioned. We continue to assume that Menger and Marshall had discovered the market and therefore put economics on the right road, when as a matter of fact they had, by discovering the market, put economics on the right road by turning away from primary concern with production and toward the study of the principles of allocation.

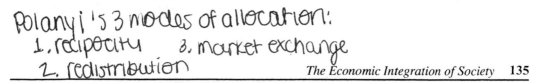
Polanyi's 3 modes of allocation:
1. reciprocity   3. market exchange
2. redistribution

The Economic Integration of Society   135

RECIPROCITY, REDISTRIBUTION, AND MARKET EXCHANGE

It is only in our own day that a daring and original economic historian, Karl Polanyi, had made it possible to study allocation cross culturally without disrupting the science of economics and without becoming its slave. Polanyi has not been popular with most economists, probably because he chose guns instead of butter in planning his scholarly armory. Yet he can in the long run only add to their glory because he has given us the beginning of a theory of allocation and a classification of institutions of allocation that includes the market but is not limited by it. Although comparative studies of production are of reasonable antiquity, comparative studies of allocation of goods are in their infancy.

According to Polanyi, there are three basic modes of allocation. He does not say that there are not more, but only that he has isolated three. He has given them names: reciprocity, redistribution, and market exchange. Every empirical economy exhibits at least one of these principles of distribution; most economies exhibit two; many are characterized by all three.

Market exchange is the exchange of goods at prices determined by the law of supply and demand. Its essence is free and casual contract. Only in a society in which there is an enforceable contract law can the market gain any great predominance. As we shall see, markets are present in many societies where they affect daily life only little, unlike our own society in which the market is central. In examining the other forms, it should be recognized that both supply and demand are probably present in all cases of exchange, but only in some cases is the institutionalization such that they are instrumental in determining price.

Redistribution is defined by Polanyi as a systematic movement of goods toward an administrative center and their reallotment by the authorities at the center. The limiting cases are modern tax institutions, which (even at their most Tory) redistribute wealth in society, and at the other extreme the head of a band or compound, whose followers must put their subsistence into a common store under the surveillance of its head. Just as market exchange depends on a workable and enforceable law of contract, so redistribution depends on a socially recognized hierarchal rank system, with sufficient sanctions to be effective.

Reciprocity involves exchange of goods between people who are bound in nonmarket, nonhierarchial relationships with one another. The exchange does not create the relationship, but rather is part of the behavior that gives it content. The most vivid systems of reciprocity are those based on kinship obligations, but there are many other bases to which reciprocal transfer of goods is essential.

The name that Polanyi has given to these three forms of institutionalization of exchange leave a good deal to be desired, because they do not form exclusive categories. We have already seen that supply and demand may be operative even in nonmarket exchange, but may not be primary forces in determining price. Certainly goods are redistributed in society whenever any kind of exchange, on any allocative principle, takes place. Just as certainly, all exchanges are reciprocal in some sense—reciprocity is the essense of contractual exchange, and there are reciprocal obligations of the central authority when redistribution is examined. It must be remembered, in using them, that the terms are not to be applied as if each is an exclusive phenomenon, but rather as each is a central principle in a situation in which it may be possible to discover peripheral principles.

Most empirical economies, as we have noted, display more than one of the principles of allocation. American economy of the middle twentieth century can be taken as an initial illustration of this point. American economy is dominated by the market principle. Not merely products but the factors of production themselves all enter the market. The market is at the very core of American society, and if it were to disappear, American society would either collapse or in some other way change its nature utterly. Nevertheless, there is a large area of American economy that is controlled by redistribution—taxes and fines are cases in point. Economists sometimes go to great pains to explain taxes by market principles. They try to make us think that we are buying the services of the government, on the theory that we have made a "social contract" (choice, they could say) of living under such a government, part of which choice is agreeing to pay for it. To see such a state of affairs in terms of market morality may not be wrong, but is putting the cart before the horse. It is a case of confusing allocation by the market principle with the totality of allocation.

Similarly, there is a small corner of the American economy that is dominated by the principle of reciprocity, in the form of gift exchange. The fact that Americans buy on the market most of the gifts they give does not mean that there is not a nonmarket aspect to the allocation involved in the actual giving. In fact, we are highly critical, even indignant, of the person who computes the market value of reciprocal gifts.

In the American economy, redistribution and reciprocity as principles of distribution are peripheral, whereas the market principle is central. There are other societies in which this situation is different: in which some other principle is central, and the market, if it is present at all, is peripheral. In general, the mode in which the factors of production are allocated—especially land and labor—is the central mode, whereas any others are peripheral.

TROBRIAND ECONOMY

One of the best recorded of the "primitive" economies is that of the Trobriand Islands. All of the principles of allocation are apparent there, but it is the principle of reciprocity that is central, whereas market and redistribution are both peripheral.

The economy of the Trobriand Islands appears complex, but the appearance is deceptive and derives from the fact that if this economy is to be simply explained, it must be analyzed in terms different from those used to explain Western economy. It is necessary, to explain Trobriand economy, to examine six institutions found in that culture, in order to see how allocation and production take place. It would seem, on the basis of Malinowski's descriptions (1922), that the Trobrianders themselves do not interlink these institutions, and some of them are specifically entrenched behind moral battlements so that members of the

6 types of Trobriand economy: 1. kula 2. urigubu 3. gim wali 4. pokala 5. wasi 6. sagali. [handwritten annotations]

society will not interlink them. These institutions must be given their Trobriand names, for there are no English translations of the terms. They are: (1) *kula*; (2) *urigubu*, which is counterbalanced within a single institution by *youla*; (3) *gim wali*; (4) *pokala* ("tribute" is an adequate translation); (5) *wasi* (exchange at fixed rates, between permanent partners, of yams and fish that Polanyi has playfully called fish-and-chips reciprocity); and (6) *sagali*, (a type of giveaway feast).

WASI — *exchange btwn 2 villages ie. yams for fish...* [handwritten]

There are, in the Trobriand Islands, villages in the interior that do not have fishing rights either on the lagoon or the sea. There are also seaside villages that do not have access to adequate farmland. The exchange of necessary commodities between these two sets of villages if based on a series of standing partnerships and is done at a fixed rate of exchange. At harvest time members of an inland village will bring quantities of yams to their partners in a lagoon village. Every man will set his yams in front of his partner's house. This act constitutes an indemnification on the man of the lagoon village to return an equivalent amount in fish. As soon after such a visit can be reasonably arranged, the men of the lagoon village give notice to the inland people that they are going out on a fishing expedition. By the time they return, the people from the inland village have arrived on the beach. The haul of fish is taken directly from the canoes and carried to the inland village. The equivalence between yams and fish is not measured precisely. A bunch of taro, of what Malinowski calls "the standard size," or an "ordinary" bunch of yams is given in return for a bundle of fish that weighs between three and five kilograms.

When large hauls of fish arrive in the inland villages, they are often distributed in accordance with the institution known as *sagali*. Fish is the only commodity that can be used in *sagali* giveaways in the inland villages. Conversely, the yams enter into the giveaway economy of the coastal areas, whether it be in *sagali* or in that form of giving to the sister's husband known as *urigubu*.

Wasi exchanges more or less follow the supply and undoubtedly in a good year for fishing one gets more fish per yams than in a bad year, which is to say that the bundles will be heavier in a good year than in a bad year. However, there is still a strict one-to-one equivalence between the number of bundles of yams and the number of bundles of fish. Such a situation resembles what modern merchants call packaging to price. What is important, however, is not that there may be a fluctuation in quantity and hence a change in "price." Rather, it is that "price" does not appear at all in the Trobriand evaluation of the institution. Moreover, such exchanges cannot be made with just anybody—there is no "freedom of contract." Rather, *wasi* is carried on with partners who have been "properly" come by—either through inheritance or religious pledges.

Wasi, therefore, represents a kind of reciprocal giving and receiving that is based on a special type of contract. Such a situation, if it is not adequately explained—and it is not in this case—is usually handled by anthropologists with the word "ceremonial," and Malinowski indeed speaks of *wasi* as ceremonial trade.

One further factor should be noted: *wasi* creates a debt structure among the various villages of the islands. It would be erroneous, however, to analyze this debt structure in terms of credit. Rather, it is a matter of indemnification. Although credit and indemnification provide a superficially similar debt structure, the rights and obligations—and more specifically the tone—of all such exchanges are very different.

KULA   *& ceremonial exchange of treasured items*

Very similar to *wasi* but dealing in very different goods is the institution known as *kula. Kula* is the exchange between permanent contractual partners, and no one else, of treasure items—never of subsistence items such as the fish and food in *wasi* exchanges. Treasures are of several types in the Trobriand Islands. The most exclusive and highly valued type is called *vaygua,* which Malinowski translated as "valuables." By no means do all Trobrianders engage in the *kula*. In some of the villages anyone may engage, but in others the right to take part in the *kula* is a carefully guarded prerogative of rank. As with *wasi*, a man has a set of partners to whom he gives one thing and from whom he receives another—in this case, both are *vaygua*. But the further rule is added that those people to whom he gives one class of *vaygua*—large white arm shells called *mwali*—all live in the same direction from him, whereas his partners to whom he gives the spondylous shell necklaces all live in the other direction.

As is the case in *wasi*, a man cannot keep what he gets by *kula* exchanges. Whereas in *wasi* he may consume part of it but must give the rest of it away through the institution of *sagali*, in the kula there is no way by consumption to get the *vaygua* out of the system and no moral sanction or prestige attached to keeping it, but only to getting it and giving it. Therefore, what a man must do in order to make the system work is to give away again what he has received. In so doing, he gives away to his partner to the north what he received from his partner to the south and vice versa. His own reward is in the pleasure of having had the valuable and in the reputation as a generous and powerful man, which will accrue to him.

The participants in the *kula* are located in such a way that they form a rough ring, several hundred miles in circumference. The necklaces go around the ring from one person to another in one direction whereas the arm rings go around in the other direction.[1]

With such a bald description it is difficult for Americans to realize what motivates men to participate in this particular kind of trading of treasure. The answer is to be found not in any kind of system of economic production or exchange, but rather in the social system of ranking and prestige. Thorstein Veblen (1899) has long since proved that desire for rank and prestige is one of the most moving elements in our own economy. It is certainly no less so in Melanesian economy.

As the *kula* treasures circulated around the ring, stories become attached to them—stories about the great men who had owned the treasures. The aplomb with which these men received and handed them on, and the excitement of the travel and expeditions undertaken in order to receive them. In this way the particularly handsome or fine treasures ac-

---

1. Other and similar rings have been described; see, for example, Thomson (1949).

quire not merely a patina of use, but a patina of myth and history; and every time that one of these historical pieces changes hands it is as if another chapter were added to the significant story of the valuable.

This game is complicated by the fact that every man has several *kula* partners. A commoner will have five or six in either direction along the ring. A chief may have as many as seventy or eighty. The trick is to find a way to be sure your partner gives you his newly acquired treasure instead of giving it to someone else. This may be achieved in a number of ways, the most common of which is presentation to that partner of what one might call second-grade treasures. Malinowski (1922, p. 512) refers to these second-grade treasures as "permanent *vaygua*"; they are stone blades, a certain type of belt, and pendants made from boars' tusks.[2] These second-grade treasures indemnify the owner of the treasure that is sought; he must return it with equivalent or better second-grade treasure. But more importantly, such a gift of second-grade treasure serves as "bait" to indicate your interest in your partner's *vaygua* and a public statement of your belief in your capacity to match it with an equivalent gift if he gives it to you rather than to another partner. It is interesting that the name for such a gift, given to solicit a particular gift in *kula*, is *pokala*—the same word as for tribute given to a chief. It might be assumed that in so doing a man acknowledges his partner's outranking him and solicits his good will and generosity.

The entry of valuables into the ring after their manufacture and the way in which they are removed from the ring is, of course, of primary importance to understanding it. Only two villages have adequate magical protection for making the arm shells. The shell from which the arm shell is manufactured exists all over the area, but the magic is limited to the two villages. It is also important that the "manufacture" continues as the valuables move along the *kula* ring. They may, for example, get into the *kula* when a man who finds a particularly valuable shell gives it to his brother-in-law as a return gift in the *urigubu* institution. The brother-in-law may then knock off the excess part of the shell and give it to a *kula* partner as small change, so to speak. The man who receives it may polish it and add decorative items. So begins the concomitant creation of the myth, which ultimately may make the arm shell of great value. Somewhere along the route of exchange it will get a name.

The important thing about the *kula* is not economic in any sense of providing livelihood; rather, it points up the fact that exchange, even of treasures having no practical use, can be a great motivating force. This kind of exchange, further, can be analyzed with the same set of tools as those with which *wasi* can be analyzed.

Like *wasi*, the *kula* takes place as a reciprocal giving and taking between partners who are contractual allies of permanent standing. One's prestige in the society, at least in part, depends upon the *kula* valuables one is able to receive and give away. Thus, the luck in inheriting partners and the wisdom with which one selects one's new partners are of great importance. The *kula* is done with a decorum and a seriousness that resembles modern

---

2. Mrs. Kennedy gave the President a whale's tooth incised with his portrait for Christmas, 1962. It makes a valuable addition, according to the press, to his collection of scrimshaw.

stamp auctions, where, too, people trade for treasures of no intrinsic worth. The difference is, of course, that the stamp auction is associated with the market principle whereas the *kula* is associated with reciprocity.

The *kula* is far and away the most romantic of the Trobriand exchange spheres because it involves long and dangerous overseas voyages to collect the presents that one has a right to receive. The *kula* is an extremely important mechanism of communication and social organization, as well as a quasieconomic institution, as Malinowski has shown.

GIM WALI   *practical goods bartered w/ kula*

Accompanying the *kula* expeditions, but certainly not limited to them, is another form of exchange that is very much more understandable to modern Westerners. This exchange, known as *gim wali*, is the moneyless exchange of nontreasure goods according to a market principle. Just as behavior in *kula* exchange must be decorous and "ceremonial," the accepted behavior in *gim wali* was the higgling and haggling common to the marketplace. The morality of the *kula* is to attract to oneself, and then to give away with generosity but some show of regret, the most notable of the treasures. The morality of *gim wali* is that of getting a bargain.

Too much can be made of the fact that *kula* expeditions both overseas and inland take large supplies of *gim wali* trade goods to exchange for other such goods. A man can never perform *gim wali* with his *kula* partner. However, he can perform *gim wali*, with the *kula* partners of all the other members of expedition. Therefore, during the visits it is the *kula* exchanges or gifts that get all the attention. *Gim wali*, very often noisy *gim wali*, takes place at the same time as, but at some short distance removed from, the *kula* exchanges.

kula vs. gim wali

There has been a tendency in the past for anthropologists to say that the *kula* was just an excuse for carrying out *gim wali*. The fact that they go together does not prove the one is the cover for the other, and to say that such is the case is not merely to put the entire institution of the *kula* into the crass terms of money and market economy, but to assume that *gim wali* needs a cover. The *kula* is an institution dealing in prestige items for the enhancement of one's personality and rank. *Gim wali* is trade of pedestrian household items.

There is another type of exchange related to *gim wali* called *laga*. Malinowski notes that this term means a big and important transaction. He says that if a small pig is exchanged for food or minor objects, it is called *gim wali*; but if a large pig is exchanged for treasure (*vaygua*), it is called *laga*. *Laga* is also the term used when certain tasks are "purchased" or when garden plots are transferred. Malinowski does not say what the tasks may be, but only calls *laga* a "ceremonial purchase" (1922, p. 186).

POKALA   *— tribute paid to a chief*

We have already met the term *pokala* as the word for a solicitory gift to one's *kula* partner. We noted at that time that it had something to do with relative rank. *Pokala* is also a general term for the tribute paid to a chief (Malinowski, 1922, p. 181). The word *pokala* is also used for gifts given between affines, particularly those given in exchange for the items or rights one would have eventually inherited from one's mother's brother. Malinowski states specifically that the two meanings of this word are distinguished and that the two are homonyms and not a single concept (1922, p. 186). However, he postulates that they developed out of a single concept. Perhaps the most important point that can be made about the *pokala* to the chief is that it seems to be almost indistinguishable, except by name, from the *urigubu* paid to a chief. The gifts to the chief in *pokala* are, insofar as it can be determined from the literature, subsistence goods. It is not at all clear what the chief does with them, but presumably he gives them all away again in a series of feasts similar to *sagali*. Since the Trobrianders produce an excess of food, however, it may be of little practical importance. It is also very difficult to make out the sort of gift the chief gives in return, if any, for the *pokala* he receives. It may be "services" of a political or religious sort. From some passages in Malinowski it would seem that he may return *kula* treasures; in others, there seems to be no return.

URIGUBU — annual P→ sister's husband

Urigubu is the custom in which the man makes annual contributions of food to his sister's husband. Malinowski never gives an adequate description of the *urigubu* institution, but notes only that it would be so complex as to necessitate a preliminary account of the kinship system (which he never wrote). He does say, however, that as much as three quarters of a man's crops go either as tribute to a chief or to his sister's or mother's husband and family as *urigubu*. Thus, a man is dependent for his subsistence not on himself (his own crops go to his sister's husband) but on his wife's brother.

Malinowski's greatest interest was in the points where *urigubu* and *pokala* overlap—that is, where a chief married women who were the sisters of the headmen of the various villages and thereby received from them *urigubu* in amounts that were equivalent to tribute. He seems to have received *pokala*, tribute, from many areas as well. From these combined sources of income, then, he was expected to make huge feasts and also to pay for the many services to which he had a right but for which he was nevertheless obliged to pay. Thus, turning *pokala* into *urigubu*—turning a particular type of political association into kinship ties—was the surest way for a chief to maintain his position and his capacity to demand tribute.

The gifts a chief returned to the people who gave him *urigubu* were called *youla*. It is of interest that they were never of the same type as the goods he received. *Youla* consisted primarily of small or unimportant or secondary *kula* valuables. It is difficult to discover whether or not the chief received *kula* valuables, or even the secondary ones, as *urigubu* gifts. Certainly, however, he gave them away in return.

The function, thus, of the *urigubu* is to shunt *kula* valuables among various people by means of non*kula* transactions. It is also a way to shunt these valuables down the rank order of the society.

In summary, the Trobriand Islands exhibit a set of institutions each one of which is based on its own combination of ranked goods and a mode of transaction. *Kula*, properly so-called, is a sphere limited to two types of treasure. *Gim wali* is a sphere limited to subsistence product. *Wasi* is a sphere limited to certain specific types of food.

There is another kind of institution, however, in which spheres are crossed. In the *urigubu*, which is based on a form of redistribution, the initial indemnifying payment is in subsistence goods. The return, or *youla*, is or may be in terms of treasure. Thus, the better *urigubu* that a man can make, the more likely he is to be given a treasure in return. In the same way *pokala* is payment of food to the chief or headman and seems to be returned in the form of treasure. What is lacking in *pokala* that is present in *urigubu* is the kinship rationale. Finally, we have examined *sagali*, which is the big giveaway feast—what the American Indians would have called a "blowout.'" Thus, whereas the chief receives food in the *urigubu* and returns *kula* valuables, he also returns the food in the form of feasts, although he may use it to make further *urigubu* or *pokala* payments.

There are contractual reciprocities in the area of *kula* and *wasi*; the market principle is at work in the *gim wali*; and there are definite institutions based on rank and the redistribution from recognized centers in the *urigubu*, *pokala*, and *sagali* institutions.

Trobriand economy is, in short, like our own in that a series of institutions are brought together by linked transactional principles. In America, the bonhommie of gift exchange is carried out on the basis of reciprocity, the task of financing political organization is carried out by the institutions of taxation on the principle of redistribution, and the production of substantive needs (and some other things that we have learned to see in analogy to the substantive needs) are transacted by the market principle. In the Trobriand economy, similarly, there are six interrelated institutions. The difference in the two economies lies primarily in the fact that several economic institutions of the Americans are amalgamated into a single entity by general-purpose currency and by the concept of price, whereas the amalgamation of the Trobriand institutions is of a sort that is foreign to Americans and indeed to the science of economics. The nonmonetary mode of amalgamation of the various economic institutions is the subject of the next chapter.

It remains for this chapter to carry to conclusions the idea that in every society there are dominant modes of transactions and peripheral modes of transaction, and that these modes vary from one culture to the next.

PERIPHERAL MARKETS

American society is marked by the fact that it is economically dominated by the market principle of transactions. Such a statement means that, with negligible exceptions, it is vital for at least one member of every nuclear family to "sell" one of the factors of production on the market. He must either sell his work as labor, rights in his land as rents, rights to use his money in return for interest or dividends, or else an idea, a capacity to take risks, or a managerial skill. If he fails to do so, or is unable to do so, he (and probably some of his family as well) will starve—except, of course, insofar as the government or some other body ameliorates this harsh epiphenomenon of market by "giving" him the necessities of life, which is no more than to say that relief institutions are part of the redistributive rather than the market operations of Western economy. If the combined market for factors and produce were to disappear, American society would be unrecognizable.

The market may be present, however, in many societies that it does not dominate in the way that it dominates the societies of the twentieth-century Western world. It is usual for Westerners to oppose the market society and economy to what they know as the "subsistence economy."

There has in the past been a common error in defining a subsistence economy. That error is to assume that a situation in which a people produces largely what they themselves consume is the same thing as the absence of a market. The Trobriand situation belies such an assumption. Trobrianders do not, as individuals, consume their own produce—there is extensive shifting of produce, and a family subsists on the produce grown by the brother of the wife/mother. It is not, however, a market that intervenes between the producer and the consumer. There are, moreover, other situations, such as those found in traditional West Africa, in which there is an active market, but nevertheless almost every family produces its own food, clothing, and shelter. What, then, is a "subsistence economy"?

A "subsistence economy" is one in which the factors of production are not transacted by the market mechanism. In a subsistence economy, some produce may enter the market—such a situation can be called a "peripheral market." It does not follow that simply because the factors are not transacted in the market that there are no transactions of the factors of production—we have created only a negative, residual category: the absence of market transaction of the factors of production. We have already seen that factors of production can be institutionalized in the absence of a market. It remains here to examine ways in which markets work if they do not apply to factors of production, which is to say, if factors of production are transacted by other mechanisms. Logically, of course, the institution of the market may or may not be present in a society. If it is present, it may be dominant (as in the twentieth-century West) or it may be peripheral in the sense that it is peripheral in the Trobriand institution of *gim wali*. It may indeed still be peripheral, yet be one of the most noticeable culture traits a society possesses. Such is the case in West Africa.

THE EXAMPLE OF WEST AFRICA

Market places are numerous and colorful in West Africa. They are easily appreciated by even the most amateur observer, and therefore have been described, at least superficially, over and over again. These market places do not, however, occupy the same position in African society as "the market" occupies in the West. Analyzing the difference necessitates distinguishing the market place from the market principle. As we have already established, the market principle is the determination of price by free working of the forces that create supply and demand. As any economics text testifies, *the site of the market is irrelevant to the working of the principle*. Therefore, the "market place" must be studied in analytical separation from the "market principle" and the two conjoined only where there is a good empirical basis for so doing.

The market place thrives in most of West Africa and the Congo. But until after World

War II, the market was largely peripheral, because the number of people who actually derived their livings primarily from the market was small. West Africa has had a few professional traders for centuries. Most West Africans, however, would suffer little change in their way of life were the market to disappear. Unlike the situation in the United States or in Europe, their society and culture would not be totally unrecognizable, totally changed, if the market principle were to disappear. What, then, does the market place do for West Africans?

Market places provide regular meetings of fairly large numbers of people. The attendant at markets are usually cross sections of the population. It is to be expected, therefore—and it is certainly found—that the market place is utilized for purposes far beyond those for which nominally it was established. Market places can be utilized for almost every conceivable purpose that requires a large number of people brought together in a controlled situation.

Probably the most common—because it is the most basic—noneconomic function of market places is their function as nodes in the network of communication. Undoubtedly, one of the most important points for the dissemination of information is the market place, and that dissemination can take place either on an informal, more or less unrecognized basis, or on a formal one. Chiefs, priests, administrative officers and many others make announcements in the market. In most areas, to make an announcement requires the permission of the market authorities, and it may even require that the announcement be made by one of them to signify his approval.

Of even greater importance, perhaps, is that market places provide a place to meet one's friends and kinsmen, and exchange news and gossip. Women, in particular (most of Africa, is virilocal even when it is matrilineal), meet their kinsmen at markets and keep in remarkably close touch with their natal villages by this means. Although it would be difficult to carry out, a study of markets (and perhaps other institutions) in their role of communications nodes would be extremely interesting.

The people at market provide not only listeners and gossip mongers, but also provide a ready-gathered audience. Performances of dancers and entertainers often occur in the market places. The festival aspect of markets is first pointed up by its frequent use as the place to drink beer. The market day usually falls off into a beer drink.

In a more organized fashion, the market place can be of political relevance. The reasons, obviously, are twofold: it can be politically advantageous to control the market place itself, and hence to some degree the people in it. On the other hand, it can be politically advantageous to control, in whatever degree, the produce that goes through the market place. Thus control of market places is usually in the hands of political authorities. In those parts of East and Central Africa where markets were introduced by the colonial administration, it continued to control them: the size and shape of the market place, the type and arrangement of buildings, the conditions for selling, and the composition of the sales force and the selection of goods were all to a greater or lesser degree dictated by that administration. In West Africa, on the other hand, or anywhere else that the markets antedate European control, the market places remained in the hands of indigenous authorities throughout the colonial period. Control of a market put a man at the hub of communications, where he could have immediate contact with people. It also gave him a recognized and approved *raison d'être* behind which he could hide any political chicanery that was to his advantage to hide.

In return, the political authorities in control of market places provide a "market peace," to use the old English term. This means that the markets are policed and the safety of traders and customers more or less assured. It may even be that the market place, or a portion of it, is used as a point of political asylum.

Obviously, also—this point has been made many times with reference to old European market places—it is necessary, if the economic functions of a market are to be performed, for the market peace to be observed. Successful trade demands at least a minimal degree of political stability. The man who is responsible for the market peace thus must have a police force of some description at his disposal, and he must control sufficient power actually to maintain the peace. West African market officials can either call on their families, members of their clans or other social groups, or on the police forces of their governments to police their markets.

An extremely important political consideration is the fact that the market is often used as the center of legal activities—in some areas the chiefs or other judges actually establish themselves as courts in or near the market place; in others their presence assures that when one finds one's adversary (easier at a market than any other place), the case can be laid before the official informally. No African chief can refuse to hear a case brought to his attention at market (though he may postpone it until a regular court hearing). These courts may be the same as—but are often different from—the arbitrating facilities for settling disputes that arise among sellers and customers within the market place itself.

Markets are also often accompanied by religious activities, some of which may be connected with the market peace. The peace of Ibo markets (Ottenberg and Ottenberg, 1962) and Tiv markets (Bohannan, 1963) is kept primarily in the name of and with the sanction of certain shrines and the forces they symbolize. Some African market places—particularly in those areas in which the market is indigenous—are founded with a religious ceremonial.

In summary, market places—particularly in areas in which the market is economically peripheral—fulfill many social and cultural needs of the population. Indeed, some markets are not regarded as primarily "economic" institutions by the people. They provide a meeting place where a certain minimum, at least, of security is assured and hence they can be used for political, religious, social, and personal purposes. In a society in which collections of people on nonkinship bases may prove difficult, the market place provides the setting for a wide range of social activities.

Market places are in most instances, however, primarily places for trade. Even people who produce most of their own foodstuffs are likely to respond, if they are given the opportunity, by growing extra foodstuffs to sell so that they can purchase imported articles. In such a situation a market grows up that may be of very extensive proportions, but it may nevertheless not affect the basis fact: that the family produces most of the basic subsistence it needs. West Africans, for example, produce quantities of cocoa, soybeans, peanuts, sesame, and other crops, which they sell for money. They use this money to buy imported cloth, imported dishes, hardware, and many other imported items. If the market for their produce expands sufficiently, they may in fact begin even to buy some of their food on the market. Ghanaian and Nigerian cocoa farmers, for example, obtain large portions of their food on the market. However, they have by and large not yet reached the point of no return—the individual cocoa farmer can step up food production and weather a bad year. When disease wiped out part of the cocoa plantation of Ghana, the Ghanaians did not move away and they did not starve: they adjusted to the lower cash income by growing more of their own food. The market was peripheral—they were not dependent for their subsistence on selling factors of production on the market.

Today, the factor market is gaining in importance in West Africa. It will undoubtedly continue to do so. However, there are still large areas—and there will continue to be—in which the markets are peripheral.

Prices in a peripheral market are formed in precisely the same way as in any other market: by the silent and invisible working of forces of supply and demand, and by multiplex decisions on the part of sellers and buyers. They are different only in the position the market holds in the total society. Peripheral markets are decorations on, not bulwarks of, the social organization.

A few words should also be said about the way in which the African markets are fitted together into systems or "rings" or markets. African markets do not meet every day, but rather only every four, five, or seven days. A market "ring," then, is a series of market places where meetings are held on successive days. Among the Ibo of eastern Nigeria, the market rings are made up of four markets, each meeting every fourth day. Among the Tiv to their north, the rings contain five markets, each meeting every fifth day. The phenomenon of market rings has been found in widespread parts of the world; a Mexican example has been described briefly and elegantly by Moore (1951).

> The ideas and institutions found in various parts of the world to fulfill man's material needs, and the nonmaterial ones such as prestige or rank maintenance that he sees in analogy to the material ones, are diverse. It is likely, too, that no set of institutions is so fragile and no set of ideas so ephemeral when they are brought into serious and overt question by the impact of new ideas. There is, in economic institutions, a very delicate balance among human motives, human institutions, and human ideas. When institutions change and motives do not, when ideas change and institutions do not, chaos is likely to spread. The "conflict of economies" is one of the most obvious problems in culture change, and it is also one of the vital characteristics that we must understand about the economy. When the balance of distribution changes, no corner of society, no reach of culture, is unaffected.

11 MULTICENTRIC ECONOMIES, CONVERSION, AND THE CONFLICT OF ECONOMIES

—PAUL BOHANNAN

The discussion so far has emphasized the fact that most empirical economies are collections of institutions based on a variety of transactional principles. Some economies nevertheless seem unitary, whereas others seem to be made up of the most diverse institutions with real difficulties of coordination.

The apparent unity in the organizations of the institutions of American economy arises not wholly from a simplicity or congruity of institutions, and not merely from the fact that "market mentality" (Polanyi, 1947) pervades Western thinking. Besides all these forces there is the central fact that a single cultural trait—money—permeates the whole. Money lies at the very heart of the market. It is the means by which we pay taxes or receive relief in the redistribution system; and it is the way we acquire most of the gifts we give, and in terms of which moral miscreants even evaluate the gifts they receive.

Conversely, the apparent complexity of the organization of the Trobriand economy arises from the absence of general-purpose money. The various institutions of exchange are interconnected not by monetary means primarily, but by devices and ideas that may be foreign to us and hence seem complex, the more so since money is such a simplifying device.

This chapter sets out to do two things: to examine the nature of money and its place in the coordination of economy and society, and to examine some of the ways and means by which such coordination can take place in the absence of money.

MONEY

For the last several centuries in Western society, and in a few corners of the world for millenia, exchange and distribution have been simplified by that universal solvent called money. Money is, however, a dangerous concept for the student of comparative cultures because its very simplicity creates difficulty in analyzing those situations in which it is not part of the folk image.

Economists, in their search to understand the nature of money, have determined that it can be used for three or more purposes. We shall here examine only three. In the first place,

[handwritten note at top: Money: 1. means of exchange 2. standard of value 3. means of payment]

money can be used as a means of exchange. Money allows you to exchange something you want less for something you want more without finding somebody whose situation is exactly the reverse of your own. In the absence of some sort of money, the man who has a chicken and wants a piece of cloth must find a man who has a piece of cloth and wants a chicken. Exchange in the absence of money is called "barter"—and it should be noted that barter implies nothing except lack of money in the transaction; although it is usually used with the suggestion of "price" implicit in it, such is an unnecessarily restrictive usage. Economists and savages agree that barter is a tedious and time-consuming business. *Kula*, however, is barter just as much as is *gim wali*.

In the second place, money can be used as a standard of value. Everything that can be exchanged in modern Western society can be given a money value. Money allows us to add up and to compute things of basically different sorts—items that are in their intrinsic natures incommensurable. You may add guns and butter if you do it in terms of money. No material manifestation of money is needed to utilize the idea as a standard of value: a quarter's worth of duplicates from a boy's stamp collection can be "swapped" for a quarter's worth of sea shells from another boy's collection. In most parts of the world, where extensive barter is still to be found, it is likely that this attribute of money has already been learned and tuppence worth of spinach will be bartered for tuppence worth of cooking oil.

In the third place, money is a means of payment. In fact, if money is the exchange medium, it would seem to be the perfect instrument of payment. No matter what the debt contracted, no matter what eventual product the creditor may desire, he will take money. However, payment and standard of value are not to be confused: a fine is paid in money, but the modern Western inclination to regard a standard fine, such as a two-dollar parking ticket, with the price of a misdemeanor is actively discouraged.

In the modern West, in other words, a single concept—money—with its various material manifestations (notes, coins, checks, drafts, and so on) performs all three functions. It is also noteworthy that the various manifestations of money are not distinguishable by function. In other cultures, that may not be the case: the different material items used as money *may* be distinguished by function.

Modern Western money, which performs all the functions with a single set of cultural items, can be called "general-purpose money."[1] Any cultural item that performs one or two functions, but not all three, can be called "special-purpose money."

Some economists and a few anthropologists have tried to elevate one of these money uses to a prime position in defining money—saying that anything used for payment, for example, was "money" whether any other money use was present or not. Other scholars disputed their choice and plugged for some other money use as the primary one. The result was, of course, the futile tug-of-war scholars sometimes find easier than thinking. Einzig

---

[1] General-purpose money may be put to other uses as well: in pre-Keynesian days, for instance, it was sometimes used as a means for storing wealth, and is still occasionally so used by the naïve. For the present analysis, however, the three functions described seem adequate.

(1949) says that means of exchange is the sure mark of "money," and fiercely denounces other scholars who venture to consider payment the primary defining characteristic. The whole problem is a semantic one that can be avoided by a distinction between special-purpose money and general-purpose money.

Two characteristics show up immediately in economies lacking general-purpose money. One is that the "commodities" valued and exchanged, whatever they may be, are separated into more or less self-contained categories, each category associated with a different institution. The other characteristic is the great effort that must be expended to bridge the categories and the institutions that demarcate them into a whole system; that is to say, the difficulties of "disengagement" of items from one institution and their incorporation into another.

Two examples will show clearly the sort of institutionalization that may occur in the absence of general-purpose money. They are taken from the Tiv of central Nigeria and the Kwakiutl of British Columbia.

TIV ECONOMY AND THE PHENOMENON OF CONVERSION

The most distinctive feature about the economy of the Tiv—and it is a feature they share with many, perhaps most, of the premonetary peoples—is what can be called a multicentric economy. Briefly, a multicentric economy is one in which a society's exchangeable goods fall into two or more mutually exclusive spheres, each marked by different institutionalization and different moral values. In some multicentric economies these spheres remain distinct, though in most there are more or less institutionalized means of converting wealth from one into wealth in another.

Indigenously, there were three spheres in the multicentric economy of the Tiv. The first of these spheres is that associated with subsistence, which the Tiv called *yiagh*. The commodities in it include all locally produced foodstuffs: the staple yams and cereals, plus all the condiments, vegetable side dishes and seasonings, as well as small livestock—chickens, goats, and sheep. It also includes household utensils (mortars, grindstones, calabashes, baskets, and pots), some tools (particularly those used in agriculture), and raw materials for producing any items in the category.

Within this sphere, goods are distributed either by gift giving or through marketing. Traditionally, there was no money of any sort in this sphere—all good changed hands by barter. There was a highly developed market organization at which people exchanged their produce for their requirements, and in which, today, traders buy produce in cheap markets and transport it to sell in dear markets. The morality of this sphere of the economy is the morality of the free and uncontrolled market.

The second sphere of the Tiv economy is one that is no way associated with markets. The category of goods within this sphere is slaves, cattle, ritual "offices," that type of large white cloth known as *tugudu*, medicines and magics, and metal rods. One is still entitled to use the present tense in this case; Tiv still quote prices of slaves in cows and brass rods, and of cattle in brass rods and *tugudu* cloth. The price of magical rites, as it has been described in literature, was in terms of *tugudu* cloth or brass rods (though payment might be made in other items); payment for ritual office was in cows and slaves, *tugudu* cloths, and metal rods (Akiga, 1937, p. 382). None of these goods ever entered the market. Actual transfer of such goods took place at ceremonies, at more or less ritualized wealth displays, and on occasions when doctors performed rites and prescribed medicines. Tiv refer to the items and the activities within this sphere by the word *shagba*, which can be roughly translated as prestige.

Within the prestige sphere there was one item that took on all of the money uses and hence can be called a general-purpose currency, though it must be remembered that it was of only a *very limited range*. Brass rods were used as means of exchange *within the sphere*; they also served as a standard of value (though not the only one) within it, and as a means of payment. However, this sphere of the economy was tightly sealed off from the subsistence-goods sphere and its market. After European contact, brass rods occasionally entered the market, but they did so only as means of payment, not as medium of exchange or as standard of valuation. Because of the complex institutionalization and morality, no one ever sold a slave for food; no one, save in the depths of extremity, ever paid brass rods for domestic goods.

The supreme and unique sphere of exchangeable values for the Tiv contains a single item: rights in human beings other than slaves, particularly rights in women. Even twenty-five years after official abolition of exchange marriage, it was the category of exchange in which Tiv were emotionally most entangled.

Before the coming of the Europeans all "real" marriages were exchange marriages. In its simplest form, an exchange marriage involved two men exchanging sisters. Actually, this simple form seldom or never occurred. In order for every man to have a ward (*ingol*) to exchange for a wife, small localized agnatic lineages formed ward-sharing groups. There was an initial distribution of wards among the men of this group, so that each man became the guardian (*tien*) of one or more wards. The guardian, then, saw to the marriage of his ward, exchanging her with outsiders for another woman (her "partner" or *ikyar*) who became the bridge of the guardian or one of his close agnatic kinsmen, or—in some situations—became a ward in the ward-sharing group and was exchanged for yet another woman who became a wife.

When an elopement occurred and a woman in exchange was not available, a debt was created in favor of the guardian's group. These debts sometimes lagged two or even three generations behind actual exchanges. The simplest way of paying them off was for the eldest daughter of the marriage to return to the ward-sharing group of her mother, as ward, thus canceling the debt.

Because of its many impracticalities, the system had to be buttressed in several ways in order to work: one way was to provide for "earnest" during the time of the lag, another was to recognize other types of marriage as binding to limited extents. These two elements are somewhat confused with each other, because of the fact that right up until the abolition of exchange marriage in 1927, the inclination was always to treat all nonexchange marriages as if they were "lags" in the completion of exchange marriages.

When lags in exchange occurred, they were filled with "earnests" made of brass rods or, occasionally, it would seem, of cattle. The brass rods or cattle in such situations were *never* exchange equivalents (*ishe*) for the woman. The only "price" of one woman is another woman.

Although Tiv decline to grant it antiquity, another type of marriage was common at the time Europeans first came to Tivland—it was called "accumulating a woman/wife" (*kem kwase*). It is difficult to tell today just exactly what it consisted in, because the terminology of this union has been adapted to describe the bridewealth marriage that was declared by an administrative fiat of 1927 to be the only legal form. *Kem* marriage consisted in acquisition of sexual, domestic, and economic rights in a woman—but not the rights to filiate her children to the social group of her husband. Additional payments had to be made to the woman's guardians in order to filiate the children. *Kem* payments were in brass rods. However, rights in a woman certainly had no equivalent or "price" in brass rods or any other item save identical rights in another woman.

Thus, within the sphere of exchange marriage there was no item that fulfilled any of the uses of money; when second-best types of marriage were made, payment was in an item that was specifically not used as a standard of value.

That Tiv do conceptualize exchange articles as belonging to different categories, and that they rank the categories on a moral basis, and that most but not all exchanges are limited to one sphere, gives rise to the fact that two different kinds of exchanges may be recognized: exchange of items contained within a single category, and exchange of items belonging to different categories. For Tiv, these two different types of exchange are marked by separate and distinct moral attitudes.

To maintain this distinction between the two types of exchanges Tiv mark by different behavior and different values, I shall use separate words. I shall call those exchanges of items within a single category "conveyances," and those exchanges of items from one category to another "conversions" (Steiner, 1954). Roughly, conveyances are morally neutral; conversions have a strong moral quality in their rationalization.

Exchanges within a category—particularly that of subsistence, the only one intact today—excite no moral judgments. Exchanges between categories, however, do excite a moral reaction: the man who exchanges lower-category goods for higher-category goods does not brag about his market luck but about his "strong heart" and his success in life. The man who exchanges high-category goods for lower rationalizes his action in terms of high-valued motivation (most often the needs of his kinsmen).

The two institutions most intimately connected with conveyance are markets and marriage. Conveyance in the prestige sphere centers on slave dealing, on curing, and on the acquisition of status.

Conversion is a much more complex matter. Conversion depends on the fact that some items of every sphere could, on certain occasions, be used in exchanges in which the return was *not* considered equivalent (*ishe*). Obviously, given the moral ranking of the spheres, such a situation leaves one party to the exchange in a good position, and the other in a bad one. Tiv say that it is "good" to trade food for brass rods, but that it is "bad" to trade brass rods for food; that it is good to trade your cows or brass rods for a wife, but very bad to trade your marriage ward for cows or brass rods.

Seen from the individual's point of view, it is profitable and possible to invest one's wealth if one converts it into a morally superior category: to convert subsistence wealth into prestige wealth and both into women is the aim of the economic endeavor of individual Tiv.

We have already examined the marriage system by which a man could convert his brass rods to a wife: he could get a *kem* wife and *kem* her children as they were born. Her daughters, then, could be used as wards in his exchange marriages. It is the desire of every Tiv to "acquire a woman" (*ngoho kwase*) either as wife or ward in some way other than sharing in the ward-sharing group. A wife whom one acquires in any other way is not the concern of one's marriage-ward-sharing group, because the woman or other property exchanged for her did not belong to the marriage-ward group. The daughters of such a wife are not divided among the members of a man's marriage-ward group, but only among his sons. Such a wife is not only indicative of a man's ability and success financially and personally, but rights in her are the only form of property not ethically subject to the demands of his kinsmen.

Conversion from the prestige sphere to the kinship sphere was, thus, fairly common; it consisted in all the forms of marriage—save exchange marriage—usually in terms of brass rods.

Conversion from the prestige sphere to the subsistence sphere was also usually in terms of metal rods. They, on occasion, entered the market place as payment. If the owner of the brass rods required an unusually large amount of staples to give a feast, making too heavy a drain on his wives' food supplies, he might buy it with brass rods.

However, brass rods could not possibly have been a general currency. They were not divisible. One could not receive "change" from a brass rod. Moreover, a single rod was worth much more than the usual market purchase for any given day of most Tiv subsistence traders. Although it might be possible to buy chickens with brass rods, one would have to have bought a very large quantity of yams to equal one rod, and to buy an item such as pepper with rods would be laughable. Brass rods, thus, overlapped from the prestige to the subsistence sphere on some occasion, but only on special occasions and for large purchases.

Not only is conversion possible, but it is encouraged—it is, in fact, the behavior that proves a man's worth. Tiv are scornful of a man who is merely rich in subsistence goods (or, today, in money). If, having adequate subsistence, he does not seek prestige in accordance with the old counters, or if he does not strive for more wives, and hence more children, the fault must be personal inadequacy. They also note that they all try to keep a man from making conversions; jealous kinsmen of a rich man will bewitch him and his people by fetishes, in order to make him expend his wealth on sacrifices to repair the fetishes, thus maintaining economic equality. However, once a conversion has been made, demands of kinsmen are not effective—at least, they take a new form.

Therefore, the man who converts his wealth into higher categories is successful—he has a "strong heart." He is both feared and respected.

In this entire process, metal rods hold a pivotal position, and it is not surprising that early administrators considered them money. Originally imported from Europe, they were used as "currency" in some parts of southern Nigeria in the slave trade. They are dowels about a quarter of an inch in diameter and some three feet long; they can be made into jewelry, and were used as a source of metal for castings.

Whatever their use elsewhere, brass rods in Tivland had some but not all of the attributes of money. Within the prestige sphere, they were used as a standard of equivalence, and they were a medium of exchange; they were also a mode for storage of wealth, and were used as payment. In short, brass rods were a general-purpose currency *within the prestige sphere*. However, outside of the prestige sphere—markets and marriages were the most active institutions of exchange outside it—brass rods fulfilled only one of these functions of money: payment. We have examined in detail the reasons why equivalency could not exist between brass rods and rights in women, between brass rods and food.

We have, thus, in Tivland, a multicentric economy of three spheres, and we have a sort of money that was a general-purpose money in one sphere and a special-purpose money in the special transactions in which the other two spheres overlapped it.

In the Tiv economy, conversion among ranked spheres takes the place that is occupied in a monetized economy by money. Each includes the possibility that demand schedules cover all the items one wants, as well as the obligations one has to face. The Tiv demand schedule takes a different form: it is broken into discrete categories and there are two problems—first, to manipulate items within a category; and second, to get an item disengaged from one category and into the sphere of another. A moral system pervades the practice of conversion, just as a moral system lies behind the demand schedule on the basis of which modern Americans decide how they must spend their money. Americans, however, do not have to "convert" from one category to another, because general-purpose money has entered all the categories, and hence reduced all to a common denominator.

It can be seen that Trobriand economy, too, like Tiv economy, is permeated with conversion. *Urigubu* can, for example, be seen as a mechanism for converting food into *kula* valuables.

THE KWAKIUTL ECONOMY AND THE POTLATCH

Occasionally, an economy is so bizarre as to seem unexplainable: the *potlatch* which is one of the most widely known of American Indian institutions, seems to be such. Potlatch can, however, be quite easily understood when it is seen as hyperdevelopment of conversion, and recognized that the apparent emphasis on giving away rather than on receiving may be a freakish association of Kwakiutl folk images and the European folk images of anthropologists and others, who were wont to explain it or condemn it or both.

The Kwakiutl lived on the northern shore of Vancouver Island, in British Columbia, and on the adjacent mainland, in a country with a coast line almost as long and inletted per square mile of territory as that of Norway. There were forests of giant cedar and fir; animal life abounded. The sea teemed with fish, mammals, porpoises, shellfish. Probably no other part of the world offered such riches for so little work. The Kwakiutl standard of living was among the highest the world has known. They had large amounts of material necessities, and also were the creators of an extensive and admirable art. Technology was highly developed; they had many ways of exploiting their rich environment, including adequate storage techniques. They were among the best-housed people of the New World. Their seagoing canoes held as many as fifty persons.

abundant resources

The Kwakiutl, even more than most peoples in the world, were obsessed with rank—indeed, in the midst of such plenty they created artificial shortages in the social system and their striving for high social position was an integral part of the economy. They were divided into about twenty-five village groups, each of which was politically autonomous. In one case as many as four groups lived in a single large village. In 1930, there were only about 1500 Kwakiutl, which meant that each "tribe" had no more than about sixty people in it. However, when European and American shipping concerns first began to trade with them, at the end of the eighteenth century, there were approximately ten times that number, so that a tribe of 600 people was a fairly reasonable number. The entire population was about 15,000. Each of the tribes was divided into from three to five subgroups, which nobody in the vast literature on the Kwakiutl seems ever to have been able to define, because of the fact that they were quasikinship groups which appeared to be formed almost by choice on the part of the members. We can call them subtribes.

flexible rank

In addition to this arrangement, there was an organization made up of a number of ranked but hereditary offices, each one marked by crests, ceremonial privileges, and titles. The ranking of the positions was neither automatic nor unchangeable. Rather, each position had constantly to be reaffirmed by potlatches. A potlatch (the word is from the Chinook language and means "gift") is a ceremonial occasion on which one exchanges or gives gifts to one's rival, who is a man occupying a status closest to one's own in the ranked hierarchy. The early studies of potlatch always concentrated on the fact that goods were given away. They did not linger on the more significant fact that an exchange was involved of the sort which has been called conversion. Potlatch was therefore equated with what would truly, were it actually as described, be foolhardiness. As is so often the case, however, the difficulty arose from a basic lack of understanding.

During the entire winter the Kwakiutl did little in the way of production activities, but rather turned their attention to ceremonial and potlatch. Vast feasts were common in this wealthy community, and many were accompanied by potlatching. Potlatch involves giving property by one holder of a position to the holder of another position. The former does so in order to maintain the glory of the rank he holds and of those ancestors from whom he inherited it. Potlatches were usually given on important occasions, either in the life of a person or in the activities of the community. They were frequently held in association with marriages, births, initiations. There were often potlatches in connection with winter dances or other religious rituals. A man could retire from a potlatch position and hand it down to his heir; such was an occasion for great gift giving.

The actual giving was done with vast ostentation and with vast amounts of bragging about the investment skill and the intrepidity of the position holder. The rival was openly dared to do anything half so theatrical.

Potlatching actually consisted of a whole cycle of individual potlatches, each of which was an occasion for a person ostentatiously to convert certain types of wealth into other types of wealth. However, the categories or spheres of wealth among the Kwakiutl were quite different from those involved in other economies. Because of the fact that they lived with such a vast abundance, the subsistence items themselves did not enter into the potlatching institutions. Therefore the distinction the Kwakiutl used was not one between subsistence and treasure, as the Trobriand Islanders draw it, and as indeed some of the Kwakiutl's southern neighbors, such as the Tututni, draw it. These latter make a distinction between subsistence, which is mainly food from the sea, and treasure, which was obsidian blades and large shawls made of the scalps of redheaded woodpeckers sewn together (Dubois, 1936).

Rather, among the Kwakiutl the most important potlatch counters were blankets. In the aboriginal situation, these blankets were either woven or pounded from cedar bark or else made of small animal skins sewn together. It was necessary for the potlatcher to collect as many as possible of these blankets through wise investments and precise interest rates, and then to convert the blankets into other types of goods.

In the whole potlatch literature there is only one account—Dr. Helen Codere (1950) has combed it all—of a series of transactions that can be followed through. This is a case in which a man wanted to set up his son in a potlatch position from which he himself was retiring. He arranged for several members of his tribe to give his son one hundred blankets. The boy then took the blankets and gave them to other members of his own tribe, who paid him a hundred percent interest for keeping the blankets for one year. These people also, then, at the time that they returned the hundred blankets, gave him another hundred blankets, which the boy would have eventually to return at the same hundred percent interest. Therefore, the boy on this occasion had his original one hundred blankets, his hundred blankets interest, and the hundred blankets that had been given to him. He now gave these blankets out to friends in other tribes, who returned them in a shorter time, with less interest. It gave him a total, however, of about 450 blankets. Thereupon, the father of the boy decided it was time to hold the potlatch. The boy took his 450 blankets and, amidst vast ceremonial, made his presentations. Two hundred of the blankets went to repay the original loan at one hundred percent interest. Another 200 went to repay the second loan, made when his first gifts were returned, also at a hundred percent interest. This left him with fifty blankets to give away, which seems to be the actual potlatch transaction. Giving the other blankets was a matter of repayment of debts, with interest.

Note that there are two types of exchange here. The first is among friends and tribesmen who help one to acquire large amounts of property in order that one can from the profit, so to speak, invest that property by giving it to one's rival who must return it at the same exorbitant interest rates.

However, when the rival did return the original gift, one was oneself under an obligation to make the same kind of interest payment and return. Thus, very quickly the number of blankets involved in such a series of transactions became astronomical.

As a matter of fact, there were probably nowhere near 450 actual blankets in the possession of the young man or of his people at the time the potlatch was made. In the first place, other items could be used, and their values expressed in terms of blankets. One could, for example, value a canoe at 400 blankets and give it away. Or one could even use Canadian currency as so many blankets, and give it away. Sometimes a man would receive only a tally stick, which indicated that he had already collected his blankets.

Therefore we are dealing with a situation in which all potlatch wealth is expressed in terms of blankets, not with true collections of *real* blankets. Blankets, in other words, are units of account, and whether or not they exist is beside the point. They are carrying out one of the money functions: standard of value. They are not used in exchange, and the only payment they will serve is the payment of a potlatch debt or of an investment debt leading up to potlatch. The blankets are, in short, a special-purpose money.

The question is still a very real one, however, of how such a system can persist without breaking down, without the whole economy's going to pieces. If the interest rates remained exorbitant, and if the period of time in which the investment had to double remained so relatively short, any economy would collapse. However, the system did not collapse because, through a systematic mode of conversion, the debts were cleared without actual payment. Codere (1950) had noted that if the actual blankets doubled every year, an original investment of ten blankets would, in ten years, lead to 4320 blankets[2] for purposes of potlatch. Potlatches on such scale were rare; certainly not all original loans of ten blankets led to such sums.

The whole point of Kwakiutl investment can be seen not as economic in the sense that we think of it—as dealing with subsistence goods—but with getting together, by means of blankets, sufficient purchasing power to convert out of blankets into another kind of counter or tally—the copper. Coppers were treasures of a sort similar to the *vaygua* of the Trobrianders. They were sheets of copper, slightly convex, about two and a half feet long. They were decorated with engravings of gods or crest animals of various potlatch position holders. A copper obviously had no value of its own. The value given to it depended entirely on the amount paid for it at its last transaction. Each copper was named and its history was known. Every time it was given away, its value had to increase. Boas has, probably mistakenly, compared coppers with bank notes of high denomination. High denominational bank notes are not different in quality from bank notes of small denomina-

---

2. My own computation is 5120 blankets.

tion; they merely represent greater purchasing power. Furthermore, there is no individual bank note given a specific name, although every copper had a given name. The coppers were also a substantially different thing from the blankets.

Thus, as the contest between rivals continued and the number of blankets increased until it became so totally out of proportion as to be impossible even to contemplate—at that time one of the owners gave a copper to his rival. With acceptance, the value of the copper became twice the number of blankets that had been given in the transaction the year before. The man who received the copper was obliged either to put that many blankets with it and give it back, or to give it to another of his rivals and get back another copper worth more than the original. A man's whole tribe would help him collect wealth in order to get a copper in this way, so that he could give it away to his rival, thereby increasing his own social position and perhaps ruining his rival completely.

Let us say that the rival, after a period of time, gave a potlatch in which he returned to you the copper plus interest. You then added interest to it and perhaps gave it away again to someone else who returned another that was worth more blankets. You gave that to the first rival. This process continues until one of the rivals decides that the other has extended his credit, and exhausted his resources, to the place where it was not possible for him to increase them. Then comes the coup. You destroy the copper. Amidst great ceremony, you either burn it, break it up, or throw it into the sea. However, it is important to be sure that you yourself are not too attenuated when doing this, because if the rival has reserves enough that he can destroy an equal or greater copper, then you have not won, but lost. Instead of your defeating him, you have yourself been beaten in the potlatch and your name and the name of your potlatch position covered in shame. The destruction of the copper is a means by which a symbol for computed wealth can be turned into "pure value," which itself has no symbol. It is simply glory.

The motivation of the individual Kwakiutl, then, was to get as many blankets as he could, to turn his blankets into coppers, and ultimately to destroy the coppers and turn it all into the purest value: reputation.

It was in the total destruction of the copper that the greatest misunderstanding between early European observers and the Kwakiutl is to be found. To the Europeans it was considered an utterly profitless and indeed a profligate act. Anthropologists did not recognize at this time that in the very destruction of copper, all of the debts were cleared. The debt structure that had been built up within a man's own tribe, as well as that between him and his rival, was destroyed by conversion. As Dr. Codere (1950) has put it, the Kwakiutl system, in order to exist, had to have and did have a way of destroying credit as profligate as its means of creating credit. Conversion provided such a means.

There are several other points that must be made in order fully to understand the institution of potlatch. The term "credit" is used, and used correctly, but the implications of the word are not the same as those to be found in a market-dominated economy. In a market-dominated economy, credit is initiated by the man who receives wealth to use or invest. In Kwakiutl economy, the debtor does not initiate the action—rather, it is the creditor who indemnifies the debtor. Indeed, the word indemnification might well be adopted to describe this sort of "credit," which is different in tone from the credit extended to Americans by a bank or a furniture store.

"Interest," although the word is properly used, also means something quite different in Kwakiutl economy than in capitalistic economy. In the latter, interest is the sum paid, in a market situation, for the use of the means of production or of money. In the Kwakiutl economy, "interest" is more than that: it is a reindemnification of a given partner in sparring for position. Indeed, the potlatch situation has elements of interest (the capital is repair with a price for its use) but it also has elements of "dividends" and investment. One is improving one's own social position by a constant investment in the other positions in the system of potlatch status. The interest/dividends are reinvested, along with the capital, until they are finally disengaged from the system, and turned to pure glory: something like (but also very different from) giving to a hospital a wing that will "eternally" bear one's name.

"Potlatching" of a sort goes on in American culture. One need only read the acid prose of Veblen, describing the cast-iron deer on the lawns of the Long Island estates at the turn of the century (and note, as Veblen might have done, their degeneration at mid-twentieth century into pink plaster flamingos on the lawns of prosperous artisans, whose houses are now also called "estates"). One need only read of the coming-out parties given by the wealthy for their daughters to realize that much wealth is expended on rank rather than invested. But a great deal of wealth—more and more, Americans like to think—is turned to philanthropy, to "social causes."

The important point is that there are two (or more) means of creating a unitary system from the disparate institutions of an economy. One, which leads to a "unitary economy," is by means of a general-purpose money used to evaluate everything exchanged, and used in all transactions and for all payments. The other is conversion—a more clumsy, but basically similar, device for disengaging the material and pseudomaterial items from one institution and getting them into another institution. The difference is that general purpose money breaks down the discreteness of the institutions, whereas conversion reaffirms their discreteness. Therefore, a different morality lies behind each. It is in the conflict of these two moralities that we can find the most searching revelation of each.

CONFLICT OF ECONOMIES

No more burning question has arisen in the mid-twentieth century than the impact of a homogeneous, monetized economy geared to "development" and "growth" of capital and product, on the multicentric, unmonetized economy geared to maintenance of subsistence and the aggrandizement (growth) of social prerogative. "Economic growth" has become, besides a specialty for economists, a football for politicians and an arguing point for what Americans traditionally call cracker-barrel philosophers, even after cracker barrels have disappeared before the onslaught of modern packaging. "Economic growth" is "a good thing"—and people who do not have it are said to be "underdeveloped."

It is, sometimes, not sufficiently realized that "economic growth" can occur only in association with specific types of social organization, and that an economic revolution must always be accompanied by a social revolution; or, rather, that it indeed *is* a social revolution. We shall examine briefly what happened when Tiv economy and Kwakiutl economy were brought under the dominating influence of a monetized, growing economy.

The acceptance of general-purpose money by the Tiv was accompanied by several other changes that cannot be kept separate from it; all of them are significant in understanding economic change. A general peace was imposed by the colonial administration. Before the arrival of the British, a Tiv did not venture far beyond the area of his kinsmen or friends; to do so was to court death or enslavement. With government police systems and safety, road building was also begun. Moving about the countryside was made both safe and easy. Thus, peace and the new road network led to both increased trade and a greater number of markets. Indeed, the economic institutions of the Tiv had been put in touch with world economy. Probably none of these factors, however, was as important in the economic change of the Tiv as was the introduction of general-purpose money.

General-purpose money provided a common denominator among all the various spheres and institution of the Tiv economy, thus making the commodities within each expressible in terms of a single standard and, hence, immediately exchangeable. This new money was misunderstood by Tiv. They used it as a standard of value in the subsistence category, even when—as was often the case—the exchange was direct barter. They used it as a means of payment of bridewealth under the new system, but still refused to admit that a woman had a "price" or could be valued in the same terms as food. At the same time, it became something formerly lacking in all save the prestige sphere of Tiv economy—a means of exchange. Tiv tried to categorize money with the other new imported goods and place them all in a fourth economic sphere, to be ranked morally below subsistence.

What in fact happened was that general-purpose money was introduced to Tivland, where formerly only special-purpose money had been known.

It is in the nature of general-purpose money that it standardizes the exchangeability value of every item to a common scale. It is precisely this function that brass rods, a "limited-purpose money" in the old system, did not perform. As we have seen, brass rods were used as a standard in some situations of conveyance in the intermediate or "prestige" category. They were also used as a means of payment (but specifically not as a standard) in some instances of conversion.

In this situation, the early administrative officers interpreted brass rods as "money," by which they meant a general-purpose money. It became a fairly easy process, in their view, to establish by fiat an exchange rate between brass rods and a new coinage, "withdraw" the rods, and hence "replace" one currency with another. The actual effect was to introduce a general-purpose currency in place of a limited-purpose money. By 1950, all conversions and most conveyances were made in terms of coinage. Yet Tiv constantly expressed their distrust of money. This fact, and another—that a single means of exchange had entered all the economic spheres—broke down the major distinctions among the spheres. Money created in Tivland a unicentric economy. Not only was the money a general-purpose money, but it applied to the full range of exchangeable goods.

Thus, when semiprofessional traders, using money, began trading in the foodstuffs marketed by women and formerly solely the province of women, the range of the market was very greatly increased and, hence, the price in Tiv markets came to be determined by supply and demand far distant from the local producer and consumer. Tiv reacted to this situation by saying that foreign traders "spoiled" their markets. The overlap of marketing and men's long-distance trade in staples also results in truckload after truckload of foodstuffs being exported from major markets. Food became less plentiful than in the past, even though more land was being farmed. Tiv elders deplored this situation and knew what was happening, but they did not know just where to fix the blame. In attempts to do something about it, they sometimes announced that no women should sell any food at all. But when their wives disobeyed them, men did not really feel that they were wrong to have done so. Tiv elders curse money. It is money, they said, that leads them to see their life's subsistence disappear as they produce more and more.

Of even greater concern to Tiv was the influence money has had on marriage institutions. Every woman's guardian, in accepting money as bridewealth, felt that he was converting down. Although attempts were made to spend money received in bridewealth to acquire brides for one's self and one's sons, it was most difficult to accomplish. The very nature of money makes this so. The good man still spent his bridewealth receipts for brides—but good men are not so numerous as is desirable. Tiv deplored the fact that they had to "sell" (*te*) their daughters and "buy" (*yam*) wives. There was no dignity in it since the possibility of making a bridewealth marriage into an exchange marriage has been removed.

With money, thus, the institutionalization of Tiv economy became unicentric, even though Tiv still saw it with multicentric values. The single sphere takes many of its characteristics from the market, so that the new situation can be considered a spread of the market. But throughout these changes in institutionalization, the basic Tiv value of maximization—converting one's wealth into the highest category, women and children—remained. And in this discrepancy between values and institutions, Tiv came upon what is to them a paradox, for all that Westerners understand it and are familiar with it. Today it is easy to sell subsistence goods for money to buy prestige articles and women, thereby aggrandizing one's self at a rapid rate. The food so sold is exported, decreasing the amount of subsistence goods available for consumption. On the other hand, the number of women is limited. The result is that bridewealth gets higher: rights in women have entered the market, and since the supply is fixed, the price of women has become inflated.

Because of the spread of the market and the introduction of general-purpose money, Tiv economy has become a part of the world economy, and profound changes have resulted in all the corners of Tiv culture. Tiv have had to revalue their motivations and their activities to correspond to a new reality—the market and the characteristics of general-purpose money.

The Kwakiutl experience was even more devastating because their economy and society were even further removed from the norms and principles of market and general-purpose money. The first impact, made by fur traders who came to the Pacific Northwest by sea, was to offer money in exchange for furs, and then to offer Hudson Bay blankets, as they were called, in exchange for money. The cedar-bark blankets, which had been a special-purpose money in the potlatching activities of the Kwakiutl, disappeared and were replaced by Hudson Bay blankets. For the first time, then, people began to concern themselves with money, and the whole subsistence sphere of life began, by means of the general-purpose money and the cotton blankets that were purchaseable with it, to permeate the potlatch institutions. Traditionally, subsistence and potlatch were separate—potlatchers gave feasts and sometimes made ostentatious exhibitions of destroying unneeded food, but food and the necessities for clothing and shelter did not enter into actual potlatching activities. With the goal of conversion in their minds, Kwakiutl saw a new way in which conversion could be carried out and even speeded up, advancing the day of glory. They did not know that it would also break down the system and reduce them to poverty.

A second factor was important—diseases, especially measles which was brought by the white men, and increases in tuberculosis and venereal diseases, cut the population to a fraction of what it had once been. The population was reduced to the point that the number of potlatch positions was almost equal to the adult men in the tribes. Therefore, everybody began potlatching whereas traditionally potlatching was limited to a comparatively few members of the society, each backed up by a number of tribesmen. Moreover, because of the influence of general-purpose money, all wealth, not just a few nonsubsistence items, began to emerge in potlatches. People began to give away their sustenance rather than their treasure. Again, the reason is obvious: general-purpose money, in league with other changes that accompanied it, created a situation in which a multicentric economy was made unicentric. Everything became exchangeable for everything else; disengagement of goods from one institution and their entry into another became simple. Money did it all. Without protection of activities that isolated or walled off the potlatch institutions from the other economic institutions, the staff of life was indeed "frittered away." It is small wonder that the Canadian government made potlatching illegal—Western economy had already made it ruinous.

THE NATURE OF "TRANSITION"

There has grown up as a result of the spread of the world economy, with its basic market orientation, a belief that "underdeveloped" countries have two economies: a "traditional" and a "modern" economy. It is blithely assumed that the end result of the "transition" between the two is known: that the economy of peoples undergoing this change will come to be exactly like that of Westerners. It is becoming increasingly obvious, however, that there is a point at which the "transition" ceases and a new type of economy begins, in which there are constantly warring factors, some taken from traditional values and some from the Western world. People are in the uncomfortable position of acting in accordance with their time-honored values and having the results emerge disastrous. Institutions have changed, and values and overt motivations are among the last elements to catch up with the change.

Throughout the world that was formerly marked by multicentric economies, pressure toward a unicentric economy emerges as the spread of the market. We have seen that allocation can be done on three (perhaps more) transactional principles: market, redistribution, and reciprocity. It often happens that all the principles may be used by a single society. The true "transitional" phase is the phase in which the institutions are changing and the dominance among the principles is being redetermined. The end result is not an economy such as that in the West; it is rather one in which the market (however it may be represented) plays a bigger role than it did in the traditional situation.

What changes, then, are required for the "growth" of an economy? First of all, the folk image must change in rhythm with the institutions if chaos is not to result. New types of motivation must be fostered. But there are also certain demands of the institutionalization; two will be considered here. General-purpose money brings standard of value into prominence—therefore, precise measurement devices must be introduced concomitantly with money. Institutions must be created, which allow wealth to be invested in production rather than disengaged and "converted" into social status and "pure value."

Systems of weights and measures are part of every economy. They are not always mathematically precise, and when they are not they must be understood in terms of rank rather than in terms of mathematics. The Ashanti weights are of particular interest. One of the best-known features of Ashanti culture is the gold weights that they cast in bronze for the purpose of weighing out gold dust in making certain specific kinds of payments. These weights are small *cire perdue* castings of geometric figures, or animal and human figurines, which illustrate a proverb or are merely decorative. They were necessary possessions of all chiefs and other important men. Although there is a relative ranking of weights, there is no "true weight" in the sense of the avoirdupois that we know connected with any of them. Different weights of the same name may weigh different amounts when measured in grams. What determines price in such a case—that is, what determines the amount of gold dust that must be given to make a purchase—is the rank of the man whose weights are actually used in the transaction. In a deal between the chief and an important commoner, the chief will have heavier weights than the commoner or will at least be in a position to demand that his own weights be used. The commoner can either consent to the arrangement or decline to make the transaction. Thus, as a man becomes more and more important, he can take heavier and heavier weights, thereby getting more actual gold dust in his exchanges than he gives.

This system is almost universal in the absence of a bureau of weights and standards such as that subscribed to by modern Western nations. Without such a set of recognized standards and measures, it is all but necessary to fall back on the hierarchy of the social organization to arrive at the measurements that indicate a fair price.

Not only do rich men get more for their wares when they are sold, but frequently it is also incumbent upon them to pay more for their necessities. In such a situation it is often possible to garner considerable prestige by paying more for an item than someone else could afford to pay.

With monetization and "modernization" of the economy, the weights and measures have to be standardized. Some peoples hold out against such standardization with real zeal, because their traditional modes of bargain hunting are imperiled by the system.

The greater problem is the necessity for creating institutions by means of which can be invested in production rather than converted into "noneconomic" spheres. A brief example could be discovered in Liberia as recently as 1960. In that year, because the banking facilities were inadequate, untold hundreds of thousands of dollars belonging to Liberian rubber farmers were put into American and Swiss banks at the same time that, within the country, a businessman could not borrow even modest sums of money for periods of more than a year or so. The institutions not merely discouraged "economic growth," but actually made it impossible. This situation has been changed, but there are many parts of the world in which the clash of economic institutions is such as to prevent the very "growth" that all peoples desire.

Economic "growth" results from specific types of institutionalization of man's "natural" desire to better his standard of living. It demands that investment be made more attractive than conversion to prestige items: that economic growth itself become a prestige item. Every people calls a halt to this process somewhere—a choice must be made. But, the choice is dependent in the long run on cultural values that go beyond mere economic prosperity, and on the presence of banking institutions that allow people to invest rather than to convert. The basic and fundamental idea of our own economists and politicians that we must invest is still countered with the basic and fundamental idea of our people that prestige (however defined) is worth spending money on. The anthropologist's task is to determine the balance between these factors struck by the various societies of the world.

In the last three chapters we have seen that man must exploit his environment in an organized manner—there is a specifically human set of "territorial" phenomena. There is another aspect of territoriality however, which is "dominance." Men must live together in a more or less orderly way even to be able to exploit the environment. Economy and polity can never be finally separated. And it is to political systems, the human forms of dominance, that we must now turn.

12 OF PERSONS AND THINGS: SOME REFLECTIONS ON AFRICAN SPHERES OF EXCHANGE

—CHARLES D. PIOT

This article returns to an old topic in the study of African societies—spheres of exchange—and suggests that they deserve fuller consideration than has been given them since Bohannan's analyses of the 1950s. In the particular case examined, however, that of the Kabre of northern Togo, it is suggested that analytical attention be focused on the relational implications of various exchanges rather than exclusively on the products exchanged and those products' placement into discrete spheres. This relational emphasis is consistent with recent analyses of gift societies which show that such societies value persons over things, continually converting the latter into relationships.

It is something of a puzzle that an idea as powerful and influential within anthropology as Bohannan's (1955; 1959) model of spheres of exchange, exemplified in his analysis of the economy of the Tiv of Nigeria, has been applied so rarely to other African societies. Other than Barth's (1967) somewhat different use of the model in his analysis of Darfur, and occasional elliptical references to the existence of exchange spheres elsewhere (Smith 1962: 312–13; Gray 1962: 481–9; Hill 1972: 211; Ferguson 1985: 653–5; Kopytoff 1986: 74; Shipton 1989: 63–4), I know of no comprehensive use of the model in Africa. By contrast, it has been employed extensively and productively outside of Africa, especially in Melanesia (Salisbury 1962; Meggitt 1971; Godelier 1978; Damon 1978; Rodman 1981; LiPuma 1981; Gregory 1982).[1]

One possible explanation for the model's absence from anthropological analyses of African societies, consistent with the explanation put forward by Bohannan to explain the collapse of Tiv exchange spheres, is that all over Africa such spheres simply disappeared when they came into contact with European currencies. In most cases, this would have occurred at a time—the 1920s and 30s—well before most African societies were studied by anthropologists. There are several reasons, however, why such an explanation is unconvincing. Even in societies influenced as early on or as heavily by Western penetration as the Tiv, it is hard to imagine that elders would have been unable to describe their spheres to anthropologists, as Tiv elders did to Bohannan in the 1950s (twenty-five years after Tiv spheres began to collapse). In addition, as Parry and Bloch (1989: 13–14) point out in a re-

From Man, Vol, 26, No. 3, September 1991, pp. 405-424. Reprinted by permission of the Royal Anthropological Institute.

cent discussion of Bohannan's model, the appearance of money can hardly be expected by itself to transform society and to eliminate exchange spheres. Many societies already had both exchange spheres and currencies (see, for example, Barth 1967: 155, Smith 1962: 312–13; Ferguson 1985: 653), with the latter posing no threat to the existence of the former. And today, many societies still exclude money from certain domains and spheres. Thus it is difficult to imagine that, had exchange spheres of the sort Bohannan described existed elsewhere in Africa, they would have disappeared so rapidly and so completely.

Another possible explanation is that exchange spheres are or were present in (at least some) other African societies but not in precisely the way Bohannan described them for the Tiv. My own data on exchange spheres among the Kabre (Kabiye) of northern Togo, West Africa, suggest that a slightly different set of understandings, consisting of relational rather than product spheres, is at work. In this article, I give a detailed description of the Kabre system of exchange spheres and of some of the implications of its analysis for understanding Kabre society more generally. I also attempt to show from ethnographic evidence that Kabre spheres are not an isolated case in Africa.

BOHANNAN'S MODEL

Bohannan's model of Tiv exchange spheres was a simple but powerful one. Its power derived in part from the fact that it reflected and crystallized comparative and analytical assumptions from a certain period in the history of anthropology—assumptions about the nature of the economy in non-Western societies, assumptions about the difference between Western capitalist societies and non-Western ones, and assumptions about the way in which the latter were being rapidly destroyed by the former. Many of these assumptions were incorporated into, and became a sort of platform for, the substantivist side of the 1960s debate in economic anthropology between substantivists and formalists.

Bohannan argued in two articles (1955; 1959; see also Bohannan 1963: 246–65; Bohannan & Bohannan 1968: 227–39) that Tiv divided exchangeable items into three ranked categories or 'spheres' within which they were exchangeable for one another but between which they were (usually) not. The lowest-ranking sphere consisted of subsistence products (food, pots, mortars, agricultural tools, and so on), the middle sphere included prestige items (cows, cloth, brass rods, slaves, medicine, magic, and ritual offices), and the top sphere comprised women who were exchanged between marriage-wards. Bohannan claimed that exchanges within each sphere—'conveyances'—were morally neutral while those between spheres—conversions—were morally-charged. It was desirable to convert 'up'—for example, to exchange food for prestige items and prestige items for women—but not to convert 'down'. Bohannan suggested that such downward conversions were rare and typically occurred when food was short.

An important feature of the argument, especially in the second article (Bohannan 1959), was that exchange spheres like these were highly vulnerable to the impact of colonial currencies. This seemed a logical inference to draw from the historical facts—the collapse of Tiv spheres had begun about the time of the introduction of Western money into Tivland in the 1920s. By the time of Bohannan's fieldwork in the early 1950s, Tiv were buying and selling virtually everything, including women, who were no longer exchanged for other women but were exchanged for money bridewealth. The explanation Bohannan put forward for this collapse was that money allowed the standardization of the value of all products to a common scale.

REACTIONS TO THE MODEL

As mentioned above, exchange spheres became one of the centre-pieces in the substantivists' debate with the formalists concerning the nature of the economy in non-Western societies. Exchange spheres seemed to offer clear proof of the substantivist claim that the economy and exchange were culturally-embedded. Since products were not all exchangeable for—that is, quantitatively commensurate with—one another, as they apparently are in the West (though see below), and since the use of currency (where it existed) was restricted, Western economic principles of market rationality, maximization, and so on, seemed inapplicable. Rather, the economy in non-Western societies seemed ordered by cultural principles and, therefore, required a social and contextual, rather than a strictly economic and universalist analysis (Polanyi 1968: 175–203; Bohannan & Dalton 1962: 3–7; Dalton 1968: 154, 156–68, 160–2; Sahlins 1972; 185–275, 277).

Formalists generally countered such arguments either by denying the existence of exchange spheres in the societies they studied (Schneider 1968: 426–35) or by emphasizing the permeability of spheres—the fact that conversions do occur (Barth 1967: 168–72; Joy 1967: 187; Burling 1968: 175; Leclair & Schneider 1968: 463–4). The argument here seemed to be that conversion implies a degree of commensurability (and, therefore, not so much distance between Western and non-Western economies),[2] and that 'converting up' represents a type of maximizing behaviour. In proposing the latter, however, formalists either committed themselves to the tautological assertion that any and all behaviour is a form of maximization (Cancian 1968; Donham 1985: 13) or opened themselves to the sort of social and institutional analysis demanded by substantivists (Donham 1985: 14). Even granting that Tiv are maximizing, the question still remains: what are they maximizing, and why?

In the 1970s, Africanist Marxists entered the larger debate between substantivists and formalists with specific criticisms of both sides' treatment of exchange spheres. Meillassoux (1972: 93–6) took the formalists to task for imposing Western individualist assumptions on non-Western economies and exchange systems. Along with Dupré and Rey (1973), and later Donham (1985), Meillassoux (1972: 96; 1973) also criticized the substantivists for ignoring the underlying role of production in systems of exchange, and proposed that power relations—in Africa, between elders and juniors and between men and women—were tied to, and may account for the existence of, spheres of exchange. Male elders, they suggested, were able through their control of the top-ranking exchange spheres (especially the marriage sphere), to restrict male juniors' and women's access to power, and simultaneously to reinforce the position of the latter as dependent producers.[3]

Despite certain analytical problems with this position—notably, the chicken and egg problem of whether male elders' power derived from their control of exchange spheres or whether their control of exchange spheres derived from their power—there were, as I see it, several virtues in the Marxist critique. It suggested, on the one hand, that the analysis of exchange spheres be placed into a larger social context—in this case, of productive and power relations. On the other hand, the issue was raised of motivation, of why such spheres should exist in the first place, an issue which substantivists had never specifically addressed.

Since the early 1970s, discussion of exchange spheres in the literature has been no more than intermittent. Much of this discussion has addressed issues that are important but somewhat peripheral to explaining the existence of such spheres. Certain Melanesianist commentators, for instance, have pointed out that, despite the incorporation of Melanesian societies into the larger world capitalist system, exchange spheres have not only survived but flourished (Gregory 1982: 166–209). Indeed, even in the Tiv case, as Parry and Bloch (1989: 13) point out, it is questionable whether the system of exchange spheres had collapsed as completely as Bohannan had suggested. Land, they point out, had not become a commodity, despite its increasing scarcity. Moreover, Bohannan tells us that although in the 1950s Tiv women were being exchanged for money bridewealth (instead of for other women), Tiv insisted that women did not have a price (Bohannan 1959: 500). By thus insisting on a conceptual separation between women and money, Tiv were still clearly adhering to a notion of spheres of exchange.

Parry and Bloch (1989: 13–14) also challenge Bohannan's claim that it was the mere appearance of money which brought about the erosion of Tiv exchange spheres, arguing instead that other political and economic factors more convincingly account for their apparent collapse. For instance, following the Pax Britannica and the opening up of Tiv markets to outsiders, Ibo traders descended on Tiv markets in search of agricultural produce, for which they paid cash, which Tiv needed to pay taxes. This created food shortages among the Tiv and drove up prices, thereby probably increasing the frequency of conversions which formerly had been relatively rare. This, in turn, would have threatened the relative impermeability of discrete spheres. In addition, in the 1920s British colonial administrators prohibited Tiv exchange marriage and thus abolished, by fiat, the top-ranking Tiv sphere of exchange.[4]

Two recent contributions return to issues closer to the heart of Bohannan's original model, proposing answers to the question of why discrete spheres exist to begin with in non-Western exchange systems. Kopytoff (1986: 71–2) suggests that the incommensurability of products may result from the differing amounts of labour expended in producing them and from the problems attendant upon trying to reduce types of products that are clearly different to a uniform scale. Thus, in the Tiv case, while it may be possible roughly to compute the labour that goes into producing different food items, thereby allowing them to be grouped into the same sphere and exchanged against one another, it would be much more difficult to compare labour inputs involved in producing items in the first, second, and third spheres. How, for example, could one compare the amount of time spent producing food with that spent on producing iron rods or, which would be even more difficult, with that spent on producing a woman? While this hypothesis is suggestive, there are nevertheless problems with its application to the Tiv case. For instance, it is just as hard to see how some of the items *within* spheres might be compared as it is to see how those between spheres could be. The second sphere groups together not just iron rods, cattle and cloth but also medicine, magic and ritual office. How can one compute the labour invested in producing magic, medicine and ritual office, so as to compare that to the labour involved in producing a cow?

In any case, we do not know whether Tiv in fact have a labour theory of value or not. As Turner (1989: 263–4) suggests, while a labour theory of value fits with the logic of capitalist production (where industrial capitalism demands the quantification of standardized social labour, of time, of profit, and so on), and with capitalist ideology more generally (in which there is a drive to reduce all differences to an underlying similarity), it is unlikely that non-capitalist production and exchange systems are similarly based. Indeed, the Tiv do not so much seem to be seeking to arrive at a uniform scale (and, as Kopytoff implies, settling on spheres after failing to find it), as they seem to be seeking to prevent such a scale from developing. Why, otherwise, when such 'equivalence' between spheres is found (as when rods are converted into women), do they still deny the equivalence?

Gudeman (1986: 110–28), in reanalysing data on the Gogo of East Africa, provides a more cultural interpretation for the presence of exchange spheres. He argues that the two Gogo spheres, of grain and cattle exchanges, remain separated because they represent two discrete, though complementary , cultural domains. These two domains derive from a set of oppositions (pastoralism/agriculture, male/female, ancestors/nature, and so on) at the heart of Gogo culture, which organize and reproduce social life. Gudeman's proposal has the merit of locating exchange spheres within indigenous conceptions and of tying them to the analysis of the larger social whole. The Gogo example, however, is not as complex as the Tiv one and we learn little from Gudeman's analysis of the internal logic (the theory of value, the social implications of different exchanges, and so on) operating within the different spheres.

As may be seen from this brief review, aside from Kopytoff's and Gudeman's contributions, there has not only been very little application of the model in Africa but also little further development of the original model itself. Why do spheres exist in the societies that possess them? What system of value governs exchanges within and between spheres? And how does such a system relate to the larger society? The analyses carried out thus far, for instance, leave us with the impression that exchange spheres represent little more than a curious cultural ordering of a particular domain of the economy, bearing little relation to, or interaction with, the larger society. Moreover, it is surprising, since we are concerned with societies which have repeatedly been characterized as valuing persons over things, and in which things are forever converted into relationships (Mauss 1967 [1925]; Sahlins 1972; Gregory 1982), that so little of the discussion surrounding exchange spheres in Africa has focused on the social relationships engendered through the exchanges of items included therein.[5]

In beginning to address some of these issues, I want to return to Bohannan's original model and to suggest that, if re-conceptualized, it can provide a helpful framework for analysis of Kabre material and, perhaps, of data on exchange from other African societies as well. I shall describe how Kabre exchange spheres, which bear an uncanny resemblance to Tiv spheres, exist not so much to group together exchangeable items as to identify, and to order hierarchically, certain types of exchange relationships. These relationships are indeed brought about through the exchange of particular products and persons that are associated with each sphere, but it is the relational implications of the exchanges which are paramount for Kabre. These, therefore, serve as the focus of the discussion which follows.

Before proceeding, I should address a point of epistemology. Deciding whether exchange spheres are present in a given society is not a simple empirical matter like, say, deciding whether its settlement pattern is dispersed, or whether its members practise animal husbandry. The anthropologist's claim that spheres exist is as much a product of the model used as it is of the data investigated. Differing assumptions may indeed lead to very different conclusions. For example, whereas Bohannan finds spheres among Tiv, applying the model developed by Barth (1967) to identify spheres in Darfur to the Tiv case would entail a denial of their existence. Since, for Barth, spheres of exchange are spheres of circulation, the fact that conversions occur would indicate that the Tiv have a single sphere. For Bohannan, on the other hand, what is crucial is that, despite conversions, Tiv deny value equivalence. Whatever the quantitative exchange ratio, brass rods and women are still seem as intrinsically different. Thus, by virtue of his model, Barth would deny the existence of spheres whereas Bohannan, taking his cue from indigenous categories of value, proclaims their existence.

The evolution in my own thought on Kabre spheres confirms the notion that one's model affects what one sees. While first in the field, I had Bohannan's model very much in mind. However, after spending much time looking for Kabre spheres of exchange, I decided that they did not exist—for Kabre products all appeared to be mutually exchangeable for one another. It was only much later, when I focused on the relational implications of various exchanges, and the contexts in which products were exchanged, that I was able to make sense of the data I was collecting. My ability to do so, of course, was directly related to my willingness to pay closer attention to indigenous categories.

THE KABRE

The Kabre, a Voltaic people, live in densely-packed settlements in a hilly region of northern Togo. They farm both cereals (sorghum and millet) and yams on steep, terraced fields. High population densities have produced a labour- and land-intensive system of continuous cultivation. Farming is strictly a male activity, and cooking and marketing are female ones. When small surpluses (from male farming or female marketing) are produced, they are usually converted into animals (sheep, goats or dogs), the Kabre form of wealth (*nyim*). Alternatively, and more commonly, animal wealth is obtained by borrowing a friend's female animal, tending it for several years, and keeping (some of) the offspring it produces.

Social organisation is patrilineal—though lineages ('houses') are extremely shallow, having a depth of only three to four generations—and post-marital residence is viri-neolocal. A man's preferred marriage partner is his FZD. Before getting married, a boy must perform 5–10 years of intermittent labour on his future father-in-law's fields, and must make small annual harvest prestations of his future mother-in-law. A newly married couple live with the groom's parents for from two to five years before moving out to build their own homestead in one of the husband's father's fields. At this point, the young couple constitutes a largely independent unit of production and consumption, with the man working the fields and the woman processing and cooking her husband's grains for consumption. With time, of course, they hope to give birth to many strong children who, until they marry, will help in the fields and at the homestead.

An indigenous logic linking persons and things underlies the Kabre domains of kinship and exchange, and conforms closely to that described by Gregory (1982) for 'gift' societies in general. For Kabre, it is through the production, exchange and consumption of things (food, gifts of food, and so on) that relationships among people are produced. This applies to parent-child relationships (parents are those who feed their children) as well as to relationships between non-kin (friendships are created by exchanging products). This particular indigenous understanding of converting things into persons—a process Gregory (1982: 29–35) describes as consumptive production[6]—plays a central role in the Kabre system of exchange spheres described below.

In spite of the fact that they produce no cash crops and very little surplus, Kabre do have a local, and very old, marketing system. Its principal function is to facilitate the circulation of female products among the women of different Kabre communities: cloth, pots, sauce ingredients—salt, palm oil, locust bean paste, baobab nuts—and so on. Kabre women are thus the major marketeers and the market is considered a female domain. Kabre men also go to market when they need to buy or sell animals, or to purchase various productive implements (hoe blades, baskets, etc.). A far more frequent reason, however, is to consume the beer and dog meat which is sold around the periphery of the market, and to talk with friends from their own and neighbouring communities.

The system of exchanges I discuss in this article, however, is very much separated from the market. While certain of its exchanges may occur in the marketplace—as for example when a man may buy his exchange partner some beer (see below)—these exchanges never directly involve money and are conceptually distanced from market exchange. For Kabre, market transactions, which always involve the purchase (*yapo*) of a product with money, engender no long-term relationships between transactors, while non-market exchanges, of the variety discussed below, do.

KABRE SPHERES OF EXCHANGE

Kabre exchange spheres, like those of Tiv, are associated with the exchange of particular types of products and persons—food in the lowest sphere, wealth in the second sphere, and women in the top sphere. The exchanges within each sphere have social consequences, however: they establish relationships between persons. As a relationship grows, it moves into successively higher spheres and becomes identified with different types of exchanges. This upward conversion is the goal of exchange partners and, if achieved, can produce a relationship of permanence between the two exchangers (and their houses). Kabre say of

Kabre exchange → to establish relationship

such a relationship that it 'cannot be broken' and, eventually, that the two houses have become 'one' or 'the same'.

The lowest-ranking sphere may be entered in many ways. One of these is through the direct exchange of products (*kolosoxo*). Two men[7] may exchange two chickens, or two fields, or seed yams for a chicken, because one is in need (he wants a chicken of a certain colour for a sacrifice, a field closer to his house, seed yams to plant) and asks the other to exchange with him. Such exchanges are frequent in Kabre communities and are often socially innocent, having no long-term relational implications.

Occasionally, however, an initial exchange like this will lead to a subsequent exchange. Typically, the second exchange involves a reversal in the roles of initiator and respondent: the initiator in the first exchange becomes the respondent in the second. The previous respondent may need a product that he is without and return to the person he helped out previously. The two may again exchange one product for another (of equal value), or the respondent may this time make an outright gift to his friend, telling him that he is 'just giving it to him' (*o hai kohao*).

In both cases—the exchange of two products or the outright gift—a debt and a hierarchical relation is established between the two transactors. The initiator—the one who had a 'need' (*soxolum*) and went to his friend to ask if they might work an exchange—is in the other's debt and must 'respect' him (*o hai nyamto*). He does so by responding when his friend has a need at some future time or, better yet, by anticipating his friend's request when he sees that he is in need and helping him out before being asked. When this future exchange (or gift) occurs, the hierarchical relation between the two is again reversed.

The theory of value underlying such exchanges is important and deserves elaboration. Despite the fact that Kabre are often exchanging identical products (a chicken for a chicken, a field for a field) or different products which have similar value (for example, in the standard exchange of 50 seed yams for a chicken, both items are said to be equivalent, *pa we wasaxa*), they nevertheless assert that exchanges of this sort are unequal. This is because the two transactors have differing needs. One has a serious need, causing him to ask his friend for help, while the other does not. In other words, it is the (unequal) needs of the transactors which create an unequal exchange of equal products.[8]

At the same time, however, the inequality remains concealed. It is not openly discussed at the time of the exchange—indeed Kabre assert at such times that the exchange is an equal one. Nevertheless, when questioned later, and in private, they readily admit that everyone knows—though never talks about the fact—that 'on the inside' the products are not equal, because the exchangers always have unequal needs. Indeed, it is the hidden inequality which is the more important, since it creates the hierarchies and debts which provoke future exchanges and, therefore, keep relationships going. The inequality remains hidden, however, so that if—as often occurs—the exchange goes nowhere, neither side need feel beholden to the other. When small exchange relationships like this, driven by alternating debt and hierarchy, persist through time, an *ikpanture*—a friendship—is formed.

Ikpanture is often initiated in other ways as well. It may begin at the house of a woman who has beer for sale, or in the marketplace, with one man buying and giving (*hao*) a calabash of beer to another. Weeks or months later, and ideally when the giver is 'in need', a return gift of beer is made. Alternatively, *ikpanture* may begin over one man's borrowing a product—an animal or a field—from another. Such borrowings (*sumloxo*) are extremely common. For example, every man in the community I lived in was *both* borrowing from, *and* lending fields to, others. While there is no obligation placed on the borrower of a field to return anything other than the field itself to the lender, when he has finished cultivating it he may, as a gift, decide to send the lender a pot of beer after each harvest. Such a gift not only ensures that the leader will not retract the field but may also lead to future exchanges (*kolosoxo*), or future beer gifts (*hao*) in the marketplace and, with time, may produce *ikpanture*.

Ikpanture begun in any one of these ways—through the simultaneous exchange of products, through gift and return-gift, or through the loan of an item—will probably also lead to any or all of the others. Men who exchange products and create *ikpanture*, for example, will start buying each other beer gifts in the marketplace and may loan fields and animals to one another. Similarly, those who begin with beer gifts will later exchange with, and borrow from, one another.

As this multiplying of exchange ties proceeds, the relationship may slowly build and, after several years, move into a second stage or sphere. (Of course, at any step along the

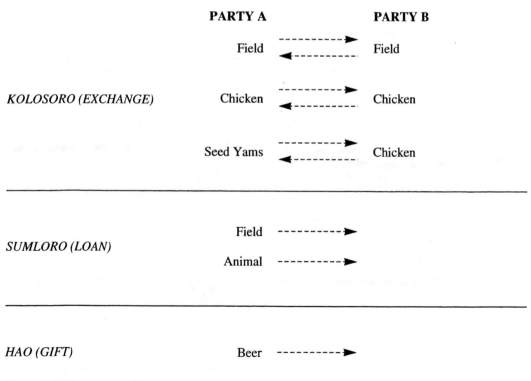

Figure 1. Different types of first sphere exchanges.

way it may, and frequently does, 'break' [*po yasa*]. Such breaks occur when, out of poverty or unwillingness, one partner no longer makes the return gifts that keep the relationship going.) The second phase in the relationship occurs when one of the partners invites ('calls') the other and his family to his homestead on one of the great holidays (*sinkaring, doxonto, cimoxo*). The host will have his wife brew a pot of beer—a small pot, since this is the first time—and kill a chicken which the two families consume together. The importance of such an invitation is indicated by the fact that the only other homesteads Kabre men will eat in, other than their own, are those of close kin.

This new phase marks several shifts in the relationship. Not only does it signify a deeper commitment to the continued growth of the relationship—a commitment symbolized through a shift from the exchange of food to the exchange of wealth items (animals)[9]—but also it brings together the entire families of the exchange partners for the first time. Kabre men say that this is important because they hope that later, when they themselves are old or dead, their children might 'carry' the *ikpanture* further. Better still, they add, it might project the relationship into a higher sphere, represented by a marriage between children of the two families (see below). This second phase is also the moment when an *ikpanture* 'goes public' for the first time, when other members of the community see that *ikpanture* exists between two partners. Since the invitation occurs on one of the great holidays, when members of the community promenade from one house to the next in search of beer, all may readily see who has been 'called' to another's homestead to eat and drink.[10]

The return invitation usually comes a year later, also on one of the great holidays, and typically involves an increase in the quantity and quality of drink and food served. Thus, a small pot of beer is replaced by a medium-sized pot, and a chicken by a guinea hen. The third time an invitation is made (again, by the original host) an even bigger pot of beer will be brewed and, perhaps, a goat or a dog killed. Finally, a large pot is served and a sheep may be killed. Each increment not only opens a new debt but also symbolizes the growing nature of the relationship. The *ikpanture* is said to be 'climbing' (*ikpanture kpa*); it is 'climbing strong' (*ikpanture kpa qung*).

Note here that exchanges within spheres, as in Bohannan's model, remain discrete. Once a relationship has moved into the second sphere, though first place exchanges will almost certainly continue between partners, they do not in any way cancel the obligation to invite one's partner to his homestead at some future time. Exchanges of wealth thus remain discrete from exchanges of food, beer, fields, and so on (and, if the relationship moves into the third sphere, from exchanges of women).

It is clearly more costly to maintain a relationship in the second stage than it was in the first, and many Kabre simply do not have the surplus animals to kill or the money to buy the grain for making beer. (Most Kabre men I talked to had between one and three partners in this stage, and all said that it would be too costly to have any more.) Hence there is a greater possibility that the relationship may founder, because several years may go by before a return invitation is made. At the same time, however, both parties have already invested much time and many products, and would like to see the relationship continue.

Thus, it is often the case that if one of the parties is unable to increase the scale of presta-
tion from its previous level, but still wants to continue the relationship, he will go to his
friend and tell him that he would like to kill a goat but can only afford a chicken. Usually,
since it is the intention of the donor that is paramount, the partner will accept and the relationship will continue. Another common outcome is that both parties agree to eliminate the
increment and exchange equivalent products each time—a medium sized pot of beer and a
dog.[11]

Many friendships remain at this second level indefinitely. Yet it is the aim of exchange
partners to move the relationship to a yet higher level. This may be accomplished by arranging a marriage between children of the two families. As informants pointed out to me,
these children are those who played together ('got to know one another') on the great holidays when their fathers were entertaining each other. If such a marriage between children
of exchange partners can be arranged, Kabre say, the *ikpanture* can 'no longer be broken'
(*pii yasuxe*). Not only have the years of gift-giving and accumulated good-will built something so solid that it is not easily shaken, but also the two houses now become tied together
through a series of obligatory affinal exchanges that endure for several generations.

Having reached this third, unbreakable stage of the relationship, it is everyone's desired goal, as it is among Tiv, that the two houses effect a return-marriage. However,
whereas the Tiv ideal is the exchange of women between two houses in the same generation (sister-exchange), Kabre say that it is better to wait until the second generation to effect the return (FZD marriage).[12] This is consistent with Kabre ideas of gift exchange, for
FZD marriage introduces a delay in the return, thereby temporally extending the relationship. But Kabre also say that sister-exchange leads too easily to a double divorce: if one of
the wives leaves, it is likely that the other will side with her brother (the departed wife's
spouse) and leave too. With FZD marriage, on the other hand, should the woman decide to
leave, she would be leaving her mother's natal house (and her own maternal grandparents'
house), a move which would be discouraged by everyone, including the mother.

Kabre see the two women as being exchanged for one another, for the second marriage
is described as a 'return' (*omula ogbiqi ro*, 'she has returned to her cooking-stool').[13] It is
therefore accurate to follow Bohannan's model in seeing both marriages as part of a third
sphere in which persons are exchanged (rather than, say, to see the first marriage as comprising a third sphere and the return as comprising a yet higher, fourth, sphere). Nevertheless, it is important to note that Kabre describe the relationship between two houses in very
different terms after the return marriage has occurred. They say now that the two houses
have become 'the same' or 'one' (*pa we korum*), by which they mean that they are like kin
to one another. They now share food on quotidian occasions, routinely help each other with
fieldwork, and share each other's secrets. This closeness is also reflected in how they describe one of the benefits of FZD marriage: having (unwillingly) given up his sister to another, a man now has back the next best thing, her daughter; it is almost as if, they say, the
sister had never left. FZD marriage also indicates, of course, that the relationship (*ikpanture*) has been passed to one's children, for it is the children who arrange the return.

Kabre also say of return (FZD) marriage that it turns a hierarchical relationship into an

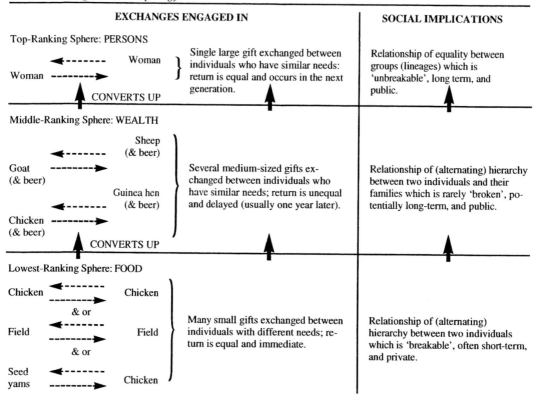

EXCHANGES ENGAGED IN

SOCIAL IMPLICATIONS

Top-Ranking Sphere: PERSONS

Single large gift exchanged between individuals who have similar needs: return is equal and occurs in the next generation.

Relationship of equality between groups (lineages) which is 'unbreakable', long term, and public.

CONVERTS UP

Middle-Ranking Sphere: WEALTH

Several medium-sized gifts exchanged between individuals who have similar needs; return is unequal and delayed (usually one year later).

Relationship of (alternating) hierarchy between two individuals and their families which is rarely 'broken', potentially long-term, and public.

CONVERTS UP

Lowest-Ranking Sphere: FOOD

Many small gifts exchanged between individuals with different needs; return is equal and immediate.

Relationship of (alternating) hierarchy between two individuals which is 'breakable', often short-term, and private.

Figure 2. Kabre spheres of exchange.

equal one. Since wife-giver is superior to wife-receiver, to let a full-fledged *ikpanture* lie with only one marriage between the houses is to leave them in an unbalanced, hierarchical relationship. But to effect a return is to bring them into a relationship of mutual or reciprocal hierarchy in which they are both beholden to one another at the same time.[14] Both houses now treat each other equally, with 'respect'.[15]

Thus, for Kabre, years of building *ikpanture* culminate in the creation of a relationship that is equal, unbreakable and enduring, and one that has transcended the exchanges of two individuals alone, involving now two houses and all their members.[16] Begun through the exchange of food gifts (seed yams, beer, fields), relationships grow, 'climb', and come to be associated with the exchange of wealth items (animals) and, finally, are made solid and enduring through the exchange of women. This move from things to persons which defines the trajectory of a relationship is also underwritten by a changing set of consumptive metaphors. Indeed at one level the whole system may be seen as being about people feeding one another—first from a distance and then close at hand. In the first sphere, potential partners exchange largely uncooked (or potential) food—seed yams, fields, beer—outside the home; in the second, they give each other cooked food inside the home; and, in the third sphere, they become 'one' (overcome all distance), by supplying each other with someone who actually does their cooking—Kabre explicitly define a marriage as bringing together a male cultivator and a female cook. If one of the goals of the system is to turn non-kin into kin, feeding is indeed an apt metaphor since kin among Kabre are defined as those who feed one another.

MOTIVATION AND CONTRADICTION

Two questions immediately arise from the analysis of Kabre exchange spheres in the light of some of the issues raised in earlier sections of this article. First, why are Kabre men investing so much of their wealth in this system of exchanges[17]—what motivates them? Secondly, what are the broader ramifications of the system for Kabre society as a whole? That is, what are the implications of such heavy investment of wealth in these relationships for other domains of Kabre social life? I can only comment briefly on these two issues, since an adequate exploration of each would require an essay in itself. But I hope to show that the analysis of exchange spheres needs to be carried out in terms of a much larger social field as well.

The answer to the first question—the issue of motivation—can at one level be answered by appealing to first principle: Kabre society is a 'gift' society (Gregory 1982) in which ultimate value is placed on relationships. The conversion of things into relationships is a first and unquestioned principle of social life.[18]

But this answer is not entirely adequate because it fails to account for the precise structure of the system of exchanges and for the particular cultural meanings given to it by Kabre. Whence, we might ask, comes this drive from uncertainty and impermanence to certainty and permanence? Why is there such a desire to convert non-kin into (almost) kin? And why does a return-marriage effect this transformation?

Briefly, the answer is that it is through this system that a Kabre man is able to achieve a certain sense of immortality, to produce something which endures beyond his lifetime, to inscribe his name in a lasting, more permanent, way in the social life of his community. *Ikpanture* and the making of two houses into one is not only passed to one's children but also remembered and talked about. At his funeral, the name of the man who was party to a fully-fledged *ikpanture* will be honoured and fêted in a way reserved only for those with major achievements in life. His name will also be spoken at the affinal exchanges between the houses for three generations and sung in the marketplaces and at rituals by house initiates undergoing their age-grade ceremonies.[19] Moreover a major *ikpanture* relationship that lives on affects and transforms social relations in the community in significant ways. In so doing, it writes or rewrites community history in terms of the achievements of particular individuals and the relationships they have built. It is for all these reasons that Kabre men invest so much in this system of exchange.

Turning now to the broader effects of Kabre spheres of exchange, the cost of the system is nevertheless high. Since Kabre have very little surplus, investment in this system of exchanges is also at the expense of investment elsewhere—especially in one's family and, particularly, in one's spouse. And this latter, the marital relationship, is a major source of conflict in Kabre society. The divorce rate is extremely high and the most frequent answers to my questions to divorced women regarding the reasons for their departures (it is almost exclusively women who leave their husbands rather than the other way around) were that their husbands had not given them enough food or that they had never bought them any new cloth. 'He spent money on others, outside the family (that is, on his exchange partners), but not on me', was a frequent refrain of divorced women. Indeed, it may readily be seen that a man is expected to spend, or convert into spending, on his wife the same types of things that he must spend on his *ikpanture* relationships with other men—food, money, grain and animals.

Given finite resources, however, he cannot readily do both. If, on the one hand, he spends on his wife (or wives) instead of his exchange partners, he forfeits the chance to produce something enduring. He is also liable to become the target of insulting jokes. One man I knew, for example, who had stopped going to market to drink with his friends and had instead 'become so close to his wife that he helps her bring water from the spring', was described to me as having become 'like a woman'. If, on the other hand, a man spends on his exchange partners, he risks alienating, and losing, his wife. And this, of course, means much more than just the loss of an individual. For it is through their wives that men create children and families, and thus, among other things, build the productive base which allows them to enter the world of exchange spheres to begin with.[20] Not to invest in one's wife is to neglect, and to fail to invest in, kinship. In this system, then, Kabre men are caught between two contradictory structures[21]—that of *ikpanture* and that of kinship (and, I might add, those of exchange and production). It is in this contradictory space that many Kabre histories—the histories of individuals, of marriages and even of communities—are created.

There is, however—and here we come back to the issue of motivation and to the Marxists' point about power—a potential resolution to this contradiction. If a man can arrange a marriage between houses which have *ikpanture* or, better still, if he is on the receiving end of a return (FZD) marriage, it becomes very difficult for his wife to leave. Since such a marriage has been built on something much stronger (that is, on years of smaller exchanges), his wife's family will exert enormous pressure on her to return to him if she tries to leave. Women told me, for instance, that they much preferred to marry into houses where there was no *ikpanture* and where they were not part of a return marriage because then, if they were maltreated and wished to leave, their fathers and brothers would be more inclined to side with them. This is not so when they marry into a house linked to theirs through *ikpanture*. They will almost certainly be sent back, for too much else is at stake.

For a man, then, to achieve a return marriage is to have his cake and eat it too, to resolve the contradiction of the system. But even if, through the coercion of their women, a problem in the social life of (some) Kabre men is resolved, that resolution is always an uneasy one. For even though a man's wife may be unable to leave, she will still resist any maltreatment and, through voicing her discontent, make life at the homestead a continual struggle.

CONCLUSION

The question remains whether systems of exchange spheres like that of the Kabre exist elsewhere in Africa. At least some evidence suggests that they do. Consider, for instance, the following account from Skinner (1989 [1964]: 24–5) on the Voltaic Mossi, close relatives of the Kabre:

> Most Mossi marriages were based on an exchange of women between two lineages linked by a long-term series of reciprocal exchanges of goods and services. Women were regarded as the most valuable part of this system. . . . When a man from one lineage 'made friends' with a member of another and rendered him a service or received a favour from him, their respective lineages were considered to be involved . . . . by accepting the woman as a wife for his lineage segment, the Boodkasma (lineage head) accepted the responsibility of giving a woman in return to the other lineage. . . . Since the older men of the various groups controlled the resources of their kinsmen, they usually initiated 'friendship' relations and obtained wives for their group.

Many of the Voltaic peoples of northern Togo—Konkomba, Naoudemba, Lamba— also have similar systems of return marriage built on years of smaller exchanges (Tait 1961: 215–16, on Konkomba; Tembe Assih-Aissah, personal communication, on Naoudemba and Lamba). Moreover, return marriage of the sort practised by Tiv, Mossi, and Kabre is extremely widespread in the savanna region of West Africa. The Lowiili (Goody 1967 [1956]: 48), the Samo (Héritier 1981: 73–136), the Bobo (Saul 1989: 59), and the Rukuba (Muller 1969; 1973), to mention only a few,[22] all practise one variety or another of return marriage between lineages (sister-exchange, FZD marriage, or longer term). It would seem quite possible, given the cultural proximity of these groups to Tiv, Mossi, and Kabre, that their marriage systems are also based on smaller exchanges and are part of a system of exchange spheres.[23]

If the Kabre case is at all representative, however, to show merely that other societies have exchange spheres is to miss the central, dynamic role such spheres play in the social life of these societies. As several commentators have suggested, though few have shown, the analysis of exchange spheres needs to be integrated into a much larger social context.[24] To do so—to place exchange spheres at the centre of analysis in the societies we study—might also retrieve them from the margins of anthropological theorizing about African societies more generally. In spite of the prominence exchange spheres received through Bohannan's essays, they have become little more than a footnote to the African ethnographic record. Perhaps if we broaden our notion of what exchange spheres are and what role they play, such spheres will become much more central to our understanding of African societies.

NOTES

Field research among the Kabre during 1982–84, and during the summers of 1985 and 1989, was supported by grants from the Social Science Research Council, the National Science Foundation, the Wenner-Gren Foundation, the Institute for Intercultural Studies, and the University of Virginia's Carter G. Woodson Institute. I wish also to thank the Togolese Ministère de l'Education National et de la Recherche Scientifique for granting research permission.

I am indebted to Fred Damon for much of the inspiration behind this article. I should also like to thank Anne Allison, Don Donham, Nancy Ehrenreich, Sharon Hutchinson, and Paul Shankman for their comments, and Tim Ingold, who provided a very perceptive set of editorial remarks.

1. Of course, exchange spheres were described for Melanesian (and Polynesian) societies much earlier than for African ones (Malinowski 1961 [1922]; Armstrong 1924; Firth 1967 [1939]). But it was not until Bohannan formalized the model in the African context that it received wide currency in anthropology. In several cases (Damon 1978; Gregory 1982), the more recent use of the model in Melanesia owes as much to Bohannan's formalization of it as to its Melanesian precursors.

2. Note, however, that even when converting up, Tiv deny the equivalence of the exchange (Bohannan 1959: 496–7).

3. See also Ferguson (1985) for a more recent, richly-textured, version of the same argument. He suggests that the southern African Sotho cultural prohibition on the sale of cattle derives from male elders' desire to maintain and reinforce their position of dominance in a hierarchy of gender relations.

4. A different issue raised in the literature challenges the antinomy between Western and non-Western societies built into Bohannan's original position. Polanyi (1957) and Bohannan and Dalton (1962) had argued that non-Western economies are 'multicentric' whereas Western ones are 'unicentric'. In the latter, money, 'one of the shatteringly simplifying ideas of all time', reduces the commodities to a common scale (Bohannan 1959: 503). In a recent essay, however, Kopytoff (1986) shows that we in the West in fact also have multiple spheres of exchange in which, for instance, persons, gifts, favours, family heirlooms, and so on, circulate within non-monetized exchange circuits. Of course, Marx (1977 [1867]) suggested long ago, with his celebrated discussion of commodity circulation, that there are exchange spheres at the heart of the capitalist economy itself. To argue, however, that capitalism also has exchange spheres is not to suggest that they are similar to those found in non-capitalist societies in any other than a formal sense. It would indeed be surprising if the uses or social implications of exchange spheres in non-Western societies were at all similar to those found in the West.

5. Nevertheless, around the edges of Bohannan's discussion of Tiv spheres, we catch glimpses of the importance of relationships within the Tiv scheme itself. For instance, those exchanges associated with the top two spheres—of prestige and marriage—have obvious relational implications. These implications are, however, never fully drawn out by Bohannan.

6. While employing Gregory's categories, I nevertheless recognize that, as several commentators have pointed out (Appadurai 1986: 11–13; Parry & Bloch 1989: 8–12), the contrast he develops between 'gift' and 'commodity' economies is perhaps too sharply drawn.

7. Similar exchanges and exchange relationships do occur between women, and between men and women. However, they are less frequent, typically last for a shorter period of time, rarely enter the second sphere of exchange, and never enter the third sphere (since it is only men who arrange marriages). The analysis that follows, therefore, focuses strictly on the more formalized exchange relationships between men.

8. Foster (1990), in a stimulating analysis which builds on work by Strathern (1984; 1987), suggests that in New Ireland the notion of difference is a prerequisite for exchange and underlies the indigenous theory of value. The same is true of the Kabre system of exchange: to create relationships through the exchange of identical products, Kabre individuals must differentiate themselves. They do so through this notion of differing needs.

9. Sharon Hutchinson perceptively pointed out to me that Nuer, among whom she conducted fieldwork, consider living animals to be 'wealth', but not cooked meat. Thus a gift of meat would be a 'food' gift. My

guess is that Kabre would make a similar distinction. However, I retain the term 'wealth' for this category of exchanges because not only is a gift of meat considered quite different from that of everyday food but also Kabre explicitly identified this sphere with wealth by claiming that an individual had to have animal wealth to enter it.

10. Even though some of the first sphere exchanges, such as buying beer for someone, are carried out in a public place (the marketplace, the homestead of a woman who sells beer), others who are present never know whether the beer given is, for example, a simple return for a favour, an attempt to overly indebt and humiliate an enemy, or a step towards *ikpanture*.

11. While conceptually, if not always in practice, unequal gifts (and debt) continue to move the relationship, many Kabre emphasized that these second sphere exchanges are not competitive (like, say, the potlatch). The goal of Kabre is to make a relationship, and to keep it going, not to break or outdo a partner.

12. In the Tiv case, if a same generation return (sister-exchange) cannot be arranged, lineage elders will attempt to make the return in the next generation (FZD marriage) (Bohannan & Bohannan 1953: 69–71). Kabre, too, admit several possible ways of fulfilling the return obligation. While the real FZD is the most desirable return, any classificatory house sister may be substituted if the real one marries elsewhere. And, if a second generation (FZD) return cannot be arranged, they may look to the next generation (FFZSD marriage) to effect the return. Every 'house' (lineage) in the community I lived in had from one to three return marriages (of one type or another) with other houses in the community.

13. Kabre insist that brideservice and harvest prestations are *not* exchanged for a woman in marriage. The field labour and harvest gifts are, rather, used to help 'feed' a woman, they say, so that when she is of age to marry she will be a strong worker and producer of children. Through thus feeding his wife—'producing' her—a husband gains rights over the children she bears.

14. While the two houses, and the relations between the original exchange partners, are considered 'equal', the relationship between son-in-law and father-in-law initiated by the return marriage nevertheless remains hierarchical.

15. While my data are incomplete on this issue, there appears to be a transformation in the theory of value operating in each of the three spheres. Whereas first sphere exchanges involve the exchange of equal products between persons with unequal needs, second sphere exchanges involve the precise opposite: unequal products exchanged between individuals who have equal needs (for the invitation to someone's house is not described as a response to a specific need). The third sphere, in turn, represents a transformation and negation of the theory of value operating in the first two spheres, since it involves the exchange of equal products between persons (houses) with equal needs.

1st Sphere	2nd Sphere	3rd Sphere
equal products	unequal products	equal products
unequal needs	equal needs	equal needs

The encompassing equality (of products and needs) of the third sphere is, of course, consistent with the equality which Kabre claim exists between two houses at this stage of the relationship.

16. All members of the two houses are now considered to have *ikpanture* with one another. Thus, they might ask one another for help in the fields, side with one another in disputes, and so on.

17. In addition to exchanging a large number of products they themselves have produced (beer made from their grain, animals), many of the men I surveyed in a year-long census of thirteen households spent half of their annual money income (obtained by selling tree crops and animals in the markets) on gifts for exchanging partners.

18. This has little to do, I believe, either with the social need to create ties in order to overcome the fragility of social relations (e.g., Tait 1961: 211, 217), or with the ecological need to create relationships that can be called on in times of food shortages (e.g., Gulliver 1955: 211–12). While these functions are, perhaps, also served by the Kabre system of exchanges, they cannot account for the system's complexity or its cultural elaboration (Sahlins 1976).

19. While the cultural importance of establishing (and remembering) an individual's 'name' is often remarked upon in the ethnographic literature on African societies (e.g., Evans-Pritchard 1956: 162–4; Middleton 1965: 82), its theoretical importance has not, perhaps, been adequately appreciated.

20. A gap in the present analysis is indicated here, consistent with the claim of Meillassoux, and other Marxist critics, that production underlies exchange. I cannot pursue this claim here, but should note that, while accepting its general validity, the Kabre case is slightly different from the cases described by Meillassoux and others. Contrary to what Meillassoux (1972; 1973) has suggested, Kabre elders control the production and dependency of juniors not so much through the bridewealth system (Kabre have a brideservice system) as through their age-grade system. Kabre fathers, for instance, are the ones who decide when to release their sons for initiation, a decision which fixes when they emerge (ten years later) to become relatively independent producers. By delaying a son's initiation, and by making sure that only one son at a time is initiated—a cultural rule which is strictly observed—a father can (and does) retain dependent labour in the household (see Piot [1988] for a fuller analysis of the relationship between Kabre production and age-grades).

21. I use 'contradiction' here in the Marxian sense, in which two related components of a social system are seen as being unable to 'progress together toward the goals inherent in their respective relations' because those goals are in conflict with one another (Ollman 1978 [1971]: 56–7).

22. See, for example, Muller (1980: 518–9) on the more than thirty different peoples of northern Nigeria who practise sister-exchange.

23. The exchange relationships described herein also bear certain similarities to what have been referred to as 'bond' friendships in the East African literature (see, for example, Gulliver 1955: 209–12; Carr 1977: 118–19). Such friendship relations are also described in West African ethnographies (Fortes 1949: 337; Tait 1961: 210–20), though they are not there typically referred to as 'bond' friendships. Discussion of such relationships, however, is never given the centrality I am suggesting they deserve.

24. In addition to those larger context addressed here, others are important as well, though they lie beyond the purview of the present article. For instance, the regional system of product exchanges and markets within which Kabre communities are located interdigitates with the exchanges described here, affecting them in complex ways. (See, for example, Piot [in press], where I have dealt with aspects of the marketing and regional systems.) I also have some evidence to suggest that the types of exchange relationships described here both multiplied and extended to people beyond the boundaries of individual communities during the period of forced labour (1925–1950).

REFERENCES

Appadurai, A. (ed.) 1986. *The social life of things: commodities in cultural perspective*. Cambridge: Univ. Press.

Armstrong, W.E. 1924. Rossel Island money: a unique monetary system. *Econ. J.* **34**, 423–9.

Barth, F. 1967. Economic spheres in Darfur. In *Themes in economic anthropology* (ed.) R. Firth. London: Tavistock.

Bohannan, L. & P. Bohannan 1953. *The Tiv of central Nigeria*. London: International African Institute.

Bohannan, P. 1955. Some principles of exchange and investment among the Tiv. *Am. Anthrop.* **57**, 60–70.

—1959. The impact of money on an African subsistence economy. *J. econ. Hist.* **19**, 491–503.

—1963. *Social anthropology*. New York: Holt, Rinehart & Winston.

—& L. Bohannan 1968. *Tiv economy*. Evanston: Northwestern Univ. Press.

Bohannan, P. & G. Dalton (eds) 1962. *Markets in Africa*. Evanston: Northwestern Univ. Press.

Burling, R. 1968. Maximization theories and the study of economic anthropology. In *Economic anthropology: readings in theory and analysis* (eds) E. Leclair & H. Schneider. New York: Holt, Rinehart & Winston.

Cancian, F. 1968. Maximization as norm, strategy, and theory: a comment on programmatic statements in economic anthropology. In *Economic anthropology: readings in theory and analysis* (eds) E. Leclair & H. Schneider. New York: Holt, Rinehart & Winston.

Carr, C. 1977. *Pastoralism in crisis: the Dasanetch and their Ethiopian lands*. Chicago: Dept. of Geography, Univ. of Chicago.

Dalton, G. 1968. Economic theory and primitive society. In *Economic anthropology: readings in theory and analysis* (eds) E. Leclair & H. Schneider. New York: Holt, Rinehart & Winston.

Damon, F. 1978. Modes of production and the circulation of value on the other side of the kula ring. Thesis, Princeton University.

Donham, D. 1985. *Work and power in Maale, Ethiopia*. Ann Arbor: UMI Research Press.

Dupré, G. & P.P. Rey 1973. Reflections on the pertinence of a theory of the history of exchange. *Econ. Soc.* **2**, 131–163.

Evans-Pritchard, E.E. 1956. *Nuer religion*. Oxford: Univ. Press.

Ferguson, J. 1985. The bovine mystique. *Man* (N.S.) **20**, 647–74.

Firth, R. 1967 [1939]. *Primitive Polynesian economy*. London: Routledge & Kegan Paul.

Fortes, M. 1949. *The web of kinship among the Tallensi*. Oxford: Univ. Press.

Foster, R. 1990. Value without equivalence: exchange and replacement in a Melanesian society. *Man* (N.S.) **25**, 54–69.

Godelier, M. 1978. 'Salt money' and the circulation of commodities among the Baruya of New Guinea. In M. Godelier: *Perspectives in marxist anthropology*. Cambridge: Univ. Press.

Goody, J. 1967 [1956]. *The social organization of the Lowiili*. Oxford: Univ. Press.

Gray, R.F. 1962. Economic exchange in a Sonjo village. In *Markets in Africa* (eds) P. Bohannan & G. Dalton. Evanston: Northwestern Univ. Press.

Gregory, C.A. 1982. *Gifts and commodities*. New York: Academic Press.

Gudeman, S. 1986. *Economics as culture: models and metaphors of livelihood*. London: Routledge & Kegan Paul.

Gulliver, P.H. 1955. *The family herds: a study of two pastoral tribes in East Africa, the Jie and Turkana.* London: Routledge & Kegan Paul.

Héritier, F. 1981. *L'exercise de la parenté*. Paris: Gallimard.

Hill, P. 1972. *Rural Hausa: a village and a setting*. Cambridge: Univ. Press.

Joy, L. 1967. An economic homologue of Barth's presentation of economic spheres in Darfur. In *Themes in economic anthropology* (ed.) R. Firth. London: Tavistock.

Kopytoff, I. 1986. The cultural biography of things: commoditization as process. In *The social life of things* (ed.) A. Appadurai. Cambridge: Univ. Press.

Leclair, E. & H. Schneider (eds) 1968. *Economic anthropology: readings in theory and analysis*. New York: Holt, Rinehart & Winston.

LiPuma, E. 1981. Cosmology and economy among the Maring of Papua New Guinea. *Oceania* **61**, 266–85.

Malinowski, B. 1961 [1922]. *Argonauts of the Western Pacific*. New York: Dutton.

Marx, K. 1977 [1867]. *Capital*, Vol. 1. New York: Vintage.

Mauss, M. 1967 [1925]. *The gift*. New York: Norton.

Meggitt, M. 1971. From tribesmen to peasants: the case of the Mae-Enga of New Guinea. In *Anthropology in Oceania: essays presented to Ian Hogbin* (eds) L.R. Hiatt & C. Jayawardena. Sydney: Angus & Robertson.

Meillassoux, C. 1972. From reproduction to production: a marxist approach to economic anthropology. *Econ. Soc.* **1**, 93–103.

—1973. The social organisation of the peasantry: the economic basis of kinship. *J. Peasant Stud.* **1**, 81–90.

Middleton, J. 1965. *The Lugbara of Uganda*. New York: Holt, Rinehart & Winston.

Muller, J.C. 1969. Preferential marriage among the Rukuba of Benue-Plateau State, Nigeria. *Am. Anthrop.* **71**, 1057–61.

—1973. On preferential/prescriptive marriage and the function of kinship systems: the Rukuba case. *Am. Anthrop.* **75**, 1563–76.

—1980. Straight sister-exchange and the transition from elementary to complex structures. *Am. Ethnol.* **7**, 518–29.

Ollman, B. 1978 [1971]. *Alienation*. Cambridge: Univ. Press.

Parry, J. & M. Bloch (eds) 1989. *Money and the morality of exchange*. Cambridge: Univ. Press.

Piot, C. 1988. Fathers and sons: domestic production, conflict and social forms among the Kabre. In *Research in economic anthropology*, vol. **10** (ed.) B. Isaac. Greenwich: JAI Press.

—in press. Wealth production, ritual consumption and center/periphery relations in a West African regional system. *Am. Ethnol.*

Polanyi, K. 1957. Aristotle discovers the economy. In *Trade and market in the early empires* (eds) K. Polanyi *et al.* Glencoe: Free Press.

—1968. *Primitive, archaic, and modern economies* (ed.) G. Dalton. Boston: Beacon Press.

Rodman, M. 1981. A boundary and a bridge: women's pig killing as a border-crossing between spheres of exchange in East Aoba. In *Vanuatu: politics, economics and ritual in island Melanesia* (ed.) M. Allen. New York: Academic Press.

Sahlins, M. 1972. *Stone age economics*. Chicago: Aldine.

—1976. *Culture and practical reason*. Chicago: Univ. Press.

Salisbury, R.F. 1962. *From stone to steel*. London: Cambridge Univ. Press.

Saul, M. 1989. Corporate authority, exchange, and personal opposition in Bobo marriages. *Am. Ethnol.* **16**, 57–74.

Schneider, H. 1968. Economics in East African aboriginal societies. In *Economic anthropology: readings in theory and analysis* (eds) E. Leclair & H. Schneider. New York: Holt, Rinehart & Winston.

Shipton, P. 1989. *Bitter money: cultural economy and some African meanings of forbidden commodities*. Washington: American Anthropological Association.

Skinner, E. 1989 [1964]. *The Mossi of Burkina Faso: chiefs, politicians and soldiers*. Prospect Heights, Ill: Waveland.

Smith, M.G. 1962. Exchange and marketing among the Hausa. In *Markets in Africa* (eds) P. Bohannan & G. Dalton. Evanston: Northwestern Univ. Press.

Strathern, M. 1984. Marriage exchanges: a Melanesian comment. *Ann. Rev. Anthrop.* **13**, 41–73.

—1987. Conclusion. In *Dealing with inequality: analysing gender relations in Melanesia and beyond* (ed.) M. Strathern. Cambridge: Univ. Press.

Tait, D. 1961. *The Konkomba of northern Ghana* (ed.) J. Goody. London: Oxford Univ. Press.

Turner, T. 1989. A commentary (on T.O. Beidelman, agonistic exchange, Homeric reciprocity and the heritage of Simmel and Mauss). *Cult. Anthrop.* **4**, 260–4.

13 THE CULTURE OF POVERTY

—OSCAR LEWIS

Poverty and the so-called war against it provide a principal theme for the domestic program of the present Administration. In the midst of a population that enjoys unexampled material well-being—with the average annual family income exceeding $7,000—it is officially acknowledged that some 18 million families, numbering more than 50 million individuals, live below the $3,000 "poverty line." Toward the improvement of the lot of these people some $1,600 million of Federal funds are directly allocated through the Office of Economic Opportunity, and many hundreds of millions of additional dollars flow indirectly through expanded Federal expenditures in the fields of health, education, welfare and urban affairs.

Along with the increase in activity on behalf of the poor indicated by these figures there has come a parallel expansion of publication in the social sciences on the subject of poverty. The new writings advance the same two opposed evaluations of the poor that are to be found in literature, in proverbs and in popular sayings throughout recorded history. Just as the poor have been pronounced blessed, virtuous, upright, serene, independent, honest, and happy, so contemporary students stress their great and neglected capacity for self-help, leadership and community organization. Conversely, as the poor have been characterized as shiftless, mean, sordid, violent, evil and criminal, so other students point to the irreversibly destructive effects of poverty on individual character and emphasize the corresponding need to keep guidance and control of poverty projects in the hands of duly constituted authorities. This clash of viewpoints reflects in part the in fighting for political control of the program between Federal and local officials. The confusion results also from the tendency to focus study and attention on the personality of the individual victim of poverty rather than on the slum community and family and from the consequent failure to distinguish between poverty and what I have called the culture of poverty.

The phrase is a catchy one and is used and misused with some frequency in the current literature. In my writings it is the label for a specific conceptual model that describes in positive terms a subculture of Western society with its own structure and rationale, a way of life handed on from generation to generation along family lines. The culture of poverty

SOURCE: Oscar Lewis, *La Vida* (*New York: Random House, 1966*). Copyright © 1965, 1966 by Oscar Lewis. Reprinted by permission of Random House, Inc. This article originally appeared in *Scientific American* 215, no. 4, October 1966: 19–25.

Reprinted by permission of Harold Ober Associates Incorporated. Copyright © 1966 by Oscar Lewis.

is not just a matter of deprivation or disorganization, a term signifying the absence of something. It is a culture in the traditional anthropological sense in that it provides human beings with a design for living, with a ready-made set of solutions for human problems, and so serves a significant adaptive function. This style of life transcends national boundaries and regional and rural-urban differences within nations. Wherever it occurs, its practitioners exhibit remarkable similarity in the structure of their families, in interpersonal relations, in spending habits, in their value systems and in their orientation in time.

Not nearly enough is known about this important complex of human behavior. My own concept of it has evolved as my work has progressed and remains subject to amendment by my own further work and that of others. The scarcity of literature on the culture of poverty is a measure of the gap in communication that exists between the very poor and the middle-class personnel—social scientists, social workers, teachers, physicians, priests and others—who bear the major responsibility for carrying out the antipoverty programs. Much of the behavior accepted in the culture of poverty goes counter to cherished ideals of the larger society. In writing about "multiproblem" families social scientists thus often stress their instability, their lack of order, direction and organization. Yet, as I have observed them, their behavior seems clearly patterned and reasonably predictable. I am more often struck by the inexorable repetitiousness and the iron entrenchment of their lifeways.

The concept of the culture of poverty may help to correct misapprehensions that have ascribed some behavior patterns of ethnic, national or regional groups as distinctive characteristics. For example, a high incidence of common-law marriage and of households headed by women has been thought to be distinctive of Negro family life in this country and has been attributed to the Negro's historical experience of slavery. In actuality it turns out that such households express essential traits of the culture of poverty and are found among diverse peoples in many parts of the world and among peoples that have had no history of slavery. Although it is now possible to assert such generalizations, there is still much to be learned about this difficult and affecting subject. The absence of intensive anthropological studies of poor families in a wide variety of national contexts—particularly the lack of such studies in socialist countries—remains a serious handicap to the formulation of dependable cross-cultural constants of the culture of poverty.

My studies of poverty and family life have centered largely in Mexico. On occasion some of my Mexican friends have suggested delicately that I turn to a study of poverty in my own country. As a first step in this direction I am currently engaged in a study of Puerto Rican families. Over the past three years my staff and I have been assembling data on 100 representative families in four slums of Greater San Juan and some 50 families of their relatives in New York City.

Our methods combine the traditional techniques of sociology, anthropology and psychology. This includes a battery of 19 questionnaires, the administration of which requires 12 hours per informant. They cover the residence and employment history of each adult; family relations; income and expenditures; complete inventory of household and personal possessions; friendship patterns, particularly the *compadrazgo*, or godparent, relationship that serves as a kind of informal social security for the children of these families and establishes special obligations among the adults; recreational patterns; health and medical history; politics; religion; world view and "cosmopolitanism." Open-end interviews and psychological tests (such as the thematic apperception test, the Rorschach test and the sentence-completion test) are administered to a sampling of this population.

All this work serves to establish the context for close-range study of a selected few families. Because the family is a small social system, it lends itself to the holistic approach of anthropology. Whole-family studies bridge the gap between the conceptual extremes of the culture at one pole and of the individual at the other, making possible observation of both culture and personality as they are interrelated in real life. In a large metropolis such as San Juan or New York the family is the natural unit of study.

Ideally our objective is the naturalistic observation of the life of "our" families, with a minimum of intervention. Such intensive study, however, necessarily involves the establishment of deep personal ties. My assistants include two Mexicans whose families I had studied; their "Mexican's-eye view" of the Puerto Rican slum has helped to point up the similarities and differences between the Mexican and Puerto Rican subcultures. We have spent many hours attending family parties, wakes and baptisms, responding to emergency calls, taking people to the hospital, getting them out of jail, filling out applications for them, hunting apartments with them, helping them to get jobs or to get on relief. With each member of these families we conduct tape-recorded interviews, taking down their life stories and their answers to questions on a wide variety of topics. For the ordering of our material we undertake to reconstruct, by close interrogation, the history of a week or more of consecutive days in the lives of each family, and we observe and record complete days as they unfold. The first volume to issue from this study is to be published next month under the title of *La Vida, a Puerto Rican Family in the Culture of Poverty—San Juan and New York* (Random House).

There are many poor people in the world. Indeed, the poverty of the two-thirds of the world's population who live in the underdeveloped countries has been rightly called "the problem of problems." But not all of them by any means live in the culture of poverty. For this way of life to come into being and flourish it seems clear that certain preconditions must be met.

The setting is a cash economy, with wage labor and production for profit and with a persistently high rate of unemployment and underemployment, at low wages, for unskilled labor. The society fails to provide social, political and economic organization, on either a voluntary basis or by government imposition, for the low-income population. There is a bilateral kinship system centered on the nuclear progenitive family, as distinguished from the unilateral extended kinship system of lineage and clan. The dominant class asserts a set of values that prizes thrift and the accumulation of wealth and property, stresses the possibility of upward mobility and explains low economic status as the result of individual personal inadequacy and inferiority.

Where these conditions prevail the way of life that develops among some of the poor is the culture of poverty. That is why I have described it as a subculture of the Western social order. It is both an adaptation and a reaction of the poor to their marginal position in a class-stratified, highly individuated, capitalistic society. It represents an effort to cope with feelings of hopelessness and despair that arise from the realization by the members of the marginal communities in these societies of the improbability of their achieving success in terms of the prevailing values and goals. Many of the traits of the culture of poverty can be viewed as local, spontaneous attempts to meet needs not served in the case of the poor by the institutions and agencies of the larger society because the poor are not eligible for such service, cannot afford it or are ignorant and suspicious.

Once the culture of poverty has come into existence it tends to perpetuate itself. By the time slum children are six or seven they have usually absorbed the basic attitudes and values of their subculture. Thereafter they are psychologically unready to take full advantage of changing conditions or improving opportunities that may develop in their lifetime.

My studies have identified some 70 traits that characterize the culture of poverty. The principal ones may be described in four dimensions of the system: the relationship between the subculture and the larger society; the nature of the slum community; the nature of the family, and the attitudes, values and character structure of the individual.

The disengagement, the nonintegration, of the poor with respect to the major institutions of society is a crucial element in the culture of poverty. It reflects the combined effect of a variety of factors including poverty, to begin with, but also segregation and discrimination, fear, suspicion and apathy and the development of alternative institutions and procedures in the slum community. The people do not belong to labor unions or political parties and make little use of banks, hospitals, department stores or museums. Such involvement as there is in the institutions of the larger society—in the jails, the army and the public welfare system—does little to suppress the traits of the culture of poverty. A relief system that barely keeps people alive perpetuates rather than eliminates poverty and the pervading sense of hopelessness.

People in a culture of poverty produce little wealth and receive little in return. Chronic unemployment and underemployment, low wages, lack of property, lack of savings, absence of food reserves in the home and chronic shortage of cash imprison the family and the individual in a vicious circle. Thus for lack of cash the slum householder makes frequent purchases of small quantities of food at higher prices. The slum economy turns inward; it shows a high incidence of pawning of personal goods, borrowing at usurious rates of interest, informal credit arrangements among neighbors, use of secondhand clothing and furniture.

There is awareness of middle-class values. People talk about them and even claim some of them as their own. On the whole, however, they do not live by them. They will declare that marriage by law, by the church or by both is the ideal form of marriage, but few will marry. For men who have no steady jobs, no property and no prospect of wealth to pass on to their children, who live in the present without expectations of the future, who want to avoid the expense and legal difficulties involved in marriage and divorce, a free union or consensual marriage makes good sense. The women, for their part, will turn down offers of marriage from men who are likely to be immature, punishing and generally unreliable. They feel that a consensual union gives them some of the freedom and flexibility men have. By not giving the fathers of their children legal status as husbands, the women have a stronger claim on the children. They also maintain exclusive rights to their own property.

Along with disengagement from the larger society, there is a hostility to the basic institutions of what are regarded as the dominant classes. There is hatred of the police, mistrust of government and of those in high positions and a cynicism that extends to the church. The culture of poverty thus holds a certain potential for protest and for entertainment in political movements aimed against the existing order.

With its poor housing and overcrowding, the community of the culture of poverty is high in gregariousness, but it has a minimum of organization beyond the nuclear and extended family. Occasionally slum dwellers come together in temporary informal groupings; neighborhood gangs that cut across slum settlements represent a considerable advance beyond the zero point of the continuum I have in mind. It is the low level of organization that gives the culture of poverty its marginal and anomalous quality in our highly organized society. Most primitive peoples have achieved a higher degree of sociocultural organization than contemporary urban slum dwellers. This is not to say that there may not be a sense of community and *esprit de corps* in a slum neighborhood. In fact, where slums are isolated from their surroundings by enclosing walls or other physical barriers, where rents are low and residence is stable and where the population constitutes a distinct, ethnic, racial or language group, the sense of community may approach that of a village. In Mexico City and San Juan such territoriality is engendered by the scarcity of low-cost housing outside of established slum areas. In South Africa it is actively enforced by the *apartheid* that confines rural migrants to prescribed locations.

The family in the culture of poverty does not cherish childhood as a specially prolonged and protected stage in the life cycle. Initiation into sex comes early. With the instability of consensual marriage the family tends to be mother-centered and tied more closely to the mother's extended family. The female head of the house is given to authoritarian rule. In spite of much verbal emphasis on family solidarity, sibling rivalry for the limited supply of goods and maternal affection is intense. There is little privacy.

The individual who grows up in this culture has a strong feeling of fatalism, helplessness, dependence and inferiority. These traits, so often remarked in the current literature as characteristic of the American Negro, I found equally strong in slum dwellers of Mexico City and San Juan, who are not segregated or discriminated against as a distinct ethnic or racial group. Other traits include a high incidence of weak ego structure, orality and confusion of sexual identification, all reflecting maternal deprivation; a strong present-time orientation with relatively little disposition to defer gratification and plan for the future, and a high tolerance for psychological pathology of all kinds. There is widespread belief in male superiority and among the men a strong preoccupation with *machismo,* their masculinity.

Provincial and local in outlook, with little sense of history, these people know only their own neighborhood and their own way of life. Usually they do not have the knowledge, the vision or the ideology to see the similarities between their troubles and those of their counterparts elsewhere in the world. They are not class-conscious, although they are sensitive indeed to symbols of status.

The distinction between poverty and the culture of poverty is basic to the model described here. There are numerous examples of poor people whose way of life I would not characterize as belonging to this subculture. Many primitive and preliterate peoples that have been studied by anthropologists suffer dire poverty attributable to low technology or thin resources or both. Yet even the simplest of these peoples have a high degree of social organization and a relatively integrated, satisfying and self-sufficient culture.

In India the destitute lower-caste peoples—such as the Chamars, the leather workers, and the Bhangis, the sweepers—remain integrated in the larger society and have their own panchayat institutions of self-government. Their panchayats and either extended unilateral kinship systems, or clans, cut across village lines, giving them a strong sense of identity and continuity. In my studies of these peoples I found no culture of poverty to go with their poverty.

The Jews of eastern Europe were a poor urban people, often confined to ghettos. Yet they did not have many traits of the culture of poverty. They had a tradition of literacy that placed great value on learning; they formed many voluntary associations and adhered with devotion to the central community organization around the rabbi, and they had a religion that taught them they were the chosen people.

I would cite also a fourth, somewhat speculative example of poverty dissociated from the culture of poverty. On the basis of limited direct observation in one country—Cuba—and from indirect evidence, I am inclined to believe the culture of poverty does not exist in socialist countries. In 1947 I undertook a study of a slum in Havana. Recently I had an opportunity to revisit the same slum and some of the same families. The physical aspect of the place had changed little, except for a beautiful new nursery school. The people were as poor as before, but I was impressed to find much less of the feelings of despair and apathy, so symptomatic of the culture of poverty in the urban slums of the U.S. The slum was now highly organized, with block committees, educational committees, party committees. The people had found a new sense of power and importance in a doctrine that glorified the lower class as the hope of humanity, and they were armed. I was told by one Cuban official that the Castro government had practically eliminated delinquency by giving arms to the delinquents!

Evidently the Castro regime—revising Marx and Engels—did not write off the so-called *lumpenproletariat* as an inherently reactionary and anti-revolutionary force but rather found in them a revolutionary potential and utilized it. Frantz Fanon, in his book *The Wretched of the Earth,* makes a similar evaluation of their role in the Algerian revolution: "It is within this mass of humanity, this people of the shantytowns, at the core of the *lumpenproletariat,* that the rebellion will find its urban spearhead. For the *lumpenproletariat,* that horde of starving men, uprooted from their tribe and from their clan, constitutes one of the most spontaneous and most radically revolutionary forces of a colonized people."

It is true that I have found little revolutionary spirit or radical ideology among low-income Puerto Ricans. Most of the families I studied were politically conservative, about half of them favoring the Statehood Republican Party, which provides opposition on the right to the Popular Democratic Party that dominates the politics of the commonwealth. It seems to me, therefore, that disposition for protest among people living in the culture of poverty will vary considerably according to the national context and historical circumstances. In contrast to Algeria, the independence movement in Puerto Rico has found little popular support. In Mexico, where the cause of independence carried long ago, there is no longer any such movement to stir the dwellers in the new and old slums of the capital city.

Yet it would seem that any movement—be it religious, pacifist or revolutionary—that organizes and gives hope to the poor and effectively promotes a sense of solidarity with larger groups must effectively destroy the psychological and social core of the culture of poverty. In this connection, I suspect that the civil rights movement among American Negroes has of itself done more to improve their self-image and self-respect than such economic gains as it has won although, without doubt, the two kinds of progress are mutually reinforcing. In the culture of poverty of the American Negro the additional disadvantage of racial discrimination has generated a potential for revolutionary protest and organization that is absent in the slums of San Juan and Mexico City and, for that matter, among the poor whites in the South.

If it is true, as I suspect, that the culture of poverty flourishes and is endemic to the free-enterprise, pre-welfare-state of capitalism, then it is also endemic in colonial societies. The most likely candidates for the culture of poverty would be the people who come from the lower strata of a rapidly changing society and who are already partially alienated from it. Accordingly the subculture is likely to be found where imperial conquest has smashed the native social and economic structure and held the natives, perhaps for generations, in servile status, or where feudalism is yielding to capitalism in the later evolution of a colonial economy. Landless rural workers who migrate to the cities, as in Latin America, can be expected to fall into this way of life more readily than migrants from stable peasant villages with a well-organized traditional culture, as in India. It remains to be seen, however, whether the culture of poverty has not already begun to develop in the slums of Bombay and Calcutta. Compared with Latin America also, the strong corporate nature of many African tribal societies may tend to inhibit or delay the formation of a full-blown culture of poverty in the new towns and cities of that continent. In South Africa the institutionalization of repression and discrimination under *apartheid* may also have begun to promote an immunizing sense of identity and group consciousness among the African Negroes.

One must therefore keep the dynamic aspects of human institutions forward in observing and assessing the evidence for the presence, the waxing or the waning of this subculture. Measured on the dimension of relationship to the larger society, some slum dwellers may have a warmer identification with their national tradition even though they suffer deeper poverty than members of a similar community in another country. In Mexico City a high percentage of our respondents, including those with little or no formal schooling, knew of Cuauhtémoc Hidalgo, Father Morelos, Juárez, Díaz, Zapata, Carranza and Cardenas. In San Juan the names of Rámon Power, José de Diego, Baldorioty de Castro, Rámon Betances, Nemesio Canales, Lloréns Torres rang no bell; a few could tell about the late Albizu Campos. For the lower income Puerto Rican, however, history begins with Muñoz Rivera and ends with his son Muñoz Marin.

The national context can make a big difference in the play of the crucial traits of fatalism and hopelessness. Given the advanced technology, the high level of literacy, the all-pervasive reach of the media of mass communications and the relatively high aspirations of all sectors of the population, even the poorest and most marginal communities of the U.S. must aspire to a larger future than the slum dwellers of Ecuador and Peru, where the actual possibilities are more limited and where an authoritarian social order persists in city and country. Among the 50 million U.S. citizens now more or less officially certified as poor, I would guess that about 20 percent live in a culture of poverty. The largest numbers in this group are made up of Negroes, Puerto Ricans, Mexicans, American Indians and Southern poor whites. In these figures there is some reassurance for those concerned, because it is much more difficult to undo the culture of poverty than to cure poverty itself.

Middle-class people—this would certainly include most social scientists—tend to concentrate on the negative aspects of the culture of poverty. They attach a minus sign to such traits as present-time orientation and readiness to indulge impulses. I do not intend to idealize or romanticize the culture of poverty—"it is easier to praise poverty than to live in it." Yet the positive aspects of these traits must not be overlooked. Living in the present may develop a capacity for spontaneity, for the enjoyment of the sensual, which is often blunted in the middle-class, future-oriented man. Indeed, I am often struck by the analogies that can be drawn between the mores of the very rich—of the "jet set" and "café society"—and the culture of the very poor. Yet it is, on the whole, a comparatively superficial culture. There is in it much pathos, suffering and emptiness. It does not provide much support or satisfaction; its pervading mistrust magnifies individual helplessness and isolation. Indeed, poverty of culture is one of the crucial traits of the culture of poverty.

The concept of the culture of poverty provides a generalization that may help to unify and explain a number of phenomena hitherto viewed as peculiar to certain racial, national or regional groups. Problems we think of as being distinctively our own or distinctively Negro (or as typifying any other ethnic group) prove to be endemic in countries where there are no segregated ethnic minority groups. If it follows that the elimination of physical poverty may not by itself eliminate the culture of poverty, then an understanding of the subculture may contribute to the design of measures specific to that purpose.

What is the future of the culture of poverty? In considering this question one must distinguish between those countries in which it represents a relatively small segment of the population and those in which it constitutes a large one. In the U.S. the major solution proposed by social workers dealing with the "hard core" poor has been slowly to raise their level of living and incorporate them in the middle class. Wherever possible psychiatric treatment is prescribed.

In underdeveloped countries where great masses of people live in the culture of poverty, such a social-work solution does not seem feasible. The local psychiatrists have all they can do to care for their own growing middle class. In those countries the people with a culture of poverty may seek a more revolutionary solution. By creating basic structural changes in society, by redistributing wealth, by organizing the poor and giving them a sense of belonging, of power and of leadership, revolutions frequently succeed in abolishing some of the basic characteristics the culture of poverty even when they do not succeed in curing poverty itself.

14 THE "WIZARD OF OZ" AS A MONETARY ALLEGORY

—HUGH ROCKOFF

The *Wonderful Wizard of Oz*, perhaps America's favorite children's story, is also an informed comment on the battle over free silver in the 1890s. The characters in the story represent real figures such as William Jennings Bryan. This paper interprets the allegory for economists and economic historians, illuminating a number of elements left unexplained by critics concerned with the politics of the allegory. It also reexamines Bryan and the case for free silver. Far from being monetary cranks, the advocates of free silver had a strong argument on both theoretical and empirical grounds.

I. INTRODUCTION

The *Wizard of Oz*, is perhaps the best-loved American children's story. The movie, starring Judy Garland, Bert Lahr, Ray Bolger, and company, is an annual television ritual. The book on which the movie is based, L. Frank Baum's *The Wonderful Wizard of Oz*, however, is not only a child's tale but also a sophisticated commentary on the political and economic debates of the Populist Era.[1] Previous interpretations have focused on the political and social aspects of the allegory. The most important of these is Littlefield ([1966] 1968), although his interpretation was adumbrated by Nye (1951), Gardner and Nye (1957), Sackett (1960), and Bewley ([1964] 1970). My purpose is to unlock the references in the *Wizard of Oz* to the monetary debates of the 1890s. When the story is viewed in this light, the real reason the Cowardly Lion fell asleep in the field of poppies, the identity of the Wizard of Oz, the significance of the strange number of hallways and rooms in the Emerald Palace, and the reason the Wicked Witch of the West was so happy to get one of Dorothy's shoes become clear. Thus interpreted, the *Wizard of Oz* becomes a powerful pedagogic device. Few students of money and banking or economic history will forget the battle between the advocates of free silver and the defenders of the gold standard when it is explained through the *Wizard of Oz*.

This paper also serves a more conventional purpose. William Jennings Bryan and his supporters in the free silver movement, who play a central role in the story, have been treated as monetary cranks even by historians who are sympathetic to them on other

I must thank Marcia Anszperger, Michael Bordo, Charles Calomiris, Stephen DeCanio, Stanley Engerman, Milton Friedman, Robert Greenfield, Jonathan Hughes, Fred C. Meyer, James Seagraves, Michael Taussig, Richard Timberlake, Geoffrey Wood, and the participants in a seminar at Rutgers for many useful comments. I owe a special debt to Eugene White not only for his comments but also for encouraging me to put part of Rutgers's "oral tradition" on paper.

1. What follows is based on the book, Metro-Goldwyn-Mayer made numerous changes in the text, some of which, such as changing the silver slippers of the book into the famous ruby slippers of the movie, obscure the allegory.

issues.[2] Here I show that Bryan's monetary thought was surprisingly, sophisticated and that on most issues his positions, in the light of modern monetary theory, compare favorably with those of his "sound money" opponents.[3]

L. Frank Baum's early life proved to be ideal preparation for writing a monetary allegory.[4] Born to a wealthy family in Chittenango, New York, in 1856, Baum while still in his early 20s wrote and produced a successful play that made it to Broadway. In 1882 he married Maud Gage, the daughter of one of the leading suffragettes, Matilda Joslyn Gage. Later Baum and his family moved to Aberdeen, South Dakota, where he viewed at close hand the frontier life that gave rise to the populist movement. He was unsuccessful in South Dakota, where among other things he published a small paper, the *Saturday Pioneer,* and several issues of the *Western Investor.* In 1890, the Baums moved to Chicago. While pursuing a number of jobs, he frequented the Chicago Press Club and met some of the city's leading writers. There he undoubtedly heard a great deal about the battle for the free coinage of silver, especially in 1896 when Chicago hosted the Democratic National Convention at which William Jennings Bryan made his famous "Cross of Gold" speech. Baum's first book of children's stories was published in 1897 and, in 1900, *The Wonderful Wizard of Oz* followed. After moving to Hollywood, Baum devoted himself to writing children's stories, the most successful being sequels to his masterpiece.

Table 1 contains data basic to an understanding of the world that produced the *Wizard of Oz.* The key fact was deflation. The gross national product deflator, shown in column 1, fell steadily from the end of the 1860s until the United States returned to the gold standard in 1879. After a brief upsurge the deflator resumed its fall, reaching its nadir in 1896. Farm prices, shown in column 2, fell even more rapidly, also reaching a post-Civil War low in 1896. Thus part of the farm problem was the decline in the relative price of farm products. It is a fair criticism of the Populists, to which Bryan is not immune, that they did not adequately distinguish between general price trends that resulted from relatively slow growth in the stock of money compared with real output and relative price trends that would be impervious to monetary remedies.[5]

Between 1869 and 1879 the stock of money grew at about 2.6 percent per year and real output at about 5.0 percent per year, so the deflationary pressure from the lack of monetary growth is easy to understand. In the same period, high-powered money—gold and

---

2. For the purposes of this paper, it is sufficient to lump the Populists, free silver Democrats, and other supporters of free silver together. But it should be noted that while the Populist party nominated Bryan, many hard-line Populists advocated more radical measures such as greenbacks or a commodity-backed currency and supported free silver only as the best that could be gotten in the current political climate. See Goodwyn (1976) and the appendix by Yohe (1976) for a detailed discussion of populist monetary ideas and their relationship to free silver.

3. There are many biographies of Bryari. Two of the best, on the issues covered here, are Coletta (1964–69) and Koenig (1971).

4. This paragraph is based on Baum and MacFall (1961), the major biography of L. Frank Baum.

5. Harvey ([1894] 1963, pp. 198–214), e.g., illustrates the deflation with series on wheat, cotton, and silver. Then in answering the criticism that prices other than wheat had fallen by an equal percentage, he points first to debts but then (p. 214) to a variety of prices—streetcar fares, a hotel room, and so on—that were not fixed in nominal terms.

TABLE 1
Prices and Related Data, 1869–1906

Year	Implicit Price Deflator (1)	Whole-sale Farm Prices (2)	Ratio of Price of Gold to Price of Silver (3)	Percentage Civilian Labor Force Unem-ployed (4)	Money Stock ($ Billion) (5)	High-powered Money ($ Billions) (6)	Real Income ($ Billions 1869) (7)
1869	100	100	20.7		1.28	.760	7.242
1870	9	88	17.9		1.35	.766	7.369
1871	96	80	17.4		1.50	.778	7.240
1872	91	84	17.6		1.61	.782	8.909
1873	90	80	18.1		1.62	.789	8.958
1874	89	80	18.0		1.65	.795	8.726
1875	87	77	19.2		1.72	.773	8.802
1876	83	70	19.9		1.68	.754	9.411
1877	80	70	18.1		1.65	.758	10.078
1878	74	56	18.1		1.58	.763	10.791
1879	72	56	18.5		1.66	.801	11.902
1880	79	63	18.0		2.03	.949	13.646
1881	77	70	18.3		2.44	1.077	13.911
1882	80	77	18.1		2.63	1.140	14.500
1883	79	68	18.6		2.80	1.186	14.237
1884	75	64	18.6		2.80	1.204	14.555
1885	70	56	19.4		2.87	1.233	14.510
1886	69	53	20.8		3.10	1.213	15.282
1887	70	55	21.1		3.31	1.271	15.656
1888	71	59	22.0		3.40	1.318	15.126
1889	71	52	22.1		3.60	1.342	15.578
1890	70	55	19.8	4.0	3.92	1.390	16.820
1891	69	60	20.9	5.4	4.08	1.461	17.506
1892	66	54	23.6	3.0	4.43	1.533	19.117
1893	68	56	26.4	11.7	4.26	1.561	18.373
1894	64	49	32.8	18.4	4.28	1.582	17.259
1895	63	48	31.7	13.7	4.43	1.499	19.248
1896	61	44	30.8	14.4	4.35	1.451	18.758
1897	61	47	34.6	14.5	4.64	1.554	20.563
1898	63	49	35.5	12.4	5.26	1.682	20.924
1899	65	50	34.7	6.5	6.09	1.812	23.353
1900	68	56	33.7	5.0	6.60	1.954	24.121
1901	68	58	35.1	4.0	7.48	2.096	26.928
1902	70	64	39.6	3.7	8.17	2.168	26.883
1903	71	61	38.6	3.9	8.68	2.278	28.090
1904	72	64	36.1	5.4	9.24	2.243	27.487
1905	73	62	34.2	4.3	10.24	2.489	29.676
1906	75	63	30.9	1.7	11.08	2.646	33.624

Source—Col. 1: Friedman and Schwartz (1982), pp. 122–23, table 4.8 col. 4 (set equal to 100 in 1869). Col. 2: U.S. Bureau of the Census (1975), pt. 1, ser. E42, p. 200 (linked to ser. E53, p. 201, in 1890). Col. 3: For gold: Jastram (1977), p. 143, table 6; for silver: U.S. Bureau of the Census (1975), pt. 1, ser. M270, p. 606. Col. 4: U.S. Bureau of the Census (1975), pt. 1, ser. D86, p. 135. Cols. 5–7: Friedman and Schwartz (1982), pp. 122–23, table 4.8, cols. 1, 10, and 3, respectively (converted to 1869 dollars).

silver moneys, other Treasury obligations that could serve as bank reserves, and national bank notes[6]—increased at a rate of only 0.5 percent per year. so the deflation can be traced ultimately to the slow growth in high-powered money. In the following decade, however, the story is somewhat different. High-powered money actually grew at 5.2 percent per year and the total money stock at 7.7 percent, while the rate of growth of real income slowed to 2.7 percent. Since the United States was linked after 1879 to other gold standard countries by fixed exchange rates, one might expect, on the basis of the actual money and real income figures and the velocity trend, in the previous decade, a high U.S. inflation rate paralleled by inflation in other gold standard countries. Otherwise rapid U.S. monetary growth would have been cut short by an outflow of gold. But instead all that happened during the 1880s was a leveling off of prices: the rate of deflation declined from −3.3 percent per year in the 1870s to a modest −0.1 percent per year in the 1880s. In other words, after falling at the relatively low rate of 0.9 percent per year in the 1870s, velocity fell a surprising 5.2 percent per year in the 1880s.

The 1880s were a period perhaps something like the 1980s, in which the economy exhibited a surprisingly strong demand for additional money balances. It would take us too far afield to attempt an explanation of this phenomenon. Suffice it to say that in the 1880s as in the 1980s, there are a number of candidate explanations: interest rates were falling, partially reflecting the fall in prices, but perhaps for other reasons as well; and institutional developments such as the rapid development of the state banking systems may have played a role.

The Panic of 1893 and the subsequent depression were superimposed on these long-term price trends. The depression shows up dramatically in the unemployment data in column 4. Although there is a wide margin of error, it appears that unemployment exploded from 3 percent in 1892 to 11.7 percent in 1893, peaking at 18.4 percent in 1894. The exact cause of the panic is in doubt. One factor was concern over maintenance of the gold standard. In 1890, Congress had passed the Sherman Silver Purchase Act, which provided for the regular purchasing and coining of silver in limited quantities. Silver had been purchased under earlier legislation, but Sherman's act increased the amount. Along with other proposed legislation, it stimulated fears that the United States might leave the gold standard, and this led to a depletion of Treasury gold stocks. In addition, there was a stock market crash prompted by several business failures and a growing tide of bank failures, particularly in the West. Together these developments produced a banking panic, the suspension of gold payments, and a severe depression of an order not seen since the 1830s and not be seen again until the 1930s.

The response of President Grover Cleveland was to seek (successfully) the repeal of the Sherman Silver Purchase Act. But a brief cyclical expansion that began in June 1894

---

6. The inclusion of national bank notes in high-powered money is debatable since they were a liability of commercial banks analogous to deposits. But Milton Friedman and Anna Schwartz (who developed the basic series) included the notes in high-powered money, basing their decision on several considerations. The most important was simply that national bank notes were indirectly obligations of the federal government since they had to be backed by federal government bonds.

petered out, the peak coming in December 1895. According to Friedman and Schwartz (1963, p. 111), it was one of the weakest expansions in the cyclical history of the United States. When the Democrats met at Chicago in the summer of 1896 to nominate a candidate for president, the economy, to put it mildly, was in terrible shape and apparently was getting worse. The closest parallel, perhaps, is with 1932. Unemployment was 14.4 percent. This was one of the most famous conventions in American history. The Democrats were locked in a battle between those favoring the gold standard and those favoring a bimetallic standard. After numerous votes, they finally nominated William Jennings Bryan. He and his supporters called for the free and unlimited coinage of silver at mint prices that made the value of 16 ounces of silver equivalent to 1 ounce of gold.

As can be seen in column 3 of table 1, this ratio was far below the ratio then prevailing in the market, about 31 to 1. Had the United States returned to a bimetallic standard at 16 to 1, there probably would have been some outflows of gold and inflows of silver, although the exact amount is hard to quantify. Critics denounced the plan as wildly inflationary. This criticism was weak on two counts. First, it is unclear that resumption at 16 to 1 would have left the United States with an inflated and purely silver stock of high-powered money. The remonetization of silver by the United States would have substantially increased the world demand for silver and brought the bimetallic ratio down toward the ratio set by the U.S. mint, especially if other countries followed the United States back to the bimetallic standard. Note that as late as 1890 the ratio had been at 20 to 1; the extreme departure of the bimetallic ratio from 16 to 1 was a product of recent events.

Second, some increase in the monetary base was justified. As noted, unemployment stood at 14.4 percent; the business failure rate was 133 per thousand (U.S. Bureau of the Census 1975, p. 912), one of the highest in the postbellum era. The same could be said for the number of bank suspensions, which stood at 155, down from the record-breaking 496 in 1893 but up from 89 in 1894 and 124 in 1895. Failure rates of the larger, more prestigious national banks paralleled those of the state and private banks (p. 1038). The implicit price deflator was down 10.9 percent and farm prices were down 24.1 percent from 1893 after 3 years of steady deflation. To reject monetary expansion in such an environment because it might be inflationary seems excessive, reminding us of the concerns over inflation voiced by the Federal Reserve in the 1930s. However, despite the appeal of free silver, Bryan lost a bitterly contested election to Republican William McKinley.

Meanwhile, the economy began to improve rapidly. Four years later, when Bryan and McKinley had their second contest, prices were up—farm prices more than the deflator—and unemployment was down to 5 percent. In part, the rapid recovery was caused by the failure of European harvests, which created a strong market for American crops. The U.S. balance of trade turned from a deficit to a surplus, and gold flowed in. The expansion was fueled by a 41.7 percent increase in the stock of money and by a 29.8 percent increase in high-powered money. Increased supplies of gold from South African and other areas were now generating a steady rise in the world's stock of monetary gold.

II. FROM KANSAS TO FAIRY LAND

The *Wizard of Oz,* conceived over several years, was written mostly in 1899. It is a cautionary tale, recounting "the first battle" of 1896 (the title of Bryan's [1896] immensely popular account of that election) and warning of the dangers that lay ahead. The story is rich in references to the current scene, but it is not mathematical puzzle. Baum's main purpose was to tell a good story, and his need for symmetry, interesting characters, and so on took precedence over historical accuracy. Nevertheless, the references to the current scene are sufficiently numerous to make looking for them rewarding and informative. The heroine is Dorothy, a little girl who lives with her Aunt Em on an impoverished farm in Kansas. Dorothy represents America—honest, kindhearted, and plucky.[7] Her best friend is her dog, Toto.[8] The populist movement began in the West, so it is natural that the story begins there. But there may also be a reference here to Kansas City, Missouri, where the Democratic convention of 1900 would be held. In 1900, going "from Kansas to Fairyland" (an early title) meant following the campaign trail from Kansas City to Washington, D.C.

Dorothy is in her home when it is carried by a cyclone (tornado) to the land of Oz. This is Baum's fantasy counterpart to America, a land in which, especially in the East, the gold standard reigns supreme and in which an ounce (Oz) of gold has almost mystical significance. The cyclone is the free silver movement itself. It came roaring out of the West in 1896, shaking the political establishment to its foundations. A cyclone is an apt metaphor. Bryan was first elected to Congress in 1890 and made his first important speech in Congress on the silver question in 1893. Three years later he was the leader of a national movement. Dorothy's house lands on the Wicked Witch of the East. The Witch dries up completely, leaving only her silver shoes. These represent the silver component of a bimetallic standard and are given to Dorothy to wear by the Good Witch of the North, who has been summoned to the scene.[9] The silver shoes have a magical power that the Wicked Witch of the East understood but which the Munchkins (citizens of the East) do not.

On a general level the Wicked Witch of the East represents eastern business and financial interests, but in personal terms a Populist would have had one figure in mind: Grover Cleveland. It was Cleveland who led the repeal of the Sherman Silver Purchase Act, and it was his progold forces that had been defeated at the 1896 convention, making it possible for America to vote for Bryan and free silver. But the American people, like the Munchkins, never understood the power that was theirs once the Wicked Witch was dead. Timberlake (1978) argues that the repeal of the Sherman Silver Purchase Act, rather than the campaign

---

7. Recently, Dorothy has ben identified by Leslie Kelsey with the famous populist orator known as the "kansas Tornado," Mary Elizabeth Lease ("Raise more hell and less corn") (Meyer 1987, p. 32).

8. Toto represents the Prohibition party. *Toto* being a play on *teetotaler* (Jensen 1971, p. 283). Prohibitionists' hearts were in the right place on many issues; in addition to opposing alcohol, they supported free coinage of silver in 1896. But they were a minor and eccentric group, always pulling in the wrong direction, and not be taken all that seriously.

9. Free silver had some support in New England. Bryan's running mate in 1896 was Arthur Sewall, a businessman and banker from Maine. But I have not been able to identify the Good Witch of the North clearly with one particular politician.

of 1896, was the real end of the possibility of a bimetallic standard. He shows in detail that repeal was a bipartisan movement. He then asks the following question: "Why should anyone then [in 1896] have believed that a Democratic vote would have any greater effect in promoting silver monetization that it had in 1892?" (p. 42). The free silver Democrats had a simple but not naive answer: The Wicked Witch of the east was (politically) dead.

The friendly inhabitants of the land Dorothy enters cannot tell her how to return to Kansas. She is advised to seek the answer in the Emerald City, which can be found at the end of the yellow brick road. The road, of course, is a symbol of the gold standard. Following it will lead to the Emerald City (Washington, D.C.), but the solution to Dorothy's problems will not be found there. Thus the silver shoes and the yellow brick road are Baum's primary symbols of the the two metals. But there are many others.

The first person whom Dorothy meets along the way is the Scarecrow. As Littlefield (1968, p. 376) notes, the Scarecrow is the western farmer. He thinks that he has no brains because his head is stuffed with straw. But we soon learn that he is shrewd and capable. He brings to life a major theme of the free silver movement: that the people, the farmer in particular, were capable of understanding the complex theories that underlay the choice of a standard. They did not have to accept a monometallic gold standard simply because the experts said that it was necessary. This attitude is best illustrated in the leading tract of the free silver movement, W. B. Harvey's *Coin's Financial School* ([1894] 1963). The imaginary Coin is a small boy who conducts a series of lectures in Chicago attended by some of the leading sound money men, including Lyman Gage, a Chicago banker who became secretary of the Treasury, and James Laurence Laughlin, a professor of economics at the University of Chicago. Although first contemptuous of the untutored boy, they gradually find their arguments for a gold standard refuted. Laughlin, for one, was outraged by the use of his name, and a letter by him denying any association with Coin was reprinted in Horace White's answer to Harvey, Coin's *Financial Fool*.

It is one of the ironies of monetary history that William Jennings Bryan gave his 1896 Cross of Gold speech on the South Side of Chicago, only a short distance from the University of Chicago. At the time the university was home to Laughlin, one of free silver's most acerbic critics and a strong opponent of the quantity theory of money, Bryan's basic framework. Later, under Henry Simons, Lloyd Mints, and Milton Friedman, the university's Department of Economics became the intellectual center for the revival of the quantity theory. In *A Monetary History of the United States,* Friedman and Schwartz (1963, p. 134) take a cautious, although ultimately favorable, view of the free silver position when contrasted with maintenance of a monometallic gold standard.[10] They argue that a firm national commitment to either a bimetallic standard or gold would have been preferable to the "uneasy compromise" that existed until Bryan's defeats. But they then consider the effects of an early adoption of a bimetallic standard and argue that, on the whole, the trend of the price level would have been preferable to the trend that actually prevailed. They also sug-

---

10. A standard based on government-issued fiat money controlled by a monetary rule was not a politically viable alternative in this period. Interestingly, the position of the radical Populists came closer to this formula, although their rule would have imposed a significant inflation (Yohe 1976).

gest, in a cautious way, that the abandonment of a monometallic gold standard might have made sense in the 1890s (p. 115).

Next, Dorothy and the Scarecrow meet the Tin Woodman. Baum's symbol for the workingman. He was once flesh and blood but was cursed by the Wicked Witch of the East. As he worked, his ax would take flight and cut off part of his body. A tinsmith would replace the missing part, and the Tin Woodman could work as well as before. Eventually, there was nothing left but tin. This is why the claws of the Cowardly Lion can make no "impression" on him, just as Bryan failed to make an impression on urban industrial workers in the campaign of 1896. But for all his increased power to work, the Tin Woodman was unhappy for he had lost his heart. As Littlefield (1968, p. 375) points out, this tale is a powerful representation of the populist and socialist idea that industrialization had alienated the workingman, turning an independent artisan into a mere cog in a giant machine. The joints of the Tin Woodman have rusted, and he can no longer work. He has joined the ranks of those unemployed in the depression of the 1890s, a victim of the unwillingness of the eastern goldbugs to countenance an increase in the stock of money through the addition of silver. After his joints are oiled, the Tin Woodman wants to join the group to see if the Wizard can give him a heart. He, too, will learn that the answer is not to be found at the end of the yellow brick road.

The last character to join the group is the Cowardly Lion. This character is William Jennings Bryan himself.[11] The sequence is not accidental. Baum is following history in suggesting that the movement was started first by the western farmers, was joined (to a limited extent) by the workingman, and then, once it was well under way, was joined by Bryan. The roaring lion is a good choice for one of the greatest American orators. At the convention of 1896, his stirring speech on the silver plank of the platform, ending with his challenge to the Republicans, "Thou shalt not crucify mankind upon a cross of gold," won him the nomination. In the words of one observer whom Baum may have known, John T. McCutcheon, "When he sat down, the convention went wild. . . . We who watched saw a man march relatively unknown to the platform, and march down again the leader of a national party" (1950, pp. 88–89).

Bryan was a lion, but why a cowardly lion? In the late 1890s, as I noted, the world gold supply began to increase rapidly, reversing the long deflation. As a result, the usefulness of silver as a political issue declined. It was obvious almost immediately after the election of 1896 that Bryan would again be the standard-bearer in 1900. But with the return of prosperity, he continually received advice to soft-pedal silver and concentrate on new issues such as opposition to the trusts and anti-imperialism, which would appeal to the eastern wing of the party, advice that to an extend he heeded. After the successful conclusion of the Spanish-American War, the United States, to retain control of the Philippines, was forced to put down a bloody rebellion. Like many regular Democrats and Republicans, the Populists were opposed to the United States fighting to hold the Philippines. But there were many Populists who were afraid that Bryan would push this issue to the exclusion of silver. They

---

11. The Populists liked to give politicians outlandish nicknames. John W. Daniel, a silver Democrat from Virginia, was known as the "Lame Lion" (Hollingsworth 1963, p. 54).

considered this line of action pure cowardice. They wanted the Great Commoner to fight for silver in 1900 as he had in 1896.

The little party heading toward the Emerald City reminds me of "Coxey's army" of unemployed workers that marched on Washington, D.C., in 1894. Jacob Coxey was a green-backer, and his idea was simple: The federal government should build public works and pay for them by printing money (Hicks [1931] 1961, p. 322). At the time the idea seemed to be the wildest kind of extremism. But given unemployment of 18.4 percent and the monetary and fiscal options then open to the government, few modern economists would be prepared to dismiss such a proposal out of hand. Indeed, at the height of the Keynesian period, it would have been taken to be the essence of sound macroeconomics. Although the march addressed serious problems, Coxey's army took on an opera bouffe quality. Characters such as "Cyclone" Kirtland, a Pittsburgh astrologer, showed up to take part (Nye 1951, p. 91). So it is not surprising that Coxey's army should suggest a fairy tale.

Along the way Dorothy and her friends meet a series of challenges that show that each character really has the quality he feels he is missing. The Scarecrow proves intelligent although he thinks he has no brain; the Tin Woodman proves to be kinder than an ordinary man; and the Cowardly Lion is prepared to fight to the death against the deadly Kalidahs, frightening monsters with the body of a bear and the head of a tiger.[12] The most mysterious challenge is the Deadly Poppy Field. The Cowardly Lion falls asleep in the field and is pulled to safety, but with the greatest difficulty. This is another reference to the dangers of putting anti-imperialism ahead of silver. Poppies are the source of opium, and falling asleep in a field of poppies symbolizes the populist fear that Bryan would fall asleep in the midst of these new issues. Anti-imperialism was predominantly a middle-class and intellectual issue. Bryan's Populist advisers were concerned that if he failed to stress the issues of greatest concern to rank-and-file Populists (particularly silver), he would fail to win the overwhelming support from them that was crucial to his election. It is therefore appropriate that it is the field mice, little folk concerned with everyday issues (such as the price of corn), who pull the Cowardly Lion from the Deadly Poppy Field.

At last the little group arrives at the Emerald City. The Guardian of the Gate assures them that the Wizard can solve their problems. The Wizard has, for example, a pot of courage (a colloquial term for liquor) for the Cowardly Lion. The pot is prevented from overflowing by a plate made of gold, another reference to the gold standard and its effects. But before Dorothy and her friends can enter the city they must don a pair of green-colored glasses. Everyone, in the city must wear them and they must be locked on with a gold buckle by order of the Wizard. The conservative financiers who run the Emerald City, in other words, force its citizens to look at the world through money-colored glasses.

Dorothy and her friends are taken to the Emerald Palace, the White House itself, where they must stay the night before they can have their audience with the Wizard. Dorothy is led to the room through seven passages and up three flights of stairs. It is not surprising that the layout of the Emerald Palace should reflect the numbers seven and three.

---

12. Michael Taussig has suggested to me that the Kalidahs might represent newspaper reporters. Most of the papers were strongly opposed to Bryan and his cause, and they violently denounced the Populists.

The Crime of '73 was a crucial event in populist monetary history. Legislation in that year eliminated the coinage of the silver dollar. At that time the price of silver bullion was well above the traditional mint price, so the decision to eliminate the silver dollar had no immediate impact and aroused little public opposition. But in later years, when the bullion price fell below the mint price, the decision taken in 1873 began to appear as the source of all future difficulties.[13]

The next day Dorothy and her friends are brought to see the Great Oz. First they have to pass through a great hall in which there are many ladies and gentlemen of the court, all dressed in rich costumes . . . [who] had nothing to do but talk to each other" (Baum, 1973, p. 205), a reference to the bureaucrats to be found in any seat of government, but not amiss in a description of Washington, D.C. One by one, each is taken into a big round room (the oval office?) to meet the Wizard. Each sees a different character Dorothy sees an enormous head, the Scarecrow sees a lovely lady, the Tin Woodman sees a terrible beast, and the Cowardly Lion sees a ball of fire. Each of them receives the same message: the Wizard will help them, but first they must do something for the Wizard. "In this country," the Wizard explains, "everyone must pay for everything he gets" (p. 208). But who is the Wizard who speaks through various figureheads and adheres to such a purely Republican world view? To a Populist at the turn of the century, there is only one answer: Marcus Alonzo Hanna. A close adviser of McKinley and the chairman of the Republican National Committee, he was, in populist mythology, the brains behind McKinley and his campaigns. It was the money that Hanna raised from giant corporations, according to the Populists, that defeated Bryan. To satisfy the Wizard, the group must travel to the West and destroy his enemy the Wicked Witch of the West. That the Wizard wanted them to leave and go West, there can be no doubt. But that he was really an enemy of the Wicked Witch of the West is another matter. The Wizard does not always tell the truth, a lesson that Dorothy will soon learn.

III. THE WICKED WITCH OF THE WEST

The Wizard's demand is analogous to Hanna's advice to journalists, politicians, and plain citizens to visit McKinley at his home in Ohio. In 1896, McKinley conducted a "front porch" campaign, extolling the virtues of "sound" money to visiting crowds. If Cleveland was the Wicked Witch of the East, slain in 1896, McKinley in 1896 and 1900 was the very much alive Wicked Witch of the West. Dorothy and her friends must face biblical plagues—wolves, crows, and black bees—thrown at them by the Witch. But they defeat each of them. The Wicked Witch is thus forced to turn to her Golden Cap, another symbol of the gold standard, which gives her the power to call the Winged Monkeys. According to Littlefield (1968, p. 378), the Winged Monkeys represent the Plains Indians, free spirits brought to

---

13. According to O'Leary (1960), the decision to eliminate the silver dollar was a deliberate attempt to avoid the possibility of a de facto silver standard, based on the understanding that secular forces might undermine the price of silver.

earth by the relentless western march of the frontier. They, too, cannot avoid the overarching power of the gold standard.

The owner of the Golden Cap is allowed three wishes, but the Wicked Witch of the West has already used two, one to drive the Wizard out of the West and one to enslave the yellow Winkies. Although Hanna was a westerner living in the East, he had not really been driven out. Here Baum has departed, apparently, from a strict allegory.[14] But the enslavement of the yellow Winkles is clear enough. After winning the Philippines, the United States, as I noted above, had to put down a bloody rebellion to maintain control of the Islands. The Wicked Witch of the West's enslavement of the yellow Winkies is a not very well disguised reference to McKinley's decision to deny immediate independence to the Philippines. To a modern ear there is a condescending tone to "yellow Winkies," but clearly Baum was sympathetic to the plight of the Philippines (and other Plains Indians).[15]

The Wicked Witch commands the Winged Monkeys to attack Dorothy and her friends. They drop the Tin Woodman on jagged rocks and pull out the Scarecrow's straw. The Lion is taken to the castle and penned up. Dorothy is taken there as well and made to do household chores. The Witch covets Dorothy's silver shoes, for the Witch knows their power. At last she devises a scheme: she trips Dorothy over an invisible iron bar and snatches one of the silver shoes. The Wicked Witch is greatly pleased with this trick, for she realizes that with the silver shoes divided, Dorothy cannot use them. This refers to McKinley's position on silver. McKinley and the Republicans in 1896 did not argue that only gold monometallism would do. Their position was that bimetallism should be reestablished, but only after an international agreement. The Republicans argued that this would raise the world demand for silver sufficiency to prevent the United States from being flooded with silver and protect the dollar from being devalued when bimetallism was reestablished. This position had a number of respectable academic supporters, and McKinley followed through on his promise to support an international conference on bimetallism. But the Populists believed, perhaps correctly, that this was merely so much talk designed to hide the real intention of the Republicans: to maintain a monometallic gold standard. Most of Bryan's Cross of Gold speech and much of his campaign in 1896 were devoted to attacking the Republican position on international bimetallism.

Dorothy is so angry with the Wicked Witch for tripping her that she pours a bucket of water over her. To her surprise, the Witch melts away. For Littlefield (1968, p. 379), to whom the Wicked Witch represents the malign forces of nature in the West, the point is that all it takes is some water to make the dry plains bloom. In the 1890s the "rain line" moved east, causing farmers in Kansas, Nebraska, and the Dakotas who had moved west in the

---

14. This is one of the few points at which the allegory does not work straightforwardly. I would be interested in hearing alternative interpretations of this piece of Oz history.

15. Several readers of a previous draft suggested that there might also be a reference here to the plight of Asian immigrants in California. The coincidence of the events in The Philippines with the composition of the Wizard of Oz leads me to discount this possibility. But the analogy is broadly consistent with the populist view of the relationship between western financial interests and the immigrants. But although sympathetic, the Populists supported efforts to limit Asian immigration on the grounds that it undermined the wages and working conditions of native Americans; support for unrestricted immigration generally came from the Republican side.

1880s, on the basis of a few good years, great hardships in addition to those generated by the depression in agricultural prices. Kansas was one of the areas hardest hit. To the western farmer, it appeared that what he needed to get out of debt was some good rain and some good crops.

Inflation was to some extent simply a substitute for rain. But the usefulness of inflation to the farmer depended in large measure on its, effects on farm debt. Although the percentage of farmland that was mortgaged was low for the nation as a whole, western farmers, especially in certain areas, were heavily mortgaged. Kansas had one of the heaviest levels of indebtedness, with 60 percent of taxed acres under mortgage (Emerick 1896, p. 603). But not all the indebted farmers would have benefited from inflation. One of the most telling criticisms of free silver was that the prospect of inflation would lead to the renewal of mortgages at higher interest rates many farmers would be no better off than before. One important statement of this point was made by Fisher (1896). His paper, one of the most influential in the history of monetary economics, argued that anticipated increases in the rate of inflation would be reflected in higher interest rates, although he acknowledged that as a historical matter debtors did tend to lose during periods of deflation and gain during periods of inflation.

Fisher pointed out that most farm mortgages were relatively short. He gave 4.67 years as the average length so that the typical mortgage had only 2.33 years left. It is obvious that a large proportion of existing mortgages would mature, and have to be renewed, between the time when free silver became a fait accompli and when farmers saw any benefits in the form of higher farm prices. The expected inflation would be incorporated in interest rates, so for many farmers there would be little or no debt relief. Bryan was aware of this argument but had no convincing answer. In his Madison Square Garden speech, he tried to meet this criticism by arguing that the lag between the election and the adoption of free silver could be shortened by calling a special session of Congress (1896, p. 336).[16] But he quickly moved on to other issues.

With the Wicked Witch dead, Dorothy is able to free her friends. Tinsmiths repair the Tin Woodman, and he is given a new ax. The handle is made of gold, and the blade is polished until it "glistens like burnished silver." The new ax is a good symbol of a point often made by the Populists: that they did not want to replace a gold standard with a silver standard; they wanted a genuine bimetallic standard. In *Coin's Financial School*, Harvey likened the gold standard to a one-legged man and the bimetallic standard to a two-legged man. Baum's image is even more vivid. The Tin Woodman is also given a silver oilcan inlaid with gold and precious stones, just the thing to prevent a recurrence of unemployment. Toto and the Cowardly Lion are given gold collars without any silver, and the Scarecrow is given a walking stick with a gold head. Here Baum did not follow through explicitly on the bimetallic theme (although given the purpose of a collar this

---

16. The Madison Square Garden speech was Bryan's most complete analysis of the money issue during the campaign. The speech, eagerly anticipated after his stirring Cross of Gold speech in Chicago, was expected to be filled with fire and brimstone. Instead, to allay fears of his radicalism, he wrote a detailed defense of free silver, treating his audience to a lecture on the quantity theory of money, the meaning of the purchasing power of money, and related issues.

may not be surprising), and we are not told what the stick itself was made of. Bryan frequently received gifts of this sort to portray the battle of the standards. There was an ink bottle made of gold and silver, a gold pen with a silver holder, gold-headed canes like the one given to the Scarecrow, and so forth (Bryan 1896, pp. 537, 629–20). The advocates of a gold standard argued that bimetallism was unworkable because a rise in the bimetallic ratio could produce an outflow of gold and an inflow of silver that left only silver in circulation; a fall in the ratio might leave only gold in circulation. There could be alternating gold and silver standards, but there could not be a true bimetallic standard in the sense of two metals circulating side by side, except in the accidental case in which the mint ratio was equal to relative prices in world markets. Although not always consistent, the Populists at times made correct counterarguments. First, with a nation as large as the United States on the standard, the world ratio might adapt to the U.S. ratio, and gold and silver might circulate simultaneously for a long period of time. Second, the really important things about a standard are the implications for the stock of money and the price level. Under a bimetallic standard, a decline in the production of one monetary metal would not necessarily imply a drastic fall in the supply of money because the other metal was ready to fill the gap.

These arguments were laid out clearly by William Stanley Jevons and other scholars whom Bryan read. The extent of the increase in price stability to be expected is debatable. Fisher ([1922] 1971, pp. 325–26), who accepted the theoretical argument and had his own gift for the telling analogy, likened the benefits from a bimetallic standard to "two tipsy men locking arms. Together they walk somewhat more steadily than apart, although if one happens to be much more sober, his own gait may be made worse by the union." In short, bimetallism offered no more than an "indifferent remedy" to the problem of long-term price instability.[17]

IV. THE DISCOVERY OF OZ THE TERRIBLE

Dorothy and her friends return to the Emerald City confident that the Wizard will grant them their wishes. But they soon unmask the Wizard and learn that he is nothing but a humbug who has been fooling the people. It is clear that the Wizard has been lying, but how much of the story that he now begins to tell is true is open to question. He claims to be from Nebraska, Bryan's state. But this is doubtful. There may be a reference here to Hanna's own transition after the election of 1896. He entered politics behind the scenes and soon became the sinister figure of populist mythology. Shortly after the election, he was appointed to the Senate from Ohio. But to win a full term, he was forced to take to the stump. Here he was a surprising success. His down-to-earth "I'm just a common man" (Baum 1973, p. 264) style was a hit, effective even with farmers and workers. If I read Baum correctly, he accepts this transformation, up to a point. The Wizard is to be accepted

---

17. Fisher, although mildly sympathetic to bimetallism, was strongly opposed to its adoption in 1896 at the ratio of 16 to 1.

as an ordinary man, but that does not mean that we can believe everything he says. With a little shrewd psychology, the Wizard solves the problems of Dorothy's friends. The Scarecrow is given brains in the form of a mixture of bran and pins and needles (to be sharp-witted), the Tin Woodman is given a heart lined with silk and filled with sawdust, and the Lion is given courage in the form of a green liquid. But Dorothy still cannot get back to Kansas. The Wizard promises to take her in a hot air balloon. But at the last moment, the line holding the balloon breaks and the Wizard is carried away, leaving Dorothy behind. The promises of the Wizard of Oz (like those of the newly reformed Hanna) are partly hot air.

Dorothy then decides to seek out Glinda, the Good Witch of the South. The South was generally sympathetic to free silver, so it is not surprising that it is ruled by a good witch. All her friends join Dorothy, including the wise Scarecrow, who has been made ruler over the Emerald City. The inhabitants of the city are proud to have the Scarecrow as their leader because it makes them, as far as they know, the only city to be ruled over by a stuffed man. Along the way, Dorothy and her friends encounter the Dainty China Country, a land in which the inhabitants are actually figurines made of bone china. To enter the Dainty China Country, the party must crawl over a high wall that has been likened to the Great Wall of China (Hearn 1973, p. 303). Once inside, Dorothy and her party accidentally damage some of the figures, and after a China Princess explains how delicate the figures are, Dorothy and her friends decide to leave so that they will do no more damage. The attitude of the China Princess has been compared to that of the Dowager Empress of China, Tzu Hsi. Chinese resistance to the West culminated in the Boxer Rebellion in the summer of 1900. But, as Hearn notes (p. 311), all the damage in Baum's story is done by the foreign invaders. This point of view, like Baum's attitude toward the Winkles, is a reflection of his populist anti-imperialism.[18]

After further adventures the party reaches Glinda, the Good Witch of the South, where, incidentally, the favorite color is red like much of the soil in the American South. Glinda solves all the party's remaining problems. The Scarecrow returns to rule the Emerald City, the Tin Woodman becomes ruler of the Winkies, and the Cowardly Lion becomes ruler of a jungle. The populist dream of achieving political power with the help of the South is realized. Dorothy is told how to return to Kansas. All that is necessary is that she click the heels of her silver shoes together three times. The power to solve her problems (by adding silver to the money stock) was there all the time.

When Dorothy awakes in Kansas, she finds that the silver shoes have disappeared, just as the silver issue was disappearing in the late 1890s. As Littlefield (1968, p. 380) notes, another lesson here may be that the battle for silver added a measure of excitement to the lives of the westerners, even if in the end the battle could not be won. In any case,

---

18. China, as well as several other Asian nations, was on a silver standard during the period 1879–96 when the United States, along with the rest of the gold bloc, was experiencing deflation (Fisher 1971, pp. 243–45). The silver standard countries experienced, predictably, a mild inflation. Bryan and his allies in the free silver movement, however, do not appear to have made much use of the argument, perhaps because they wanted to avoid being labeled as inflationists or because they did not want to reinforce the argument that it was the "advanced" countries that were moving to the monometallic gold standard.

Baum's observation that the silver cause would become a distant memory proved to be true. The Gold Standard Act, committing the United States firmly to the gold standard, was passed in 1900.

V. SOME THOUGHTS FOR THE SKEPTICS

There is always a danger that a critic may see symbols where the author has merely placed the concrete reference points of his story. Baum left no hard evidence that he intended his story to have an allegorical meaning: no diary entry, no letter, not even an off-hand remark to a friend. But this need not be conclusive. He probably considered his references to current events to be a series of sly jokes, like the puns that dot the text, rather than something to be worried about by future generations. The creative process, moreover, is highly complex. An author's experience may be transformed in ways he is only dimly aware of, before it issues forth in a work of art. The critic may be uncovering elements beyond the explicit intentions of the author.[19]

There is, moreover, considerable circumstantial evidence for the populist interpretation. It has been recognized independently by a number of thoughtful readers, it is consistent with what we know of Baum's politics, for although he was not an activist, it is known that he marched in torchlight parades for Bryan and voted Democratic (Baum and MacFall, 1961, p. 85). References to current affairs appear in a number of his later works. The most obvious are a comic opera Baum worked on in 1901, *The Octopus* or *The Title Trust,* and *The Marvelous Land of Oz* (1904), which was a satire of the suffragist movement.

An allegorical interpretation of a story can be viewed as something like a model in economics. The test of an economic model is whether it can be extended in a "natural" way to explain additional phenomena. Here I have tried to extend Littlefield's populist interpretation by using what we know of populist monetary thought to explain additional episodes in Baum's story. That this can be done with a relatively moderate amount of pushing and pulling strengthens the case for the populist interpretation. If this interpretation is right, then Baum's story gives us some real insight into how a detached but informed Populist viewed free silver. In any case. economists should not have any difficulty accepting, at least provisionally, an elegant but controversial model.

VI. WILLIAMS JENNINGS BRYAN AND FREE SILVER

Bryan was not a deep or original thinker; he was a politician with a gift for the telling analogy in an age of high oratory. But historians have been too hard on Bryan the monetarist, influenced more perhaps by their antipathy to the religious beliefs that engaged his attention in later years or other aspects of the populist creed than to a real examination of

---

19. Just how complex that process can be is illustrated by Lowes's (1927) account of how Samuel Taylor Coleridge's imagination fashioned some of his most memorable poetry from the books he had been reading.

his monetary views. An early statement by Bryan, to the effect that he was for silver because Nebraska was for it and he would look up the arguments later, has been often quoted against him. But he did his homework better than most politicians. He read Jevons, Laughlin, and other scholars well enough to understand the case for a bimetallic standard and for expanding the stock of money in periods of deep depressions. He understood the rudiments of the quantity theory of money, including the relationship between velocity and the rate of price change. He understood the mechanics of a bimetallic standard. He recognized that a bimetallic standard could keep both metals circulating side by side for long periods of time and that the problem of alternating metallic flows was secondary, in any case, to the problem of maintaining price-level stability. If he sometimes claimed too much for monetary expansion, he was at least on as strong a theoretical basis as his critics.[20]

Not all economists who started from the quantity theory agreed that an inflation resulting from the free coinage at 16 to 1 would restore prosperity. Clark (1896a, 1896b) imagined a stagnation: prices would rise, alleviating debt burdens as the advocates of free silver claimed, but the uncertainty would rock credit markets and produce a business "convulsion." The counterclaim that an increase in the stock of money generated by the introduction of large elements of silver into the monetary base would have effects similar to a sudden increase in gold—that prices and real output would both rise—was soundly based on historical experience and an interpretation of the quantity theory of money acceptable to many monetary economists even today.

Changing the monetary constitution to cure the depression opened the door to discretionary policies. There was a danger that milder recessions would be met with changes in the mint prices or other devices, Clark (1896a) speculated that the transitional inflation would encourage farmers to go further into debt. The inflation would end and farmers would again be agitating for monetary expansion to alleviate their new debt burdens. The only bailout the second time around would be paper money. Bryan and his allies recognized the danger of a discretionary policy. It was one reason they gave for rejecting the greenback and commodity-backed standards favored by radical Populists. But in the circumstances of 1896, using reentry to the bimetallic standard at a ratio that overvalued silver as a substitute for a central bank operating in its role of lender of last resort made a good deal of sense. It is only because we now know that rising gold supplies would solve the monetary problems of the day, a fact not known at the time, that we can be sure that Bryan's reforms were unnecessary.

Bryan was aware that the expansion of gold supplies had undermined the case for free silver. But as he noted (1900, p. 179), the expansion of gold supplies had dramatically vindicated his basic framework: the quantity theory of money. The stock of money had risen rapidly, and prices, employment, and real output had responded. The case for a bimetallic standard, moreover, remained intact, according to Bryan. For one thing, the monetary

---

20. In a series of recent papers, Milton Friedman has reexamined the case for free silver. He agrees that the general case for bimetallism, as opposed to a monometallic gold standard, was strong (1990a), and he argues that returning to a bimetallic standard at 16 to 1 would have made sense in 1873 (1990b). But he argues that it would have been a mistake to return at 16 to 1 in 1896 (1989).

stringency that followed the Boer uprising in South Africa showed that the gold standard was vulnerable to threats to the supply of gold (pp. 171–72). More fundamentally, the increased supplies of gold might be exhausted, and prices could again head down.

Others were observing the trend in prices, associating it with rising gold supplies, and concluding that this supported the quantity theory. But if others saw the logic, Bryan still had the gift for expressing his point with a simple metaphor:

> Suppose the citizens of a town were divided, nearly equally on the question of water supply, one faction contending that the amount should be increased, and suggesting that the increase be piped from Silver Lake, the other faction insisting no more water was needed; suppose that at the election the opponents of an increase won (no matter by what means); and suppose, soon after the election, a spring which may be described as Gold Spring, broke forth in the very center of the city, with a flow of half as much water as the city had before used; and suppose the new supply was turned into the city reservoir to the joy and benefit of all the people of the town. Which faction would, in such a case, have been vindicated?
>
> Just such a result has followed a similar increase in the nation's supply of money to the joy of all—thus proving the contentions of the bimetallists. [Bryan and Bryan 1925, p. 471]

Is it any wonder that in an age in which politicians would be willing to describe monetary policy in such wondrous terms, Baum would incorporate the monetary controversies of the day in his fairy tale?

REFERENCES

Baum, Frank Joslyn, and MacFall, Russell P. *To Please a Child: A Biography of L. Frank Baum, Royal Historian of Oz.* Chicago: Reilly & Lee, 1961.

Baum. L. Frank. *The Wonderful Wizard of Oz.* New York: Hill, 1900. Reprinted in *The Annotated Wizard of Oz*, edited by Michael Patrick Hearn. New York: Potter, 1973.

———. *The Marvelous Land of Oz., Being an Account of the Further Adventures of the Scarecrow and the Tin Woodman. . . .* Chicago: Reilly & Britton, 1904.

Bewley, Marius. "Oz Country." New York Rev, Books 3 (December 3, 1964): 18–19. Reprinted as "The Land of Oz: America's Great Good Place." In *Masks and Mirrors: Essays in Criticism.* New York: Atheneum, 1970.

Bryan, William Jennings. *The First Battle: A Story of the Campaign of 1896.* Chicago: Conkey, 1896.

———. *The Second Battle; or, the New Declaration of Independence, 1776–1900.* Chicago: Conkey, 1900.

Bryan, William Jennings, and Bryan, Mary Baird. *The Memoirs of William Jennings Bryan.* Chicago: Winston, 1925.

Clark, John B. 'The After Effects of Free Coinage of Silver." *Polit. Sd. Q.* 11 (September 1896): 493–501. (*a*)

———. "Free Coinage and Prosperity." *Polit. Sci. Q.* 11 (June 1896): 248–58, (*b*)

Coletta, Paolo E. *William Jennings Bryan*. 3 vols. Lincoln: Univ. Nebraska Press, 1964–69.

Emerick, C. F. "An Analysis of Agricultural Discontent in the United States. *Polit. Sci. Q.* 11 (December 1896): 601–39.

Fisher, Irving. Appreciation and Interest. Publications of the American Economic Association, vol. 11. New York: Macmillan, 1896.

———. *The Purchasing Power of Money*. 2d cd. New York: Macmillan, 1922. Reprint. New York: Kelley, 1971.

Friedman, Milton, "WIlliam Jennings Bryan and the Cyanide Process." Manuscript. Stanford, Calif.: Hoover Inst., 1989.

———. "Bimetallism Revisited." *J. Econ. Perspectives* (1990), in press. (*a*).

———. "The Crime of 1873." *J.P.E.* 98 (December 1990), in press, (*b*).

Friedman, Milton, and Schwartz, Anna J. *A Monetary History of the United States, 1867–1960*. Princeton Univ. Press (for NBER), 1963.

———. *Monetary Trends in the United States and the United Kingdom: Their Relation to Income, Prices, and Interest Rates, 1867–1975*. Chicago: Univ. Chicago PRess (For NBER), 1982.

Gardner, Martin, and Nye, Russel B. *The Wizard of Oz and Who He Was*. East Lansing: Michigan State Univ. Press, 1976.

Harvey, William H. *Coin's Financial School*. Chicago: Coin, 1894. Reprint. Edited by Richard Hofstadter. Cambridge, Mass.: Harvard Univ. Press, 1963.

Hearn, Michael Patrick, ed. *The Annotated Wizard of Oz*. New York: Potter, 1973.

Hicks, John D. *The Populist Revolt: A History of the Farmer's Alliance and the People's Party*. Minneapolis: Univ. Minnesota Press, 1931; Lincoln: Univ. Nebraska Press, 1959.

Hollingsworth, Joseph Rogers. *The Whirligig of Politics: The Democracy of Cleveland and Bryan*. Chicago: Univ. Chicago press, 1963.

Jastram, Roy W. *The Golden Constant: The English and American Experience, 1560–1976*. New York: Wiley, 1977.

Jensen, Richard. *The Winning of the Midwest: Social and Political Conflict, 1888–1896*. Chicago Press, 1971.

Koenig, Louis W. *Bryan: A Political Biography of William Jennings Bryan*. New York: Putnam, 1971.

Littlefield, Henry M. "The Wizard of Oz: Parable on Populism." *American Q.* 16 (Spring 1964): 47–58. Reprinted in *The American Culture: Approaches to the Study of the United States*, edited by Hennig Cohen. Boston: Houghton Mifflin, 1968.

Lowes, John Livingston. *The Road to Xanadu: A Study in the Ways of the Imagination*. Boston: Houghton Mifflin, 1927.

McCutcheon, John T. *Drawn from Memory.* Indianapolis: Bobbs-Merrill, 1950.

Meyer, Fred M. "Oz in the News." *Baum Bugle* 31 (Autumn 1987): 32.

Nye, Russel B. *Midwestern Progressive Politics: A Historical Study of Its Origins and Development, 1870–1950.* East Lansing: Michigan State College Press, 1951.

O'Leary, Paul M. "The Scene of the Crime of 1873 Revisited: A Note." *J.P.E.* 68 (August 1960): 388–92.

Sackett, S. J. "The Utopia of Oz." *Georgia Rev.* 14 (Fall 1960): 275–91.

Timberlake, Richard H., Jr. "Repeal of Silver Monetization in the Late Nineteenth Century." *J. Money, Credit and Banking* 10 (February 1978): 27–45.

U.S. Bureau of the Census. *Historical Statistics of the United States, Colonial Times to 1970.* Washington: Government Printing Office, 1975.

Yohe, William P. "An Economic Appraisal of the Sub-Treasury Plan." App. B in *Democratic Promise: The Populist Moment in America,* by Lawrence Goodwyn. New York: Oxford Univ. Press, 1976.

15 POOR MAN, RICH MAN, BIG-MAN, CHIEF: POLITICAL TYPES IN MELANESIA AND POLYNESIA*

—MARSHALL D. SAHLINS

With an eye to their own life goals, the native people of Pacific Islands Unwittingly present to anthropologists a generous scientific gift: an extended series of experiments in cultural adaptation and evolutionary development. They have compressed their institutions within the confines of infertile coral atolls, expanded them on volcanic islands, created with the means history gave them cultures adapted to the deserts of Australia, the mountains and warm coasts of New Guinea, the rain forests of the Solomon Islands. From the Australian Aborigines, whose hunting and gathering existence duplicates in outline the cultural life of the later Paleolithic, to the great chiefdoms of Hawaii, where society approached the formative levels of the old Fertile Crescent civilizations, almost every general phase in the progress of primitive culture is exemplified.

Where culture so experiments, anthropology finds its laboratories—makes its comparisons.[1]

From COMPARATIVE STUDIES IN SOCIETY AND HISTORY, Vol. 5, No. 3 (1963), pp. 285–303. Copyright © 1963 by Cambridge University Press. Reprinted with the permission of Cambridge University Press.

* The present paper is preliminary to a wider and more detailed comparison of Melanesian and Polynesian polities and economics. I have merely abstracted here some of the more striking political differences in the two areas. The full study—which, incidentally, will include more documentation—has been promised the editors of *The Journal of the Polynesian Society,* and I intend to deliver it to them some day.

The comparative method so far followed in this research has involved reading the monographs and taking notes. I don't think I originated the method, but I would like to christen it—The Method of Uncontrolled Comparison. The description developed of two forms of leadership is a mental distillation from the method of uncontrolled comparison. The two forms are abstracted sociological types. Anyone conversant with the anthropological literature of the South Pacific knows there are important variants of the types, as well as exceptional political forms not fully treated here. All would agree that consideration of the variations and exceptions is necessary and desirable. Yet there is pleasure too, and some intellectual reward, in discovering the broad patterns. To (social-) scientifically justify my pleasure, I could have referred to the pictures drawn of Melanesian big-men and Polynesian chiefs as "models" or as "ideal types". If that is all that is needed to confer respectability on the paper, may the reader have it this way.

I hope all of this has been sufficiently disarming. Or need it also be said that the hypotheses are provisional, subject to further research, etc.?

1. Since Rivers' day, the Pacific has provided ethnographic stimulus to virtually every major ethnological school and interest. From such great landmarks as Rivers' *History of Melanesian Society,* Radcliffe-Brown's *Social Organization of the*

In the southern and eastern Pacific two contrasting cultural provisions have long evoked anthropological interest: *Melanesia,* including New Guinea, the Bismarcks, Solomons, and island groups east to Fiji; and *Polynesia,* consisting in its main portion of the triangular constellation of lands between New Zealand, Easter Island, and the Hawaiian Islands. In and around Fiji, Melanesia and Polynesia intergrade culturally, but west and east of their intersection the two provinces pose broad contrasts in several sectors: in religion, art, kinship groupings, economics, political organization. The differences are the more notable for the underlying similarities from which they emerge. Melanesia and Polynesia are both agricultural regions in which many of the same crops—such as yams, taro, breadfruit, bananas, and coconuts—have long been cultivated by many similar techniques. Some recently presented linguistic and archaeological studies indeed suggest that Polynesian cultures originated from an eastern Melanesian hearth during the first millenium B.C.[2] Yet in anthropological annals the Polynesians were to become famous for elaborate forms of rank and chieftainship, whereas most Melanesian societies broke off advance on this front at more rudimentary levels.

It is obviously imprecise, however, to make out the political contrast in broad culture-area terms. Within Polynesia, certain of the islands, such as Hawaii, the Society Islands and Tonga, developed unparalled political momentum. And not all Melanesian polities, on the other side, were constrained and truncated in their evolution. In New Guinea and nearby areas of western Melanesia, small and loosely ordered political groupings are numerous, but in eastern Melanesia, New Caledonia and Fiji for example, political approximations of the Polynesian condition become common. There is more of an upward west to east slope in political development in the southern Pacific than a step-like, quantum progression.[3] It is quite revealing, however, to compare the extremes of this continuum, the western Melanesian underdevelopment against the greater Polynesian chiefdoms. While such comparison does not exhaust the evolutionary variations, it fairly established the scope of overall political achievement in this Pacific phylum of cultures.

Measurable along several dimensions, the contrast between developed Polynesian and underdeveloped Melanesian polities is immediately striking for differences in scale. H. Ian Hogbin and Camilla Wedgwood concluded from a survey of Melanesian (mostly western Melanesian) societies that ordered, independent political bodies in the region typically include seventy to three hundred persons; more recent work in the New Guinea Highlands

---

Australian Tribes, Malinowski's famous Trobriand studies, especially *Argonauts of the Western Pacific,* Raymond Firth's pathmaking *Primitive Economics of the New Zealand Maori,* his functionalist classic, *We, the Tikopia,* and Margaret Mead's *Coming of Age in Samoa,* one can almost read off the history of ethnological theory in the earlier twentieth century. In addition to continuing to provision all these concerns, the Pacific has been the site of much recent evolutionist work (see, for example, Goldman 1955, 1960; Goodenough 1957; Sahlins 1958; Vayda 1959). There are also the outstanding monographs on special subjects ranging from tropical agriculture (Conklin 1957; Freeman 1955) to millenarianism (Worsley 1957).

2. This question, however, is presently in debate. See Grace 1955, 1959; Dyen 1960; Suggs 1960; Golson 1961.

3. There are notable bumps in the geographical gradient. The Trobriand chieftainships off eastern New Guinea will come to mind. But the Trobriand political development is clearly exceptional for western Melanesia.

suggests political groupings of up to a thousand, occasionally a few thousand, people.[4] But in Polynesia sovereignties of two thousand or three thousand are run-of-the-mill, and the most advanced chiefdoms, as in Tonga or Hawaii, might claim ten thousand, even tens of thousands.[5] Varying step by step with such differences in size of the polity are differences in territorial extent: from a few square miles in western Melanesia to tens or even hundreds of square miles in Polynesia.

The Polynesian advance in political scale was supported by advance over Melanesia in political structure. Melanesia presents a great array of social-political forms: here political organization is based upon patrilineal descent groups, there on cognatic groups, or men's club-houses recruiting neighborhood memberships, on a secret ceremonial society, or perhaps on some combination of these structural principles. Yet a general plan can be discerned. The characteristic western Melanesian "tribe," that is, the ethnic-cultural entity, consists of many autonomous kinship-residential groups. Amounting on the ground to a small village or a local cluster of hamlets, each of these is a copy of the others in organization, each tends to be economically self-governing, and each is the equal of the others in political status. The tribal plan is one of politically unintegrated segments—segmental. But the political geometry in Polynesia is pyramidal. Local groups of the order of self-governing Melanesian communities appear in Polynesia as subdivisions of a more inclusive political body. Smaller units are integrated into larger through a system of intergroup ranking, and the network of representative chiefs of the subdivisions amounts to a coordinating political structure. So instead of the Melanesian scheme of small, separate, and equal political blocs, the Polynesian polity is an extensive pyramid of groups capped by the family and following of a paramount chief. (This Polynesian political upshot is often, although not always, facilitated by the development of ranked lineages. Called *conical clan* by Kirchhoff, at one time *ramage* by Firth and *status lineage* by Goldman, the Polynesian ranked lineage is the same in principle as the so-called *obok* system widely distributed in Central Asia, and it is at least analogous to the Scottish clan, the Chinese clan, certain Central African Bantu lineage systems, the house-groups of Northwest Coast Indians, perhaps even the "tribes" of the Israelites.[6] Genealogical ranking is its distinctive feature: members of the same descent unit are ranked by genealogical distance from the common ancestor; lines of the same group became senior and cadet branches on this principle; related corporate lineages are relatively ranked, again by genealogical priority.)

Here is another criterion of Polynesian political advance: historical performance. Almost all of the native peoples of the South Pacific were brought up against intense European cultural pressure in the late eighteenth and the nineteenth centuries. Yet only the Hawaiians, Tahitians, Tongans, and to a lesser extent the Fijians, successfully defended

---

4. Hogbin and Wedgwood 1952-53, 1953-54. On New Guinea Highland political scale see among others, Paula Brown 1960.

5. See the summary account in Sahlins 1958, especially pp. 132-33.

6. Kirchhoff 1955; Firth 1957; Goldman 1957; Bacon 1958; Fried 1957.

themselves by evolving countervailing, native-controlled states. Complete with public governments and public law, monarchs and taxes, ministers and minions, these nineteenth century states are testimony to the native Polynesian political genius, to the level and the potential of indigenous political accomplishments.

Embedded within the grand differences in political scale, structure and performance is a more personal contrast, one in quality of leadership. An historically particular type of leader-figure, the "big-man" as he is often locally styled, appears in the underdeveloped settings of Melanesia. Another type, a chief properly so-called, is associated with the Polynesian advance.[7] Now these are distinct sociological types, that is to say, differences in the powers, privileges, rights, duties, and obligations of Melanesian big-men and Polynesian chiefs are given by the divergent societal contexts in which they operate. Yet the institutional distinctions cannot help but be manifest also in differences in bearing and character, appearance and manner—in a word, personality. It may be a good way to begin the more rigorous sociological comparison of leadership with a more impressionistic sketch of the contrast in the human dimension. Here I find it useful to apply characterizations—or is it caricature?—from our own history to big-men and chiefs, however much injustice this does to the historically incomparable backgrounds of the Melanesians and Polynesians. The Melanesian big-man seems to thoroughly bourgeois, so reminiscent of the free enterprising rugged individual of our own heritage. He combines with an ostensible interest in the general welfare a more profound measure of self-interested cunning and economic calculation. His gaze, as Veblen might have put it, is fixed unswervingly to the main chance. His every public action is designed to make a competitive and invidious comparison with others, to show a standing above the masses that is product of his own personal manufacture. The historical caricature of the Polynesian chief, however, is feudal rather than capitalist. His appearance, his bearing is almost regal; very likely he just *is a* big man—"Can't you see he is a chief? See how big he is?"[8] In his every public action is a display of the refinements of breeding, in his manner always that *noblesse oblige* of true pedigree and an incontestable

7. The big-man pattern is very widespread in western Melanesia, although its complete distribution is not yet clear to me. Anthropological descriptions of big-man leadership vary from mere hints of its existence, as among the Orokaiva (Williams 1930), Lesu (Powerdermaker 1933) or the interior peoples of northeastern Guadalcanal (Hogbin 1937-1938a), to excellent, closely grained analyses, such as Douglas Oliver's account of the Siuai of Bougainville (Oliver 1955). Big-man leadership has been more or less extensively described for the Manus of the Admiralty Islands (Mead 1934, 1937); the To'ambaita of northern Malaita (Hogbin 1939, 1943-44); the Tangu of northeastern New Guinea (Burridge 1960); the Kapauku of Netherlands New Guinea (Pospisil 1958, 1959-60); the Kaoka of Guadalcanal (Hogbin 1933-34, 1037-38); the Senaing District of Malekula (Deacon 1934); the Gawa' of the Huon Gulf area, New Guinea (Hogbin 1951); the Abelam (Kaberry 1940-41, 1941-42) and the Arapesh (Mead 1937a, 1938, 1947) of the Sepik District, New Guinea; The Elema, Orokola Bay, New Guinea (williams 1940); the Ngarawapum of the Markham Valley, New Guinea (Read 1946-47, 1949-50); the Kiwai of the Fly estuary, New Guinea (Landtman 1927); and a number of other societies, including, in New Guinea Highlands, the Kuma (Reay 1959), the Gahuka-Gama (Read 1952-53, 1959), the Kyaka (Bulmer 1960-61), the Enga (Meggitt 1957, 1957-58), and others. (For an overview of the structural position of New Guinea Highlands' leaders see Barnes 1962.) A partial bibliography of Polynesian chieftainship can be found in Sahlins 1958. The outstanding ethnographic description of Polynesian chieftainship is, of course, Firth's for Tikopia (1950, 1957)—Tikopia, however, is not typical of the more advanced Polynesian chiefdoms with which we are principally concerned here.

8. Gifford 1929:124

right of rule. With his standing not so much a personal achievement as a just social due, he can afford to be, and he is, every inch a chief.

In the several Melanesian tribes in which big-men have come under anthropological scrutiny, local cultural differences modify the expression of their personal powers.[9] But the indicative quality of big-man authority is everywhere the same: it is *personal* power. Big-men do not come to office; they do not succeed to, nor are they installed in, existing positions of leadership over political groups. The attainment of big-man status is rather the outcome of a series of acts which elevate a person above the common herd and attract about him a coterie of loyal, lesser men. It is not accurate to speak of "big-man" as a political title, for it is but an acknowledged standing in interpersonal relations—a "prince among men" so to speak as opposed to "The Prince of Danes". In particular Melanesian tribes the phrase might be "man of importance" or "man of renown", "generous rich-man", or "center-man", as well as "big-man".

A kind of two-sidedness in authority is implied in this series of phrases, a division of the big-man's field of influence into two distinct sectors. "Center-man" particularly connotes a cluster of followers gathered about an influential pivot. It socially implies the division of the tribe into political in-groups dominated by outstanding personalities. To the in-group, the big-man presents this sort of picture:

The place of the leader in the district group [in northern Malaita] is well summed up by his title, which might be translated as "center-man". . . He was like a banyan, the natives explain, which, though the biggest and tallest in the forest, is still a tree like the rest. But, just because it exceeds all others, the banyan gives support to more lianas and creepers, provides more food for the birds, and gives better protection against sun and rain.[10]

But "man of renown" connotes a broader tribal field in which a man is not so much a leader as he is some sort of hero. This is the side of the big-man facing outward from his own faction, his status among some or all of the other political clusters of the tribe. The political sphere of the big-man divides itself into a small internal sector composed of his personal satellites—rarely over eighty men—and a much larger external sector, the tribal galaxy consisting of many similar constellations.

As it crosses over from the internal into the external sector, a big-man's power undergoes qualitative change. Within his faction a Melanesian leader has true command ability, outside of it only fame and indirect influence. It is not that the center-man rules his faction

---

9. Thus the enclavement of the big-man pattern within a segmented lineage organization in the new Guinea Highlands appears to limit the leader's political role and authority in comparison, say, with the Siuai. In the Highlands, intergroup relations are regulated in part by the segmented lineage structure; among the Siuai intergroup relations depend more on contractual arrangements between big-men, which throws these figures more into prominence. (Notable in this connection has been the greater viability of the Siuai big-man than the native Highlands leader in the face of colonial control.) Barnes' (1962) comparison of Highland social structure with the classic segmentary lineage systems of Africa suggests an inverse relation between the formality of the lineage system and the political significance of individual action. Now, if instances such as the Siuai be tacked on to the comparison, the generalization may be further supported and extended: among societies of the tribal level (cf. Sahlins 1961, Service *in press*), the greater the self-regulation of the political process through a lineage system, the less function that remains to big-men, and the less significant their political authority.

10. Hogbin 1943–44:258.

by physical force, but his followers do feel obliged to obey him, and he can usually get what he wants by haranguing them—public verbal suasion is indeed so often employed by center-men that they have been styled "harangue-utans". The orbits of outsiders, however, are set by their own center-men. "'Do it yourself. I'm not *your* fool,'" would be the characteristic response to an order issued by a center-man to an outsider among the Siuai.[11] This fragmentation of true authority presents special political difficulties, particularly in organizing large masses of people for the prosecution of such collective ends as warfare or ceremony, Big-men do instigate mass action, but only by establishing both extensive renown and special relations of compulsion or reciprocity with other center-men.

Politics is in the main personal politiking in these Melanesian societies, and the size of a leader's faction as well as the extent of his renown are normally set by competition with other ambitious men. Little or no authority is given by social ascription: leadership is a creation—a creation of followership. "Followers", as it is written of the Kapauku of New Guinea, "stand in various relations to the leader. Their obedience to the headman's decisions is caused by motivations which reflect their particular relations to the leader."[12] So a man must be prepared to demonstrate that he possesses the kinds of skills that command respect—magical powers, gardening prowess, mastery of oratorical style, perhaps bravery in war and feud.[13] Typically decisive is the deployment of one's skills and efforts in a certain direction: towards amassing goods, most often pigs, shell monies and vegetable foods, and distributing them in ways which build a name for cavalier generosity, if not for compassion. A faction is developed by informal private assistance to people of a locale. Tribal rank and renown are developed by great public giveaways sponsored by the rising big-man, often on behalf of his faction as well as himself. In different Melanesian tribes, the renown-making public distribution may appear as one side of a delayed exchange of pigs between corporate kinship groups; a marital consideration given a bride's kinfolk; a set of feasts connected with the erection of a big-man's dwelling, or a clubhouse for himself and his faction, or with the purchase of higher grades of rank in secret societies; the sponsorship of a religious ceremony; a payment of subsidies and blood compensations to military allies; or perhaps the give away is a ceremonial challenge bestowed on another leader in the attempt to outgive and thus outrank him (a potlatch).

The making of the faction, however, is the true making of the Melanesian big-man. It is essential to establish relations of loyalty and obligation on the part of a number of people such that their production can be mobilized for renownbuilding external distribution. The bigger the faction the greater the renown; once momentum in external distribution has been generated the opposite can also be true. Any ambitious man who can gather a following can launch a societal career. The rising big-man necessarily depends initially on a small core of

---

11. Oliver 1955:408. Compare with the parallel statement for the Kaoka of Guadalcanal in Hogbin 1937-38:305.

12. Pospisil 1958:81.

13. It is difficult to say just how important the military qualifications of leadership have been in Melanesia, since the ethnographic researches have typically been undertaken after pacification, sometimes long after. I may underestimate this factor. Compare Bromley 1960.

followers, principally his own household and his closest relatives. Upon these people he can prevail economically: he capitalizes in the first instance on kinship dues and by finessing the relation of reciprocity appropriate among close kinsmen. Often it becomes necessary at an early phase to enlarge one's household. The rising leader goes out of his way to incorporate within his family "strays" of various sorts, people without familial support themselves, such as widows and orphans. Additional wives are especially useful. The more wives a man has the more pigs he has. The relation here is functional, not identical: with more women gardening there will be more food and pigs and more swineherds. A Kiwai Papuan picturesquely put to an anthropologist in pidgin the advantages, economic and political, of polygamy: " 'Another woman go garden, another woman go take firewood, another woman go catch fish, another woman cook him—husband he sing out plenty people come kaikai [i.e., come to eat].' "[14] Each new marriage, incidently, creates for the big-man an additional set of in-laws from whom he can exact economic favors. Finally, a leader's career sustains its upward climb when he is able to link other men and their families to his faction, harnessing their production to his ambition. This is due to calculated generosities, by placing others in gratitude and obligation through helping them in some big way. A common technique is payment of bridewealth on behalf of young men seeking wives.

The great Malinowski used a phrase in analyzing primitive political economy that felicitously describes just what the big-man is doing: amassing a "fund of power". A big-man is one who can create and use social relations which give him leverage on others' production and the ability to siphon off an excess product—or sometimes he can cut down their consumption in the interest of the siphon. Now although his attention may be given primarily to short-term personal interests, from an objective standpoint the leader acts to promote long-term societal interests. The fund of power provisions activities that involve other groups of the society at large. In the greater perspective of that society at large, big-men are indispensable means of creating supralocal organization: in tribes normally fragmented into small independent groups, big-men at least temporarily widen the sphere of ceremony, recreation and art, economic collaboration, of war too. Yet always this greater societal organization depends on the lesser factional organization, particularly on the ceilings on economic mobilization set by relations between center-men and followers. The limits and the weaknesses of the political order in general are the limits and weaknesses of the factional in-groups.

And the personal quality of subordination to a center-man is a serious weakness in factional structure. A personal loyalty has to be made and continually reinforced; if there is discontent it may well be severed. Merely to create a faction takes time and effort, and to hold it, still more effort. The potential rupture of personal links in the factional chain is at the heart of two broad evolutionary shortcomings of western Melanesian political orders. First, a comparative instability. Shifting dispositions and magnetisms of ambitious men in a region may induce fluctuations in factions, perhaps some overlapping of them, and fluctuations also in the extent of different renowns. The death of a center-man can become a regional political trauma: the death undermines the personally cemented faction, the group

14. Landtman 1927:168.

dissolves in whole or in part, and the people re-group finally around rising pivotal big-men. Although particular tribal structures in places cushion the disorganization, the big-man political system is generally unstable over short terms: in its superstructure it is a flux of rising and falling leaders, in its substructure of enlarging and contracting factions. Secondly, the personal political bond contributes to the containment of evolutionary advance. The possibility of their desertion, it is clear, often inhibits a leader's ability to forceably push up his followers' output, thereby placing constraints on higher political organization, but there is more to it than that. If it is to generate great momentum, a big-man's quest for the summits of renown is likely to bring out a contradiction in his relations to followers, so that he finds himself encouraging defection—or worse, an equalitarian rebellion—by encouraging production.

One side of the Melanesian contradiction is the initial economic reciprocity between a center-man and his followers. For his help they give their help, and for goods going out through his hands other goods (often from outside factions) flow back to his followers by the same path. The other side is that a cumulative build-up of renown forces center-men into economic extortion of the faction. Here it is important that not merely his own status, but the standing and perhaps the military security of his people depend on the big-man's achievements in public distribution. Established at the head of a sizeable faction, a center-man comes under increasing pressure to extract goods from his followers, to delay reciprocities owing them, and to deflect incoming goods back into external circulation. Success in competition with other big-men particularly undermines internal-factional reciprocities: such success is precisely measurable by the ability to give outsiders more than they can possibly reciprocate. In well delineated big-man polities, we find leaders negating the reciprocal obligations upon which their following had been predicated. Substituting extraction for reciprocity, they must compel their people to "eat the leader's renown," as one Solomon Island group puts it, in return for productive efforts. Some center-men appear more able than others to dam the inevitable tide of discontent that mounts within their factions, perhaps because of charismatic personalities, perhaps because of the particular social organizations in which they operate.[15] But paradoxically the ultimate defense of the center-man's position is some slackening of his drive to enlarge the funds of power. The alternative is much worse. In the anthropological record there are not merely instances of big-man chicanery and of material deprivation of the faction in the interests of renown, but some also of overloading of social relations with followers: the generation of antagonisms, defections, and in extreme cases the violent liquidation of the center-man.[16] Developing internal con-

---

15. Indeed it is the same people, the Siuai, who so explicitly discover themselves eating their leader's renown who also seem able to absorb a great deal of deprivation without violent reaction, at least until the leader's wave of fame has already crested (see Oliver 1955:362, 368, 387, 394).

16. "In the Paniai Lake region (of Netherlands New Guinea), the people go so far as to kill a selfish rich man because of his 'immorality'. His own sons or brothers are induced by the rest of the members of the community to dispatch the first deadly arrow. *'Aki to tonowi beu, inii idikima enadani kodo to niitou* (you should not be the only rich man, we should all be the same, therefore you only stay equal with us)' was the reason given by the Paniai people for killing Mote Juwopija of Madi, a *tonowi* [Kapauku for 'big-man'] who was not generous enough". (Pospisil 1958;80, cf. pp. 108-110). On another egalitarian conspiracy, see Hogbin 1951:145, and for other aspects of the Melanesian contradiction note, for example, Hogbin 1939:81; Burridge 1960:18-19; and Reay 1959:110, 129-30.

straints, the Melanesian big-man political order brakes evolutionary advance at a certain level. It sets ceilings on the intensification of political authority, on the intensification of household production by political means, and on the diversion of household outputs in support of wider political organization. But in Polynesia there constraints were breached, and although Polynesian chiefdoms also found their developmental plateau, it was not before political evolution had been carried above the Melanesian ceilings. The fundamental defects of the Melanesian plan were overcome in Polynesia. The division between small internal and larger external political sectors, upon which all big-man politics hinged, was suppressed in Polynesia by the growth of an enclaving chiefdom-at-large. A chain of command subordinating lesser chiefs and groups to greater, on the basis of inherent social rank, made local blocs or personal followings (such as were independent in Melanesia) merely dependent parts of the large Polynesian chiefdom. So the nexus of the Polynesian chiefdom became an extensive set of offices, a pyramid of higher and lower chiefs holding sway over larger and smaller sections of the polity. Indeed the system of ranked and subdivided lineages (conical clan system), upon which the pyramid was characteristically established, might build up through several orders of inclusion and encompass the whole of an island or group of islands. While the island or the archipelago would normally be divided into several independent chiefdoms, high-order lineage connections between them, as well as kinship ties between their paramount chiefs, provided structural avenues for at least temporary expansion of political scale, for consolidation of great into even greater chiefdoms.[17]

The pivotal paramount chief as well as the chieftains controlling parts of a chiefdom were true office holders and title holders. They were not, like melanesian big-men, fishers of men: they held positions of authority over permanent groups. The honorifics of Polynesian chiefs likewise did not refer to a standing in interpersonal relations, but to their leadership of political divisions—here "The Prince of Danes" *not* "the prince among men". In western Melanesia the personal superiorities and inferiorities arising in the intercourse of particular men largely defined the political bodies. In Polynesia there emerged suprapersonal structures of leadership and followership, organizations that continued independently of the particular men who occupied positions in them for brief mortal spans.

As these Polynesian chiefs did not make their positions in society—they were installed in societal positions. In several of the islands, men did struggle to office against the will and stratagems of rival aspirants. But then they came *to* power. Power resided in the office;

---

17. Aside from the transitional developments in eastern Melanesia, several western Melanesian societies advanced to a structural position intermediate between under-developed Melanesian polities and Polynesian chiefdoms. In these western Melanesian protochiefdoms, an ascribed division of kinship groups (or segments thereof) into chiefly and nonchiefly ranks emerges—as in Sa'a (Ivens 1927), around Buka passage (Blackwood 1935), in Manam Island (Wedgwood 1933-34, 1958-59), Waropen (Held 1957), perhaps Mafulu (Williamson 1912), and several others. The rank system does not go beyond the broad dual division of groups into chiefly and nonchiefly: no pyramid of ranked social-political divisions along Polynesian lines is developed. The political unit remains near the average size of the western Melanesian autonomous community. Sway over the kin groups of such a local body falls automatically to a chiefly unit, but chiefs do not hold office title with stipulated rights over corporate sections of society, and further extension of chiefly authority, if any, must be achieved. The Trobriands, which carry this line of chiefly development to its highest point, remain under the same limitations, although it was ordinarily possible for powerful chiefs to integrate settlements to the external sector within their domains (*cf.* Powell 1960).

it was not made by the demonstration of personal superiority. In other islands, Tahiti was famous for it, succession to chieftainship was tightly controlled by inherent rank. The chiefly lineage ruled by virtue of its genealogical connections with divinity, and chiefs were succeeded by first sons, who carried "in the blood" the attributes of leadership. The important comparative point is this: the qualities of command that had to reside in men in Melanesia, that had to be personally demonstrated in order to attract loyal followers, were in Polynesia socially assigned to office and rank. In Polynesia, people of high rank and office *ipso facto* were leaders, and by the same token the qualities of leadership were automatically lacking—theirs was not to question why—among the underlying population. Magical powers such as a Melanesian big-man might acquire to sustain his position, a Polynesian high chief inherited by divine descent as the *mana* which sanctified his rule and protected his person against the hands of the commonalty. The productive ability the big-man laboriously had to demonstrate was effortlessly given Polynesian chiefs as religious control over agricultural fertility, and upon the ceremonial implementation of it the rest of the people were conceived dependent. Where a Melanesian leader had to master the compelling oratorical style, Polynesian paramounts often had trained "talking chiefs" whose voice was the chiefly commands.

In the Polynesian view, a chiefly personage was in the nature of things powerful. But this merely implies the objective observation that his power was of the group rather than of himself. His authority came from the organization, from an organized acquiescence in his privileges and organized means of sustaining them. A kind of paradox resides in evolutionary developments which detach the exercise of authority from the necessity to demonstrate personal superiority: organizational power actually extends the role of personal decision and conscious planning, gives it greater scope, impact, and effectiveness. The growth of a political system such as the Polynesian constitutes control of human affairs. Especially significant for society at large were privileges accorded Polynesian chiefs which made them greater architects of funds of power than ever was any Melanesian big-man.

Masters of their people and "owners" in a titular sense of group resources, Polynesian chiefs had rights of call upon the labor and agricultural produce of households within their domains. Economic mobilization did not depend on, as it necessarily had for Melanesian big-men, the *de novo* creation by the leader of personal loyalties and economic obligations. A chief need not stoop to obligate this man or that man, need not by a series of individual acts of generosity induce others to support him, for economic leverage over a group was the inherent chiefly due. Consider the implications for the fund of power of the widespread chiefly privilege, related to titular "ownership" of land, of placing an interdiction, a tabu, on the harvest of some crop by way of reserving its use for a collective project. By means of the tabu the chief directs the course of production in a general way: households of his domain must turn to some other means of subsistence. He delivers a stimulus to household production: in the absence of the tabu further labors would not have been necessary. Most significantly, he has generated a politically utilizable agricultural surplus. A subsequent call on this surplus floats chieftainship as a going concern, capitalizes the fund of power. In certain islands, Polynesian chiefs controlled great storehouses which held the goods congealed by chiefly pressures on the commonalty. David Malo, one of the great native custodians of old Hawaiian lore, felicitously catches the political significance of the chiefly magazine in his well-known *Hawaiian Antiquities:*

> In was the practice for kings [i.e., paramount chiefs of individual islands] to build store-houses in which to collect food, tapas [bark cloth], malos [men's loin cloths], pa-us [women's loin skirts], and all sorts of goods. These store-houses were designed by the Kalaimoku [chief's principal executive] as a menas of keeping the people contented, so they would not desert the king. They were like the baskets that were used to entrap the *hinalea* fish. The *hinalea* thought there was something good within the basket, and he hung round the outside of it. In the same way the people thought there was food in the store-houses, and they kept their eyes on the king. As the rat will not desert the pantry . . .where he thinks food is, so the people will not desert the king while they think there is food in his store-house.[18]

Redistribution of the fund of power was the supreme art of Polynesian politics. By well-planned *noblesse oblige* the large domain of a paramount chief was held together, organized at times for massive projects, protected against other chiefdoms, even further enriched. Uses of the chiefly fund included lavish hospitality and entertainments for outside chiefs and for the chief's own people, and succor of individuals or the underlying population at large in times of scarcities—bread and circuses. Chiefs subsidized craft production, promoting in Polynesia a division of technical labor unparalleled in extent and expertise in most of the Pacific. They supported also great technical construction, as of irrigation complexes, the further returns to which swelled the chiefly fund. They initiated large-scale religious construction too, subsidized the great ceremonies, and organized logistic support for extensive military campaigns. Larger and more easily replenished than their western Melanesian counterparts, Polynesian funds of power permitted greater political regulation of a greater range of social activities on greater scale.

In the most advanced Polynesian chiefdoms, as in Hawaii and Tahiti, a significant part of the chiefly fund was deflected away from general redistribution towards the upkeep of the institution of chieftainship. The fund was siphoned for the support of a permanent administrative establishment. In some measure, goods and services contributed by the people precipitated out as the grand houses, assembly places, and temple platforms of chiefly precincts. In another measure, they were appropriated for the livelihood of circles of retainers, many of them close kinsmen of the chief, who clustered about the powerful paramounts. These were not all useless hangers-on. They were political cadres: supervisors of the stores, talking chiefs, ceremonial attendants, high priests who were intimately involved in political rule, envoys to transmit directives through the chiefdom. There were men in these chiefly retinues—in Tahiti and perhaps Hawaii, specialized warrior corps—whose force could be directed internally as a buttress against fragmenting or rebellious elements of the chiefdom. A Tahitian or Hawaiian high chief had more compelling sanctions than the harangue. He controlled a ready physical force, an armed body of executioners, which

18. Malo 1903:257-58.

gave him mastery particularly over the lesser people of the community. While it looks a lot like the big-man's faction again, the differences in functioning of the great Polynesian chief's retinue are more significant than the superficial similarities in appearance. The chief's coterie, for one thing, is economically dependent upon him rather than he upon them. And in deploying the cadres politically in various sections of the chiefdom, or against the lower orders, the great Polynesian chiefs sustained command where the Melanesian big-man, in his external sector, had at best renown.

This is not to say that the advanced Polynesian chiefdoms were free of internal defect, of potential or actual malfunctioning. The large political-military apparatus indicates something of the opposite. So does the recent work of Irving Goldman[19] on the intensity of "status rivalry" in Polynesia, especially when it is considered that much of the status rivalry in developed chiefdoms, as the Hawaiian, amounted to popular rebellion against chiefly despotism rather than mere contest for position within the ruling-stratum. This suggests that Polynesian chiefdoms, just as Melanesian big man orders, generate along with evolutionary development countervailing anti-authority pressures, and that the weight of the latter may ultimately impede further development.

The Polynesian contradiction seems clear enough. On one side, chieftainship is never detached from kinship moorings and kinship economic ethics. Even the greatest Polynesian chiefs were conceived superior kinsmen to the masses, fathers to their people, and generosity was morally incumbent upon them. On the other side, the major Polynesian paramounts seemed inclined to "eat the power of the government too much," as the Tahitians put it, to divert an undue proportion of the general wealth toward the chiefly establishment.[20] The diversion could be accomplished by lowering the customary level of general redistribution, lessening the material returns of chieftainship to the community at large—tradition attributes the great rebellion of Mangarevan commoners to such cause.[21] Or the diversion might—and I suspect more commonly did—consist in greater and more forceful exactions from lesser chiefs and people, increasing returns to the chiefly apparatus without necessarily affecting the level of general redistribution. In either case, the well developed chiefdom creates for itself the dampening paradox of stoking rebellion by funding its authority.[22]

19. Goldman 1955; 1957; 1960.

20. The great Tahitian chiefs were traditionally enjoined not to eat the power of government too much, as well as to practice open-handedress towards the people (Handy 1930:41). Hawaiian high chiefs were given precisely the same advice by counselors (Malo 1903:255).

21. Buck 1938:70–77, 160, 165.

22. The Hawaiian traditions are very clear on the encouragement given rebellion by chiefly exactions—although one of our greatest sources of Hawaiian tradition, David Malo, provides the most sober caveat regarding this kind of evidence. "I do not suppose", he wrote in the preface of *Hawaiian Antiquities*, "the following history to be free from mistakes, in that material for it has come from oral traditions; consequently it is marred by errors of human judgment and does not approach the accuracy of the word of God."

Malo (1903:258) notes that "Many kings have been put to death by the people because of their oppression of the *makaainana* (i.e., commoners)." He goes on to list several who "lost their lives on account of their cruel exactions", and follows the list with the statement "It was for this reason that some of the ancient kings had a wholesome fear of the people." The propensity of Hawaiian high chiefs for undue appropriation from commoners is a point made over and over

In Hawaii and other islands cycles of political centralization and decentralization may be abstracted from traditional histories. That is, larger chiefdoms periodically fragmented into smaller and then were later reconstituted.

Here would be more evidence of a tendency to overtax the political structure. But how to explain the emergence of a developmental stymie, of an inability to sustain political advance beyond a certain level? To point to a chiefly propensity to consume or a Polynesian propensity to rebel is not enough; such propensities are promoted by the very advance of chiefdoms. There is reason to hazard instead that Parkinson's notable law is behind it all: that progressive expansion in political scale entailed more-than-proportionate accretion in the ruling apparatus, unbalancing the flow of wealth in favor of the apparatus. The ensuing unrest then curbs the chiefly impositions, sometimes by reducing chiefdom scale to the nadir of the periodic cycle. Comparison of the requirements of administration in small and large Polynesian chiefdoms helps make the point.

A lesser chiefdom, confined say as in the Marquesas Islands to a narrow valley, could be almost personally ruled by a headman in frequent contact with the relatively small population. Melville's partly romanticized—also for its ethnographic details, partly cribbed—the account in *Typee* makes this clear enough.[23] But the great Polynesian chiefs had to rule much larger, spatially dispersed, internally organized populations. Hawaii, an island over four thousand square miles with an aboriginal population approaching one hundred thousand, was at times a single chiefdom, at other times divided into two to six independent chiefdoms, and at all times each chiefdom was composed of large subdivisions under powerful subchiefs. Sometimes a chiefdom in the Hawaiian group extended beyond the confines of one of the islands, incorporating part of another through conquest. Now, such extensive chiefdoms would have to be coordinated; they would have to be centrally tapped for a fund of power, buttressed against internal disruption, sometimes massed for distant, perhaps overseas, military engagements. All of this to be implemented by means of communication still at the level of word-of-mouth, and means of transportation consisting of human bodies and canoes. (The extent of certain larger chieftainships, coupled with the limitations of communication and transportation, incidentally suggests another possible source of political unrest: that the burden of provisioning the governing apparatus would

---

again by Malo (see pp. 85, 87-88, 258, 267-68). In Fornander 1880:40-41, 76-78, 88, 149–150, 270–271). In addition, Fornander at times links appropriation of wealth and ensuing rebellion to the provisioning of the chiefly establishment, as in the following passage: "Scarcity of food, after a while, obliged *Kalaniopuu* (paramount chief of the island of Hawaii and half brother of Kamehameha I's father) to remove his court (from the Kona district) into the Kohala district, where his headquarters were fixed at Kapaau. Here the same extravagant, *laissez-faire*, eat and be merry policy continued that had been commenced at Kona, and much grumbling and discontent began to manifest itself among the resident chiefs and cultivators of the land, the 'Makaainana'. *Imakakaloa*, a great chief in the Puna district, and *Nuuampaahu*, a chief of Naalehu in the Kau district, became the heads and rallying-points of the discontented. The former resided on his lands in Puna [in the southeast, across the island from Kohala in the northwest], and openly resisted the orders of *Kalaniopuu* and his exagant demands for contributions of all kinds of property; the latter was in attendance with the court of *Kalaniopuu* in Kohala, but was strongly suspected of favouring the growing discontent" (Fornander 1880:200). Aside from the Mangarevan uprising mentioned in the text, there is some evidence for similar revolts in Tonga (Mariner 1827i:80; Thomson 1894:294f) and in Tahiti (Henry 1928:195-196, 297).

23. Or see Handy 1923 and Linton 1939.

tend to fall disproportionately on groups within easiest access of the paramount.[24]) A tendency for the developed chiefdom to proliferate in executive cadres, to grow top-heavy, seems in these circumstances altogether functional, even though the ensuing drain on wealth proves the chiefdom's undoing. Functional also, and likewise a material drain on the chiefdom at large, would be widening distinctions between chiefs and people in style of life. Palatial housing, ornamentation and luxury, finery and ceremony, in brief, conspicuous consumption, however much it seems mere self-interest always has a more decisive social significance. It creates those invidious distinctions between rulers and ruled so conducive to a passive—hence quite economical!—acceptance of authority. Throughout history, inherently more powerful political organizations than the Polynesian, with more assured logistics of rule, have turned to it—including in our time some ostensibly revolutionary and proletarian governments, despite every pre-revolutionary protestation of solidarity with the masses and equality for the classes.

In Polynesia then, as in Melanesia, political evolution is eventually shortcircuited by an overload on the relations between leaders and their people. The Polynesian tragedy, however, was somewhat the opposite of the Melanesian. In Polynesia, the evolutionary ceiling was set by extraction from the population at large in favor of the chiefly faction, in Melanesia by extraction from the big-man's faction in favor of distribution to the population at large. Most importantly, the Polynesian ceiling was higher. Melanesian big-men and Polynesians chiefs not only reflect different varieties and levels of political evolution, they display in different degrees the capacity to generate and to sustain political progress.

Especially emerging from their juxtaposition is the more decisive impact of Polynesian chiefs on the economy, the chiefs' greater leverage on the output of the several households of society. The success of any primitive political organization is decided here, in the control that can be developed over household economies. For the household is not merely the principal productive unit in primitive societies, it is often quite capable of autonomous direction of its own production, and it is oriented towards production for its own, not societal consumption. The greater potential of Polynesian chieftainship is precisely the greater pressure it could exert on household output, its capacity both to generate a surplus and to deploy it out of the household towards a broader division of labor, cooperative construction, and massive ceremonial and military action. Polynesian chiefs were the more effective means of societal collaboration on economic, political, indeed all cultural fronts. Perhaps we have been too long accustomed to perceive rank and rule from the standpoint of the individuals involved, rather than from the perspective of the total society, as if the secret of the subordination of man to man lay in the personal satisfactions of power. And then the breakdowns too, or the evolutionary limits, have been searched out in men, in "weak" kings or megalomaniacal dictators—always, "who is the matter?" An excursion into the

---

24. On the *difficulty* of providing the Hawaiian paramount's large establishment see the citation from Fornander above, and also Fornander 1880: 100–101; Malo 1903: 92–93, *et passium.* The Hawaiian great chiefs developed the practice of the circuit—like feudal monarchs—often leaving a train of penury behind as they moved in state from district to district of the chiefdom.

field of primitive politics suggests the more fruitful conception that the gains of political developments accrue more decisively to society than to individuals, and the failings as well are of structure not men.

REFERENCES

Bacon, Elizabeth E., *Obok.* (= *Viking Fund Publications in Anthropology* No. 25) (New York: The Wenner-Gren Foundation, 1958).

Barnes, J. A., "African Models in the New Guinea Highlands", *Man* 62(2):5–9 (1962).

Blackwood, Beatrice, *Both Sides of Buka Passage* (Oxford: Clarendon Press, 1935).

Bromley, M., "A Preliminary Report on Law Among the Grand Valley Dani of Netherlands New Guinea", *Nieuw Guinea Studien* 4;235–259 (1960).

Brown, Paula, "Chimbu Tribes: Political Organization int he Eastern Highlands of New Guinea", *Southwestern Journal of Anthropology* 16:22-35 (1960).

Buck, Sir Peter H., *Ethnology of Mangareva* (= *Bernice P. Bishop Mus. Bull.* 157) (Honolulu, 1938).

Bulmer, Ralph, "Political Aspects of the Moka Exchange System Among the Kyaka People of the Western Highlands of New Guinea", *Oceania* 31:1–13 (1960–61).

Burridge, Kenelm, *Mambu: A Melanesian Millenium* (London: Methuen & Co., 1960).

Conklin, Harold C. *Hanunoó Agriculture* (= *FAO Forestry Development paper* No. 12) (Rome: Food and Agricultural Organization of the United Nations, 1957).

Deacon, A. Bernard, *Malekula: A Vanishing People in the New Hebrides.* (C. H. Wedgwood, ed.) (London: Geo. Routledge and Sos. 1934).

Dyen, Isidore, Review of *The Position of the Polynesian Languages within the Austronesian (Malayo-Polynesian) Language Family* (by George W. Grace). *Journal of the Polynesian Society* 69:180–184 (1960).

Firth, Raymond, *Primitive Polynesian Economy* (New York: Humanities Press, 1950). ,*We, the Tikopia.* Second ed. (London: Allen and Unwin, 1957).

Fornander, Abraham, *An Account of the Polynesian Race.* Vol. II (London: Trübner, 1880).

Freeman, J. D., *Ibban Agriculture* (= *Colonial Research Studies* No. 18) (London: Her Majesty's Stationery Office, 1955).

Fried, Morton, H., "The Classification of Corporate Unilineal Descent Groups". *Jour. of the Royal Anthrop. Instit.* 87:1–29 (1957).

Gifford, Edward Winslow, *Tongan Society* (= *Bernice P. Bishop Mus. Bull.* 61) (Honolulu, 1929).

Goldman, Irving, "Status Rivalry and Cultural Evolution in Polynesia", *American Anthropologist* 57:680–697 (1955).

—, "Variations in Polynesian Social Organization", *Journal of the Polynesian Society* 66:374–390 (1957).

—, "The Evolution of Polynesian Societies", *Culture and History* (S. Diamond, ed.) (New York: Columbia University Press, 1960).

Golson, Jack, "Polynesian Culture History", *Journal of the Polynesian Society,* 70:498–508 (1961).

Goodenough, Ward, "Oceania and the Problem of Controls in the Study of Cultural and Human Evolution", *Journal of the Polynesian Society* 66:146–155 (1957).

Grace, George, "Subgroupings of Malayo-Polynesian: A Report of Tentative Findings", *American Anthropologist* 57:337–39 (1955).

—, *The Position of the Polynesian Languages within the Austronesian (Malayo-Polynesian) Family (= Indiana University Publications in Anthropological Linguistics* 16) (1959).

Handy, E. S. Craighill, *The Native Culture in the Marquesas* (= *Bernice P. Bishop Museum Bull.* 9) (Honolulu, 1923).

—, *History and Culture in the Society Islands* (= *Bernice P. Bishop Mus. Bull.* 79) (Honolulu, 1930).

Held, G. J., *The Papuas of Waropen* (The Hague: Koninklijk Instituut Voor Taal-, Land- En Volkenkunde, 1957).

Henry, Teuira, *Ancient Tahiti* (= *Bernice P. Bishop Mus. Bull.* 48) (Honolulu, 1928).

Hogbin, H. Ian, "Culture Change in the Solomon Islands: Report of Field Work in Guadalcanal and Malaita", *Oceania 4:233-267* (1933-34).

—, "Social Advancement in Guadalcanal, Solomon Islands", *Oceans 8:289–305 (*1937-38).

—, "The Hill People of North-eastern Guadalcanal", *Oceania* 8:62-89 (1937–38a).

—, *Experiments in Civilization* (London: Geo: Routledge and Sos, 1939).

—, "Native Councils and Courts in the Solomon Islands", *Oceania* 14:258–283 (1943–44).

—, *Transformation Scene: The Changing Culture of a New Guinea Village* (London: Routledge and Kegan Paul, 1951).

Hogbin, H. and Camilla H. Wedgwood, "Local Groupings in Melanesia", *Oceania* 23:241-276; 24:58-76 (1952-53, 1953-54).

Ivens, W. G., *Melanesians of the Southeast Solomon Islands* (London: Kegan, Paul, Trench, Trubner and Co. 1927).

Kaberry, Phyllis M. "The Abelam Tribe, Sepik District, New Guinea: a Preliminary Report", *Oceania* 11:233-258, 345-367 (1940-41).

—, "Law and Political Organization in the Abelam Tribe", *Oceania* 12:79–95, 209–255, 331–363 (1941-42).

Kirchhoff, Paul, "The Principles of Clanship in Human Society", *Davidson Anthropological Journal* 1:1-11 (1955).

Landtman, Gunnar, *The Kiwai Papuans of British New Guinea* (London: Macmillan, 1927).

Linton, Ralph, "Marguesan Culture", *The Individual and His Society* (Ralph Linton and A. Kardiner) (New York: Columbia University Press, 1939).

Malo, David, *Hawaiian Antiquities* (Honolulu: Hawaiian Gazette Co, 1903).

Mariner, William, *An Account of the Natives of the Tonga Islands* (John Martin, compiler) (Edinburgh: Constable & Co, 1827).

Mead, Margaret, "Kinship in the Admiralty Islands", *Amer. Mus. Nat. Hist. Anthrop. Papers* 34:181–358 (1934).
—, "The Manus of the Admiralty Islands", *Cooperation and Competition among Primitive Peoples* (m. Mead, ed.) (New York and London: McGraw-Hill, 1937).
—, "The Arapesh of New Guinea", *Cooperation and Competition Among Primitive Peoples* (M. Mead, ed.) (New York and london: McGraw-Hill, 1937a).
—, "The Mountain Arapesh I. An Importing Culture", *Amer. Mus. Nat. Hist. Anthrop. Papers* 36:139–349 (1938).
—, "The Mountain Arapesh III. Socio-Economic Life", *Amer. Mus. Nat. Hist. Anthrop. Papers* 40:159–232 (1947).

Meggitt, Mervyn, "Enga Political Organization: A Preliminary Description", *Mankind* 5:133–137 (1957).
—, "The Enga of the New Guinea Highlands: Some Preliminary Observations", *Oceania* 28:253–330 (1957–58).

Oliver, Douglas, *A Solomon Islands Society* (Cambridge: Harvard University Press, 1955).

Pospisil, Leopold, *Kapauku Papuans and Their Law* (= *Yale University Publications in Anthropology,* No. 54) (New Haven: Yale University Press, 1958).
—, "The Kapauku Papuans and their Kinship Organization", *Oceania* 30:188–205 (1958–59).

Powdermaker, Hortense, *Life in Lesu* (New York: W. W. Norton, 1933).

Powell, H. A., "Competitive Leadership in Trobriand Political Organization", *Jour. Royal Anthrop. Instit.* 90:118–145 (1960).

Read, K. E., "Social Organization in the Markham Valley, New Guinea", *Oceania* 17:93–118 (1946-47).
—, "The Political System of the Ngarawapum", *Oceania* 20:185-223 (1949–50).
—, "The Nama Cult of the Central Highlands, New Guinea", *Oceania* 23:1–25 (1952–53).
—, "Leadership and Consensus in the New Guinea Society" *American Anthropologist* 61:425–436 (1959).

Reay, Marie, *The Kuma* (Melbourne University Press, 1959).

Sahlins, Marshall D., *Social Stratification in Polynesia* (= *American Ethnological Society Monograph*) (Seattle: University of Washington Press, 1958).
—, "The Segementary Lineage: An Organization of Predatory Expansion", *American Anthropologist* 63:322–345 (1961).

Service, Elman, R., *Primitive Social Organization: An Evolutionary Perspective* (New York: Random House, in press).

Suggs, Robert C., *Ancient Civilizations of Polynesia* (New York: Mentor, 1960).

Thomson, Sir Basil, *The Diversions of a Prime Minister* (Edinburgh and London: William Blackwood & Sos, 1894).

Vayda, Andrew Peter, "Polynesian Cultural Distributions in New Perspective", *American Anthropologist* 61:817–828 (1959).

Wedgwood, Camilia H., "Report on Research in Manam Island, Mandated Territory of new Guinea", *Oceania* 4:373–403 (1933–34).
—, "Manam Kinship", *Oceania* 29:239–256 (1958–59).

Williams, F. E., "Orokaiva Society" (Oxford University Press, London: Humphrey Milford, 1930).
—, *Drama of Orokolo* (Oxford: Clarendon Press, 1940).

Williamson, Robert W., *The Mafulu: Mountain People of British New Guinea* (London: Macmillan, 1912).

Worsley, Peter, *The Trumpet Shall Sound* (London: Macgibbon and Kee, 1957).

16 THE PRINCIPLES OF CLANSHIP IN HUMAN SOCIETY

—PAUL KIRCHHOFF

Although Kirchhoff says he is talking about clanship, he is really talking about something much broader—corporate kin groups. It is true that some of these are clans, but others are better classified as lineages or kindreds. The definition of clan continues to vary among anthropologists. The editor has suggested elsewhere that it is useful to hold the definition of clan to social units comprised of unilineally related members who trace their relationship through stipulated descent, that is, through ties which they cannot always explain genealogically. This contrasts with demonstrated descent, which involves specification of all genealogical connecting links. Unilineal groups based on this principle are better termed lineages. Both kinds of groups, can exist at the same time in the same society. However, there are societies in which one or the other predominates or is the sole kind of organization at the appropriate social level. This is said to be related to the divergent functions of stipulated and demonstrated descent. The former accords with easier access to the corporate holdings of the group; the latter tends to be associated with increasing use of the principle of economic scarcity and the narrowing of rights of access to basic resources.

The Kirchhoff essay lays the basis for understanding the previous generalization. It suggests some of the processes by which relative equalitarianism was replaced in some societies by increasing the significance of ranking and stratification. As such, it contributes further to our understanding of the evolution of society.

1

If one were asked to single out one outstanding social phenomenon which dominates the early evolution of human society the answer would undoubtedly have to be that this phenomenon is the clan. Proof for this assertion will hardly be necessary. The decisive role of the clan in early human history manifests itself in a striking manner in the fact that its disappearance as the dominating form of social organization marks the end of a whole historical phase, and the beginning of another, i.e., that dominated by social classes and their struggles.

It would, of course, be incorrect to say that the history of human society begins only with the emergence of the clan. A very important chapter precedes this event. But while the beginning of this chapter of the evolution of human society is still characterized by the

Originally published in the *Davidson Journal of Anthropology* (1955), pp. 1–10. Reprinted with permission of the Department of Anthropology, University of Washington.

comparative shapelessness of all social forms, in its later part the subsequent emergence of the clan casts its shadow ahead as it were: here the main theme, and consequently the main problem confronting the student, are the various facts and forms leading towards the emergence of the clan.

One of the outstanding tasks before the student of early human society is, therefore, the study of the various forms the clan has taken in the course of its development, of the factors which brought the clan in its various forms into existence, and of the factors which led to its replacement, as the dominating form of social organization, by other forms.

The study of this complex of problems has dominated the first decades of anthropological research. Within the last two decades, however, it has almost completely receded into the background as a result of the present anti-evolutionist trend of anthropology.

The early evolutionist school in anthropology, with Morgan as its most gifted spokesman, fell into an error for which anthropology subsequently had to pay a heavy fine, i.e., the fine of experiencing the growth of anti-evolutionist tendencies, the unchecked growth of which today threatens anthropology with ever-increasing sterility. This error consists in replacing the concept of *multi*lineal evolution, as applied by leading students to both natural history and the *later* phases of the history of society, by the concept of *uni*lineal evolution, as far as early society is concerned. The application of this mistaken concept led to the distortion of many facts—and it may be said that anthropology since Morgan has to a very large extent lived on these distortions. It has become the fashionable pursuit of many a writer to demonstrate that the unilineal evolutionism of Morgan and others operated with distorted or misinterpreted facts, and that—therefore!—the facts unearthed by anthropology, both before, and even more so since Morgan, prove the inapplicability of the concept of evolution to primitive society—and therefore to society generally. All that has to be done, on the contrary, in order to demonstrate its applicability is to replace the unilineal concept of Morgan by the multilineal concept as applied in other sciences.

One of the tasks, therefore, which confronts us in studying the evolution of the clan and its role in the history of society is to inquire which different *forms of the clan* are found to exist, and what *their mutual genetic relation is*. The present paper is in the main confined to this task.

2

The most primitive stage of societal development known shows relatively small communities with a non-productive economy. The communities, several of which are united by bonds of common speech, customs and beliefs into what usually is called a tribe, apparently everywhere consist of a nucleus of near relatives (relatives both by blood and by marriage)—to which nucleus are frequently attached more distant relatives and unrelated individuals who for one reason or other have left their original community. Everywhere, however, the decisive element is the group of relatives, by blood and by marriage. Very frequently the community consists only of this group: a married couple and their unmarried and some of their married children—usually the married sons only, or the married daughters only, together with their husbands and wives and unmarried children.

This group, and the whole community, if larger than the kernel of relatives, is by no means a permanent unit. Ever again it splits up into smaller units of similar composition, be it at the death of the leading member of the community, as the result of the impossibility of the existence of a group above a certain size in one locality at this stage of economy and organization, or be it as the result of friction between members of the group, e.g., between brothers or sisters. Marriage of a member of the community frequently leads to his settling apart. This lays the foundation for a new community which in the course of time will go through the same process as the original one.

No bond beyond that of sentiment ties the members of this community to the one in which they were born. What matters is where people live at a given moment: in other words, *the concept of descent is still completely absent.*

Relatives by blood and relatives by marriage are here, as to their place in the community, on a far more equal footing than at any subsequent stage of societal development.

The ties and obligations of kinship cut, of course, across several such communities, where there is intermarriage between several of them. But these ties and obligations do not themselves constitute communities. They do, therefore, not enter into our problem directly.

It is, on the other hand, only these ties of kinship which apparently everywhere at this stage regulate marriage. If we confine the term exogamy to the rule that marriage must be outside of a group larger than that composed of relatives in the first degree, and if we mean by group a constant body of people whose extent is the same for any of its members, then there is no such thing as exogamy to be found at this stage. Society here can still do without the concept of descent and consequently without the rule of exogamy.

The conditions described here are found mainly amongst mere food-gatherers and hunters, and may be said to be typical for them.

In certain cases, however, as, e.g., in many tribes in the Amazon area of South America, where the tilling of the soil has already replaced the mere hunting and collecting of food, and where the communities are considerably larger than, let us say, those of the Shoshoni or Apache, the concept of descent is nevertheless still unknown. Such cases undoubtedly present exceptions to the rule that mere foodgathering and hunting go together with the absence of groups based on the concept of descent. Lowie has quoted these South American cases as proof for his contention that there is "little evidence of complex laws of sequence." It would, however, seem to be very unsafe to base such a far-reaching contention on what so obviously are exceptional cases. Similarly futile it would be to arrive at general conclusions from the reverse cases of, e.g., many Australians or the tribes of the North American northwest coast where we find more advanced forms of kinship organization combined with lower forms of economy. These cases have to be explained on the individual merits of the case, and clearly understood as exceptions due to exceptional historical circumstances which in most cases we probably shall be able to demonstrate.

3

In the overwhelming majority of cases higher forms of economic activity are found together with higher forms of kinship organization.

The increasing cooperative character of economic activity requires forms of kinship organization which assure greater stability of the cooperating groups (which in primitive society predominantly means groups of relatives). Greater stability of the cooperating groups of relatives requires some principle which more clearly sets off one such group from the other, and which at the same time, assures their continuity in time.

The principle of clanship, based on the concept of descent, does both. In other words, the function of the clan is to assure stable and continuous cooperation. It takes a number of different forms, but its essence appears to be the same everywhere: to group together in one permanent unit all those persons, living or dead, who can claim common descent. This group is commonly called a clan or sib. Its invention, if we may call it that, is one of the greatest achievements of early man. It provided the form of social organization under which the forces of production could grow, slowly but steadily, to the comparative height attained, e.g., by the mountain tribes of Luzon, with their magnificent terraced fields and irrigation works, or, higher still, by Homeric society.

In this respect, however, and in the complexity and perfection attained by the developing forms of kinship organization themselves, there are important, even striking differences between some of the main forms which the principle of clanship took concretely. To anticipate one of the main results of our survey: some of these forms seem to lead comparatively early to the stage of stagnation, or into a blind alley if we may say so, while others seem to possess far greater possibilities of development.

At the present stage of the investigation of the problem, I conceive of these various forms of clans not as of consecutive stages, so that one could be explained as developing out of the other, but rather as stemming from the same root, i.e., from the more amorphous type of kinship organization outlined before. Whether they actually grew out of this common root *at the same time* is quite another question. In fact, it would seem that they, or at least some of them, rather represent *successive* branches off the same tree. In other words, while none can be explained out of the others, still some appear to be more archaic, others more recent. This concept is, of course, thus far but a working hypothesis, and may remain so for a good time, until a complete survey has been made of the known forms of kinship organization and the other cultural forms accompanying them in every specific case. The detailed evidence on which these provisional conclusions are based can unfortunately not be given here for reasons of space. I hope to be able to present this evidence, in part at least, soon in a second article dealing with this question.

Out of the several forms of clans which have to be distinguished I shall here omit some, especially that found in most Australian tribes, and single out for discussion two only. It appears that the overwhelming majority of tribes whose social units are known to be based on descent, belong to one or the other of these two types.

4

The first of these two types is that of *unilateral exogamous clans*, either of the patrilineal or matrilineal variety. Since these two varieties are alike in all other points except that one is matrilineal, the other patrilineal no attention needs to be paid here to this difference, since our main aim is to show what distinguishes *both* of them from the other type of clan which is neither unilateral nor exogamous.

The formative features of the first type of clan, in both of its varieties, are: (1) The clan consists of people who are related to each other either through women only or through men only—according to the customs of the tribe; (2) every member of the clan is, as far as clan membership goes, on an absolutely equal footing with the rest: the nearness of relation to each other or to some ancestor being of no consequence for a person's place in the clan; (3) members of the clan may not marry each other.

In other words, the principles underlying this type of clan are: unilateral, "equalitarian," exogamous. They constitute one indivisible whole. It is no accident that practically everywhere where we find one of them we find the other two. Neither of them would, in fact, by itself, produce the same result.

These principles of clanship, or rather this threefold principle, leads to sharply defined, clearly separate units, comparable to so many blocks out of which society is built. There have to be always at least two such blocks—two clans living in connubium. Usually there are more than two.

The most striking aspect of this threefold principle of clanship is its extreme rigidity. It is hard to imagine in which direction this type of clan could develop further. The classical form in which we know it from hundreds of tribes seems to exhaust all its possibilities, and no forms leading beyond it seem to have been reported from anywhere—unless the Australian systems should fall into this category.

This type of clan makes possible a kind of economic and general cultural cooperation which in its way seems perfect. But, as the term perfect implies, it seems to be the highest type of cooperation which can be achieved along *this* line of development. The growing forces of production at a certain stage demand important readjustments in the form of kinship organization of which this type appears to be incapable. Its absolute equalitarianism, combined with the complete subordination of each of its members to the interests of the clan as a whole, while making possible a certain type of primitive cooperation, obstructs very effectively the evolution of these tight forms of cooperation which are based upon economic and social differentiation. Where, therefore, with this type of clan higher forms of economy have come into existence, as, e.g., those based on animal breeding, the development of which requires higher forms of cooperation, there this new economy has usually not gone beyond rather meagre beginnings. It is, on the other hand, significant that the forms of irrigated agriculture found amongst so-called primitive tribes appear to be in the main confined to tribes with the second type of clan, the characteristics of which we will describe presently.

The first type of clan, the unilateral, equalitarian, exogamous clan, is, in the main, typical of tribes with migratory agriculture or with primitive forms of animal breeding. It is probably no accident that it is found above all in those parts of the world where cultural development seems to have reached a point of stagnation, except where subject to foreign stimuli, i.e., in the Americas, in large parts of Negro Africa, in Melanesia and New Guinea, etc.

The form of kinship organization which the unilateral-exogamous principle of clanship creates appears definitely as a blind alley, and more than that; at a certain stage of economic and general cultural evolution as an obstacle to further development. What constitutes its greatness at the same time constitutes its limits.

5

We are presented with a strikingly different picture the moment we turn to the second type of clan, found amongst the early Indo-European and Semitic tribes, amongst the Polynesians and most of the Indonesians, including the inhabitants of the Philippines, and a few tribes in other parts of the world. At whatever stage of development we find these tribes, we discover in their economic and social life, factors making for further development, everywhere in the direction of further economic and social differentiation.

What, then, is the type of clan found among these tribes? The answer to the question is not a simple one, at any rate, not if a simple designation like "unilateral," "exogamous," etc., is expected. In fact, the very names "clan," "Sippe," "gens," etc., while taken from the vocabulary of tribes having the *second* type of clan, have been for such a long time and so exclusively used for clans of the first, i.e., the unilateral-exogamous type, that it is very difficult indeed to break down the confusion which anthropologists themselves have created. This confusion consists in the belief that the unilateral-exogamous clan is *the* clan, and that everything else, including the clan of the Gaels, the Sippe of Germans, and the gens of the Romans, is a deviation, or at any rate a special development, from the type of clan found among the Iroquois or in the Trobriand islands. If there is one question in which there is full continuity from Morgan to our own days, then it is this misconception.

Very few indeed are the anthropologists who have tried to understand the clans, e.g., of the Polynesians as a type in itself, as opposed to that, e.g., of the Melanesians. And there is hardly any modern anthropologist who has tried to re-evaluate the principles underlying the clans and sibs and gentes of the early Indo-European tribes. In fact, it has somehow become a habit to shun tribes which have this type of clan, both in library research and in field work. They do not fit into the accustomed pattern. Yes, it is precisely the study of these tribes which will allow us to bridge the still existing gulf between the facts of anthropology and those of early European history. These tribes are closer to our own past than any others, and if anthropology aims at being a "useful" science in the sense that its researches and findings fit into a larger body of scientific knowledge, then we must undoubtedly pay more attention to tribes the study of which promises to give us the key to the earliest written history of the Jews, the Greeks, the Romans, the Germans, etc. Thus far, anthropology has completely failed in this task which Morgan regarded as one of the main tasks of our science. In fact, there are probably very few anthropologists today who would agree that this is one of the main tasks of anthropology.

The decisive difference between the first and the second type of clan is that what matters in the one is relationship *through* either men or women (according to the customs of the tribe), irrespective of the nearness of such relationship to the other members of the group or to some ancestor—whereas, on the contrary, in the other type it is precisely the *nearness* of relationship to the common ancestor of the group which matters. The first of the two principles of clanship results in a group the members of which are of absolutely equal standing, as far as this standing is determined by membership in the group (leaving aside the question of age). The second principle results in a group in which every single member, except brothers or sisters, has a different standing: the concept of the *degree of relationship* leads to *different degrees of membership* in the clan. In other words, some are members to a higher degree, than others.

The logical consequence of this state of affairs is that at a certain point it becomes doubtful whether a person is still to be regarded a member of a certain clan—a question that could never arise in a unilateral-exogamous clan. Clan membership so-to-speak shades off the farther one is away from the center-line of the clan—the real core of the group. This core, the *aristoi*, consists of those who are the nearest descendants of the common ancestors of the clan.

In most tribes descent is customarily either through men or, more rarely, through women, but very frequently, especially in the case of the *aristoi*, descent may be counted through either of them. That side being chosen which gives a person a higher descent, i.e., a closer relationship with the ancestor of the group. The term "ambilateral" has been coined for this system.

Genealogies, unknown and unnecessary in a unilateral clan, are here the means of establishing the "line" of descent of the nobles—this "line" being another concept unknown in unilateral clans.

A corollary of the second principle of clanship is that there is no exogamy in the sense defined above. In fact, there could be none, since there are no groups with definite and fixed "boundaries." On the contrary, we frequently find close endogamy—however, usually only for the *aristoi*. Marriage between relatives of high descent assures that their offspring will be of still higher descent.

The type of preferential marriage most characteristic for this type of clan is that with parallel relatives:—the brother's daughter and/or the father's brother's daughter. We find this marriage all the way from ancient Prussia, Greece, and Arabia, to the Kwakiutl of the North American northwest coast who together with the Nootka seem to be the only representatives of this type of clan organization on North American soil. Marriage with either the brother's daughter or the father's brother's daughter may almost be regarded as a "leit-fossil" of this type of clan.

Another type of preferential marriage found frequently with it is marriage with a half-sister, i.e., a sister by the same father, but a different mother. Neither of these two types of preferential marriage seems to be ever found in societies organized into unilateral-exogamous clans.

The distinction between rules of behavior for the noble core of the clan and for its outer membership runs through all societies organized into clans of the second type. It is the feature which most clearly and sharply sets off this type of clan from the "equalitarian" unilateral-exogamous clan, and it is this feature which lies at the root of the very different role which tribes organized into the one or the other type of clan have played in the history of mankind. In fact, this difference inevitably flows from the opposite principles which determine the structure of these two types of clans. The one divides the tribe into a number of solid blocks with clear cut boundary lines, each homogenous within. The other results in a type of society which may be likened to a cone, the whole tribe being one such cone, with the legendary ancestor at its top,—but within it are a larger or smaller number of similar cones, the top of each coinciding with or being connected with the top of the whole cone. The bases of these cones, representing the circles of living members of the various clans at a given moment, overlap here and there.

The tribe as a whole has essentially the same structure as each of its component parts: it is, therefore, only a question of a choice of words whether we call both of them "tribe," or both of them "clan," or the larger one "tribe" and the smaller ones "clans." Professor Boas' presentation of Kwakiutl kinship organization illustrates this point.

Any one of these cones, large or small, can exist by itself. With the unilateral-exogamous type of clan, on the other hand, always at least two such clans must exist, and the body comprising two, or more, of them together does not have the structure of a clan.

In other words, the two types of clan differ in every single aspect, except the basic one, namely that they are *both based on the principle of descent* (though a different one).

6

In societies of the "conical" clan type, it is regarded as a matter of course that all leading economic, social, religious functions are reserved to those of highest descent, i.e., those closest to the ancestor of the clan and tribe, who frequently is regarded as a god. With the development of production and of culture as a whole, the role of these *aristoi* within the life of the clan and the tribe becomes ever more important. The nearer in descent to the godlike ancestor a person is, the greater are his chances in the process of ever-growing economic and social differentiation. Social differentiation, at this stage of evolution of society, the *condition sine qua non* of the development of higher forms of cooperation, not only finds no obstacle in this type of clan, but on the contrary an extremely flexible medium, namely a hierarchy of relatives, based on the principle of nearness of descent.

For a long period to come this principle of clanship is able to adapt itself to the ever-growing complexity of social relations. A survey of the tribes organized into clans of this type shows a whole scale of such adaptations to the increasing degree of social differentiation within the tribes; mainly along the line of a more marked stratification of the members of one and the same group. Thus, some members of the clan may be chiefs and near-gods, while others, at the opposite end of the scale, may be slaves; yet all of them are regarded as relatives, and in many cases, are able to prove it.

The process of differentiation within the clan, while for a long time taking place within this flexible unit, finally reaches the point where the interests of those of equal standing, in *all* the clans of the tribe, come into such sharp conflicts with the interests of the other strata that their struggles, the struggle of by now fully-fledged social classes, overshadows the old principles of clanship and finally leads to the break-up of clan, first as the dominating form of social organization and then to its final disappearance. This point, the end of one phase of human history, and the beginning of another, had just been reached when the Greeks, the Romans and the Germans enter into the light of documented history.

However, none of the tribes with which anthropology usually deals have reached this stage. The highest stage found here is, on the contrary, one where it is still to the advantage of the *aristoi* to keep the clan organization intact because it still serves them as the best instrument in their struggle against the lower orders. The reason for this is not difficult to see. In clans of the unilateral-exogamous type the obligations and privileges of every clan member in the final account equal each other. Whatever benefits the individual benefits the clan as a whole, and reversely; whatever strengthens the clan strengthens every one of its members in an equal measure. In this lies the greatness, but at the same time, the limitation of this type of clan. In the cone-shaped clan, on the contrary, everything that strengthens the clan strengthens, above all, its core and correspondingly, whatever any member contributes to the welfare of the clan as a whole benefits above all, the *aristoi*.

Up to a certain point of economic and general cultural development, this strengthening of the core of the clan means, at the same time, a strengthening of the whole clan. But, in the course of time, this becomes less and less true. The interests of the *aristoi*, and to a lesser degree, those of the middle strata where these have come into existence, become ever more separate from and finally opposed to the interests of the group as a whole. But, the bonds of clanship still exist, and, again up to a certain point, it is to the advantage of the *aristoi* to utilize them against the other strata within the clan.

7

A most instructive example of this state of affairs is offered by the Igorot tribes of the northernmost of the Philippine Islands, Luzon. Amongst these tribes whose economy is based on terraced agriculture and irrigation, we are able to study certain still rather embryonic forms of struggle between the developing classes of landlords and landless. Both sides fight here completely within the confines of the old clan organization which is still fully intact. The struggle has certain outward forms of a religious character which, however, do not conceal from the observer the essentials of the struggle.

Both weddings and funerals necessitate amongst these tribes the sacrificial slaughtering of a pig by the nearest relative. The majority of the population, however, have no pigs.

If they still own a piece of land, they have to pawn it to a rich man in order to get the required pig. If they have already, at the previous occasion, lost their land, they have to work off the price of the pig. Thus the concentration of land in the hands of a few proceeds at a rapid pace.

The mechanism through which this process operates is the equality of the obligations, on the surface religious in character, for every member of the clan, be he rich or poor. The continuation of equal obligations unquestionably works to the advantage of some against others, at a moment when the development of the forces of production has already led to far-reaching economic and social differentiation. Now, the important point for our problem in all this lies in the fact that both contending sides are very frequently, possibly in the majority of cases, members of the same clan. In fact, they are under the mutual obligation of blood vengeance. But his obligation, too, under the conditions of economic inequality and of the peculiar ties of this type of clan system, works to the advantage of the *aristoi* who can, more or less, force the lesser members of the clan to come to their assistance, and thus, through composition fines extracted from the offender, are able continuously to increase their resources, which in turn gives them a still greater hold over their poorer clan fellows.

The role which this principle of clanship plays here, at a comparatively advanced stage of the evolution of economy and social relations, shows its extraordinary flexibility and adaptability. Its contrast to the rigid unilateral-exogamous principle of clanship is striking. However, this contrast should not induce us to overlook the fact that both of these principles of clanship and the form of clan to which they lead, belong essentially to the same phase of the evolution of society. If we compare them either with the stage of kinship organization which preceded it, or with the breakdown of kinship organization which followed it, the common features, which by grouping the living and the dead together into stable and permanent units, permit of higher forms of cooperation than those known before.

One of these, however, seems, through its rigidity, to lead into a blind alley, while the other, more flexible, has become the form within which social differentiation in a long course of evolution reached the point where it led to the formation of social classes and its own consequent destruction.

17 ME KO COURT: THE IMPACT OF URBANIZATION ON CONFLICT RESOLUTION IN GHANAIAN TOWN

—MICHAEL J. LOWY

Much urban anthropological research is based on the implicit supposition that an open-ended holistic approach yields the most valuable information on how people, as individuals and in groups, adjust to city life. "Me Ko Court" offers an alternative perspective: a specific theoretical problem is examined by testing a set of hypothesis in a carefully selected field site. In this analysis of urbanization and law in Koforidua, Ghana, Michael J. Lowy employed a wide variety of research techniques to gather the data he needed, but he examined traditional anthropological categories like social class, ethnicity, kinship, politics, economics, and migrant-or-nonmigrant status only insofar as they related to conflict resolution and dispute settlement. Lowy's study illustrates the potential utility of a "problems and process" approach to urban anthropology. For example, his discovery that urban Ghanaians effectively resolve interpersonal conflicts through nonjudicial mechanisms suggests that similar alternatives to formal courts might improve the legal system in other urban settings, including the overburdened courts of large American cities.

As Freilich has pointed out (1970:15), the budding anthropologist's first experience as a *rite de passage,* the crossing of a professional threshold from which he emerges as if reborn. My turn to validate my claim to membership in the anthropological fraternity came toward the end of October, 1967, when my wife, Ruth, and I left Berkeley for a year in Ghana. After more than two years of graduate seminars, courses, and independent reading projects, I had proved—by successfully passing my Ph.D. oral qualifying examination—that I had enough theoretical anthropological knowledge to hope to become a full-fledged professional. Now it was time to demonstrate that my book learning could be converted into original research.

I had been drawn to Berkeley for graduate study to work with Professor Laura Nader's Berkeley Comparative Village Law Project, and under her direction, in the company of a handful of other students, I had read about and discussed the ways in which cross-cultural research might be carried out on the problems of conflict resolution. A field manual outlining areas of common concern and describing specific techniques to be followed in gathering case material emerged from this project, and through adherence to it we expected to achieve a degree of comparability in the data that we would collect.

But my desire to gather data on law in a non-Western society went deeper than mere intellectual curiosity. I believe that "the way things are" is not always the best way, and that they need not always remain the same. This seems to me to be particularly true of legal procedures in the United States, where personal conflicts are regularly referred to the courts for resolution. Under the banner of "due process" in an adversary system, which presupposes a guilty and an innocent party, and a clear-cut division between right and wrong, we attempt to arrive at an absolute that we call justice. Yet the data from anthropological research among many societies have revealed that alternative forms of conflict resolution, many based on a consensus model, de-emphasize the concepts of guilt and innocence. I believed that data on these alternate forms of conflict resolution might assist in generating new and imaginative approaches to the problems of interpersonal conflict in the United States.

My research hypotheses derived from the contrasting views of Sir Henry Maine and E. A. Hoebel. More than a hundred years ago Maine argued that "the movement of the progressive societies has hitherto been a movement from Status to Contract" (1963 [1861]:165), and that changes in relationships within the family lead to changes in the form of legal relationships between people outside the family. Hoebel, on the other hand, points out that this shift does not really become important before urbanization occurs, and that it is this process—and not a shift from status to contract—that dissolves the strength of kinship ties. Urbanization "concomitantly steps up the need for centralized legal control by throwing together multitudes of persons whose local or tribal backgrounds are different and whose customs and their underlying postulates are frequently in conflict at many points. *City life proliferates law*" (Hoebel 1954:328-329. My emphasis).

Hoebel's argument, which supports the American legal system, implies two interconnected propositions:

1. Individuals in urban society are predominantly involved in "simplex," "contractual" relationships and will, therefore, not have social ties which can be mobilized to produce solutions to conflicts without a public remedy agent.
2. The heterogeneity that characterizes urban society implies inequalities of power and resources, as well as differences in custom and sometimes in language; hence, public remedy agents become essential to settle disputes and to achieve justice.

Since the contrasting views of Maine and Hoebel had not been tested by anthropologists carrying out legal research *in cities,* I felt that this would make an ideal project. Specifically, I wished to test the hypothesis that change from an extended family form to a nuclear family form as the primary unit of social organization, which generally accompanies a shift from a subsistence to a market economy, leads to extrafamilial relationships that are contractual rather than based on status. The corollary to this hypothesis—really an integral part of the hypothesis—was that the settlement of conflicts in contractual relationships would tend to be by public rather than private remedy agents.

To test this hypothesis I needed an urban research setting in which recent migrants would be in the process of shifting from a village-based corporate family structure, with all of its attached obligations and expectations, to city life in which individual achievement underlies making a living. I assumed that these changes do not occur uniformly in a given population, and that some individuals and groups would more readily discard the old corporate ties than others, even though they would be living under similar urban conditions. I reasoned that if individuals had relatively free choice in selecting a forum for settling conflicts, individuals responding differently to the challenges of urban life—and particularly with respect to their family ties—would follow different patterns in their choices of remedy agents.

I decided to go to Africa in large part because during the years immediately preceding my graduate work the most important research in legal anthropology had been carried out there. Initially I settled on the Yoruba of Nigeria, traditionally farmers who depended on lineage loyalties for access to land. But when the Yoruba move to rapidly growing cities, they become wage earners, and are presumably less concerned with their lineage ties. The ways in which these wage-earning migrants resolve disputes, I felt, should help me test the relationship between urbanization and conflict resolution. These plans, however, were never to be executed.

Five months prior to my planned departure for the field, and after I had received research support from the National Institute of Mental Health (Grant No. USPHS-MH-11211), the Nigerian civil war was erupting. my advisers urged me to select an alternate site and begin preparations immediately. With a pardonable student bias, I felt my time was better spent preparing for my examinations. When I later turned to my advisers for aid in selecting a new site, they resisted the temptation to say "I told you so." It was Professor Elizabeth Colson who provided the guidance I needed: she suggested two towns, one in Uganda and the other in Ghana, both of which seemed to fit my research requirements.

By chance, Professor Raymond Apthorpe from Makerere University in Kampala, Uganda, was visiting Berkeley at this time, and over lunch we discussed the possibilities of support for my research at his institution. Although I was better prepared ethnographically for Ghana, I was strongly attracted by this offer of institutional affiliation and support, and had it not been for a delay in telegraphic communication with Makerere University, my research would have been carried out in that East African country. But when the expected support did not materialize, I turned to Ghana.

The site Professor Colson had suggested was Koforidua, a southern Ghanaian Ashanti town of 40,000 that had been studied by Daniel McCall in the early 1950's (McCall 1956, 1962). He had reported that both the increasing independence of market women, and the growing importance of wage labor and commerce at the expense of traditional subsistence agriculture, were weakening the corporate quality of traditional family life. This sounded much like the conditions I believed I needed, so that after personal communications and a very helpful meeting with Professor McCall, I decided on Koforidua.

After the traditional good-bye party, Ruth and I left for New York, where we looked forward to two weeks visiting friends and relatives, obtaining visas, and buying equipment. Before proceeding to Accra, we planned to spend a week in London reading the District Commissioner reports pertaining to Koforidua. Unfortunately, these weeks stretched into three months, and we did not reach our destination until mid-January, 1972.

Visa difficulties were the principal reason for the delay. I had been told in Berkeley that Ghana requires a two-year residence visa for field research, but the Ghanaian Consulate in New York could issue us only a thirty-day visitor's visa without authorization from Accra. While waiting for this clearance, which we assumed would be routine, we bought cameras, anti-malarial medicine and other supplies, and continually changed our air reservations from one departure date to another. Meanwhile I visited the Consulate almost daily and was assured that they had "checked with Accra." Since our language preparation in Twi, which we would use in Koforidua, had been limited to Peace Corps tapes and a manual which we had acquired just before leaving Berkeley, we decided we could profitably use our enforced leisure learning that language. Although we were fortunate to find a Ghanaian in New York who would teach us the language, we were able to spend no more than ten hours with her before we departed. Consequently, we arrived in Ghana with only a rudimentary knowledge of Twi.

When the situation began to appear hopeless, I wrote to several Stanford University graduate students conducting research in Ghana, asking them what to do. They agreed that the accepted practice was to travel to Ghana on the thirty-day visa, receive support from the University and then apply personally for the residence visa. Much encouraged by this breakthrough, we departed for London, arriving in the unusually cold and snowy month of January, 1968. Although the inclement weather precluded visits with London anthropologists—they were not even in their offices at this time—letters of introduction from the University of California gave me access to the Library of the British Museum and the Public Records Office. I hoped to find reports of British District Commissioners who served on the Gold Coast, as Ghana was known prior to independence, but five days of searching proved fruitless, and I was told to look instead in Ghanaian archives.

Thus, at 5:30 A.M. on January 16, 1968, we circled the Accra airport, tired, depressed, and miserably overdressed for the heat and humidity. During the all-night trip across southern Europe and the Sahara Desert I had had plenty of time to reflect on the chance combination of theoretical interests, world affairs, and poor communications that had combined to bring me almost half way around the world. I was still not certain that my original research proposal, designed for a Yoruba town, would be applicable to conditions in Ghana. But I was sure that my utilizing participant observation, survey research, and archival materials, I would be able to gather data on the sociocultural impact of urbanization and urbanism, and I remained fairly confident that the strategies for collecting law cases would provide the data I needed to complete my research. Occupied with these problems of theory and method, I was less concerned than was Ruth with basic creature comforts—a house and transportation—and the uncertainties that go with entry into a new life.

GETTING SETTLED

After we cleared customs, the cab ride to our hotel through the outskirts and then the central streets of Accra at six o'clock in the morning gave us our first look at the field. Both of use were shocked at the poverty and (to us) unsanitary conditions that we saw. Several months later, however, the same scenes evoked images of security and sophistication, the consequence of our new-found familiarity with the country. During our first few days in Accra we were skillfully guided by Naomi Quinn, a Stanford University anthropology graduate student who generously had interrupted her own fieldwork among Fanti fisherman to help us get settled. Through her efforts we found quarters in a residence hall at the University of Ghana, from which strategic point we developed networks within the university community which eventually satisfied our needs. New friends in the Faculty of Law assisted us in getting our two-year visas, and they extended library privileges to us as well as a permanent mailing address while we were in Ghana. Dr. Peg Peil of the Department of Sociology helped me construct a census form and a social survey questionnaire, and a staff member of the Archaeology Department introduced me to my first research assistant. One of Naomi's Ghanaian friends, Mr. Yeboah, aided me in buying a used car and in making our first social contacts in Koforidua. The University community, which for us consisted of a dozen expatriate teachers and researchers in various disciplines, offered friendship and valuable assistance during our seventeen months in Ghana. Periodic escapes from my field site to the University provided an opportunity to share my problems and frustrations with sympathetic listeners, in the relative comfort of a large city.

We spent six weeks at the University prior to leaving for Koforidua, and even though preparations appeared to be going very well, I experienced periods of alternating depression and elation, accompanied by weight loss. Each time I was thwarted in my attempt to achieve a goal, I saw it as a conspiracy to sabotage my research; but each time I succeeded in something, I was again reassured that I would complete my work. Nevertheless more than once during those first weeks I seriously considered leaving Ghana and returning to the physical and intellectual comforts of Berkeley. Without fully appreciating it, I was experiencing culture shock.

The following except from my diary of January 19, 1968, written shortly after I discovered that a Ghanaian bank official had given me misinformation about the transfer of dollars into the country, is a good example of the paranoia I experienced:

> He told us that we *could* have what is called an *external account!* Contrary to what we were told at the bank here! Man—the Ghanaians lie with a smile—I really trusted him—no *more.* I will keep mistrusting everyone until I know them well! Tomorrow I will call the bank manager and tell him if he doesn't switch our account to an external account, I will switch my funds to another bank and get one for the rest of my money coming in! We don't trust *anyone anymore!*

Several devices helped me keep my moodiness within acceptable limits. First, my diary allowed me to take revenge upon those I saw as thwarting my research. I enjoyed the feeling of being able to classify them as the "bad guys." Second, my wife helped me maintain my balance by assuming much of the burden of buying equipment. And the third method of coping with my initial bout of culture shock was discussing fears and hopes with other researchers facing similar problems. Those who had already passed through the crisis of depression socialized those of us who had more recently arrived, assuring us that our temporary feelings of paranoia were normal.

The time had now come to move to the field site. By good fortune Mr. Yeboah, who had been so helpful in our car purchase, was able to accompany us the fifty-six miles to Koforidua where he introduced us to Mr. Appiah, an official in the local Department of Social Welfare, who had been a research assistant to anthropologist David Brokensha during his study of a nearby town in the early 1960's. He became a close friend to whom we turned in times of illness or other emergency. Professor McCall had given me the name of the chairman of the Koforidua Municipal Council, who had been his research assistant many years earlier. We were grateful to these men for helping us meet officials of the District and Regional Ministries, and especially the chiefs of the New Juaben Traditional area, in which we had settled.

Adequate accommodations for anthropologists are not easy to find in a rapidly urbanizing town like Koforidua. Here again Mr. Appiah came to our rescue. Traditional houses, called "compounds," were roughly rectangular, one-story dwellings around a central courtyard. I would have liked to have lived in a compound in a migrant neighborhood where I could observe the daily routine of people, But there were other considerations of privacy and comfort, as well as the perception by the local population of our status as "Europeans." Consequently we considered other possibilities before making up our minds. First we looked at a European-style house enclosed by a high wall on the outskirts of town. We were attracted to this house because it had hot and cold running water and electricity, but since it was isolated from the Ghanaian population, we gave up the idea. A second "apartment" in a typical compound had two rooms, a hall and chamber (i.e., living room and bedroom). Although it had electricity, the toilet, running water, and cooking facilities had to be shared with other tenants. We decided not to rent it because of lack of privacy. On our third try we found exactly what we needed: six rooms on the second floor of a modern, compound-type house, with electricity, kitchen, toilet, and cold running water. The building was in the center of Nsukwao, one of the fastest growing migrant neighborhoods in the town, and from our balcony I could watch the daily activities of neighbors, and the coming and going of people on the busy footpath beneath us. We had pleasant neighbors downstairs—a Ghanaian schoolteacher, his wife, and family—and privacy and comfort without real isolation.

Since both Ruth and I planned to do research we hired a young man, Johnny, as cook/steward, to prepare meals, and do washing and cleaning, for the equivalent of $16.50 a month, plus room and board. Johnny quickly became a close friend, and he contributed much to the first three months of my research; his death after a sudden illness and surgery was the greatest personal tragedy of our field experience. Johnny's replacement, however, did not fit into our household routine, and so we found him comparable work elsewhere.

Our third and final cook/steward not only was a reliable source of gossip, but he turned out to be very useful in helping me interview informants who spoke his language, Ewe.

WHAT WORK DO YOU DO?

In order to work effectively in the field, the anthropologist must establish a plausible role for himself. In small communities that is not too difficult; one quickly becomes known to everyone, and after that the people themselves explain one's presence to visitors and other outsiders. But in a city of 40,000 I found it necessary to explain continually who I was. People would ask, "Are you Peach Corps?" "Are you a priest?" "What work do you do?" It seemed as if each day I had to start anew, explaining who I was and what I was. Over and over I patiently explained to people—in the market, at the post office, in the homes of informants—that I did "research." The answer was always the same, but the level of specificity varied according to who asked. For government and University officials I gave very much the same answers that I might give to persons in comparable positions in the United States. Copies of my research proposal were delivered to the judicial Secretary of Ghana (roughly equivalent to the American Attorney General) and to the heads of several University faculties. They, of course, understood more clearly than others the theoretical nature of what I was doing. In contrast, in talking with magistrates, lawyers, chiefs, and other educated Koforiduans, I called attention to my affiliation with the law faculty but explained the nature of my research in more general terms. With informants and neighbors, some of whom lacked formal schooling, I stressed my status as a "scholar." When I learned that a neighbor's brother was attending Columbia University on a scholarship, I explained that I also had a scholarship to study the history and current way of life in Koforidua.

In carefully identifying myself in a new community, I was simply following traditional Ghanaian norms. Most adults in Koforidua have spent varying lengths of time away from home, and they knew a stranger pays his respects to the local chief or elder by explaining his presence. When I began a round of visits to introduce myself to the chiefs, subchiefs, and influential men in the town and vicinity, it was understood that I offered my allegiance in exchange for their protection and support. Although it quickly became clear that a bottle of "schnapps" (usually gin) was more highly valued than allegiance by some, others were genuinely flattered that their status as an important person was validated by my visit. Those initial contacts were relatively easy to arrange, but lasting relationships and assistance depended upon many factors including my personality and generosity. I believe I ultimately established good rapport with most of the people with whom I had dealings because I demonstrated a sincere and consistent interest in Ghanaian life. Many informants, including the Omanhene (Paramount Chief) of Koforidua told me they were flattered that I learned to speak Twi, even though my imperfect knowledge of the highly important tones in this complex language often made it difficult for them to understand me. I dressed in "cloth" and sandals, i.e., native garb, when appropriate, attended funerals, drank and ate local food and drink, and danced and played music. Ghanaians, like anthropologists, are inquisitive, and they approve of individuals who are "free" and receptive of new experiences.

My permanent reputation as "The white man who likes cases too much" began one evening during our first week in Koforidua, when a fight between two children broke out in front of my compound. People quickly gathered to talk about it, and when discussion ended, my assistant explained that I came from America especially to learn about disputes. A lantern was brought, and the adults began to question me: "Why do you want to hear such things?" They were curious to know why I was interested in what they were doing. I said that learning how Koforiduans settle disputes might help my people settle *their* disputes without violence. Knowledge of recent assassinations in the United States increased the credibility of this argument. A small table was brought, and then and there I interviewed the children in the street, while adults added helpful bits of information.

As my language proficiency increased, I spent more time drinking with individuals such as court clerks, whom I had identified as key informants. I became quite good at a card game called *spa*, which was played at palm wine bars and photographers' studios. During the game I often explained my research and increased my social network. Several otherwise hostile informants who appeared in court cases allowed me to interview them as a result of the social relations we had developed over the card table and bottle. Very few of my friends or informants were directly compensated for their assistance, although we often shared drinks with them. However, we did express our gratitude to the many people who helped make our stay pleasant and enjoyable by hosting a New Year's celebration on January 1, 1969. Neighbors, friends, and informants were invited to eat and drink in our compound. The affair lasted all day, and included music, dancing, and entertainment supplied by friends.

RESEARCH ASSISTANTS

Because of the complexity of my project and my initial limitations in the Twi language, research assistance was essential. Although I might have been able to use English to communicate with about half of the people with whom I would be dealing, I decided to use Twi whenever possible. Peter, my first interpreter/assistant, was introduced to me by an archaeologist while we were living at the University. He seemed ideal: single, thirty years of age, and a secondary school "leaver" from Kumasi, he had had previous research experience with a Ph.D. art history candidate. Peter spent three months with me before he took a research position at the University. Quite honestly, our relationship was not all that either of us had expected. Subsequently he come to the United States, and we have had opportunities to examine our relationship without the stress of the field situation. He explained that he often wanted to quit because I frequently challenged his honesty. And he was quite right. Before I understood Twi well, I doubted the competence of all my interpreter/assistants; I was convinced that they were not asking my questions correctly. But as I grew more comfortable with the language, I began to appreciate the difficulties of translating questions that often made little sense to informants. Without realizing it, during my first few months of research I wanted informants to give answers to *my* questions, rather than respond to other questions that were more meaningful in the context of their lives.

By the time Peter left I realized I would need two assistants, one to collect statistical information, and another to accompany me during interviews. For the first task I hired Mr. Eugene Walker, a seventy-four-year-old man from Larteh, who had spent many years working as a research assistant to anthropologists. I was pleased when he adopted a grandfatherly attitude in our relationship, often helping me to understand "proper" local behavior. He worked for me full-time for six months, and part-time for an additional two months. For the second task—formal interviews, and observations of conflict resolution situations—I selected Manu, a Juaben Ashanti, born and raised in Koforidua, thirty years of age, married, and former engineering student at the University of Kumasi. Recommended by a local shopkeeper, he had never before worked as a research assistant. Although we didn't always agree on methods, he remained in my employ until I left the field, and I still consider him one of my closest friends. Neither of these men spoke Ewe, Hausa, or Yoruba, so when I interviewed speakers of these languages I was assisted by our young, middle-school educated cook/steward and by a twenty-eight-year-old Yoruba secondary school "leaver."

In addition to these "regulars,"I quickly realized that I would need high skilled assistants to carry out the census and social survey of Koforidua, scheduled for the end of the summer. For this task I hired four third-year University sociology students with previous experience who worked for me all during the month of August. Then, when I unearthed a sixty-year sequence of uncataloged court records in the "Grade II" Court Clerk's office, I knew I needed even more skilled help. This I obtained in the form of two third-year law students from the University, who spent their four-month summer vacation in Koforidua coding information from these records. My wife supervised this project, continuing the work for several months after the students returned to their studies.

RESEARCH DESIGN REFORMULATION

In Berkeley, and until the time we settled in Koforidua, I assumed that my research would focus on a relatively homogeneous neighborhood in which migrants from the same ethnic group were settling. I had in mind a closely knit neighborhood within the urban area which I could quickly come to know through participant observation and other standard anthropological research techniques. To my dismay, I soon found that—with few exceptions—ethnic residence patterns did not conform to my expectations. The exceptions were a few homogeneous Ashanti neighborhoods, but even there the hierarchical organization of authority over disputes I had expected to find—from family heads to subchiefs responsible for the neighborhood to town-wide agencies (such as the court)—was absent. I searched without success for disputes between migrants and long-term city-dwellers settled by neighborhood authorities. The few conflicts I observed or heard about did not include the "mix" of migrants and nonmigrants that I wanted, and neighborhood remedy agents were not involved.

Finally, after two months of uncertainty, and many sleepless nights, I had to admit that the conditions necessary to complete my original research design did not exist. I therefore decided to collect cases from town-wide agencies rather than to concentrate on the very few cases that were heard by neighborhood authorities. The decision to switch the structural level of my enquiry caused me great anxiety. I doubted my research ability because the reality I perceived around me did not fit what I had anticipated. Were my informants hiding the real structure of conflict resolution from me, I wondered? Rationally I knew this was not true, since I was reminded daily from what I saw around me that common neighborhood residence was not necessary to enduring social relationships. Compound mates often were unrelated, and spouses, siblings, and family heads frequently lived in other neighborhoods, and even other towns. Although social relationships based on common ethnicity or village ties were not unimportant, in a majority of cases they were acted out on a town-wide basis. I concluded that occupational, religious, and other nonkinship relationships in Koforidua were situationally more important than social relationships based on common residence, and that consequently, authority for dispute settlement within a limited area such as a neighborhood would not be significant. At the same time I came to the conclusion that patterns of conflict resolution would not be significantly influenced by the migrant status of the litigants. Kinship and common ethnicity, I came to see, *were* important seasonally, or at dramatic stages in the life cycle, when a group's corporateness was reaffirmed by its members' physical presence; in this way leaders of kinship and ethnic units retained the legitimate right to settle disputes between their constituents. But most social relationships were open to people from every neighborhood, and town-wide authorities played the dominant role in conflict resolution. Police and welfare officers, judges, employers, and lawyers all were important agents of conflict resolution, not only for established city-dwellers, but for recent migrants as well. Given these facts, I realized I would have to describe changes in the social organization of the entire town, and not just that of one neighborhood; only against this background could I compare the use of remedy agents between individuals differentially affected by sociocultural changes.

This major change in research design affected the data I collected and, therefore, the results of the project. For example, the census and social survey I had planned for a single neighborhood now had to be applied to the entire town. By widening the enquiry I had to confront much more difficult problems of sampling and time management. During this agonizing period of uncertainty and reappraisal I again became badly depressed. The number of conflicts I was observing was small, and my language proficiency was proceeding more slowly than I had anticipated. I confided to Ruth that I was afraid to return from the field empty-handed, but what could I do? To help organize my thoughts I wrote long letters to the members of my dissertation committee and to other friends. I did this initially because I felt a strong need to justify the change in my plans to people I held in high regard. As matters turned out, this was the most fortunate thing I could have done; when I forced myself to write what I was seeing in a coherent and organized manner, I not only felt justified in changing my research focus, but I began to see how I would now proceed.

In retrospect I see that the first few months in the field corresponded roughly to Freilich's "passive stage" (Freilich 1970: 18–19), in which a basic adjustment to field conditions and a restructuring of the anthropologist's reality take place. Although I recorded field notes during this period, systematic collection of data began only after I reconciled my research design with the social reality of Koforidua.

SUATRA: LEARNING AN URBAN LIFE STYLE

Old inhabitants could still remember when Koforidua was a small town at the railroad's end, and they took pleasure in describing the changes that had produced the present state of *suatra* ("civilization"). Koforidua had, in fact, grown from a small agricultural settlement of Juaben Ashanti in 1875 to become the fifth largest town in Ghana. Its 40,000 inhabitants are engaged in large-scale marketing of cocoa and other foodstuffs, and wage labor has increased greatly during recent years. Koforidua is headquarters for Regional and District government services, it has an important rail line, good roads, many schools, and scores of churches. Thus, it is not without reason that people refer to it as civilized.

In view of these rapid and pervasive changes, I felt my first job was to learn as much as I could about the details of the transformation process. Fortunately, in former British colonies like Ghana, masses of documents have been left behind. The earliest reports I consulted on the town were those of the Methodist mission, which began with the minutes of their annual synod meetings in 1895. Although these documents were concerned largely with the problems of religious conversion, they shed light on educational and economic developments following the establishment of the mission.

The District Commissioners' quarterly reports began in 1913, and they documented the increase in British Government services, litigation, and political control. These reports were almost as difficult to locate in Ghana as they had been in London, and it was only after I could ask the clerk for then in Twi that I gained access. The Koforidua Regional Archives proved to be invaluable for throwing light on the political relationships between the British and the Native Authorities. Quite by accident I found in the Courthouse the Paramount Chief's "Letter Book," with correspondence between the British and Native Authorities during the period 1915-1926. This highly useful source contained records of the complaints and problems of the townspeople during a period of rapid socioeconomic change.

While written records were useful in discovering trends and major changes, I had to rely on the memory of elderly informants to provide the cultural significance of the statistics I was recording. The selection of these individuals was governed by such factors as age, former occupation, ethnicity, ability to communicate intelligently, and by the degree of rapport I was able to establish with them. Some, such as the former Paramount Chief, were logical and obvious choices. Others, such as a former cocoa buyer and a carpenter, were identified by their reputations among the historically knowledgeable townsmen. The problems of bias in these accounts was never fully resolved, but my means of cross-checking, and from the recollections of my seventy-four-year-old assistant who had worked as a clerk in Koforidua before World War I, I believe that the picture that emerged is reasonably accurate.

TAKING A CENSUS

After learning something about the history of Koforidua, my second job was to learn more about the contemporary community. Because of the large size of the city, I felt that a census of a sample of the community was the best first step. The 1960 government census showed that 34,856 people lived in 1,628 compounds in 17 enumeration areas. Since the town had grown a good deal since that date, and since the government census did not contain all of the information I wanted, I resolved to carry out my own census. The Municipal Council, some of those members had become good friends, made available to me a copy of the tax roll for 1967-1968. I numbered these compounds, and then selected a random sample of 20 per cent for censusing, all of which had to be located on a town map.

The magnitude of the task made an informed public and official support essential. Fortunately, I gained the approved of the Commissioner of the Eastern Region, and of chiefs, subchiefs, and headmen of five major ethnic groups, including the Hausa headman, who publicly announced his support in the central mosque. The *Omanhene* ("Paramount Chief") delegated his messenger, the Gong-gong man, to inform townsmen by beating his gong at major intersections in Koforidua. And two days prior to the census, the local radio station broadcast a series of announcements I had written explaining the project and identifying the interviewers.

Since the four university sociology students who assisted me with the census had used substantially the same interview schedule on two earlier occasions, I anticipated no more than routine problems. When they arrived from Accra on July 30, 1968, we reviewed the forms and discussed the definition of a *household head* ("the most senior member of the household," or the individual who held the "tenancy") and a *household* ("a group of people living together. . .who keep house together. . .sharing their meals and expenses") (cf. Marris 1962). I asked the students to interview everybody in the compound who could respond intelligently, and to accept information from household heads only for those who could not. After the assistants had pretested the census forms, our full-scale survey yielded 3,598 people living in 178 compounds in 7 different neighborhoods.

Two major problems developed in the course of the census: poor cooperation from many respondents, and careless interviewing by the students. Females were less willing to cooperate than men. For example, one old lady told an interviewer, "I cannot talk until my husband returns." *Interviewer:* "When will he be back?" *Lady*" "I cannot tell, he is in the hospital." *Interviewer:* "When did he go to the hospital?" *Lady:* "A year ago." On other occasions women said that they were visiting and did not live in the house to be censused. When difficulties arose I visited the people to "beg" for their assistance. Sometimes my personal explanation was sufficient to elicit the desired information, but more often people cooperated out of respect for my elderly assistant.

Although I had not expected such problems, given the experience of the interviewers, I found that the data of two of the students were filled with inaccuracies and omissions. To find out what was going wrong, I myself interviewed respondents in about 25 per cent of the compounds assigned to them and quickly found that they were disobeying my instructions by recording data for an entire compound from very few people. I recensused all those compounds and warned the students that I would have to dismiss them unless they followed instructions.

PARTICIPANT OBSERVATION

A census is highly useful to give a statistical structure on which to weave the fabric of daily life. But the richness and variety of culture can best be explicated through more traditional anthropological techniques, such as participant observation and less structured interviews. In collecting data on social organization and life styles, I focused primarily on the family (*abusia*), and compound (*fie*), and voluntary non-kin-based associations (*fekew)* and only secondarily on nongroup settings and behavior associated with seasons and holidays.

Within these three group settings, I focused on those actions which dramatized the changing conditions within the corporate group in this urban setting. Specifically, I attended as many *outdoorings* (infant naming ceremonies), marriages, divorce proceedings, and funerals as possible, and in compounds I observed the division of labor based on age and sex, and the routines of daily life. I was particularly interested in the interaction among tenants, and between tenants and landlords, since these relationships, while contractual in nature, often reflect noncontractual values. For instance, would a tenant, in relating to his landlord, show the same deference as to the head of his family.

Voluntary organizations in West Africa are highly important for integrating migrants to city life and in maintaining social ties among urban dwellers (cf. K. Little 1965). They are certainly important in Koforidua, where they are organized on the basis of ethnicity, hometown, occupation, religion, politics, leisure time, and burial. I attended many association meetings and questioned members about why they had joined, how they had been recruited, how one became a leader, the duties of office holders, and the services performed for the membership. I also constantly observed less structured social interaction, at bars, in the market, under shade trees, at public water taps, and at the bus and truck depot.

Since I usually attended ceremonies and meetings as the guest of a prominent participant, I dressed in a manner which I hoped would be seen as appropriate in my status. I made donations with the same consideration in mind. Almost always I could move freely about, sketching the layout and noting the position of the principal actors. When there were no objections I photographed and tape-recorded the proceedings, and afterwards I tried to learn more about what I had seen through detailed discussion with some of the participants. Sometimes I had access to written records of the groups concerned, and these were very useful. For example, records of donations and expenditures at funerals made the relationships of the hundreds of participants involved much more explicit than would have been possible through simple observation and questioning. Voluntary association membership lists and constitutions were also highly useful additions to my growing corpus of data, as were unpublished town data on births, marriages, deaths, divorces, employment applications, and business licenses.

By the end of eight months of basic data gathering I had become familiar with the general outlines of this particular urban life style. Although I occasionally gathered data of this kind throughout the remainder of my stay, I was now ready to turn to the systematic collection of case material on conflict resolution, which occupied the major part of the remaining time.

ME KO COURT

"Me ko court." During the fourteen months we lived in Koforidua I heard these words hundreds of times. Since four different Government courts—Juvenile, Magistrates Court Grade II, Magistrates Court Grade I, and Circuit Court—operate, the townsmen had plenty of opportunities to "go to court." But, in order to understand to which of these courts a litigant might turn, or which of the alternate modes of conflict resolution he might choose, it is essential to understand how Koforiduans perceive conflict. Basically, they divide disagreements into two categories: *asem* ("case, matter, word, trouble, story"), and *entokwa* ("argument, scuffle"). As the translations indicate, asem are perceived to be more serious than entokwa, but each kind of conflict can concern the same affair and can occur between the same kinds of people. The difference depends not on personnel and content, but on the mode of resolution. Asem are conflicts in which resolution is actively sought through a third party, while entowka—if settle at all—are resolved by the two parties themselves. It is with asem ("cases") that I am concerned in the remainder of this essay.

As I became more familiar with the many ways in which different kinds of disputes could be settled, I decided to group the cases according to four categories of place or context. I now conceive the following categories as analytical concepts differentiated by style of procedure and the nature of power used to resolve the case:

1. *Government courts.* These courts handle a wide variety of criminal and civil cases, including many which could not be settled in other places.
2. *Afiesem* ("household cases"). The term refers both to a physical forum for dispute settlement, usually within a compound, and in a more general sense to types of cases,

such as marriage, inheritance, and personal insults which are usually settled "within the family."

3. *Quasi-judicial agencies.* Several government agencies have been charged with settling some types of disputes. For example, the Welfare Department handles paternity and child maintenance cases, and the Rent Control Board deals with cases involving nonpayment of rent.

4. *Supernatural agencies.* This category of "remedy agent" includes both shrines and individuals who have supernatural power to end disputes.

In order to gather data on these several settings I made use of a variety of techniques: personal observation of court proceedings, interviewing of litigants, recording of "memory cases" (i.e., cases in which I was not present during the hearing), court records, and personal involvement in minor litigation. The precise technique or combination of techniques depended on the nature of the setting. Expecting the Circuit Court, I became familiar with the working of all formal courts, especially the Magistrates Court Grade II, as will be described below. In contrast, the bulk of "home" or afiesem data are derived from "memory" cases. Particularly useful was a sample of cases brought to a subchief who had a town-wide reputation for skill in settling disputes. From the files of quasi-judicial agencies, I collected at least a year's sample of cases and interviewed the personnel who regularly hear cases. My data on the supernatural mode of settling disputes is the sparsest of all; access to such cases was extremely difficult, and what little I have comes largely from second-hand accounts.

Regardless of techniques, it should be clear that my basic unit of analysis is the extended case, or situational analysis of a conflict from generation to settlement. That is, rather than carrying out a community study, I undertook a problem-oriented study in which I wanted to know about individuals only insofar as it pertained to the case at hand. I was not concerned with their personalities, their wider circles of relationships, their status within the community, and a host of other things beyond the parameters of my unit of analysis. To state the matter in extreme form, I was not really interested in people per se, but only as actors in a special drama. The process of conflict resolution—the setting, plot, and ending—was the focus of my research.

This approach stands in great contrast to the usual anthropological method, in which the fieldworker concentrates on people acting in the widest variety of settings over the longest possible time. In this more traditional research, people are the focus, and the events in which they participate, while obviously important, lack the stark relief of the disputes I analyzed according to the extended case method.

Whatever the kind of case I was investigating, I gathered as much comparable data as I could. I tried to find out the backgrounds of the litigants: age, sex, length of residence in Koforidua, ethnicity (tribe), education, occupation, and voluntary association membership. I noted the relationship between the litigants—whether kin, non-kin, or situational—as well as prior litigation between them or any of their supporters. When I asked, "How did the case come about?" I found out the substance of the complaint, when and where the case had been heard previously by a remedy agent, and the relationships to the litigants of those present at the hearings. I wanted to learn about the style and procedure of the hearing itself, including the questions asked and written, or oral evidence elicited or presented. The conclusion of a case was investigated by noting the decision or action taken by the third party, the sanctions imposed, the total cost to both parties, the degree of compliance with the decisions or sanction and the effect of the case on the relationship between the litigants.

COLLECTING CASES—AT COURT

When my informants said, "Me ko court," a majority referred to the Magistrates Court Grade II, which deals especially with debt, assault, and theft charges. Here, from January 20 to February 20, 1969, I observed 326 cases, of which 198 were civil and 128 criminal. During the next four months I intensively interviewed a sample of the litigants themselves, involved in 46 civil and 28 criminal cases. Analysis of the strategies used by these litigants formed a principal focus on my Ph.D. dissertation (Lowy 1971).

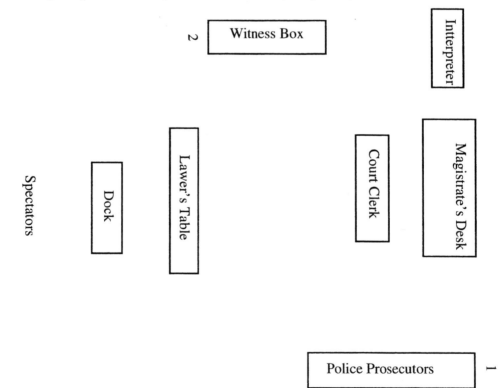

The Courtroom

I was able to begin systematic research in this court only after I knew its staff members and their routine. Armed with a letter from the Dean of the University of Ghana's Law School, and another from the Judicial Secretary of Ghana, I approached the Magistrate, asking if I might sit on his Court and take notes. He seemed unenthusiastic but agreed to provide chairs for Manu and me and give us access to current dockets. Although Ruth was allowed to photograph the court in session, the Magistrate discouraged the use of a tape recorder, no great hardship for I was not eager to transcribe five hours of recorded court cases each day for a month.

Court began at about ten o'clock each morning, but well before that hour I had copied the names, addresses, claims, and other relevant information from the civil docket, provided me by the court clerk. Since criminal case records were kept at the police station, to follow these proceedings I had to rely on what I heard in court, including information given me by the police prosecutors. In recording cases it was essential that I sit where I could see the behavior of all the principals, hear clearly, but not be identified with lawyers, court staff, or prosecutors. I settled for a spot to the left of the Magistrate's desk and just behind the police prosecutor's desk (position 1), rather over the objections of the latter, who felt it "impolite" to show me his back. (See diagram.) Here I had a fairly good view of the entire courtroom, and in addition I could hear most of the whispered interchanges between the Magistrate and the prosecutors and court clerk. My assistant, Manu, sat in position 2 beside the witness box, where he picked up most of what I lost, especially whispered interchanges between witnesses and the interpreter, and between lawyers and witnesses and the accused.

When I began my follow-up, intensive interviews of selected informants, I found that my visibility in court was a great help; people remembered me and were curious to know what I was doing. Nevertheless, it was often difficult to find the litigants, and without the bailiff, court clerk, and Manu's help, I would not have found as many as we did. As it was, of a total of 148 people in our sample, we were unable to find 19, and another 6 refused to answer questions. After we found a litigant we explained the reason for our visit and the kinds of questions we proposed to ask. By adopting a casual and informal manner, we hoped to dispel any official aura that might remain from the courtroom setting. If it were agreeable to the informant to discuss the case during our first visit, we retired to a "private" place, in his living room or bedroom, where we could work relatively undisturbed. I asked the preliminary questions about the litigant's background, and then Manu usually asked about the history of the conflict and possible previous attempts at settlement. This information, coupled with what we had learned in court, gave us fairly complete data for the entire case. Most of these interviews were conducted in Twi, and informants showed little or no reluctance at permitting me to take notes openly.

COLLECTING CASES—AT HOME

As was pointed out above, most of my cases in this category came from people's recollections, since it was difficult to find disputes in progress that I could witness. Besides collecting cases from friends and neighbors, I interviewed people who, by virtue of their positions, were often asked to adjudicate asem disputes. During the early months of my research I attempted to collect data on cases heard by household heads, but this approach was unsuccessful. I therefore estimated the number of types of cases settled by landlords for their tenants by including this question on the census. Likewise unsuccessful was an attempt to learn about cases settled out of court by lawyers, but I obtained a rough estimate of the frequency of household settlements by the police from cases listed as "refused" and "pending" in police records. The statistical information on the relative frequency of hearing before these different remedy agents was more important than the details of specific cases.

In addition, I was particularly fortunate in being able to elicit from a Juaben subchief the kinds of range of disputes in Koforidua, from which I constructed hypothetical stories for each type. By presenting them to informants, I was able to determine the kinds of remedy agents they would use to resolve them. In the course of recording this information I frequently heard about Nana Dabehene, a subchief with a reputation for skill in settling *asem*. I went to him, and he agreed to let me observe him in action. Of the seven cases he presided over in June, 1968, on the verandah of his compound, I attended four. Nana Dabehene explained who I was and why I was there, and that he had given me permission to take notes; he also permitted me to interview the participants in each case. if the chief was unable to help the parties reach a quick solution, he retired to a room with a small number of elders to work out a possible settlement, telling me about that process after the case ended.

COLLECTING CASES—QUASI-JUDICIAL AGENCIES

In this area I concentrated on hearings involving paternity, nonmaintenance of children, rent arrears, and landlord-tenant problems. Most of this information is statistical and descriptive, copied from sample cases and derived from interviews with the personnel charged with such problems. The latter were principally the members of the Reconciliation Committee of the Department of Social Welfare and Community Development, and the Rent Control Board of the Department of Works and Housing. I witnessed only a few hearings before the Reconciliation Committee, and none at all before the Rent Control Board.

With respect to supernatural remedy sources, I have the poorest information of all. By using the hypothetical case approach, and memory cases, I was able to identify a large number of such agents, and though I interviewed some, I was unable to calculate comparative frequencies of use. This mode of conflict resolution is especially important in cases of theft and cursing, although some persons prefer adversary proceedings in these kinds of cases. Since I know so little about this important side to conflict resolution, I hope to concentrate on this subject when I return to Ghana.

COLLECTING CASES—MY ACTIVE PARTICIPATION

On several occasions I was personally involved in conflict situations. Once I fulfilled my role as employer by arbitrating an employee's wife's complaint of nonmaintenance of their child. On other occasions I was the complainant myself. Once Ruth was insulted by a stranger at a funeral she attended. When I learned of the incident I returned with her and demanded to know if the accusation was true. At that moment my neighbors intervened, separating me from Ruth and my adversary. They implored Ruth to keep me from violent action, and they begged me to leave the affair at the entowka ("quarrel") level and not escalate it into an asem. On another occasion an *asafo* ("priest") of a spiritist church was annoyed because I had accepted another invitation and did not attend the thanksgiving feast at his church. During my absence he came to my compound and announced in a loud voice that I felt "too good" to come to his church, and besides, I had not made a promised donation. Faced with this challenge to my reputation, I went to his compound to verify the facts. In his absence, a female member of the church, who was a close friend of Ruth worked with her to effect a solution. These cases, although not really serious, gave me important insight into how people should react when their reputations are damaged.

THE STRATEGIES OF CONFLICT RESOLUTION

It would be a mistake to assume that aggrieved persons always turn to courts and other remedy agents in the expectation of quick and final decision. Rather, the use of *any* remedy agent is frequently part of a broader strategy, the precise form of which will depend on a great many factors, including the type of offense, the goals of the participants, the relative status of the individuals involved, costs, and the like. To resort immediately to public remedy agents in a case could easily be resolved in one's favor is considered immoral and is reflected in the proverb, "If you pursue your sweet case, you do wrong." The usual first step in dispute resolution is for the plaintiff to ask the accused if the allegation is in fact true. If it is true, or the plaintiff believes it true, even in the face of denial, he—the plaintiff—informs the defendant of his intention to pursue the matter, with the hope that court action can be avoided. If the defendant admits fault, directly or indirectly, apologizes, and makes reasonable amends, the affair should be dropped; a plaintiff who persists after such action is considered to be of bad character, and his reputation suffers in Koforidua.

Three strategies of remedy agent use emerged from any analyses of the seventy-four court cases:

1. Use of the court without prior hearings before another type of remedy agent. Charges in this category generally occur between strangers, or in nonkin, nonfriendship situations, as between buyers and sellers in the marketplace. Since continuing relationships are not at stake, money is the usual issue. Claims are realistic, and if the accused is judged guilty and pays up, the case is resolved.

2. Use of the court after prior hearings before another type of remedy agent. In these cases the court becomes the last appeal, the only remaining hope to find a solution after trying a series of actions to settle a problem.
3. Use of other types of remedy agents after bringing the case to court. This strategy is used when a plaintiff hopes that court action or the threat of court action will persuade the accused to settle out of court.

In contrast to strategy one, plaintiffs who employ strategies two and three are more concerned with their good names and reputations than with any monetary gain, as implied in the saying *Din pa ye sen ahonya* ("A good name is worth more than money").

Plaintiffs sometimes are so angered by what they feel to be threats against their reputations that they use court procedures to teach the accused "sense" and humility. In these instances, claims are often unrealistic, reflecting the plaintiff's pique more than a rational assessment of damage done. Thus, money offered by defendants is sometimes refused by plaintiffs, when the latter realized that their primary goal has been achieved. They are interested in a settlement that preserves their reputation, rather than in extracting punitive damages, which might leave the seeds for future ill feelings.

DIFFERENTIAL USES OF REMEDY AGENTS

The social, economic, and ethnic divisions within Koforidua are reflected by the choice people exercise in selecting remedy agents to solve conflicts. Thus, 90 per cent of the complainants at the Rent Control Board are landlords, although the agency entertains cases brought by tenants as well. The Welfare Department is a forum for young women in low socioeconomic positions who bring charges against older, well-paid men in order to support their children. Poor men are much less frequently defendants, since everyone recognizes that even a favorable decision will have little practical effect when there is no money to collect. In civil cases the principal plaintiffs are businessmen, professionals, and well-to-do farmers, while the defendants tend to be students, apprentices, civil servants, and clerks. Business and professional men are also the plaintiffs in criminal cases, and the unemployed are the defendants with greater frequency than their proportional numbers in the population would suggest. In almost all kinds of cases, members of ethnic groups from outside southern Ghana are underrepresented as plaintiffs and overrepresented as defendants. This may result from their relative lack of power in the city.

TESTING HYPOTHESES

Influenced by the views of Maine and Hoebel about the relationship between urbanization and conflict resolution, I was led to assume that in the city nonpublic remedy agents would be much less important in solving conflicts than public agents. I also expected that in a heterogeneous population marked by inequalities of power, access to resources, and linguistic and ethnic differences, only a public remedy agent would be capable of rendering impartial decisions.

The situation I found was much more complex than these hypotheses suggested. In Koforidua, in spite of size, density, and heterogeneity, enduring social relationships do continue to be important, and nonpublic remedy agents play an important role in the overall system of conflict resolution. The most significant element in the choice of a remedy agent, and in the strategy followed in pressing a charge, turned out to be the nature of the case itself rather than the socioeconomic, social, ethnic, or migrant-or-nonmigrant status of the complainant. Plaintiffs whose sole or primary aim was to collect money turned to the court alone, regardless of their background, whereas plaintiffs whose sole or primary objective was the preservation of their reputation or prestige used a strategy combining court with other remedy agents.

In Koforidua I found that money is viewed in nonmoral terms, but this is certainly not true of people. When money is the primary objective of a suit, remedy agent selection tends to conform to the conditions outlined by Maine and Hoebel. But in cases involving good name and prestige, a more complex pattern exists.

Other hypotheses, when tested, proved to be untrue. Thus, contrary to what I had expected, migrants, wage earners, the literate and well-educated, and the young are no more likely to turn to the courts as the only or primary remedy agent than are nonmigrants, subsistence farmers, the illiterate and uneducated, and the old. Nor did common ethnicity between the litigants lead to the use of private, rather than public remedy agents, as I had expected. While women turned out to be slightly more apt than men to use the courts, the correlation was slight and perhaps not significant. One positive finding is that people involved in simplex relationships are more likely to use only the court, rather than the court plus other agencies, in contrast to people whose relationship are multiplex, whose strategies combine both types of agents.

Retrospect

Even while leaving the field I learned further lessons—the hard way! In the kind of research I carried out, in which paid assistants copied records and aided with questionnaires and censuses, enormous quantities of field data are accumulated. Altogether I found that I had several crates of raw data, far too much to carry as baggage on an airplane. I decided to bring with me only those data I would need to write my dissertation: the case materials, personal field observations, and census sheets, sending the rest back by ship. The cost of air freight seemed prohibitive at the time, but if only I could have anticipated the future, I would have gladly paid it. While waiting on the dock my crates were broken into and some of the records were removed. What remained was repacked—in the boxes of someone going to Jamaica! A year later this material finally reached me, just when I had resigned myself to the fact that many of my data were lost forever. Even without these, processing my field data prior to writing my dissertation took a very long time, and even today I have used less than half of the information I collected. Analysis of the census alone took seven months to write the computer program, punch the cards, and work out the bugs. Based on my experience, I would urge all students who contemplate urban research to acquire some competence in computer use *prior* to gathering data.

In retrospect, I believe that in spite of all the difficulties I encountered, I accomplished most of what I had set out to do. My research results have convinced me that we can profitably rethink the use of remedy agents in our own urban areas. Even now I am encouraging my students to study the American scene, in the belief that we can isolate kinds of cases that can better be settled by private or quasi-public remedy agents, rather than by the courts. The effectiveness of nonpublic agents in a wide variety of situations in Ghana was most impressive; they can serve as a model for conflict resolution in cities in other countries. Unfortunately, a growing number of Ghanaians look upon these devices as symbols of a backward country, and in the name of "progress" and "inevitable evolution," they may suppress their use in favor of public agencies. I have sent copies of my dissertation to the Koforidua library and to the Faculty of Law at the University of Ghana. Perhaps my research findings will allow some Ghanaians to find renewed respect for the importance or usefulness of these alternative approaches to conflict resolution.

REFERENCES CITED

Freilich, Morris (ed.) 1970 *Marginal natives: Anthropologists at work* New York: Harper and Row.

Hoebel, E. Adamson 1954 *The law of primitive man: A study of comparative legal dynamics.* Cambridge: Harvard University Press.

Little, Kenneth 1965 *West African urbanization: A study of voluntary associations in social change.* London: Cambridge University Press.

Lowy, Michael 1971 *The ethnography of law in a changing Ghanian town.* Unpublished Ph.D. dissertation, U.C. Berkeley.

McCall, Daniel 1956 *The effect of family structure on changing economic activities of women in a Gold Coast town.* Unpublished Ph.D. dissertation, Columbia University.
—1962 "The Koforidua market." *In* P. Bohannan and G. Dalton (eds.), *Markets in Africa.* Evanston: Northwestern University Press. Pp. 667-696.

Maine, Sir Henry 1963 (1861) *Ancient law: Its connection with the early history of society and its relation to modern ideas.* Boston: Beacon Press.

18 NATIONALISM, MARXISM, AND WESTERN POPULAR CULTURE IN YUGOSLAVIA: IDEOLOGIES, GENUINE AND SPURIOUS

—ANDREI SIMIĆ

Laž Ima Kratke Noge

(A Lie Has Short Legs) Serbian Proverb

In 1924, linguist/anthropologist Edward Sapir published an essay entitled "Culture, Genuine and Spurious." In this now classic study, he identified two opposing societal types. He characterized what he termed "genuine cultures" as inherently harmonious in that their institutions, ideas, and values were tightly integrated into a seamless whole. In this way, life's various spheres of activity and creativity were conceived of as functionally and ideologically interrelated with respect to a widely shared overarching ethos. In such cultures nothing was spiritually meaningless and little value was attributed to such "modern" concepts as efficiency and utilitarianism. What Sapir had in mind were the small, relatively isolated societies which anthropologists had traditionally studied. In contrast to these, Sapir portrayed the cultures of contemporary urban-industrial societies as "spurious." In this context, the individual's experiences, activities, and social relationships were seen as both fragmented and shallow in content. Moreover, while genuine cultures exhibited a great deal of variation, spurious cultures tended to be geographically uniform and standardized. Of course, Sapir's dichotomy represents an ideal model, and it is clear that real societies will fall somewhere on a spectrum between these two polarities, evidencing various combinations of the characteristics hypothesized by Sapir.

In the following discussion, a model analogous to Sapir's will be proposed in respect to nationalism, Marxism, and Western popular culture, ideologies which have profoundly influenced the recent history of former Yugoslavia. In this respect, a comparison can be drawn between what can be described as contrived, self-consciously held, or deliberately propagated ideologies (spurious or *artificial* ideologies) on the one hand, and those which are discerned by ordinary people to be part of the "natural" or "God-given" order (*genuine* or *natural* ideologies). Here the term "natural order" is used in the *emic* sense, that is, as a reflection of native perceptions in contrast to an imposed *(etic)* analytical construct. In other words, this kind of ideology constitutes an artifact of folk *culture* or the *little tradition* (cf. Redfield 1956), and as such it tends to be embraced in a largely uncritical and matter-of-fact manner as an expression of conventional wisdom. Because of this, folk belief systems not only tend to evidence greater tenacity and longevity than ideologies deliberately imposed

267

from above by political and/or intellectual elites, but their assumptions are much less susceptible to empirical or experiential negation Moreover, they are to a large degree self-perpetuating since they constitute an integral element in the socialization process of children, and are subsequently reinforced by a myriad of cultural traits integrated into everyday life. As a result, such belief systems do not require the same level of deliberate reinforcement as do elite-imposed ideologies. In other words, they are not subject to the same degree of cultural entropy as are those ideologies which have been consciously propagated. Furthermore, they resemble what Carl Jung (1983: 55) has described as "collective symbols" in that they are similarly perceived to be of "divine origin" and to have been "revealed to man." In this case, "divine origin" need not necessarily have a religious connotation, but rather one which refers to a provenance within the "natural order." As is the case with origin myths, such folk ideologies are "sacred" narratives which address the broader meaning of life, the cosmos, and human morality (cf. Custred 2001:17).

In this essay, I will argue that ethno-nationalism among the South Slavs conforms generally to what has been defined above as a *genuine ideology*. As a consequence, it constitutes an overarching ethos which tends to be reified and embraced in an uncritical manner. Thus, as a shared world view it proffers a comfortable and familiar medium within which people define themselves and lead their everyday lives. However, it is not my intent to interpret South Slav nationalism exclusively in primordialist terms, nor to negate instrumentalist and constructionist interpretations. In this respect, it should be noted that not only do many aspects of popular nationalist belief have great-tradition origins, but that recent history amply demonstrates that these sentiments can be easily co-opted by intellectual and political elites.

In stark contrast to the tenacity of the various South Slav nationalisms, I hold that Marxism's relatively brief period florescence and subsequent demise in Yugoslavia was due at least in part to the widely perceived artificial or spurious nature of its ideology as revealed by the evident dissonance between its expressed values and its practice. In this sense, it can be conceptualized as a failed *revitalization movement*[1] whose promise of a Utopian future was increasingly belied by the realities of everyday experience. Thus, rather than being integrated syncretically into the national and individual ethos, Marxism remained cynically and precariously compartmentalized, external to both.

A third and more recent force paralleling both Marxism and nationalism in Yugoslavia has been the influence of Western popular culture. Although the idealization of the West and in particular things American is hardly a new phenomenon in the Balkans, in recent times, it has assumed a far greater significance due to both the ubiquitous nature of mass communication and the anomic social and economic conditions engendered by the fall of communism. I make reference here to the role of Western commercially produced popular culture, not so much as an ideology per se, but as a medium for the dissemination of ideas and fantasies which are for the most part inimical to traditional South Slav culture. These representations do, nevertheless, constitute a world view which by its very nature will be shown to conform to the definition of a spurious *ideology*.

---

1. In regard to the characteristics of *revitalization movements*, see Wallace (1956).

CORE VALUES AND THE RESURGENCE OF SOUTH SLAV NATIONALISM

Sociologist Jefrzy Smolicz (1979: 57–58) has identified what he labels "core values," that is, those elements "forming the most fundamental components of a group's culture." In the case of the South Slavs, these primary markers of identity are comprised of a series of dyadic cross-linkages which subsume in different combinations religious and linguistic affiliations. Since the Serbs, Croats, and Slav Muslims speak the same language (in spite of efforts by Slav Muslim and Croat nationalists to deny this unity), religion (not necessarily religiosity) marks the perceptual boundaries between them.

When in June of 1981, six children in the impoverished Hercegovinian village of Medjugorje began reporting a series of visitations by the Virgin Mary, this phenomenon was quickly co-opted by the Franciscans (Bax 1995: 10–20), a Catholic order which had enthusiastically embraced the pro-Nazi Independent State of Croatia during World War II (Balen 1952 and Lauriere 1993, among many others). At about the same time, construction began in Belgrade to complete what was to become the largest Orthodox church in the Balkans. Its dedication to Saint Sava, the Patron of Serbia, clearly underscored its nationalist implications. Both these events heralded the emergence into the public arena of religion as an ethnic marker after more than four decades of semi-obscurity under the Titoist regime.

It would be erroneous to interpret religion in the Balkans as simply an elite, great-tradition phenomenon. In this regard, the dogmas and practices of official religious bodies are paralleled by and intertwined with a plethora of folk beliefs and practices, the majority of which are confined within the boundaries of the respective religio-ethnic communities. In the case of the Serbs, for example, one can cite the *krsna slava,* the commemoration of the patriline patron saint, a celebration most Serbs hold to be uniquely Serbian (although, in fact, it is also typical of some Gypsies, Vlachs, and Macedonians). As one informant so aptly stated, "You don't feel Serbian unless you have a slava." Thus, the slava simultaneously expresses through ritual and hospitality both familial and national loyalties. Moreover, the slava is usually celebrated in the home rather than the church, often in a secular manner without the participation of a priest. Similarly, among the Croats and Slav Muslims, a myriad of folk expressions of religious particularism provide a constant reminder of one's ethnic identity in a context of contrast and opposition. For example, in respect to the Croats and Serbs, their ritual cycles are regulated by different calendars, with the former employing the Gregorian and the latter the Julian. Of all the major religious holidays, only Easter falls occasionally on the same day. Similar observations can be made about the diacritical nature of the Slav Muslim ritual calendar. The point is that these customs and their attributed meanings form part and parcel of everyday life, and thus they constitute expressions of conventional wisdom. Consequently, they require little or no consciously imposed reinforcement or reification. In other words, they persevere by weight of tradition, that is, as the result of cultural inertia.

While linguistic and religious affiliations constitute overarching and fundamental determinants of national identity, they are further reinforced by a multitude of other markers which are largely though not exclusively associated with folk culture.[2] These include, among many others: historical myth; cosmology, regional dialects; ethnic stereotyping; folk rituals; family and clan lore; material culture; cuisine; literature, especially epic poetry; the arts; styles of conviviality and hospitality; and musical genres. These diacritics have a twofold impact in that they focus on ethnic differences while at the same time obscuring an abundance of characteristics shared with other groups. For example, Lockwood (1975: 160), in his study of a village in western Bosnia, found that local Muslims, Serbs, and Croats, who otherwise closely resembled each other in many respects except religion, differentiated themselves symbolically by a few seemingly insignificant traits such as subtle differences in style of dress and the types of handicrafts sold at the marketplace. Although seemingly trivial, these signs served as effective boundary-maintenance mechanisms in contexts outside the village.

Musical genres provide an illustration of how effectively and precisely national and even regional identities are delineated and symbolized by elements of folk culture. Since World War II, commercially produced "national music" *(komponovana narodna muzika)* in various permutations has enjoyed broadly-based popularity, and during the recent civil wars it assumed considerable political significance (cf. Gordy 1999: 103–164). The predilection for this genre has been particularly strong among the provincial and working classes in Serbia, Bosnia-Hercegovina, Montenegro, and Macedonia, and to a lesser extent in Croatia and Slovenia (cf. Simić 1979). The terms "national" and "folk" are employed here to signify those musical expressions which do not generally transcend ethnic boundaries in contrast to transnational forms such as those associated with Western popular culture. While the various types of Yugoslav national music are only subtly distinguishable from those of neighboring peoples (aside from language differences in the lyrics), internal variation within former Yugoslavia is enormous. Thus, while Macedonian music is often barely distinguishable from Bulgarian, and Slovene from Austrian, the vast gulf between the styles of Slovenia and Macedonia is readily perceived by even the most casual listener. Thus, within the realm of national music, almost no composition is without ethnic or regional specificity. In this way, the concept of national and regional identity is given overt expression in the enjoyable and highly evocative and emotive context of artistic expression.

NATIONALISM AS A WORLD VIEW

Nationalism and ethnicity can be conceptualized as a multi-stranded *world* view which contextualizes, and encompasses a wide range of life's ordinary and extraordinary concerns. In this sense, it shapes the way in which people think about themselves and others, their surroundings, their origins, life's goals, and so forth (cf. Kearney 1984:1). Although nationalism is commonly thought of as the creation of nineteenth-century literary and political elites, it also had its roots among ordinary people, especially in Eastern Europe

---

2. The term *folk* is employed here to mean "those traits associated with everyday life," that is, with the so-called little tradition. While the term, *popular culture* might also be appropriate in this context, I have reserved it exclusively for reference to "commercially produced Western popular culture."

and the Balkans. At the grass-roots level, it can be explained as the logical extension and abstraction of those sentiments which unite members of families, clans, tribes, and other small face-to-face communities. Thus, the values of ethno-nationalism represent a kind of ideological *charter* underwriting what Anderson (1991) has termed "imagined communities," that is, social systems which have grown too large to be validated by the kind of intimate personal relationships typical of so-called *simple societies*. Although more abstract, ethnically based sentiments appear to differ little qualitatively from those characterizing family and kinship ties. Indeed, the relationship between co-ethnics is often phrased symbolically in kinship terms. Thus, at the folk level, ethno-nationalism conforms closely to Geertz's (1963) and Isaacs's (1975) definition of *primordialism*. In contrast, *instrumentalist* and *constructionist* approaches conceive of nationalism as a modem invention exploited by elites to further their economic and political ambitions (cf. Cohn 1974, Gellner 1983, and Walker and Stern 1993). However, the Yugoslav case demonstrates that these contrasting concepts can function symbiotically within the same context.

One way that the development of South Slav nationalism can be conceptualized is as a process which melded an emerging sophisticated cultural and political movement with themes and institutions long present in the indigenous folk cultures (cf. Sugar 1969).[3] For example, in the Serbian lands, as was also the case elsewhere in nineteenth-century Europe, language and folklore became salient markers of ethnic identity. However, among the Serbs, religion (Orthodoxy) combined with elements of common law and kinship, on the one hand, and new artistic and literary creativity, on the other, to form the ideological basis of a nascent national consciousness (cf. Bogisić 1874; Halpern and Hammel 1969).

For many, perhaps most Serbs, the conceptual contrast between the nation and the family is largely one of degree. This is in opposition to the state which is viewed as belonging to another order of reality, and as such not associated with kinship values. The relationship between the family and the nation is eloquently expressed by Milovan Djilas in his epic work. *Land without Justice* (1958:3):

> The story of a family can also portray the soul of the land. This is especially true in Montenegro where the people are divided in clans and tribes to which each family is indissolubly bound. The life of the family reflects the broader community of kin, and through it the entire nation.

The extension of the familial ethos to the nation[4] reflects a perception of co-ethnicity as a form of quasi-kinship. One way in which this relationship can be modeled is as a series of concentric circles whose center is the family, and whose outermost ring encompasses the nation and defines the final limits of moral obligation. In other words, the conceptual space occupied by both the family and the nation constitutes a single, gradated *moral field,* with areas beyond its purview forming an *amoral sphere* where theoretically behavior is not subject to the imposition of in-group moral judgments or sanctions (Simić 1991: 27–32). In terms of this theory, the blood feud, once widespread in Dinaric Mountains of the western Balkans, differs markedly from interethnic conflict. The feud, which was usually waged

---

3. For recent works on South Slav nationalism, see among many others: Denitch (1994); Lederer (1996); and Vučković" (1997: 54–81).

between clans belonging to the same ethnic group, was regarded as a moral, even sacred institution, and was conducted according to mutually agreed upon rules (cf. Boehm 1984; Karan 1986). In contrast, no set of mutual understandings or laws governed the conduct of interethnic conflict other than the obligation to inflict damage on the enemy. In this light, much of the cruelty reported in the recent Yugoslav civil wars can be explained by the fact that those belonging to other ethnic groups fell outside the realm of moral imperatives. Even the influence of religion has not significantly mitigated this behavior since, as history demonstrates. Orthodoxy, Catholicism, and Islam in the Balkans have tended to at least tacitly endorse the values of the folk society.

FOLK CULTURE AND THE DEMISE OF MARXISM IN YUGOSLAVIA

The dissolution of Yugoslavia provides a striking example of the ways in which folk concepts of ethnicity were able to subvert the best efforts of the Titoist regime to create a pan-Yugoslav identity. The relative brevity of the apparent reconciliation on the part of Serbs, Croats, and Slav Muslims following World War II, in retrospect, speaks to both the tenacity of ethnic loyalties and the cyclical nature of their overt expression. In regard to Serb-Albanian relationships during this period, one cannot even speak of a period of reconciliation.

The tenacity of the nationalist ethos in former Yugoslavia stands out in sharp contrast to the failure of Marxism to achieve the same level of popular commitment and cultural integration, that is, to conform to what was previously defined as a "genuine ideology." Nevertheless, a great deal of effort was expended to realize this goal. Among other symbols employed in this respect were: Yugoslavia as the leader of the so-called nonaligned nations; Tito as the ethnically undifferentiated inheritor of the South Slav heroic tradition; the glorification of the role of Partisans in the National Liberation Struggle *(Narodna Oslobodilačka Borba)* during World War II; the concept of a unique Yugoslav form of socialism; the notion of "worker self-management" and, not least of all, the catch-all slogan "brotherhood and unity" (bratstvo *ijedinstvo*).

Arguments have been made that the incidence of ethnically mixed marriages in former Yugoslavia suggests that the role of ethnicity in the recent civil wars was not as great as many have held (cf. Gagnon 1994). However, statistics regarding this can be quite misleading if taken at face value. For example, the Montenegrins have the highest incidence of outmarriage, but the vast majority of these unions are with Serbs with whom they share such close historical and cultural ties as to virtually constitute the same people (cf. Petrovic 1985). Of particular significance was the inclusion of the category "'Yugoslav" as a nationality in the census data. In this respect, it can be inferred that fearing discrimination, many Bosnian and Croatian Serbs opted for this designation in order to hide their ethnic identity. Thus, a union between a "Yugoslav" and a member of any other category would appear sta-

---

4. The term *nation is* employed throughout this essay as virtually synonymous with *ethnic group*, that is, in the Slavic sense of *narod*.

tistically to be an "ethnically mixed" marriage when in fact it may have been homogenous (Simić 1994: 33–34). Furthermore, culture and social structure also tend to shed doubt on the significance of mixed marriages. Given the strong patrilineal bias of South Slav culture and the tendency in rural areas for postmarital residence to be patrilocal, in many cases interethnic marriages probably simply provided a mechanism for recruiting women into the husbands' kinship groups with children assuming the ethnic identity of their fathers (cf. Petrović and Simić 1990). As Barth (1969: 21) has noted, "examples of stable and persisting ethnic boundaries that are crossed by a flow of personnel are clearly more common than the ethnographic literature would lead us to believe."

The strength of ethno-nationalist sentiments can be largely attributed to the fact that they are expressed in a multitude of familiar ways and are manifested both implicitly and explicitly in a broad spectrum of institutions and behaviors. They are taken as "natural" in that they are inculcated from earliest childhood and infused with an aura of sacredness. Moreover, they have no evident externally imposed source, although they may be appropriated and amplified by cultural elites and power brokers for their own purposes. In contrast, Marxism in Yugoslavia was never deeply internalized by the masses of people who became increasingly aware that its Utopian promises of social justice, egalitarianism, and material well-being had not been borne out in practice. For instance, almost thirty years ago, Doder (1974: 75) observed that Yugoslavs regarded public life as a fraud. Similarly, Denitch (1994: 158) describes the widespread disillusionment with and cynicism about Marxism:

> It was responsible for all that ailed the society. Communism was now widely considered responsible for economic backwardness, low personal incomes, poor access to consumer goods, disintegration of traditional values, disrespect from the young, *repressed national grievances and resentments,* poor working habits, and everything else that prevented life in the Yugoslav republics from resembling that of the much-idealized Western Europe. [italics mine]

What the above observations make clear is that Marxism came to be regarded as a dysfunctional ideology antithetical to traditional culture and national aspirations. Nevertheless, it succeeded in maintaining its ascendancy for over four decades by means of constant propagation in the schools, the workplace, and the mass media, as well as through a system of sanctions and rewards within the context of a relatively authoritarian and repressive political structure. Despite these efforts to create a sense of legitimacy, it never attained a position of genuine moral authority in the society. With the demise of Yugoslav Marxism, an ideological vacuum was created, a vacuum which was quickly filled by the more enduring and deeply inculcated ethos of nationalism. However, because this ethos required very little external validation, it was easily exploited by political and economic opportunists.

POPULAR CULTURE AND THE IDEALIZATION OF THE WEST

As mentioned previously, the idealization and emulation of the West is hardly a new phenomenon in the Balkans, in fact, it has a venerable history dating from at least the beginning of the nineteenth century. For instance, with the final liberation of Belgrade from Turkish rule in 1817, the city began a profound physical transformation with the destruction of mosques, Turkish baths, and other remnants of the Ottoman period. By the end of the nineteenth century, Europeanization had touched at least superficially all segments of Belgrade society. Its urban nucleus had been physically metamorphosed into what resembled a provincial Central European town (Andric' et al. 1967). However, this veneer of urbanism and Europeanization barely obscured the city's peasant foundations and the substratum of rural Balkan values which continued to dominate social life. However, today the influence of the West, especially that of America, differs profoundly from the foreign impact on Serbian life during any previous epoch. In this respect, while I will focus mainly on Serbia, it is my presumption that in a general way the following comments can be extrapolated to other Balkan and East European peoples as well.

In addressing the issue of Western influence, Denitch (1994: 134) speaks Of "East Europeans seeking to become just like their idealized versions of West Europeans or Americans." The key word here is *idealized*. The significance is that these representations do not represent a true picture of American and West European life, nor do they respond in any realistic way to the substantive economic needs and social concerns of East Europeans. However, they do act as a powerful tool for the erosion of the traditional cultural and social order. In this sense. Western popular culture provides a conduit for the transmission of certain values, values which do not so much constitute a coherent ideology per se, but rather communicate a vaguely defined and decontextualized world view. In regard to former Yugoslavia, it is clear that popular culture has constituted one of the tools—ostensibly a benign one—for the neocolonial cultural, political, and economic domination of Southeast Europe by the United States and its allies, especially Germany.

Drawing on George Orwell's classic *1984* and Aldous Huxley's *Brave New World* and *Brave New World Revisited*, Neil Postman (1986: vii–vii) points out the insidious and coercive nature of popular culture (what he subsumes under the rubric of amusement):

As Huxley remarked in *Brave New World Revisited*, the civil libertarians and rationalists who are ever on the alert to oppose tyranny failed to take into account man's almost infinite appetite for distractions. In 1984 . . . people are controlled by inflicting pain. In *Brave New World*, they are controlled by inflicting pleasure. In short, what Orwell feared was that what we hate will ruin us. Huxley feared that what we love will ruin us.

This image of pleasure is perhaps most effectively communicated by television. As in much *of* the world, people in Serbia are sitting in darkened rooms fixed on a glowing screen viewing images, more often than not intellectually vacuous ones, transmitted over thousands of miles from a culture with little historical connection to their own. And what exactly are they watching? As the Turning Point Project described it in a paid statement in the *New York Times* of June 19, 2000 (as part of a series entitled "Megatechnology"):

Even in places on the earth where there are still no roads—tiny tropical islands, icy tundras of the north, or in the mountains of the Himalayas—people are sitting in their grass houses or log cabins watching Americans in Dallas driving sleek cars, or standing around swimming pools drinking martinis, plotting ways to do-in one another. Or they are seeing "Bay Watch," the most popular series in the world. Life in Texas, California, New York is made to seem the ultimate in life's achievements while local culture . . . can seem backward.

These images not only communicate an illusion of excitement, luxury, and material well-being, but also glamorize crime, violence, and sexual promiscuity. In essence, the values projected are those of moral relativism, unfettered individualism, consumerism, blatant materialism, and above all, pleasure. Moreover, these messages are disseminated in a spectrum of appealing ways: in films, television, advertising, fashions, fast food, the print media, radio, the music industry, and less directly by religious missionaries of non-native sects and the representatives of a spectrum of foreign-based NGOs. The implicit message here is clear: "Embrace the concept of *democracy and free markets,* and you will have all these things." In other words, the subtext is a political and economic one (cf. Schiller 1989).

The influence of various forms of rock music in Serbia provides a case in point. In his study of the "culture of power" in Serbia under Milošević, Gordy (1999),[5] negatively contrasts the traditionalists, whom he stereotypes as nationalists "less open to democratic possibilities" (203), with those who advocate the Western values of democracy in both public and private life as an expression of individualism, self-determination and unbridled personal freedom. For Gordy, among those who espouse the latter are young Belgrade rock musicians. While lavishing praise on them, the author directs his scorn at the various forms of national music which he associates with retrograde political and cultural attitudes. He sees such genres as shutting off sophisticated, cosmopolitan cultural alternatives from the West. In his words (108), "Neofolk was marginalized in the cities, as was its audience, regarded as composed of 'peasants' (seljaci) and 'primitives' (primitivci)." The relative musical value of these two forms of musical expression is not at issue here, but simply the fact that rock music is indisputably the carrier of certain Western values, principally American ones.

What kind of values are embedded in the rock movement which Gordy so lionizes? If the lyrics are any indication, they are ego-centered and hedonistic, or in the author's own words, they constitute a *culture of pleasure.* This hedonistic idol is succinctly given substance in his concluding remarks wherein he comments upon the various symbols which he observed at an anti-Milošević demonstration in Belgrade (208):

The protesters seemed to suggest with their flags that the countries of the world, its *entertainment* spectacles, and *commercial* products share a value—and that the places and *pleasures* of the world, the taste of its bourbon, and the strategies of Michael Jordan belong to them also [italics mine].

Gordy's words are echoed in a more general context by Rothstein (2002: 19), who comments:

American popular culture is capitalist culture. In capitalism commodities are produced that will spur desire for more commodities. Capitalism seduces through sheer force of marketing and sheer promise *of pleasure* [italics mine].

The question remains in the case of former Yugoslavia, as well as in the rest of the former Eastern Block, as to whether this promise of pleasure and material well-being can be

5. For a detailed analysis of Gordy's work, see Simić (2000).

delivered. The evidence to date suggest a prophetic parallel with Marxism, the decline of which resulted to a significant degree from the dissonance between its ideology and its perceived reality. The case of Serbia's impoverished and demoralized neighbor, Bulgaria, can perhaps provide some instructive insights. For example, Blagovesta Doncheva (1999) comments that the Bulgarians were cruelly deceived by the West, and that democracy has only created hordes of unemployed workers, the closing of factories, beggars on the streets, and old people digging in the trash (cf. Balikci 1998: 4). This stands out in stark contrast to the profusion of consumer goods displayed in the shop windows along Sofia's Vitosha street, goods far out of the reach of most Bulgarians.

It is in the disparity between the promise and the reality that Marxism and free-market capitalism (as portrayed in popular culture) exhibit a common feature as ideologies. In Sapir's words, they are both "spurious." In contrast to nationalism, both are far more susceptible to empirical and experiential negation. In the case of Western popular culture, it has a fragmenting effect in that it is oriented primarily toward the youth. This is particularly significant in the case of former Yugoslavia where traditional culture has stressed the solidarity and corporacy of family and kinship relations (cf. Hammel 1968, Simic 1973, among many others). Moreover, popular culture is generic and homogenizing. In this way, it links the individual conceptually not to local culture and institutions, but rather to an imagined and often ill-perceived global society.

In his book, *One Market under God,* Frank (2000: xiv–xv) speaks of "market populism," a system which claims to "express the popular will more articulately and more meaningfully" than do mere elections. He further points to the role of Hollywood in tandem with Madison Avenue in the propagation of this ideology. However, he notes the concomitant presence of elements of class warfare with the elevation of the rich and the disregard of the poor. Nowhere is this more evident than on the streets of Belgrade where expensively dressed nouveaux-elites and would-be elites stand out in sharp contrast to those unfortunates struggling to survive by selling sundries on Knez Mihailo Street late into the night. It is the latter who are emblematic to one degree or another of the impoverished general population. Thus, the ideology embodied in "market populism" works only for a minority, and surely the dissonance between belief and practice must be manifest even to the privileged few. In contradiction to this, the strength of nationalism does not lie in the fulfillment of certain explicit promises, but stems from the power of transcendent historical and racial myth as well as from a sense of individual and group connection to the real or imagined glories of the nation. Such sentiments are, in fact, often strengthened by shared adversity. In times of chaos and economic and political instability, they provide a last defense against the forces of nihilism and anomie. This inherent durability of nations and nationalism is incisively summarized by Smith (1998: 159):

> I have argued that, despite the capacity of nationalisms to generate widespread terror and destruction, the nation and nationalisms provide the only realistic socio-cultural framework for a modern world order. They have no rivals today. National identity too remains widely attractive and effective and is felt by many people to satisfy their needs for cultural fulfillment, security and fraternity. Many people are still prepared to answer the call of the nation and lay down their lives for its cause. Finally,

nations are linked by chains of memory, myth and symbol to the widespread and enduring type of community, the *ethnic*, and this is what gives them the unique character and their profound hold over the feelings and imaginations of so many people.

The function of nationalist ideology as an individual psychological resource was once very simply but profoundly expressed to me some thirty years ago by a shabbily dressed elderly man on the streets of Sofia whom I asked for directions:

"I don't know sir, but you see I am just a poor street sweeper, but thanks to God, a Bulgarian street sweeper."

REFERENCES

Anderson, Benedict

1991 Imagined Communities. London and New York: Verso Press.

Andrić, Nada et al.1967. *Beograd u XIX Veku*. (Belgrade in the XDC Century).Belgrade: Muzej Grada Beograda.

Balen, Šime 1952 *Pavelić*. Zagreb: Biblioteka DrAva Novinara. Balikci, Asen

1998 A Qualitative Assessment of the Living Standards of the Bulgarian Elderly. A report commissioned for the Social Assessment of Bulgaria by the Social Assessment Team of the Europe and Central Asia Region of the World Bank.

Barth, Frederik 1969. Introduction." In Barth, Frederik (ed.), Ethnic Groups and Ethnic Boundaries. Boston: Little, Brown.

Bax, Mart *1995. Medjugorje: Religion, Politics, and Violence in Rural Bosnia*. Amsterdam: VU Uitgeverij.

Bogisić, Valtazar *1874. Zbornik Sadašnjih Praynih Običaja u Južnih Slavena* (A Compendium of Contemporary Legal Customs among the South Slavs). Zagreb: Jugoslovenska Akademija.

Boehm, Christopher

1984. Blood Revenge: The Anthropology of Feuding in Montenegro and Other Tribal Societies. Lawrence: University of Kansas Press.

Cohen, Abner 1974. "Introduction: The Lessons of Ethnicity." In Cohen, Abner (ed.). *Urban Ethnicity*. London: Tavistock. Pp. ix–xxi.

Custred, Glynn 2001. "Oral Traditions and the Rules of Evidence." *Mammoth Trumpet* (June): 17.

Denitoh, Bogdan 1994. *Ethnic Nationalism: The Tragic Death of Yugoslavia*. Minneapolis: University of Minnesota Press.

Doder, Dusko 1978. *The Yugoslavs*. New York: Random House. Doncheva, Blagovesta

1999. "In Bulgaria 10 Years of Misery." *New York Times* (November 11—Op-Ed Section).

Frank, Thomas 2000. *One Market under God: Extreme Capitalism, Market Populism, and the End of Economic Democracy*. New York: Doubleday.

Gagnon, V.P. Jr. 1994. "Reaction to the Special Issue of AEER, War among the Yugoslavs." *Anthropology of East Europe Review* 12(1): 50–51.

Geertz, Clifford 1963 . "The Integrative Revolution: Primordal Sentiments and Civic Politics in the Anthropology of East Europe Review New States." In Geertz, Clin'ord (cd.). *Old Societies and New States*. New York: Free Press.

Gellner, Ernest 1983. *Nations and Nationalism*. Ithaca: Comell University Press.

Gordy, Eric D. 1999. *The Culture of Power in Serbia: Nationalism and the Destruction of Alternatives*. University Park: The Pennsylvania State University Press.

Halpern, Joel M. and E.A. Hammel 1969. "Observations on the Intellectual History of Ethnology and Other Social Sciences in Yugoslavia." *Comparative Studies in Society and History 2:* 17–26.

Hammel, Eugene A. 1968. *Alternate Social Structures and Ritual Relations in theBalkans*. Englewood Cliffs: Prentice Hall.

Issacs, Harold P. 1975. *Idols of the Tribe: Group Identity and Political Change*. New York: Harper and Row.

Jung, Carl G. 1983. *Man and His Symbols*. Garden City: Doubleday.

Karan, Milenkol 1986. *Krvna Osveta* (Blood Revenge). Ljubljana: Partizanska, Krijiga. Keamey, Michael

1984 *World View:* Novato, California: Chandler and Sharp.

Lauriere, Heme 1993. *Assassins au Norn de Dieu* (Assassins in the Name of God). Paris: L'Age D'Homme.

Lederer, Ivo J. 1969. "Nationalism and the Yugoslavs." In Sugar, Peter F. and Ivo J. Lederer (eds.), *Nationalism in Eastern Europe*. Seattle: University of Washington Press.

Lockwood, William 1975. *European Moslems: Economy and Ethnicity in Western Bosnia*. New York: Seminar Press.

Petrović, Edit 1995. "Ethnicity Deconstructed: The Breakup of the Former Yugoslavia and Personal Reflections on Nationalism, Identity, and Displacement." *Culture* 15(2): 117–124.

Petrovic Edit and Andrei Simić 1990. "Montenegrin Colonists in Vojvodina: Objective and Subjective Measures of Ethnicity." *Serbian Studies* 5(4): 5–20.

Postman, Neil 1986. Amusing Ourselves to Death: Public Discourse in the Age of Show Business. New York: Penguin Books.

Redfield, Robert 1956. *Peasant Society and Culture: An Anthropological Approach to Civilization.* Chicago: University of Chicago Press.

Rothstein, Edward 2002. "Damning (Yet Desiring) Mickey and the Big Mac." *New York Times* (March 2): 17–19.

Sapir, Edward 1924. "Culture, Genuine and Spurious." *American Journal of Sociology* 29: 401–429.

Schiller, Herbert I. 1989. *Culture Inc.: The Corporate Takeover of Public Expression.* New York: Oxford University Press.

Simić, Andrei 1973. *The Peasant Urbanites.* New York: Seminar Press.

1979. "Commercial Folk Music in Yugoslavia: Idealization and Reality." *Journal of the Association of Graduate Dance Ethnologists* 2: 25–37.

1991. "Obstacles to the Development of a Yugoslav National Consciousness: Ethnic Identity and Folk Culture in the Balkans." *Journal of Mediterranean Studies* 1(1): 18–36.

1994 "The Civil War in Yugoslavia: Do Ostensibly High Rates of Intermarriage Obviate Ethnic Hatreds as a Cause?" *Anthropology of East Europe Review* 12(2): 33–34.

2000. "Conventional Wisdom and Milošević's Serbia: A Review Essay." *The Anthropology of East Europe Review* 18(1): 87–95.

Smith, Anthony D. 1998. *Nations and Nationalism in a Global Era.* Cambridge, UK: Polity Press.

Smolicz, Jerzy J.I 979. *Culture and Education in a Plural Society.* Adelaide: University of Adelaide Curriculum Development Center.

Sugar, Peter F. 1969. "External and Domestic Roots of East European Nationalism." In Sugar, Peter F. and Ivo J. Lederer (eds.). *Nationalism in Eastern Europe.* Seattle: University of Washington Press.

Turning Point Project 2000. "Monocultures of the Mind." *New York Times* (June 12).

Vučković, Goiko 1997 Ethnic Cleavages and Conflict: The Sources of National Cohesion and Disintegration—The Case of Yugoslavia. Brookfield, Vermont: Ashgate Publishing Company.

Walker, Lee and Paul C. Stem (eds.) 1993 *Balancing and Sharing Political Power in Multiethnic Societies.* Washington, D.C.: National Academy Press.

Wallace, Anthony F.C.I 956. "Revitalization Movements." *American Anthropologist* 58: 264–281.

NOTES

The observations in this essay are based in part on my over thirty-five years of field work and periodic residence in Yugoslavia, principally in rural and urban Serbia, but also in Bosnia-Hercegovina, Croatia, and Montenegro. This essay was presented at The International Symposium on Ethnic Identity sponsored by the Demokritos Foundation and the Laboratory of Anthropology of the University of Thrace at Xanthi, Greece, July 6 to July 9, 2002.

19 THE FATE OF LOT'S WIFE: STRUCTURAL MEDIATION IN BIBLICAL MYTHOLOGY

—D. ALAN AYCOCK

A theme recurrent in mythology is the immobilization of a hero or villain, together with his/her transformation into an inanimate object.[1] To my knowledge, however, Lévi-Strauss is the first to have offered a satisfactory explanation of this immobilization/transformation theme, in his analysis of the Tsimshian 'Asdiwal' cycle: the hunger Asdiwal's transmutation into stone comes as the final result of a complex series of symmetrical geographic, social, economic, and cosmological oppositions expressed in the myth and developed through a dialectic, in which the actions of Asdiwal himself represent the dynamic mediation of thesis and antithesis (1967: 1–47). Even Mary Douglas, who is by no means uncritical of Lévi-Strauss, is obliged to remark of his analysis that: 'Some may have doubted that myths can have an elaborate symmetrical structure. If so, they should be convinced of their error' (1967: 56).

To interpret an instance of immobilization and transformation, therefore, it seems that we must invoke the wider symbolic structure of the myth, insofar as that structure expresses contradictory events or tendencies. We must then inquire whether the character who becomes immobilized and changed embodies a midpoint between these contradictions, in such a way that the mythic plot cannot further unfold unless this dramatic resolution occurs.[2]

My purpose in this paper is to argue that the 'recipe' I have outlined in the above paragraph is entirely adequate to enable us to understand what must otherwise remain a mysterious mythological event, namely, the transformation of Lot's wife into a pillar of salt. Lest the attainment of this goal be viewed as more trivial than triumphant, I hasten to add that I perceive the myth of Lot to be a structural analogue of many other, more significant myths in the Old and New Testaments, and that I expect my unravelling of the fate of Lot's wife, together with an explication of the accompanying symbolic structure, to suggest interesting resonations throughout Hebraic and Christian mythology.

In view, however, of Professor Julian Pitt-Rivers' recent (1977) critique of 'structuralist' Biblical exegeses, I wish to enter three *caveats* at this point. First, although I regard this essay as inspired by the work of Claude Lévi-Strauss (as well as by that of Sir Edmund

Leach), I am not claiming either to be acting within any theoretical parameters he may have set out, or to be producing an analysis that Lévi-Strauss himself might identify as 'structural'. What I have written here ought to be judged on its own merits and limitations. Second, I am not proposing that this analysis unravels the *only* message to be discovered in the myth of Lot and his wife; it is entirely possible that there might be as many exegetically valid messages as there are persons inclined towards hermeneutics. My only canon of success is to generate an interpretation which, among others, may be regarded as intellectually and aesthetically satisfying by myself and at least some of my readers. Third, I do not accept Pitt-Rivers' prohibition upon the structural analysis of any text falling toward the consciously prescriptive end of his continuum between myth and 'real' history (1977: 140ff.). I think that the 'irreversibility' and 'progression' of moral history is another part of its message(s), not a factor somehow extrinsic to the text itself, and therefore subject to the same approach as any other part of the text. I have correspondingly incorporated that factor into my analysis.

I shall not recount the myth of Lot, since it is readily available to any reader not familiar with its details.[3] In studying the myth, I was immediately struck by a series of contradictory events which 'bracket' the changing of Lot's wife into a pillar of salt.

First, the myth begins with a recounting of the hospitality offered by Lot to the two angles in disguise sent by God to inform him of the extent of iniquity in Sodom. The hospitality, prescribed by the *mores* of ancient (as well as modern) Semitic-speaking peoples, consisted of a feast together with unleavened bread.[4] The end of the myth, on the other hand, tells of the drunkenness of Lot as a consequence of the wine given him by his daughters. Thus a sequence which commences with restraint and social formality concludes with intemperance and social insensibility.

A second theme closely related to the first involves the identities of Lot's companions. At the beginning of the myth, these companions are two males,[5] disguised, and strangers to Lot. At the ending of the myth, the companions are two females, 'disguised' by Lot's drunkenness, and his intimates in more than one sense.

Third, the myth starts with the impending destruction of Sodom by God, but ends with the creation of the tribes of the Moabites and Ammonities, descended from the incestuous relationship of Lot with his daughter.

Fourth, the myth is initially located within the city walls of Sodom, and ultimately set in a cave in the hills above Zoar. This geographical movement might best be understood as a contrast of the 'Culture' of the city with the 'Nature' of the wilderness, an opposition familiar to students of Lévi-Strauss (1969) and Sir Edmund Leach (1976).

Finally, the myth begins in a society of homosexuals, who by virtue of their (apparently exclusive) sexual preference *cannot* produce children (we may also note the symbolic blinding/castration of the men of Sodom by the angles in disguise). The myth ends in an incestuous association precipitated by Lot's daughters, who justify their actions by asserting that they *must* bear children (the womb-link locale of this event, in the caves in the hills above Zoar, is most appropriate).

Turning now to the problem of mediation, how is it that the miraculous transformation of Lot's wife into a pillar of salt 'resolves' the contradictions posed above?

The key to my argument is that Lot's wife became, specifically, a pillar of *salt*: this particular fate may be interpreted most clearly in the context of the ethnography of the ancient Mediterranean. Salt, to the ancient Hebrews, had three main connotations: first, it was a symbol of purification, preservation, and immortality; second, it was a symbol of barrenness and sterility; third, it was a symbol of covenant, as between parties concluding a peace treaty or a marriage agreement (Gaster 1969: 301–2, 428–30, 516–17, 628–19; Smith 1927: 270, 454). All three of these meanings are relevant to my demonstration (I consider the actual presence of considerable quantities of salt in the geographical region indicated by the myth neither to substantiate nor to vitiate the explanations offered here).

Let us consider, first, salt in relation to the social control implied by Lot's hospitality to the disguised angels, and in relation to the social excess implied by Lot's drunkenness. A well-known Semitic metaphor equates hospitality with salt shared between guest and host; indeed, every instance of commensality, *including* sacrifices offered to God, is to be accompanied by appropriate seasoning with salt (Gaster 1969 and Smith 1927; *loc. cit.*). In effect, I suppose we could say that the fate of Lot's wife is an extraordinary affirmation of sociability: she has been offered up as a sacrifice to God in much the same way Lot offered food to the disguised angles, and offered his daughters to the men of Sodom,[6] as testimony to his hypertrophied sense of *politesse*. In contrast, we might point to the lack of social control instanced by Lot's drunkenness, and equate this with the disobedience of his wife, with its saline consequence. More to the point, I think, are the divine interventions which constitute a direct response to the instances of social control and social excess: the disguised angels miraculously deliver Lot and his family from Sodom and its inhabitants as a reward for his hospitality; God, accepting Lot's 'sacrificial' offering, simultaneously punishes Lot's wife for her excessive attachment to a doomed city; Lot's 'sacred' drunkenness (Dumézil 1973: 21ff. has much to say on this subject in Norse and Indic contexts) spares him culpability for his incest, which itself was linked to the imagery of divinity and elitism in the ancient Near East. Salt is important here, therefore, to evoke the idea of mediation between God and man.

The contrast between the identities of Lot's guests and those of his daughters is precisely resolved by Lot's wife. The plot logically requires a means of transition from Lot's interaction with the two angels to Lot's interaction with his two daughters. His wife provides such a transition, or mediation, since she embodies qualities of both daughters and angels: like his daughters, Lot's wife is an intimate and a member of his household, but unlike most characterizations in Pentateuchal mythology, Lot's wife is never named, nor is she genealogically attached to one of the patriarchs. In this latter respect, therefore, she is more like the strangers who prove to be angles; indeed, we might even say that Lot's wife attains an apotheosis in her fate which is not unlike that of other figures of the mythology of classical antiquity.

The contradition between the destruction of Sodom and the creation of the Moabites and Ammonites, which arises from the structure of the myth, leads us again to the imagery of salt which the fate of Lot's wife presents: both the discontinuity implied by the obliteration of the cities of Sodom and Gomorrah, and the continuity implied by the divine blessing required for the creation of new social groups, are subsumed for the ancient Hebrews by the idea of covenants attested through the sharing of salt. We may say that on the one hand a covenant implies discontinuity: since it entails mutual obligations newly recognized by the parties, these obligations must not have previously existed (as in a marriage contract or a peace treaty). On the other hand, a covenant required the *imprimatur* of ancestral approval ultimately derived from God's authority, and here the continuity involved in the creation of any social form must be acknowledged. Thus, the metamorphosis of Lot's wife embodies a covenant between God and Lot which must formally be accompanied by a communion of salt. Salt, of course, may also here be viewed as symbolic of the preservation of the covenant.

I think, then, that we ought to accept the geographical journey of Lot and his family from Sodom to the hills above Zoar as a metaphoric rite of passage from an old society to a new one. Here it is tempting to refer to the symbolic immobilizations which many cultures impose to emphasize the non-social character of persons undertaking the liminal phase of a rite of passage (Turner 1967: 93–111). The permanent geographical immobilization of Lot's wife in the wilderness of Nature between the old Culture of Sodom and the new Culture emanating from the caves in the hills above Zoar should thus be interpreted as a moral analogy of her permanently liminal status in the rite of passage she chose to abort. Here again, the preservative function of salt was employed during rites of passage by the ancient Hebrews in an attempt to safeguard the purity and permanence of the status about to be entered upon (see references already cited in Gaster 1969).

We may go further than this, and argue that Lot's wife, by virtue of her statuses of wife and mother, is anomalous both in the society of homosexuals she has abandoned, and in the incestuous ménage à trois which eventuates. Her mediating position, therefore, must be one of immobilization, since she would be in a contradictory situation were she to go either forward or back. Perhaps the barrenness of salt is a uniquely suitable image for Lot's wife as wife or mother in either society, since her reproductive functions are irrelevant to both.

Finally, the statuses of Lot's wife as woman and as a genealogical 'stranger' also doom her to immobility between the initial and final events of the myth. If we study the 'abominations' of Leviticus, it is clear that rules about food and rules about sexuality are equated by the ancient Hebrews, as by so many other peoples. In particular, the rules stress the 'separateness' of interaction in both cases, and assign a 'clean' or 'pure' condition to those who conscientiously observe the rules which separate various kinds of foods on the one hand, and various kinds of sexual partners on the other (Douglas 1966). Both intercourse with a person of one's own sex and intercourse with a person of one's own kin group are therefore 'abominable' and 'unclean'. Lot's wife, as a *female*, is thus anomalous in Sodomite society: as a member (presumably) of a kin group *separate* from Lot's own, she is anomalous also in his incestuous relationship with his daughters. It may be supposed that the salt into which she is transformed has therefore not only the connotation of sterility, but also the connotation of purity, since she cannot, by definition, participate in the abominations and impurity of either Sodom or the caves in the hills.

I shall now suppose, however presumptuously, that I have established both the symmetry and the contradictions in the myth of Lot, and further that I have shown that the fate of Lot's wife is appropriate and necessary to her role as mediator of these contradictions. As I have already suggested, this exercise would be of limited value if it had no further application. However, even a modest inquiry assures us of the proliferation of immobilized or suspended heroes in Biblical mythology: Noah in his ark upon Ararat, Isaac tied to the altar below Abraham's knife and the ram caught in the bushes who substitutes for him, and Jesus on the cross are some prominent examples. Furthermore, the oppositions I have elicited from this myth are likewise standard themes: excess and restraint applied to food and sexuality, the city and the wilderness, the ambiguous status of women in a formally patrilineal society and the relation of covenant to sacrifice are ideas which inform key metaphors throughout the Old and New Testaments.

NOTES

1. For other examples of immobilization/transformation, see the examples and bibliography cited in Gaster 1969: 160–1, 366 (n. 1).

2. Although the transformation of Asdiwal is the conclusion of that specific story in the cycle, Lévi-Strauss argues in effect that its sequel, which concerns Waux, the son of Asdiwal, cannot be justified without that particular dénouement (1967: 23ff.).

3. All references in this essay to the myth of Lot are taken from Gen. 19: 1–38, in the Revised Standard Edition of the Christian Bible.

4. This specification of the offering of unleavened (and unsalted) bread seems significant in the light of subsequent events. Perhaps I ought to suggest a contrast between the *unsalted* bread at the beginning of the myth, and the wine (which in ancient times would have been made *with* salt) at its ending?

5. The 'twoness' of the angels is part of the Old Testament manifestation of divinity, regarded there as a plural noun.

6. A confrontation of purity with abomination which is both dramatically satisfying, and, as later events prove, entirely ironic. I am indebted to Dr. Brent Shaw for pointing out to me this facet of the myth.

REFERENCES

Douglas, Mary 1966 *Purity and Danger; an Analysis of Concepts of Pollution and Taboo*, London: Routledge and Kegan Paul

1967 'The meaning of myth, with special reference to "La Geste d'Asdiwal' ", in Edmund Leach (ed.), *The Structural Study of Myth and Totemism*, London: Tavistock Publications Ltd

Dumézil, Georges 1973 *Gods of the Ancient Northmen* (E. Haugen, ed. and trans.), Berkeley: University of California Press

Gaster, Theodor H. 1969 *Myth, Legend, and Custom in the Old Testament* (2 vols.), New York: Harper and Row

Leach, Edmund 1976 *Culture and Communication: the Logic by Which Symbols are Connected.* Cambridge: Cambridge University Press.

Lévi-Strauss, Claude 1967 'The story of Asdiwal' (N. Mann, trans.), in Edmund Leach (ed.), *The Structural Study of Myth and Totemism*, London: Tavistock Publications Ltd.

1969 *The raw and the cooked; introduction to a science of mythology* (J. and D. Weightman, trans.), New York: Harper and Row

Pitt-Rivers, Julian 1977 'The Fate of Shechem or the Politics of Sex,' in Pitt-Rivers, *The Fate of Shechem or the Politics of Sex: Essays in the Anthropology of the Mediterranean*, Cambridge: Cambridge University Press.

Smith, W. Robertson 1889 *Lectures on the Religion of the Semites*, 1st Edition (London, A. & C. Black), 2nd Edition 1894. 3rd Edition (edited by S. A. Cook) 1927

Turner, Victoria 1967 'Betwixt and between: the liminal period in *rites de passage*', in *The Forest of Symbols*, Ithaca, New York: Cornell University Press

20 THE MEANING OF MYTH
WITH SPECIAL REFERENCE TO 'LA GESTE D'ASDIWAL'

—MARY DOUGLAS

Social anthropology, as we know it, was born of a professedly empirical approach. And it was first developed in Britain. These two marks, of being British and empirical, are not accidentally linked. This is the home of philosophical scepticism, an attitude of thought which has insulated us more effectively than the North Sea and the Channel from Continental movements of ideas. Our intellectual climate is plodding and anti-metaphysical. Yet, in spite of these traditions, we cannot read much of Lévi-Strauss without feeling some excitement. To social studies he holds out a promise of the sudden life that new methods of science could give. He has developed his vision so elaborately and documented it so massively from so many fields of our subject that he commands our attention.

He has developed most explicitly in connection with myth his ideas of the place of sociology within a single grand discipline of Communication. This part of his teaching draws very broadly on the structural analysis of linguistics, and on cybernetics and communication theory in general, and to some extent on the related theory of games. Briefly, its starting-point is that it is the nature of the mind to work through form. Any experience is received in a structured form, and these forms or structures, which are a condition of knowing, are generally unconscious (as, for example, unconscious categories of language). Furthermore, they vary little in modern or in ancient times. They always consist in the creation of pairs of opposites, which are balanced against one another and built up in various (algebraically representable) ways. All the different kinds of patterned activity can be analysed according to the different structures they produce. For example, social life is a matter of interaction between persons. There are three different types of social communication. First, there is kinship, the structure underlying the rules for transferring women; second, there is the economy, that is the structure underlying transfer of goods and services; third, there is the underlying structure of language. The promise is that if we can get at these structures, display and compare them, the way is open for a true science of society, so far a will-o'-the-wisp for sociologists.

So far myth has not been mentioned. Lévi-Strauss recognizes that its structures belong to a different level of mental activity from those of language, and the technique of analysis must be correspondingly different. The technique is described in his 'Structural Study of Myth' (1955) and is also made very clear in Edmund Leach's two articles (1961, 1962) in which he applies the technique to the Book of Genesis. It assumes that the analysis of myth should proceed like the analysis of language. In both language and myth the separate units have no meaning by themselves, they acquire it only because of the way in which they are combined. The best comparison is with musical notation: there is no musical meaning in a single isolated note. Describing the new science of mythologics which is to parallel linguistics, Lévi-Strauss unguardedly says that the units of mythological structure are sentences. If he took this statement seriously it would be an absurd limitation on analysis. But in fact, quite rightly, he abandons it at once, making great play with the structure underlying the meaning of a set of names. What are sentences, anyway? Linguists would be at a loss to identify these units of language structure which Lévi-Strauss claims to be able to put on punched cards and into a computing machine as surely and simply as if they were phonemes and morphemes. For me and for most of us, computer talk is a mysterious language very apt for prestidigitation. Does he really mean that he can chop a myth into semantic units, put them through a machine, and get out at the other end an underlying pattern which is not precisely the one he used for selecting his units? The quickness of the hand deceives the eye. Does he further believe that this underlying structure is the real meaning or sense of the myth? He says that it is the deepest kind of sense, more important than the uninitiated reader would suspect. However, I do not think it is fair to such an ebullient writer to take him literally. In other contexts it is plain that Lévi-Strauss realizes that any myth has multiple meanings and that no one of them can be labelled the deepest or the truest. More of this later.

From the point of view of anthropology, one of his novel departures is to treat all versions of a myth as equally authentic or relevant. This is right, of course. Linguistic analysis can be applied to any literary unit, and the longer the better, so long as there is real unity underlying the stretches of language that are analysed together. Why stop short at one of Shakespeare's historical plays? Why not include the whole of Shakespeare? Or the whole of Elizabethan drama? Here Lévi-Strauss gives one of his disturbing twists of thought that make the plodding reader uneasily suspect that he is being duped. For by 'version' we find that Lévi-Strauss means both version and interpretation. He insists that Freud's treatment of the Oedipus myth must be put through the machine together with other earlier versions. This challenging idea is not merely for the fun of shocking the bourgeois mythologist out of his search for original versions. Freud used the Oedipus myth to stand for his own discovery that humans are each individually concerned with precisely the problem of 'birth from one' or 'birth from two' parents. On Lévi-Strauss's analysis of its structure, this problem is revealed as underlying the Oedipus cycle. So there is no inconsistency between Freud and Sophocles. But the reference to Freud interestingly vindicates Lévi-Strauss on a separate charge. Some must feel that the themes which his technique reveals are too trivial and childish either to have been worth the excavation, or to have been worth the erecting of an elaborate myth series in the first place. But after Freud no one can be sure that an individual's speculation about his own genesis is a trivial puzzle without emotional force.

I admit that the use of all interpretations of a great myth might not always so triumphantly vindicate this method. Meyer Fortes (1959) treated Oedipus rather differently in *Oedipus and Job in West Africa.* Compare St. Augustine, Simone Weil (1950), and Edmund Leach (1962) on the Biblical story of Noah drunk in the vineyard: for one the drunken, naked Noah is Christ humiliated; for the other he is the dionysian mysteries too austerely rejected by the Jewish priesthood, and for the last the tale is a trite lesson about Hebrew sexual morality. I will say more below of how these 'versions' would look coming out of the mythologic computer. At this stage of the discussion we should treat the computer as a red herring and forget for the moment the quest for the real meaning. We can then begin seriously to evaluate Lévi-Strauss's approach to mythology.

First, we should recognize his debt to the dialectical method of Hegelian-Marxist philosophy. The dialectic was Hegel's speculation about the nature of reality and about the logical technique by which it could be grasped. When Lévi-Strauss says that mythic thought follows a strict logic of its own, he means a Hegelian logic of thesis, antithesis, and synthesis, moving in ever more complex cycles to comprehend all the oppositions and limitations inherent in thought. According to Lévi-Strauss, the structure of myth is a dialectic structure in which opposed logical positions are stated, the oppositions mediated by a restatement, which again, when its internal structure becomes clear, gives rise to another kind of opposition, which in its turn is mediated or resolved, and so on.

On the assumption that it is the nature of myth to mediate contradictions, the method of analysis must proceed by distinguishing the oppositions and the mediating elements. And it follows, too, that the function of myth is to portray the contradictions in the basic premises of the culture. The same goes for the relation of myth to social reality. The myth is a contemplation of the unsatisfactory compromises which, after all, compose social life. In the devious statements of the myth, people can recognize indirectly what it would be difficult to admit openly and yet what is patently clear to all and sundry, that the ideal is not attainable.

Lévi-Strauss does not stick his neck out so far as to say that people are reconciled better or worse to their makeshift arrangements and contradictory formulae—but merely that myth makes explicit their experience of the contradictoriness of reality.

A summary of 'La Geste d'Asdiwal'[1] best demonstrates how this is to be understood. It is a cycle of myths told by the Tsimshian tribes. These are a sparse population of migratory hunters and fishers who life on the Pacific coast, south of Alaska. They are culturally in the same group with Haida and Tlingit, northernmost representatives of Northwest Coast culture. Topographically their territory is dominated by the two parallel rivers, Nass and Skeena, which flow southwest to the sea. In the summer they live on vegetable products collected by women, and in winter on marine and land animals and fish killed by the men. The movements of fish and game dictate their seasonal movements between sea and mountains, and the northern and southern rivers. The Tsimshian were organized in dispersed matrilineal clans and lived in typical Northwest Coast composite dwellings which housed several families. They tended to live with their close maternal kin, generally practising avunculocal residence at marriage and the ideal was to marry a mother's brother's daughter.

The myth begins during the winter famine in the Skeena valley. A mother and daughter, separated hitherto by their marriages but now both widowed by the famine, set out from East and West, one from upstream and one from downstream of the frozen Skeena, to meet each other half-way. The daughter becomes the wife of a mysterious bird who feeds them both and when she gives birth to a miraculous child, Asdiwal, its bird father gives him a magic bow and arrow, lance, snow-shoes, cloak, and hat which make him invisible at will, invincible, and able to produce an inexhaustible supply of food. The old mother dies and the bird father disappears. Asdiwal and his mother walk West to her natal village. From there he follows a white bear into the sky where it is revealed as Evening-Star, the daughter of the Sun. When Asdiwal has succeeded, thanks to his magic equipment, in a series of impossible tasks, the Sun allows him to marry Evening-Star, and, because he is homesick, to take his wife back to the earth generously supplied with magic food. On earth, because Asdiwal is unfaithful to her, his sky wife leaves him. He follows her half-way to the sky, where she kills him with a thunderbolt. His father-in-law, the Sun, brings him to life and they live together in the sky until Asdiwal feels homesick again. Once home, Asdiwal finds his mother is dead and, since nothing keeps him in her village, he continues walking to the West. This time he makes a Tsimshian marriage, which starts off well. Asdiwal using his magic hunting-weapons to good effect. In the spring he, his wife, and her four brothers move along the coast northwards, towards the River Nass, but Asdiwal challenges his brothers-in-law to prove that their sea-hunting is better than his land-hunting. Asdiwal wins the contest by bringing home four dead bears from his mountain hunt, one for each of the four brothers, who return empty handed from their sea expedition. Furious at their defeat, they carry off their sister and abandon Asdiwal, who then joins some strangers also going North towards the Nass for the candlefish season. Once again, there are four brothers, and a sister whom Asdiwal marries. After a good fishing season, Asdiwal returns with his in-laws and wife to their village, where his wife bears them a son. One day, however, he boasts that he is better than his brothers-in-law at walrus-hunting. Put to the test, he succeeds brilliantly, again infuriating his wife's brothers, who abandon him without food or fire to die on a rocky reef. His bird father preserves him through a raging storm. Finally, he is taken by a mouse to the underground home of the walruses whom he has wounded. Asdiwal cures them and asks in exchange a safe return. The King of the Walruses lends Asdiwal his stomach as a boat, on which he sails home. There he finds his faithful wife, who helps him to kill her own brothers. But again Asdiwal, assailed by homesickness, leaves his wife and returns to the Skeena valley, where his son joins him. When winter comes, Asdiwal goes hunting in the mountains, but forgetting his snow-shoes, can go neither up nor down and is changed into stone.

This is the end of the story. In the analysis which follows, Lévi-Strauss draws out the remarkably complex symmetry of different levels of structure. Asdiwal's journeys take him from East to West, then North to the Nass, then Southwest to the sea fishing of walrus, and finally Southeast back to the Skeena River. So the points of the compass and the salient points of order of Tsimshian migration are laid out. This is the geographical sequence. There is another sequence concerned with residence at marriage, as follows.

The two women who open the tale have been separated by the daughter's virilocal residence at marriage. Living together, they set up what Lévi-Strauss calls a 'matrilocal residence of the simplest kind, mother and daughter'. Lévi-Strauss counts the first marriage of the bird father of Asdiwal as matrilocal. Then the sky marriage of Asdiwal himself with Evening-Star is counted as matrilocal, and matrilocal again the two human marriages of Asdiwal, until after he has come back from the walrus kingdom, when his wife betrays her brothers. So, Lévi-Strauss remarks that all the marriages of Asdiwal are matrilocal until the end. Then the regular pattern is inverted and 'patrilocalism triumphs' because Asdiwal abandons his wife and goes home, accompanied by his son. The story starts with the reunion of a mother and daughter, liberated from their spouses (and paternal kin in the case of the daughter), and ends with the reunion of a father and son, liberated from their spouses (and maternal kin in the case of the son). To the English anthropologist some of this symmetry and inversion seems rather far-fetched. The evidence for counting the bird marriage as matrilocal is dubious and the sky marriage is plain groom service. The rejection of the third wife is hardly 'patrilocalism'. But more about inversion below. I want to go into details of another sociological sequence which produces two more pairs of oppositions which are also inverted at the end.

The same symmetry is traced in the cosmological sequence. First, the hero sojourns in the sky where he is wounded and cured by the sky people; then he makes an underground sojourn where he finds underground people whom *he* has wounded, and whom *he* cures. There is a similar elaboration of recurring themes of famine and plenty. They correspond faithfully enough to the economic reality of Tsimshian life. Using his knowledge of another myth of the region, Lévi-Strauss explains their implication. The Northwest Coast Indians attribute the present condition of the world to the disturbances made by a great Crow, whose voracious appetite initiated all the processes of creation. So hunger is the condition of movement, glut is a static condition. The first phase of the Asdiwal tale opposes Sky and Earth, the Sun and the earthly human. These oppositions the hero overcomes, thanks to his bird father. But Asdiwal breaks the harmony established between these elements: first he feels homesick, then, once at home, he betrays his sky wife for a terrestrial girl, and then, in the sky, he feels homesick again. Thus the whole sky episode ends on a negative position. In the second phase, when Asdiwal makes his first human marriage, a new set of oppositions are released: mountain-hunting and sea-hunting; land and sea.

Asdiwal wins the contest as a land-hunter, and in consequence is abandoned by his wife's brothers. Next time Asdiwal's marriage allies him with island-dwellers, and the same conflict between land and sea takes place, this time on the sea in a boat, which Asdiwal has to leave in the final stage of the hunt in order to climb onto the reef of rock. Taken together, these two phases can be broken down into a series of unsuccessful mediations between opposites arranged on an ever-diminishing scale: above and below, water and earth, maritime hunting and mountain-hunting. In the sea hunt the gap is almost closed between sea- and mountain-hunting, since Asdiwal succeeds where his brothers-in-law fail because he clambers onto the rock. The technique by which the oppositions are reduced is by paradox and reversal: The great mountain-hunter nearly dies on a little half-submerged rock;

the great killer of bears is rescued by a little mouse; the slayer of animals now cures them; and, most paradoxical of all, the great provider of food himself has provender become—since he goes home in the stomach of a walrus. In the final dénouement, Asdiwal, once more a hunter in the mountains, is immobilized when he is neither up nor down, and is changed to stone, the most extreme possible expression of his earthly nature.

Some may have doubted that myths can have an elaborate symmetrical structure. If so, they should be convinced of their error.

Lévi-Strauss's analysis slowly and intricately reveals the internal structure of this myth. Although I have suggested that the symmetry has here and there been pushed too hard, the structure is indisputably there, in the material and not merely in the eye of the beholder. I am not sure who would have argued to the contrary, but myths must henceforth be conceded to have a structure as recognizable as that of a poem or a tune.

But Lévi-Strauss is not content with revealing structure of its own sake. Structural analysis has long been a respectable tool of literacy criticism and Lévi-Strauss is not interested in a mere literary exercise.

He wants to use myth to demonstrate that structural analysis has sociological value. So instead of going on to analyse and compare formal myth structures, he asks what is the relation of myth to life. His answer in a word is 'dialectical'. Not only is the nature of really dialectical, and the structure of myth dialectical, but the relation of the first to the second is dialectical too.

This could mean that there is a feedback between the worlds of mythical and social discourse—a statement in the myth sets off a response which modifies the social universe, which itself then touches off a new response in the realm of myth, and so on. Elsewhere, Lévi-Strauss (1962b, pp. 283–284) has shown that this complex interaction is indeed how he sees the relation between symbolic thought and social reality. And he even attempts to demonstrate with a single example how this interaction takes place (1963b; cf. 1962b, Ch. IV). But in his analysis of myth itself he leaves out this meaning of dialectic. This is a pity, but perhaps inevitable because there is so little historical information about the tribes in question, and still less about the dating of different versions of the myth.

Rather, he develops the idea that myth expresses a social dialectic. It states the salient social contradictions, restates them in more and more modified fashions, until in the final statement the contradictions are resolved, or so modified and masked as to be minimized. According to Lévi-Strauss, the real burden of the whole. Asdiwal myth and the one burning issue to which all the antinomies of sky and earth, land and sea, etc., are assimilated, is the contradiction implicit in patrilocal, matrilateral cross-cousin marriage. This comes as a surprise, since there has never been any mention whatever of matrilateral cross-cousin marriage in the myth of Asdiwal. But the Asdiwal story has a sequel. His son, Waux, grows up with his maternal kin, and his mother arranges for him to marry a cousin. He inherits his father's magic weapons and becomes, like him, a great hunter. One day he goes out hunting, having forgotten his magic spear which enables him to split rocks and open paths through the mountains. There is an earthquake. Waux sees his wife in the valley and shouts to her to make a sacrifice of fat to appease the supernatural powers. But his wife gets it wrong and thinks he is telling her to eat the fat, on which she proceeds to stuff herself until, gorged, she bursts and turns into a rock. Waux, now without either his father's spear or his wife's help, also turns into stone. With this story the Asdiwal cycle is completed. Waux's wife dies of glut, thus reversing the opening gambit in which Asdiwal's mother is started on her journey by a famine. So the movement set going by famine ends in the immobility of fullness. Asdiwal's marriages were all with strangers. Waux makes the approved Tsimshian marriage with his maternal cousin, but she ends by ruining him; the myth makes thus the comment that matrilateral cross-cousin marriage is nothing but a feeble palliative for the social ills it seeks to cure.

Lévi-Strauss points out that the Tsimshian, along with other Northwest Coast cultures, do not benefit from the equilibrium which cross-cousin marriages could produce for them in the form of a fixed hierarchy of wife-givers and wife-receivers. They have chosen instead to be free to revise their whole system of ranking at each marriage and potlatch. So they are committed to deep-seated disequilibrium. Following Rodney Needham (1962), one suspects that this far-fetched reference to Lévi-Strauss's theory of elementary structures of kinship is misplaced. There is no reason to suppose that matrilateral cross-cousin marriage among the Tsimshian is prescribed. However, in reaching these basic antagonisms of social structure. Lévi-Strauss feels he has got to the rock bottom of the myth's meaning.

> 'All the paradoxes . . . geographic, economic, sociological, and even cosmological, are, when all is said and done, assimilated to that less obvious yet so real paradox which marriage with the matrilateral cousin attempts but fails to resolve . . . ' (*supra*, pp. 27, 28).

A great deal of this myth certainly centers on marriage, though very little on the cross-cousin marriage which is preferred. Lévi-Strauss says that the whole myth's burden is a negative comment on social reality. By examining all the possibilities in marriage and showing every extreme position to be untenable, it has as its core message to reconcile the Tsimshian to their usual compromises by showing that any other solution they attempt is equally beset with difficulty. But as I have said, we cannot allow Lévi-Strauss to claim the real meaning of such a complex and rich myth. His analysis is far from exhaustive. Furthermore, there are other themes which are positive, not negative, as regards social reality.

In the first place, this area of Northwest Coast culture combines a very elaborate and strict division of labour between the sexes with a strong expression of male dominance. The myth could well be interpreted as playing on the paradox of male dominance and male dependence on female help. The first hero, Asdiwal, shows his independence of womankind by betraying his first wife. He is betrayed by his second wife, abandons his third wife, but in the sequel his son, Waux, dies because of his wife's stupidity and greed—so the general effect is that women are necessary but inferior beings, and men are superior. Surely this is a positive comment?

In the second place, the potlatch too is built on a paradox that the receiver of gifts is an enemy. One-up-manship, in potlatch terms, brings success, rank, and followers, but two-up-manship inflicts defeat on the opponent and creates hostility. Asdiwal went too far when he brought four huge bears down from the mountain to confront his empty-handed brothers-in-law. Here again, the myth is positive and true to life, so no wonder they abandoned him. The ambivalent attitude in Northwest Coast culture to the successful shaman is a third theme that can plausibly be detected in the myth. Great shamans are always victims of jealousy. Asdiwal, the great shaman, is abandoned. So the myth is plain and simply true to life.

I feel that we are being asked to suspend our critical faculties if we are to believe that this myth mirrors the reverse of reality. I shall return again to give a closer look at the social realities of Tsimshian life.

The ideas of reversal and of inversion figure prominently in Lévi-Strauss's argument. First, he suggests that the myth is the reverse of reality in the country of its origin. Then he has formulated a curious law according to which a myth turns upside down (in relation to its normal position) at a certain distance from its place of origin. These are both developed in the Asdiwal analysis. Third, a myth which appears to have no counterpart in the ritual of the tribe in which it is told is found to be an inversion of the rites of another tribe (cf. Lévi-Strauss, 1956). On this subject the stolid English suspicion of cleverness begins to crystallize.

If ever one could suspect a scholar of trailing his coat with his tongue in his cheek, one would suspect this law of myth-inversion. The metaphor is borrowed from optics, without any explanation of why the same process should be observed in the unrelated science of mythics:

> 'When a mythical schema is transmitted from one population to another, and there exist differences of language, social organization or way of life which make the myth difficult to communicate, it begins to become impoverished or confused. But one can find a limiting situation in which, instead of being finally obliterated by losing all its outlines, the myth is inverted and regains part of its precision' (*supra*, p. 42).

So we must expect that exported myths will give a negative or upside-down picture of what the original myth portrayed. Is the scholar being ingenuous, or disingenuous? He must recognize that opposition is a pliable concept in the interpreter's hands. The whole notion of dialectic rests on the assumption that opposition can be unequivocally recognized. But this is an unwarranted assumption, as appears from a critical reading of his treatment of a Pawnee myth (Lévi-Strauss, 1956).

To demonstrate the relation of myth to rite he takes the Pawnee myth of the pregnant boy. An ignorant young boy suddenly finds he has magical powers of healing and the makings of a great shaman. An old-established shaman, always accompanied by his wife, tries to winkle his secret from him. He fails, since there is no secret learning to transmit, and then ensorcells the boy. As a result of the sorcery the boy becomes pregnant, and goes in shame and confusion to die among wild beasts. But the beasts cure him and he returns with even greater power, and kills his enemy. The analysis distinguishes at least three sets of oppositions.

Shamanistic powers through initiation : without initiation

child : old man

confusion of sex : distinction of sex

Lévi-Strauss then invites us to consider what rite this Pawnee myth corresponds to. His problem, which seems very artificial, is that there is at first sight no correlated rite. The myth underlines the opposition of the generations, and yet the Pawnee do not oppose their generations: they do not base their cult associations on age-classes, and entry to their cult societies is not by ordeals or by fee; a teacher trains his pupil to succeed him on his death. But, as he puts it, all the elements of the myth fall into place confronted with the symmetrical and opposite ritual of the neighbouring Plains Indian tribes. Here the shamanistic societies are the inverse of those of the Pawnee, since entry is by payment and organization is by age. The sponsor and his sponsored candidate for entry are treated as if in a father-son relation, the candidate is accompanied by his wife, whom he offers for ritual intercourse to his sponsor. 'Here we find again all the oppositions which have been analysed on the plane of the myth, with inversion of all the values attributed to each couple.' The initiated and uninitiated are as father to son, instead of as enemies; the uninitiated knows less than the initiated, whereas in the myth he is the better shaman; in the ritual of the Plains Societies it is the youth who is accompanied by his wife, while in the myth it is the old man. 'The semantic values are the same but changed in relation to the symbols which sustain them. The Pawnee myth exposes a ritual system which is the inverse, not of that prevailing in this tribe, but of a system which does not apply here, and which belongs to related tribes whose ritual organization is the exact opposite.'

Mere difference is made to qualify as opposition. Some of the oppositions which Lévi-Strauss detects in myth are undeniably part of the artistic structure. But opposition can be imposed on any material by the interpreter. Here we have an unguarded example of the latter process. To met it seems highly implausible that we can affirm any opposition worthy of the name between cult organization with age-grading and entrance fees, and cult organization by apprenticeship without age-grading. Old male with wife versus young man without wife, and with confusion of sex, these seem equally contrived as opposition. If the alleged opposition are not above challenge, the whole demonstration of inversion falls to the ground.

Here we should turn to the relation of myth to literature in general. Lévi-Strauss recognizes that a myth is 'a work of art arousing deep aesthetic emotion' (Jakobson & Lévi-Strauss, 1962, p. 5). But he strenuously rejects the idea that myth is a kind of primitive poetry (Lévi-Strauss, 1963a, p. 210). 'Myth,' he says, 'should be placed in the gamut of linguistic expressions at the end opposite to that of poetry. . . . Poetry is a kind of speech which cannot be translated except at the cost of serious distortions; whereas the mythical value of the myth is preserved even through the worst translation.' He goes on in terms more emotional than scientific to declare that anyone can recognize the mythic quality of myth. Why does he want so vigorously to detach myth criticism from literary criticism? It is on the literary plane that we have his best contribution to the subject of mythology. He himself wrote a splendid vindication of his own technique of literary analysis by working it out with Jakobson on a sonnet of Baudelaire (Jakobson & Lévi-Strauss, 1962). This essay is an exercise in what T. S. Eliot calls 'the lemon-squeezer school of criticism, in which the critics take a poem to pieces, stanza by stanza, line by line, and extract, squeeze, tease, press every drop of meaning out of it' (Eliot, 1957, p. 112). After reading the analysis, we perceive the poem's unity, economy, and completeness, and its tremendous range of implication.

When the lemon-squeezer technique is applied to poetry it has a high rate of extraction and the meaning flows out in rich cupfuls. Furthermore, what is extracted is not a surprise—we can see that it was there all the time. Unfortunately, something goes wrong when the technique is applied to myth: the machine seems to spring a leak. Instead of more and richer depths of understanding, we get a surprise, a totally new theme, and often a paltry one at that. All the majestic themes which we had previously thought the Oedipus myth was about—destiny, duty, and self-knowledge, have been strained off, and we are left with a worry about how the species began. When Edmund Leach applies the same technique to the Book of Genesis, the rich metaphysical themes of salvation and cosmic oneness are replaced by practical rules for the regulation of sex. When Lévi-Strauss has finished with the Tsimshian myth it is reduced to anxieties about problems of matrilateral cross-cousin marriage (which anyway only apply to the heirs of chiefs and headmen). It seems that whenever anthropologists apply structural analysis to myth they extract not only a different but a lesser meaning. The reasons for this reductionism are important. First, there is the computer analogy, for the sake of which Lévi-Strauss commits himself to treating the structural units of myth as if they were unambiguous. This takes us back to the basic difference between words and phonemes. The best words are ambiguous, and the more richly ambiguous the more suitable for the poet's or the myth-maker's job. Hence there is no end to the number of meanings which can be read into a good myth. When dealing with poetry, Lévi-Strauss gives full value to the rich ambiguity of the words. When dealing with myth he suggests that their meaning is clear cut, lending itself to being chopped into objectively recognizable, precisely defined units. It is partly in this process of semantic chopping that so much of the meaning of myth gets lost.

But there is another reason, more central to the whole programme. There are two possible objectives in analysing a piece of discourse.[2] One is to analyse the particular discourse itself, to analyse what has been said. The other is to analyse the language, seen as the instrument of what is said. No reason has so far been given to suppose that the structure of discourse is necessarily similar to that of language. But there is reason to point out that if the language analogy is adopted, research will look for a similar structure, a logic of correlations, oppositions, and differences (Ricoeur, 1963). We can say that the first kind of analysis, of what has been said in a discourse, aims at discovering a particular structure. This is what the literary critics do and what Jakobson and Lévi-Strauss did in 'Les Chats', and what Lévi-Strauss in practice does most of the time. This kind of analysis is not intended to yield a compressed statement of the theme. It is not reductionist in any sense. The other kind of analysis discovers a formal or general structure which is not particular to any given stretch of language. For instance, the alexandrine or the sonnet form is not particular to a given poem, and to know that a particular poem has been written in sonnet form tells you nothing about what that poem is about. In the same way, a grammatical structure is formal. A book of grammar gives the conditions under which communication of a certain kind can take place. It does not give a communication.

Lévi-Strauss claims to be revealing the formal structures of myths. But he can never put aside his interest in what the myth discourse is about. He seems to think that if he had the formal structure it would look not so much like a grammar book as like a summary of the themes which analysing the particular structure of a myth cycle has produced. Hence the reductionist tendency is built in to his type of myth analysis. He falls into the trap of claiming to discover the real underlying meanings of myths because he never separates the particular artistic structure of a particular set of myths from their general or purely formal structure. Just as knowing that the rhyme structure is a, b, b, a, does not tell us anything about the content of a sonnet, so the formal structure of a myth would not help very much in interpreting it. Lévi-Strauss comes very near this when he says (Lévi-Strauss, 1957) that the structural analysis of a Pawnee myth consists of a dialectical balancing of the themes of life and death. It might have been better to have said that it was a balanced structure of pluses and minuses, or of positive and negatives. If he had actually used algebra to present the pattern he discerned, then Edmund Leach might have been less tempted to speculate on the similarity of mythic themes all over the world. He himself had found a structure of pluses and minuses in the Garden of Eden myth (1961) and remarked that the recurrence of these themes of death versus life, procreation versus vegetable reproduction, have the greatest psychological and sociological significance. But I think that their significance is that of verb/noun relations in language. Their presence signifies the possibility of finding in them formal structures. But they are not the formal myth structures that we have been promised. These can hardly be knowable in ordinary language. If they are to be discovered special terms will have to be invented for recording them, comparable to the highly specialized terminology of grammar. To say simply that myth structures are built of oppositions and mediations is not to say what the structures are. It is simply to say that there are structures.

I will return later to the question of whether these formal myth structures are likely to be important for sociology. At this stage of publication (though three new volumes are in the press), Lévi-Strauss has not succeeded in revealing them. I should therefore do better to concentrate on the particular artistic structures he has revealed.

The meaning of a myth is partly the sense that the author intended it to convey, and the sense intended by each of its recounters. But every listener can find in it references to his own experience, so the myth can be enlightening, consoling, depressing, irrespective of the intention of the tellers. Part of the anthropologist's task is to understand enough of the background of the myth to be able to construct its range of reference for its native hearers. To this Lévi-Strauss applies himself energetically, as for example when he finds that the myth of the creative Great Crow illuminates the themes of hunger and plenty in Tsimshian life.

From a study of any work of art we can infer to some extent the conditions under which is was made. The maidservant who said of St. Peter, 'His speech betrays him as a

Galilean' was inferring from his dialect; similarly the critic who used computer analysis to show that the same author did not write all the epistles attributed to St. Paul. This kind of information is like that to be obtained from analysing the track of an animal or the finger-prints of a thief. The anthropologist studying tribal myths can do a job of criticism very like that of art critics who decide what 'attribution' to give to a painting or to figures in a painting. Lévi-Strauss, after minute analysis of the Asdiwal myth, could come forward and, like a good antiquarian, affirm that it is a real, genuine Tsimshian article. He can guarantee that it is an authentic piece of Northwest Coast mythology. His analysis of the structure of the myth can show that it draws fully on the premises of Tsimshian culture.

Inference, of course, can also be made within the culture; the native listener can infer a moral, and indeed myths are one of the ways in which cultural values are transmitted. Structural analysis can reveal unsuspected depths of reference and inference meaning for any particular series of myths. In order to squeeze this significance out, the anthropologist must apply his prior knowledge of the culture to his analysis. He uses inference the other way round, from the known culture to the interpretation of the obscure myth. This is how he discerns the elements of structure. All would agree that this is a worthwhile task. But in order to analyse particular structures, he has to know his culture well first.

At this stage we should like to be able to judge how well Lévi-Strauss knows the social reality of the Tsimshian. Alas, very little is known about this tribe. He has to make do with very poor ethnographic materials. There are several minor doubts one can entertain about his interpretation of the facts, but the information here it altogether very thin. A critic of Lévi-Strauss (Ricoeur) has been struck by the fact that all his examples of mythic thought have been taken from the geographical areas of totemism and never from Semitic, pre-Hellenic, or Indo-European areas, whence our own culture arose. Lévi-Strauss would have it that his examples are typical of a certain kind of thought, a type in which the arrangement of items of culture is more important and more stable than the content. Ricoeur asks whether the totemic cultures are not so much typical as selected, extreme types? This is a very central question which every anthropologist has to face. Is *La Pensée sauvage* as revealed by myth and rite analysis typical, or peculiar, or is it an illusion produced by the method? Here we are bound to mention Lévi-Strauss's idea of mythic thinking as *bricolage*. The *bricoleur*, for whom we have no word, is a craftsman who works with material that has not been produced for the task he has in hand. I am tempted to see him as an Emmett engineer whose products always look alike whether they are bridges, stoves, or trains, because they are always composed of odd pieces of drainpipe and string, with the bells and chains and bits of Gothic railing arranged in a similar crazy way. In practice this would be a wrong illustration of *bricolage*. Lévi-Strauss himself is the real Emmett engineer because he changes his rules as he goes along. For mythic thought a card-player could be a better analogy, because Emmett can use his bits how he likes, whereas the *bricolage* type of culture is limited by pattern-restricting rules. Its units are like a pack of cards continually shuffled for the same game. The rules of the game would correspond to the general structure underlying the myths. If all that the myths and rites do is to arrange and rearrange the elements of the culture, then structural analysis would be exhaustive, and for that reason very important.

At the outset of any scientific enterprise, a worker must known the limitations of his method. Linguistics and any analysis modelled on linguistics can only be synchronic sciences. They analyse systems. In so far as they can be diachronic it is in analysing the before-and-after evolution of systems. Their techniques can be applied to any behaviour that is systematic. But if the behaviour is not very systematic, they will extract whatever amount of regularity there is, and leave a residue. Edmund Leach has shown that the techniques of Lévi-Strauss can be applied to early Greek myths, to Buddhist, and to Israelite myths. But I suppose he would never claim that the analysis is exhaustive. In the case of his analysis of Genesis, I have already mentioned above that the residue is the greater part.

Lévi-Strauss in his publications so far seems blithely unconscious that his instrument can produce only one kind of tune. More aware of the limitations of his analysis, he would have to restrict what he says about the attitude of mythic thought to time, past and future. Structural analysis cannot but reveal myths as timeless, as synchronic structures outside time. From this bias built into the method there are two consequences. First, we cannot deduce anything whatever from it about the attitudes to time prevailing in the cultures in question. Our method reduces all to synchrony. Everything which Lévi-Strauss writes in *La Pensée sauvage* about time in certain cultures or at a certain level of thinking, should be rephrased to apply only to the method he uses. Second, if myths have got an irreversible order and if this is significant, this part of their meaning will escape the analysis. This, as Ricoeur points out, is why the culture of the Old Testament does not fit into the *bricolage* category.

We know a lot about the Israelites and about the Jews and Christians who tell and retell these stories.[3] We know little about the Australian aborigines and about the no longer surviving American Indian tribes. Would this be the anthropologist's frankest answer to Ricoeur? We cannot say whether the *bricolage* level of thought is an extreme type or what it is typical of, for lack of sufficient supporting data about the examples. But we must say that the *bricolage* effect is produced by the method of analysis. For a final judgment, then, we can only wait for a perfect experiment. For this, richly abundant mythical material should be analysed against a known background of equally rich ethnographic records. We can then see how exhaustive the structural analysis can be and also how relevant its formulas are to the understanding of the culture.

NOTES

1. See pp. 1–47 of this book. The next few pages constitute Dr. Douglas's summary of Lévi-Strauss's text (see Introduction) [E.R.L.].

2. In what follows I am indebted to the Rev. Dr. Cyril Barett, S.J. for criticism.

3. Lévi-Strauss's own justification for *not* applying his method to Biblical materials seems to rest on the proposition that we do not know enough about the ancient Israelites! (See *Esprit*, November 1963, p. 632) but cf. Leach (1966) *passim* [E.R.L.].

REFERENCES

ELIOT, T. S. 1957. *On Poetry and Poets* London: Faber & Faber.

FORTES, M. 1959. *Oedipus and Job in West African Religion*. Cambridge: Cambridge University Press.

JAKOBSON, R. & LÉVI-STRAUSS, C. 1962. 'Les Chats' de Charles Baudelaire. *L'Homme* 2: 5–21.

LEACH, E. R. 1961. Lévi-Strauss in the Garden of Eden: An Examination of some Recent Developments in the Analysis of Myth. *Transactions of the New York Academy of Sciences*. Series 2: 386–396.

—1962. Genesis as Myth. *Discovery*, May: 30–35.

—1966. The Legitimacy of Solomon: Some Structural Aspects of Old Testament History. *European Journal of Sociology* 7: 58–101.

LÉVI-STRAUSS, C. 1955. The Structural Study of Myth. *Journal of American Folklore* 28: 428–444. Reprinted with modifications in C. Lévi-Strauss, 1963a.

—1956. Structure et dialectique. In *For Roman Jakobson on the Occasion of his Sixtieth Birthday*. The Hague: Mouton. Reprinted in C. Lévi-Strauss, 1963a.

—1957. Le symbolisme cosmique dans la structure sociale et l'organisation cérémonielle des tribus améri-caines. *Serie Orientale Roma*, XIV. Institut pour l'Étude de l'Orient et de l'Extrême-Orient, Rome, pp. 47–56.

—1958. La Geste d'Asdiwal. *École Pratique des Hautes Études, Section des Sciences Religieuses*. Extr. Annu-aire 1958–1959: 3–43. Reprinted in *Les Temps modernes*, March 1961 [see pp. 1–47 of this book].

—1958a. *Anthropologie structurale*. Paris: Plon. (English translation, 1963a. *Structural Anthropology*. New York: Basic Books.)

—1962b. *La Pensée sauvage*. Paris: Plon.

—1963b. The Bear and the Barber. *Journal of the Royal Anthropological Institute* 93, Part I: 1–11.

NEEDHAM, R. 1962. *Structure and Sentiment*. Chicago: University of Chicago Press.

RICOEUR, P. 1963. Structure et hermeneutique. *Esprit*, November: 598–625.

WEIL, SIMONE. 1950. *Attente de Dieu*. Paris: La Colombe.

21 THE STORY OF ASDIWAL

—CLAUDE LÉVI-STRAUSS

Now follows a summary of the story of Asdiwal taken from Boas (1912) which will serve as a point of reference. This version was recorded on the coast at port Simpson in Tsimshian dialect. Boas published the native text together with an English translation.

Famine reigns in the Skeena valley; the river is frozen and it is winter. A mother and her daughter, both of whose husbands have died of hunger, both remember independently the happy times when they lived together and there was no dearth of food. Released by the death of their husbands, they simultaneously decide to meet and set off at the same moment. Since the mother lives down-river and the daughter up-river, the former goes eastwards and the latter westwards. They both travel on the frozen bed of the Skeena and meet half-way.

Weeping with hunger and sorrow, the two women pitch camp on the bank at the foot of a tree, not far from which they find, poor pittance that it is, a rotten berry, which they sadly share.

During the night, a stranger visits the young widow. It is soon learned that his name is Hatsenas,[2] a term which means, in Tsimshian, a bird of good omen. Thanks to him, the women start to find food regularly, and the younger of the two becomes the wife of their mysterious protector and soon gives birth to a son, Asdiwal (Asiwa, Boas, 1895; Asi-hwil, Boas, 1902).[3] His father speeds up his growth by supernatural means and gives him various magic objects: a bow and arrows which never miss for hunting, a quiver, a lance, a basket, snow-shoes, a bark raincoat, and a hat, all of which will enable the hero to overcome all obstacles, make himself invisible, and procure an inexhaustible supply of food. Hatsenas then disappears and the elder of the two women dies.

Asdiwal and his mother pursue their course westwards and settle down in her native village, Gitsalasert, in the Skeena Canyon (Boas, 1912, p. 83). One day a white she-bear comes down the valley.

Hunted by Asdiwal, who almost catches it thanks to his magic object, the bear starts to climb up a vertical ladder. Asdiwal follows it up to the heavens, which he sees as a vast prairie, covered with grass and all kinds of flowers. The bear lures him into the home of its father, the sun, and reveals itself to be a beautiful girl, Evening-Star. The marriage takes

Excerpted from "The Story of Asdiwal" by Claude Lévi-Strauss, from THE STRUCTURAL STUDY OF MYTH AND TOTEMISM, edited by Edmund Leach, published by Tavistock Publications Ltd. Reprinted by permission of Routledge.

place, though not before the Sun has submitted Asdiwal to a series of trials, to which all previous suitors had succumbed (hunting wild goat in mountains which are rent by earthquakes; drawing water from a spring in a cave whose walls close in on each other; collecting wood from a tree which crushes those who try to cut it down; a period in a fiery furnace). But Asdiwal overcomes them all thanks to his magic objects and the timely intervention of his father. Won over by his son-in-law's talents, the Sun finally approves of him.

Asdiwal, however, pines for his mother. The Sun agrees to allow him to go down to earth again with his wife, and gives them, as provisions for the journey, four baskets filled with inexhaustible supplies of food, which earn the couple a grateful welcome from the villagers, who are in the midst of their winter famine.

In spite of repeated warnings from his wife, Asdiwal deceives her with a woman from his village. Evening-Star, offended, departs, followed by her tearful husband. Half-way up to heaven, Asdiwal is struck down by a look from his wife, who disappears. He dies, but is at once regretted and is brought back to life by his celestial father-in-law.

For a time, all goes well; then, once again, Asdiwal feels a twinge of nostalgia for earth. His wife agrees to accompany him as far as the earth, and there bids him a final farewell. Returning to his village, the hero learns of his mother's death. Nothing remains to hold him back, and he sets off again on his journey downstream.

When he reaches the Tsimshian village of Ginaxangioget, he seduces and marries the daughter of the local chief. To start with, the marriage is a happy one, and Asdiwal joins his four brothers-in-law on wild goat hunts, which, thanks to his magic objects, are crowned with success. When spring approaches, the whole family moves house, staying first at Metlakatla, and then setting off by boat for the river Nass, going up along the coast. A head wind forces them to a halt and they camp for a while at Ksemaksén. There, things go wrong because of a dispute between Asdiwal and his brothers-in-law over the respective merits of mountain-hunters and sea-hunters. A competition takes place—Asdiwal returns from the mountains with four bears that he has killed, while the brothers-in-law return empty-handed from their sea expedition. Humiliated and enraged, they break camp, and, taking their sister with them, abandon Asdiwal.

He is picked up by strangers coming from Gitxatla, who are also on their way to the Nass for the candlefish season.

As in the previous case, they are a group of four brothers and a sister, whom Asdiwal wastes no time in marrying. They soon arrive together at the River Nass, where they sell large quantities of fresh meat and salmon to the Tsimshian, who have already settled there and are starving.

Since the catch that year is a good one, everyone goes home: the Tsimshian to their capital at Metlakatla and the Gitxatla to their town Laxalan, where Asdiwal, by this time rich and famous, has a son. One winter's day, he boasts that he can hunt sea-lions better than his brothers-in-law. They set out to sea together. Thanks to his magic objects, Asdiwal has a miraculously successful hunt on a reef, but is left there without food or fire by his

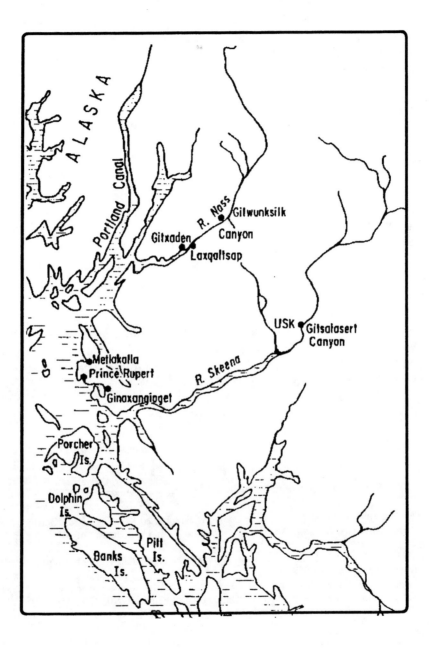

angry brothers-in-law. A storm gets up and waves sweep over the rock. With the help of his father, who appears in time to save him Asdiwal, transformed into a bird, succeeds in keeping himself above the waves, using his magic objects as a perch.

After two days and two nights the storm is calmed, and Asdiwal falls asleep exhausted. A mouse wakes him and leads him to the subterranean home of the sea-lions whom he has wounded, but who imagine (since Asdiwal's arrows are invisible to them) that they are victims of an epidemic. Asdiwal extracts the arrows and cures his hosts, whom he asks, in return, to guarantee his safe return. Unfortunately, the sea-lions' boats, which are made of their stomachs, are out of use, pierced by the hunter's arrows. The king of the sea-lions therefore lends Asdiwal his own stomach as a canoe and instructs him to send it back without delay. When he reaches land, the hero discovers his wife, and his son alike, inconsolable. Thanks to the help of this good wife, but bad sister (for she carries out the rites which are essential to the success of the operation), Asdiwal makes killer-whales out of carved wood and brings them to life. They break open the boats with their fins and bring about the shipwreck and death of the wicked brothers-in-law.

But once again Asdiwal feels an irrepressible desire to revisit the scenes of his childhood. He leaves his wife and returns to the Skeena valley. He settles in the town of Ginadâos, where he is joined by his son, to whom he gives his magic bow and arrows, and from whom he receives a dog in return.

When winter comes, Asdiwal goes off to the mountains to hunt, but forgets his snowshoes. Lost, and unable to go either up or down without them, he is turned to stone with his lance and his dog, and they can still be seen in that form at the peak of the great mountain by the lake in Ginadâos (Boas, 1912, pp. 71–146).

REFERENCES

BARBEAU, M. 1950. Totem Poles, *National Museum of Canada Bulletin,* No. 119, Anthropological Series No. 30.

BEYNON, W. 1941. The Tsimshians of Metlakatla, *American Anthropologist* 43: 83-88.

BOAS, FRANZ. 1895. *Indianische Sagen von der Nord-Pacifischen Késte Amerikas.* Berlin
—1902. Tsimshian Texts. *Bulletin of Smithsonian Institution,* No. 27. Bureau of American Ethnology, Washington.
—1911. 'Tsimshian' in *Handbook of American Indian Languages,* Part I. Smithsonian Institution, Bureau of American Ethnology, Bulletin 40, Part I.
—1912. *Tsimshian Texts (New Series).* Publication of American Ethnological Society, Vol. III. Leyden.
—1916. *Tsimshian Mythology.* Annual Report Smithsonian Institution, No. 31 (1909–1910). Washington: Bureau of American Ethnology.

DURLACH, T. M. 1928. *The Relationship of Systems of the Tlinget, Haida and Tsimshian.* Publications of American Ethnological Society, Vol. XI, New York.

EMMONS, G. T. 1910. 'Niska' in *Handbook of American Indians North of Mexico.* Smithsonian Institution, Bureau of American Ethnology, Bulletin 30, Part II.

GARFIELD, V. E. 1939. *Tsimshian Clan and Society.* University of Washington Publications in Anthropology, Vol. 7, No. 3.

GARFIELD, V. E., WINGERT, P. S. & BARBEAU, M. 1951. *The Tsimshian: Their Acts and Music.* Publications of American Ethnological Society, Vol. XVIII. New York.

GODDARD, P. E. 1934. *Indians of the Northwest Coast.* American Museum of Natural History, Handbook Series No. 10. New York.

GREENBERG, J. H. 1966. Language Universals. In T. A. Sebeok (ed.), *Current Trends in Linguistics,* Volume 3: *Theoretical Foundations.* The Hague: Mouton, pp. 62ff.

LÉVI-STRAUSS, C. 1949. *Les Structures élémentaires de la parenté.* Paris: Presses Universitaires de France.
—1958a. *Anthropologie structurale.* Paris: Plon (English translation, 1963a. *Structural Anthropology.* New York: Basic Books).
—1962b. *La Pensée sauvage.* Paris: Plon.

MALINOWSKI, B. 1932. *The Sexual Life of Savages in North-Western Melanesia,* 3rd edn. London: Routledge.

RICHARDS, J. F. 1914. Cross Cousin Marriage in South India. *Man* 14.

SAPIR, E. 1915. A Sketch of the Social Organisation of the Nass River Indians. *Museum Bulletin of the Canadian Dept. of Mines, Geological Survey,* No. XIX. Ottawa.

SWANTON, J. R. 1909. *Contributions to the Ethnology of the Haida.* Memoirs of American Museum of Natural History, Vol. VIII.
—1952. *The Indian Tribes of North America.* Smithsonian Institution, Bureau of American Ethnology, Bulletin 145.

WEDGEWOOD, C. H. 1928. Cousin Marriage in *Encyclopedia Britannica,* 14th edn.

22 CROSS CULTURAL PERSPECTIVES ON THE BODY BEAUTIFUL

—EUGENE COOPER

The impulse to decorate the body, to alter its appearance, shape or form, is probably as old as human culture itself. The human body was probably one of "the first objects of art, that is, an object of nature which people, by the addition of symbols transformed into an object of culture" (Ember and Ember 1977:271).

"All human societies use body decoration to disguise their kinship with animals; clothing, ornament and painting attempt to underline man's kinship with the world of culture, not the world of nature, with the gods and the spirits, not the animals. Decoration distinguishes us from the brutes" (Brain 1979:146).

As with all universal human propensities, however, the specific manifestations of body decoration take on a bewildering variety of forms in local cultural contexts. In addition, one finds the impulse to alter the body expressed in an equally large variety of symbolic contexts—purely aesthetic, erotic or sexual, ritual or religious, political or hierarchical.

To come to terms with this enormous variety, it is useful to adopt a stance of cultural relativism, at least at the outset. That is to say, we must attempt to set aside our own concepts of beauty and appropriate adornment, and try to understand what may appear strange, even bizarre, cosmetic practices in their own terms. Beauty is, after all, in the eyes of the beholder, and while attempts have been made to postulate objective cross-cultural standards of aesthetic judgment (Pelto and Pelto 1976:404), it just makes good methodological sense *not* to evaluate other's concepts of beauty with reference to our own. A survey of the practices by means of which people decorate, deform and mutilate their bodies reveal few if any absolutes in the consideration of what is or is not beautiful.

"Polynesian women stain their lips and file and darken their teeth to attract men; to them, European women with white, unfilled teeth and pink lips are ugly, like dogs" (Brain 1979:125).

It is well to heed the words of Charles Darwin:

"If all our women were to become as beautiful as the Venus de Medici, we should for a time be charmed; but we should soon wish for variety; and as soon as we had obtained variety, we should wish to see certain characteristics a little exaggerated beyond the then existing standards" (quoted in Rudofsky 1971:94).

Beauty then, is a relative concept, and it should not surprise us that measures taken to beautify or otherwise alter the body show enormous variation in time and space.

Upper paleolithic graves from periods of 45,000–10,000 years BP show evidence of cosmetic mutilation of the hands. Pre-neolithic inhabitants of Jericho (13,000–9,000 years BP), as well as the later civilized Egyptians (6,000–4,000 years BP) practiced deformation and elongation of the skull (Rudofsky 1971:97, Brain 1979:890). Neolithic communities in pre-historic Egypt, Babylonia and Greece show in their sculpture a preference for women with large breasts and buttocks (Brain 1979:111). While the ancient Greeks seem to have held the human body inviolate and not in need of decoration, even they were not content to leave the body as received, and plucked their pubic hair to more fully manifest the body's perfection (Rudofsky 1971:94). There is also clear evidence of tattooing among the ancient jews and Britons, although the reasons why these customs did not survive to historic times will never be clearly understood. In short, ages before the pen of Ovid immortalized Narcissus' infatuation with his own image in the pool, human beings were long used to rectifying their perceived inadequacies and dissatisfaction with nature's product.

In more modern times, anthropological investigations reveal a startling array of measures taken by contemporary human groups to beautify their natural physique and visage. The measures run the gamut from body and facial painting, to tattooing, to beauty magic, to scarification and body deformation. In this paper, we will examine some of the more dramatic of these practices drawn from the modern ethnographic record.

BODY PAINTING

Alexander von Humboldt notes that, "If painted nations had been examined with the same attention as clothed ones, it would have been perceived that the most fertile imagination and the most mutable caprice have created the fashions of painting as well as those of garments" (quoted in Rudofsky 1971:140).

Von Humboldt's assertion is certainly borne out by Claude Levi-Strauss' studies of the Guaicuru and Caduveo Indians of South America. Discussing Guaicuru cosmetic facial painting, Levi-Strauss notes that among four hundred original drawings recorded in the field, he found no two alike (Levi-Strauss 1963:251). The paintings are executed with a wooden spatula dipped in the juices of wild fruit and leaves, and are composed of "simple and double spirals, hatching, volutes, frets, tendrils, or crosses and whorls" (Ibid).

> "The design is built symmetrically in relation to two linear axes, one of them vertical, following the median plane of the face, the other horizontal, dividing the face at eye level. The eyes. . .are used as starting points for two inverted spirals, one of which covers the right cheek and the other the left side of the forehead. A motif in the shape of a compound bow, which is located in the lower part of the painting represents the upper lip and is applied on it" (Levi-Strauss 1963;252).

This "grafting of art on to the human body" (Levi-Strauss 1973:201) constitutes for Levi-Strauss a kind of "pictorial surgery". The decorations are created for the face, "but in another sense, the face is predestined to be decorated, since it is only by means of decoration that the face receives its social dignity and mystical significance. Decoration is conceived for the face, but the face itself exists only through decoration" (1963:261).

A somewhat different perspective is provided by the New Guinea Hagen. Hagen society is immensely competitive. With no hereditary chiefs, there is a constant competition between self-styled "big men" in elaborate ceremonial exchanges and feasts in which groups try to outdo each other in lavishing gifts on their neighbors. Ceremonial displays of group prowess in mobilizing resources reflect upon the status of one group vis a vis its neighbors, and body and facial painting contribute to the overall effect. In addition, such ceremonies provide an opportunity for a group to display the attractiveness of its members as potential marital partners and allies, and "a sequence of exchange festivals...triggers off courting parties" (Strathern and Strathern 1971:54).

Unlike the Guaicuru, Hagen facial paint is multicolored, women and boys applying swatches of blue and white against a red ochre base, men usually applying white designs on a black charcoal base. Since men are normally bearded, there is generally less facial surface available for decoration, and men stress that "face paint should not clash too much with the dark color of their beards" (Strathern and Strathern 1971:118). "The mustache may be sprayed lightly with white, and the mouth rimmed also in white, but facial hair is never painted with colors" (Ibid).

> "Men . . . prefer restrained designs executed in white, with only a limited area brightly pigmented in blue, red or yellow; women choose lavish designs predominately in bright colors, with only the eyes ringed in white" (Strathern and Strathern 1971:119).

The ceremonial display of group status implicit in Hagen body decoration is also a "medium through which people demonstrate their relationship to ancestral spirits" (Ibid:1), the well being of which is closely associated with the success of the living in competitive exchanges.

Among the Nuba of the East African Sudan, the rationale for body painting lies in the celebration of the strong and healthy body. Nuba society "demands and rewards physical strength, prowess and beauty" (Faris 1972:19). Not only the face, but the entire body is covered in such a way as to accentuate, complement and enhance its physical features. Designs may be representational, in which the human body is portrayed as an antelope, jackal or leopard with key anatomical features of the specific species rendered on the analogous human body part — stripes over the eyes for antelope, stripes on the legs and/or arms for jackal, spots on the body for leopard (Faris 1972:75). However, the critical form variables are the preservation of balance and culturally acceptable symmetry, and it is clear that "the natural world simply furnishes an addition to the repertory of design forms — additions to the non-representational imagination of the artist within the paramount dictates of cultural style" (Faris 1972:84).

The paint is concocted from a variety of oils and ochres, and is applied to the young male body only after it has been cleaned, shaved of both facial and pubic hair, and oiled. Elderly men whose bodies show the effects of old age cease decorating, and "almost all old men...wear shorts or a loose Arab garment to cover their bodies" no longer worth calling attention to. Similarly, "men of any age who are sick or injured, or whose bodies are otherwise incapacitated will wear clothing or some kind of cover for the duration of the illness or until the injury heals" (Faris 1972: 54).

A young man's design will last a couple of days, after which it must be renewed. The most flamboyant decorators will usually have a new design each day which may take up to an hour to execute (Faris 1972:162). "An artist normally avoids repeating a design on successive days, although his repertory will be limited by his abilities and the colors available" (Faris 1972:70).

Of perhaps greatest interest in Nuba decorative art is the fact that the designs have no apparent connection to religious beliefs or social structure. "Body painting is not a cosmological art; the body and its celebration is primary" (Brain 1979:42).

TATTOOING

Tattooing as a means of body decoration is widespread among the world's peoples, and was apparently much more common in ancient Europe than at present. Surviving as it did in the west until very recently only as a means of displaying one's toughness and virility, tattooing has nevertheless become more common among women in our society of late, and occupies a much more central place as a beautifying technique in many cultures.

Relatively simple facial tattoos are applied to Hagen girls by pricking the skin and rubbing in charcoal and blue dye. "Most commonly the . . . [designs] consist of dots over the forehead or arching over the eyebrows, and under-eye dots or short streaks at the top of the cheek" (Strathern and Strathern 1971:40). Tattooing was a relatively casual affair among Northwest Coast American Indians as well, consisting of simple designs.

Among the Haida, however, it was common to tattoo young persons of high rank with designs of the crest symbols of their clan.

> "The Haida who used the most elaborate and extensive patterns, . . . applied them on ceremonial occasions — that is major potlatches. A high ranking Haida man or woman was considered fully tattooed when the back of the hands, both arms from wrist to shoulder, the chest, thighs, and lower legs, and upper surfaces of the feet bore crest designs. Sometimes the cheeks and back were also decorated" (Drucker 1955:92).

Such elaborate tattooing was also common among the New Zealand Maori, among whom tattoos were also a symbol of rank. "The Maoris decorated their bodies with inspired genius. Their tattooing was central to their whole aesthetic outlook and to their appreciation of the beautiful body" (Brain 1979;61). Maori tattooing, called *moko,* is unusual in that a low relief design is actually carved into the skin, with a black pigment rubbed into the cuts. "Instead of a needle-like instrument, a chisel was used to make the incisions, driven into the skin with a light mallet" (Brain 1979:59-60). Designs consisted of complicated geometric forms, parabolic curves, involutes of circles and Ionic involutes with no trace of confusion in the designs. "The artist has as clear a conception of the finished design as a European fresco painter" (Brain 1979:61).

The technique was learned in apprenticeship during which the initiate got a chance to practice on slaves or commoners. "To secure our services of an expert tattooer, men showered the gifts of guns, canoes, clothes — even slaves — on a renowned artist" (Brain 1979:60). Great chiefs had their faces and their bodies tattooed with delicacy and beauty, and "it was the ambition of all free men to have a finely tattooed face, which made them conspicuous in war and attractive to women" (Ibid:59). The work of some artists was so highly prized, that corpses were purchased and the skins preserved (Brain 1979:60).

This may strike our western consciousness as a bizarre human aberration, but this practice is also found in association with another tattooing tradition — Japanese *irezumi*. Irezumi tattoos are genuine works of art created over months of arduous labor by an artist working with an awl and gouge "on a canvas of flesh" (Brain 1979:62). Indeed, a private museum in Japan is devoted entirely to the display of fine skins, for which a down payment is made during the lifetime of the bearer, and the skin collected upon his or her death (Brain 1979:64).

> "The artist works with a variety of colors, taking more than a year to finish a whole body tattoo. First the design is selected. usually from a collection of traditional patterns...[and] is drawn on the skin in black ink. The dye is then applied. Following the outlines, the artist uses a series of triangle shaped gouges and chisels. The brush, full of dye, is kept steady by the little finger of the left hand, while the gouge is held in the right, rubbed against the brush and pushed up under the skin. When a thick clear line has been achieved. the artist, using the full traditional range of colours, works the design into the skin. The visits last for several hours, or as long as the client can endure the pain" (Brain 1979: 64-66).

The results are genuinely impressive, covering the back, the buttocks, both arms to the elbow and the upper thighs, leaving the middle of the chest, the stomach and the abdomen undecorated. The designs call to mind the elaborate landscapes, floral designs, folk heroes, deities and other motifs usually associated with classical Japanese print making on paper. Close attention is given to the laws of perspective, and "the motion of the lines and figures on the living skin is taken into consideration; such that trees may be seen to bend with the wind, fish to swim with the lazy lash of the tail, and birds to swoop gracefully on the wing (Brain 1979:66).

BEAUTY MAGIC

Among the steps taken by many of the world's people to beautify themselves, magical means are not uncommon. An interesting example of such practices is provided by the Trobriand islanders of the western Pacific, described in Malinowski's classic works. Like the Hageners described above, a central component of Trobriand society is a competitive trade network, the kula, in which men participate in an attempt to acquire and then pass on a variety of non-utilitarian trade valuables, *vaygu'a,* the temporary possession of which confers high prestige. One does not hoard these valuables, but rather passes them onto other trading partners in the course of time, thereby obligating one's partners to reciprocate with a valuable of equal magnitude at some later date.

The *kula* expeditions involve elaborate preparations for ocean going canoe voyages to distant islands, and magic is employed at various stages in an attempt to assure the success of the enterprise. At the final stage of the expedition, just prior to their canoes' arrival at the islands of their trading partners, a brief stop is made at an outlying island for the final stage of magical preparations. At this point, the older men utter magical formula over a variety of cosmetic substances. All members of the party wash with sea water and apply medicated coconut oil which gives the skin a shiny gloss.

> "A comb is chanted over, and the hair teased out with it. Then, with crushed betel-nut mixed with lime, they draw red ornamental designs on their faces, while others use...an aromatic resinous stuff, and draw similar lines in black...All the magic which is spoken over the natives cosmetics is the...magic of beauty. The main aim of these spells is...to make the man beautiful, attractive and irresistible to his Kula partner. . . . 'Our partner looks at us, sees our faces are beautiful; he throws the *vaygu'a* at us'" (Malinowski 1922:335-6).

Malinowski explains that the deep belief in the efficacy of the magic makes it quite effective, not that actual beauty can be imparted by the spells. However, the feeling of being beautiful gives assurance and may influence people in their behavior and deportment, and since the confidence with which the trading party approaches their partners is enormously important, the magic may be said to achieve its purpose at a deeper psychological if not physiological level (Malinowski 1922:336).

Beauty magic is also performed on other ceremonial occasions in Trobriand life. Trobrianders are overwhelmingly concerned that their children develop into beautiful, strong young men and women.

> "A straight nose, thick hair, smooth, unwrinkled light skin, firm breasts, flashing eyes, delicately painted facial designs, red and white shell decorations, coconut oil and flowers filled with love magic are elements that induce desire" (Weiner 1976:131).

At a special dance ritual and feast, held after the annual yam harvest, young people in particular are on display, and each has beauty magic performed over them by their father's sister. The paternal aunt has a key role to play on behalf of her brother's children when beauty is most desired. The feasting which accompanies the dancing, provides occasion as well for the adults to seek out strategic political alliances either through the liaisons of their children, or through direct contacts with adults in neighboring groups who come to witness the beautiful dancers.

Trobriand society thus provides a concrete example of the centrality of magically induced beauty to social life. Here we find confirmation of the idea that it is feeling beautiful more than any objective measures of beauty that is of the essence.

However, as we shall see below, objective standards of the most extreme form also characterize the concepts of beauty of many of the world's people. Scarification, mutilation and deformation of various body parts is seen as integral to achieving beauty in many cultures, and it is to such practices that we now turn.

SCARIFICATION

We have already had an opportunity to discuss the Nuba of southeastern Sudan in the context of body painting, primarily practiced by men. But Nuba concepts of female beauty involve an elaborate series of scarifications applied to the body throughout a woman's life.

> "The first of these is a series of scars cut on either side of the abdomen below the navel — joining above the navel and continuing to a point between the breasts. These scars are made at the first signs of puberty as the breasts begin to fill out. A second set takes place after the start of menses. This is a series of lateral parallel rows of scars under the breasts to the back over the entire length of the torso. This is the last scarification until after the weaning of the first child, when final scarring takes place all over the back, the neck, the back of the arms, buttocks and back of the legs to the knee" (Faris 1972:33).

The scarring is carried out at a considerable distance from the village since the blood resulting from the slicing of the skin is deemed extremely polluting, and must be kept away from tools, cooking equipment or weapons. Kept in seclusion in the mountains while the scars heal for four to five days, women resume active social life, oiling and coloring their skin within a week following the operation.

> "Scarring involves two instruments — a hooked thorn with which the skin is hooked and pulled up and a small blade with which the raised skin is sliced, to produce a slightly protruding scar. The more the skin is pulled up before cutting, the more raised will be the resulting scar, and not only is this considered more attractive, but it also lasts longer — for a woman's scars wear down through time, so that when old, hardly more than a slight surface distinction is visible where each raised scar was formerly" (Faris 1972:33-34).

The scarrer works quickly, executing about one scar per second, proceeding vertically or horizontally as she covers the area with small raised scars. She pauses occasionally to check to see that the alignment is correct, to wipe away blood, or to give the girl a chance to rest (Faris 1972:36).

Scarring is justified as a cosmetic practice, closely associated with ideas of beautification. The final scarring which takes place after the weaning of the first child, in addition to marking the transition to full womanhood, is regarded primarily as a beauty treatment, following which a young girl is believed to be at the peak of her seductive power. Both males and females undergo cosmetic scarification of the face at puberty, the scars of which are renewed again after a few years.

Needless to say, the operations are enormously painful, especially the final scarring of the women, during which it is not uncommon for the subjects to become faint, or even pass out from loss of blood and pain. Nevertheless, the women are expected to bear up without complaint. To be without scars in such a society is to be close to an outcast, an undesirable spouse, or conceptually naked.

An explicit statement of the relationship between pain and the achieving of beauty was provided to anthropologist Paul Bohannan who studied scarification in the conceptions of beauty of the Tiv of Nigeria. "Of course it is painful. What girl would look at a man if his scars had not cost him pain", they reported. For the Tiv, "the pain is proof positive that decoration is an unselfish act, and that it is done to give pleasure to others as well as oneself" (Bohannan 1956:121).

Tiv scarification, however, is also noteworthy for a number of singular aspects. For one thing, scarification among the Tiv is subject to stylistic variation from generation to generation. Rather than marking a person as a member of a certain clan or tribe, Tiv scars mark one's generation (Bohannan 1956:118). During Bohannan's fieldwork there were four generations of scarification style present in the population. Specific techniques, motifs and marking styles pass in and out of fashion as the generations pass.

Within these styles, designs and patterns are chosen to highlight the best aspects of one's face or torso. "A girl who is lucky enough to be born with 'good' legs (full calves and prominent heels) will probably call attention to them by having a design put on them" (Ibid). Successful scars call attention to one's strong points and are even said to fit one's face or to augment one's personality (Ibid:121).

The design motifs are common to men and women and are cut with a sharpened nail or razor, wounds being made into raised scars by rubbing charcoal or camwood into them. The designs are mainly geometrical, or stylized representations of swallow, water monitor, scorpion, catfish or chameleon. A fully decorated Tiv will also oil his or her body to achieve a "glow", a concept which takes in notions of beauty, clarity, brightness and a satisfactory ritual state (Bohannan 1956:117). The cosmetic chipping or extraction of the front teeth has now gone out of fashion.

Scarification may serve a variety of functions. The women of the Ila speaking groups of Zambia repeatedly cut and reopen vertical lines on their loins and inner thighs. The marks are said to enhance the arousal of one's mate during sexual intercourse, and are kept hidden by one's skirt during the day, revealed only to one's loved one during love making (Ember and Ember 1977:272).

Among the Bangwe of the Cameroon, members of the royal clan mark their status with special scarification marks on their chests and backs which are not allowed to commoners. Slaves and retainers also bear special marks or wear certain ornaments indicative of their rank (Brain 1979:19).

Scarification and mutilation may also serve ritual functions. The Dani of highland New Guinea require that women and young girls amputate a finger during the funeral service for a close relative so that the loss will not be forgotten (Friedl 1981:95).

Such practices may strike us as outrageous, but it is well to remember that "even in the west, blood-letting, flailing and scourging, and other sado-masochistic attacks on the body have been associated with [rituals of] Christian devotion and penitence" (Brain 1979:84).

BODY DEFORMATION

The inventory of practices involving deformation of various body parts ranges from simple ear piercing to accommodate ear rings among many of the world's peoples, to piercing of the nasal septum to accommodate a nose plug (Hagen), to piercing of the lips to accommodate a lip plug (Northwest coast Indians), to elongation of the lips (Ethiopian Muris), to elongation of the neck through the application of brass neck rings (Burmese Shan), to ritual fattening of nubile women and filing of the teeth (Bangwa), to clitorodectomy (Moslems) and circumcision (Jews and Australians).

The Chinook Indians of the Northwest Coast of North America were one of several groups in that culture area who practiced deformation of the head. The desired shape was achieved in infancy by swaddling a child in a straight plank, to the end of which another flat piece of wood was fastened. "This fell obliquely over the forehead and was tied down by leather thongs" to apply pressure to the still malleable skull (Brain 1979:92). The effect was to flatten the entire frontal region and to force the hair back resulting in a high back projection of the occiput.

> "As the Chinook child grew, the head resumed a more normal shape, though the excessive breadth remained. Among these Indians...it was only the freeborn who deformed their heads, slaves had round, natural, 'ugly' heads, although even they were allowed to elongate their children's skulls (Brain 1979:92).

Head deformation was also practiced among the ancient Egyptians whose royal portraits frequently displayed elongated skulls, and we find the custom of head binding practiced in parts of France into the nineteenth century (Brain 1972:92, Rudofsky 1971:95). In the case of the French, the motives for deforming a child's head were linked to a desire to guide the child into a particular vocation by shaping his brain. The aesthetic motive was clearly secondary (Rudofsky 1971:95).

Perhaps one of the most intriguing deformation practices of the world's peoples is the now all but defunct custom of footbinding among the Chinese. Practiced over the period of almost 1,000 years, footbinding has only passed out of fashion in the middle twentieth century, and there are still women alive today whose feet were bound as children. Remarkable for its persistence, footbinding stands as a monument to the force of tradition, and the intensity with which concepts of beauty are adhered to.

Part of the rationale for this custom can be understood by noting the clearly erotic appeal of a woman in high heels, buttocks muscles flexed and breasts flung forward. The posture and mincing steps of a woman with bound feet was said to be most alluring in much the same way. Footbinding can be seen as a means of creating an anatomical high heel.

The binding was begun for girls between the ages of three and five, was enormously painful, inhibited circulation, causing skin and toes to occasionally slough off and small sores and scratches to fester.

> "The bandage, about two inches wide and ten feet long, was wrapped in the following way. One end was placed on the inside of the instep, and from there it was carried over the small toes so as to force the toes in towards the sole. The large toe was left unbound. The bandage was then wrapped around the heel so forcefully that heel and toes were drawn closer together. The process was then repeated from the beginning until the entire bandage has been applied. The foot of the young child was subjected to a coercive and unremitting pressure, for the object was not merely to confine the foot but to make the toes bend under and into the sole, and bring the sole and heel as close together as was physically possible. The pain continued for about a year, then diminished, until at the end of two years the feet were practically dead and painless" (Levy 1966: 25-56).

Bound feet were a mark of gentility and refinement, and were disproportionately common among, though not exclusively confined to women of gentry families. They were sexually appealing to men who were titillated by the opportunity just to steal a glance at the foot of a loved one with bindings removed.

"A woman's sexual attraction came to center in the mystery of her bound feet, which were almost never bared to view. The caressing of the diminutive foot in innumerable ways became part of the prelude to the sex act" (Levy 1966:62).

"The eye rejoiced in the tiny footstep and in the undulating motion of the buttocks which it caused; the ear thrilled to the whispered walk, while the nose inhaled the fragrant aroma from the perfumed sole and delighted in smelling the bared flesh at closer range. The ways of grasping the foot in one's palms were both profuse and varied; ascending the heights of ecstasy, the lover transferred the foot from palm to mouth. Play included kissing, sucking and inserting the foot in the mouth until it filled both cheeks" (Levy 1966:34).

"There were also women who liked to fondle the male member with their tiny feet. When intoxicated, they would remove the bindings, place the organ between their feet, and rub it back and forth until the aroused male scattered his sperm about in profusion" (Levy 1966:143).

More generally however, the binding of a woman's feet was seen as a guarantee of her chastity as daughter and fidelity as wife, making it difficult or even dangerous for her to leave her home unescorted. The natural footed girl would have difficulty contracting a proper marriage. Furthermore, the aesthetic which favored small feet in women was largely internalized by the women themselves such that they felt ashamed to show their faces in public with big feet, or ridiculed natural footed women who were brave enough to venture out. Women endured or forced their daughters to endure the pain of the bindings with stoic resignation. Such was their fate.

There were occasional attempts made over the centuries to restrict the practice by imperial decree, especially by the alien Ch'ing dynasty (1644–1911), and the late nineteenth century witnessed the emergency of Unbound Feet Associations which proselytized against the custom. Yet the tenacity of the custom is evidenced by the fact that it took two revolutions (in 1911 and 1949) to overturn the value system which justified the systematic crippling of half of the population.

These facts suggest that concepts of beauty are implicitly political, and although we began this essay with what we characterized as a healthy relativist perspective, the history of footbinding in China suggests that relativism has its limits, and that concepts of beauty do not exist outside the arena of ideological struggle. Are we to understand footbinding from the perspective of the feudal aesthetic that generated it, or from the perspective of the modernist movement which has come to see it as an institution keeping women in permanent subordination. The answer has obviously political implications, and the question could be posed with equal justification to the scarification and deformation practices examined above as well.

We may draw comfort from the observation that our own body mutilations and alterations undertaken for the sake of beauty do no seem at all extreme when compared to those of other cultures, but there is also a sense in which we remain prisoners of an aesthetic no less dramatic in its political implications than that of the pre-modern Chinese. The fashions we slavishly follow in beautifying or otherwise altering our bodies affect us in no less arbitrary a way than the magical formula uttered by the Trobriand islander, giving him the wherewithal to proceed in his endeavors with confidence, and to conduct himself with an air that supersedes his sense of self doubt.

However, we are at a considerable disadvantage since the images which are purveyed to us in fashion magazines of "beautiful" people are an every day reminder of our own failure to achieve such standards, and what is more, these standards do not flow from the exigencies of our social life as it is lived day to day, but are foisted upon us by self-appointed arbiters of fashion, in much the same way that footbinding was foisted on Chinese women.

There is, after all, something to be said for encouraging in people the personal strength of character that accepts oneself for what one is without aspiring to look like John Travolta or Brooke Shields.

BIBLIOGRAPHY

Bohannan, Paul 1956 Beauty and Scarification among the Tiv. *Man* 129: 117-121.

Brain Robert 1979 The Decorated Body. N.Y.: Harper and Row.

Douglas Mary 1975 Do Dogs Laugh: a cross cultural approach to body symbolism, in *Implicit Meanings*. London: Routledge and Kegan Paul.

Drucker, Philip 1955 Indians of the Northwest Coast. New York: McGraw Hill.

Ebin, Victoria 1979 The Body Decorated. London: Thames and Husdon.

Ember, Melvin and Carol 1977 Cultural Anthropology. Englewood: Prentice-Hall.

Faris: James C. 1972 Nuba Personal Art. Toronto: Univ. of Toronto Press.

Frank, L. K. 1972 Cultural Patterning of Tactile Experiences in L.A. Samovar and R. E. Porter, eds. *Intercultural Communication: a Reader.* N.Y.:

Friedl, John 1981 The Human Portrait. Englewood: Prentice-Hall.

Hallpike, C. R. 1979 Social Hair in William Lesser and E. Z. Vogt, eds. Reader in Comparative Religion. New York: Harper and Row.

Kunzle, David 1982 Fashion and Fetishism. Totowa, N.J.: Rownan and Littlefield.

Levi-Strauss, Claude 1963 Split Representation in the Art of Asia and America in Structural Anthropology. N.Y.: Basic Books.

—1973 Tristes-Tropiques. N.Y.: Atheneum.

Levy, Howard 1966 Chinese Footbinding: the history of a curious erotic custom. New York: Rawls.

Lowie, Robert 1935 The Crow Indians. N.Y.: Holt, Rinehart and Winston.

Malinowski, B. 1922 Argonauts of the Western Pacific. N.Y.: Dutton.

Pelto, Gretl and Pertti 1976 The Human Adventure. N.Y.: MacMillan

Rudofsky, Bernard 1971 The Unfashionable Human Body. Garden City: Doubleday.

Strathern, Andrew and Marilyn 1971 Self Decoration in Mount Hagen. Toronto: U. of Toronto Press.

Thevoz, Michel 1984 The Illusions of Reality: the painted body. N.Y.: Rizzoli International Publs.

Weiner, Annette 1976 Women of Value, Men of Renown: the perspectives on Trobriand exchange. Austin: Univ. of Texas Press.